NEGLIGENCE
FOR
'A' LEVEL

TONY WEIR

Fellow of Trinity College, Cambridge

SECOND EDITION

LONDON
SWEET & MAXWELL
1983

First edition 1981
Second edition 1983

Published by
Sweet & Maxwell Limited of
11 New Fetter Lane, London
Computerset by Promenade
Graphics Limited, Cheltenham
and printed in Scotland

British Library Cataloguing in Publication Data

Weir, Tony
    Negligence for 'A' level.—2nd ed.
    1. Negligence—England—Cases
    I. Title
    344.2063'2'0264   KD1975.A4

    ISBN 0–421–32170–9

PREFACE

The publishers of the First edition were sufficiently encouraged by the interest shown to agree readily to produce a second edition when Tony Weir revised his *Casebook*.

The topic of Negligence has proved to be sufficiently wide (and ever expanding) to justify its inclusion in the syllabus for longer than was originally envisaged. A close study of the many and varied problems which the cases—the lifeblood of the common law—generate will be rewarding for students and teachers alike. No substitute can or should be found for the original sources of law presented here together with the author's incisive comments and criticisms. It is hoped that attention to the law at this level will help to create a feel for the basic work of the civil courts—the resolution of disputes in accordance with well established but adaptable principles of law.

C. G. Blake

London,
July 1983

CHARLES G. BLAKE LL.B., LL.M. Solicitor
Senior Lecturer in Law, Ealing College of Higher Education
Chief Examiner in Law at 'A' Level for the Associated Examining Board.

PREFACE TO FIRST EDITION

The Summer of 1982 will see the first examination of the Associated Examining Board's revised 'A' level. This book is the prescribed reading for the Paper 2 topic of Negligence. It should be noted that the syllabus states that the examination will be set on the specified reading. It will be seen that as a topic for examination "Negligence" covers more than the simple tort itself and includes other aspects of the substantive law of tort, any of which can be examined. In considering this reading, students are advised to remember their studies for Paper 1, especially the principles and operation of the doctrine of *stare decisis*.

It is appropriate that this area of law has been selected as one of the first topics because it illustrates the continued vitality of judicial decisions as a source of law, which is often regarded as one of the hallmarks of the common law system. This book gives students the opportunity to examine properly primary sources of law and to acquire an appreciation of the lawyerly skills of the reconciliation and the distinguishing of cases through identification of relevant principles and facts. It is not intended that this book be regarded as a literary text for analysis. However, some of the skills of literary analysis are part of the student lawyers' armoury in their struggle with the nuances of judicial language, which reveal the policies and attitudes of the courts as they delineate the appropriate boundaries of legal restraint upon human activity.

Finally, the publishers should be thanked by all students and teachers for their decision to reproduce this text which was originally Part One of Tony Weir's *Casebook on Tort*.

R. J. Garland

Loggerheads,
April 1981

R. J. GARLAND, LL.B., LL.M.
Principal Lecturer in Law, North Staffordshire Polytechnic
Chief Examiner in Law at 'A' level for the Associated Examining Board

NEGLIGENCE FOR 'A' LEVEL

AUSTRALIA AND NEW ZEALAND
The Law Book Company Ltd.
Sydney : Melbourne : Perth

CANADA AND U.S.A.
The Carswell Company Ltd.
Agincourt, Ontario

INDIA
N. M. Tripathi Private Ltd.
Bombay
and
Eastern Law House Private Ltd.
Calcutta and Delhi
M.P.P. House
Bangalore

ISRAEL
Steimatzky's Agency Ltd.
Jerusalem : Tel Aviv : Haifa

MALAYSIA : SINGAPORE : BRUNEI
Malayan Law Journal (Pte.) Ltd.
Singapore

PAKISTAN
Pakistan Law House
Karachi

CONTENTS

INTRODUCTION

IN almost all the cases in this book the plaintiff is claiming money (damages); only occasionally does he ask the judge to stop the defendant doing something (injunction). In almost every case the plaintiff claims this money as compensation for harm he has suffered; only very rarely is the defendant required to pay more, as a punishment (*Rookes* v. *Barnard*, below, p. 281). The plaintiff's claim is grounded on the argument that the defendant (or someone for whom he is responsible) did wrong to cause this harm. Thus the law of torts determines when one person must pay another compensation for harm wrongfully caused. At any rate that is its primary function: it also helps to decide what conduct may be stopped by court order, and, quite importantly, serves as a forum for the vindication of individual rights.

A tort suit, then, is very unlike an action of debt, which is a claim for a specific sum not measured by the amount of the plaintiff's loss (*e.g.*, a tax claim, or an action for the price of goods sold). It is unlike an action on a property-insurance policy, where the debt *is* limited by the plaintiff's loss, because in such an action it is not claimed that the insurance company *caused* the loss. It is not like a claim for compensation after an expropriation; for there it is not claimed that the loss was *wrongfully* caused (*e.g. Burmah Oil Co.* v. *Lord Advocate* [1965] A.C. 75). But a tort suit is very like an action for damages for breach of contract, where also the amount claimed is claimed as compensation for harm which the defendant has caused wrongfully, by breaking his word. Indeed many actions for damages may be based indifferently on contract or on tort.

A contractual claim can arise only where there is a transaction of some kind between the parties, such as sale, employment, carriage and so on: if there is no transaction, but only a collision between strangers, then any claim must be in tort. But a collision may well take place between the parties to a transaction, and it has long been the law that in such a case the victim may have both a tort and a contract claim. Now people involved in collisions usually suffer physical harm, that is, they actually get hurt, whereas the normal outcome when a transaction goes sour is that the affected party is just worse off, that is, suffers merely economic harm. The law of tort used to be interested mainly in physical harm but recently it has become increasingly ready to redress purely economic harm, and the result of this is that more and more breaches of contract simultaneously constitute torts as well. Very many of the things people actually do they do pursuant to a transaction with someone, and if they do something wrong, that is usually a breach of their contractual duty. But under English law the only person who can sue for breach of contract is the contractor himself, and then only if he has paid in some sense for the service in question. Recent developments in the law of tort seem designed to make good these deficiencies in the law of contract, if deficiencies they be, by granting an action to people who were not parties and to parties who did not pay.

While the law of tort is basically common law, the work of judges responding to particular cases, a great deal of it is now statutory, the work of Parliament responding to pressure, from law reform bodies and others. On many occasions Parliament has intervened to reverse individual rules laid down by the judges. Thus the Fatal Accidents Act 1846 (now 1976) gave a remedy to widows and orphans which the common law had refused; the Law Reform Act of 1934 allowed a victim's claim to survive though he or the defendant had died; the Law Reform Act of 1945 allowed a plaintiff to claim (though a reduced amount) if he himself was partly to blame; and in 1947 the Crown Proceedings Act rendered the Government liable in tort nearly like everyone else. Less frequently Parliament has sought to tidy up an area of the law of tort rather than to reverse a specific rule: examples would be the Occupiers' Liability Act 1957, the Animals Act 1971 and the Torts (Interference with Goods) Act 1977. There has, however, been no serious proposal to embark on a complete codification of the law of tort.

Whether it is possible and wise to codify depends on the coherence of the area and the generality of the rules it is proposed to codify, and on whether the draftsmen possess the requisite technique. In both regards the present situation in England is unpropitious: while it is true that judicial synthesis of principle and legislative excision of anomalies have rendered the rules of tort much more general and abstract (and thereby reduced their number), tort as a whole is still far from homogeneous, thanks to the presence in it of eccentric native bodies such as defamation and conversion; and if the drafting technique displayed in the Animals Act 1971 (a product of the Law Commission itself) were adopted for codification, our code of tort alone would be nearly as long as (and less readable than) the American Restatement of 1934–39, whose 951 sections occupy four whole volumes.

Continental lawyers are more concise. The French law of delict is contained in five articles, of which the first reads: "Every act whatever of man which causes damage to another binds the person whose fault it was to repair it" (French Civil Code (1804), Art. 1382). The German Civil Code of 1900 deals with the law of unlawful acts in thirty-one paragraphs, whose principal one reads: "A person who on purpose or carelessly injures another contrary to law in his life, body, health, freedom, property or other right is liable to compensate that other for the resulting damage" (§ 823). Of course, these legislative provisions have received very many judicial glosses since their promulgation, but there has been no major legislative reformulation despite the vast changes in social structure and physical environment which have taken place since their enactment. Students might well test the results of the cases in this book against the words of these statutes.

If there is no demand for codification in England there are plenty of suggestions for further reform. The most recent proposals came from the Royal Commission on Civil Liability and Compensation for Personal Injury, set up in 1973 under the chairmanship of Lord Pearson (Cmnd. 7054, 1978). The Commission was not empowered to consider the whole of the law of tort, since *only* personal injury fell within its purview, nor yet could it investigate the compensation, by whatever means, of *all* personal injury, since apart from injuries to employees, consumers and persons on the highway, it could consider only injuries in respect of which tort liability now exists. But the Commission did review in great detail the roles and rules of tort law in relation to what might be called the total compensation situation.

The main concern of the Commission was that the law of tort be henceforth seen in relation to the other methods of alleviating harm which exist in the welfare state, especially social security. The moral value-judgment underlying the law of tort, namely that only wrongdoers need pay for the harm they cause, is at odds with the modern view, represented by social security, that all those who suffer harm should receive alleviation whether anyone is to blame or not: after all, the National Health Service does not ask *how* a patient came to need treatment.

The Commission proposed to mitigate this conflict by extending the role of social security, especially by providing all persons injured in motor accidents with benefits like those now paid to persons injured at work, and by diminishing the role of tort, not by depriving anyone of an existing right to sue, but by reducing the amount of damages payable, notably by refusing any compensation for pain and suffering during the first three months and by deducting all social security benefits.

The law of tort was thus subjected to a critical examination by the Commission, and it passed that examination, though not with flying colours: the Commission made 188 recommendations, of which the government has implemented about 15.

Those who think it wrong to discriminate in any way between persons suffering similar injuries will be displeased that a person who has only himself to blame for his injuries continues to be worse off than the person he injures, but others will be relieved that even in the welfare State some role is to be allowed to private law, especially in so far as it reflects the view that everyone should conduct himself with due regard for the physical well-being of his fellow-citizens, on pain of a monetary sanction pro-portioned to the harm he causes if he does not.

If liability in tort is to remain, we must keep the two institutions which ensure that a person who has a claim is actually paid what he is entitled to: the Motor Insurers' Bureau meets the claim of a person injured on the highway if the motorist at fault is uninsured or untraceable, and the Criminal Injuries Compensation Board gives money out of public funds to those who suffer personal injury as a result of crimes of violence.

When we turn to property damage, social security payments are unavailable and neither the Criminal Injuries Compensation Board nor the Motor Insurers' Bureau will help; the problem of alternative remedies remains, however, since the owner may well have taken out property insurance. In cases where insured property has been tortiously damaged the courts have resolutely held that the owner's claim against the tortfeasor is unaffected by the fact that the owner has insurance. Of course the owner cannot keep both the insurance proceeds and the tort damages: he must refund the insurance proceeds out of the tort damages or, as most often happens, allow the insurance company to prosecute his claim against the tortfeasor. The unsatisfactoriness of the result is concealed from us by the fact that the insurance company, by "subrogation," sues in the name of the insured owner: we therefore fail to realise that money is being claimed by a company which was paid to take the risk of losing it.

The law of tort covers a wide range of situations, from the tragic to the trivial. In this book one will come across an urchin who was blown out of a manhole (p. 190), a politician riled by criticism (p. 452), a credulous advertising agent (p. 34) and a television mogul miffed at being photographed (p. 301). Every situation, however, involves just a few structural elements which affect the outcome, and it would be right to say a preliminary word about each of them. They are (i) the victim's loss, (ii) the actor's behaviour, (iii) the relationship between the loss of behaviour, (iv) the relationship between the plaintiff and the actor or defendant and (v) the plaintiff's behaviour. As each case in this book is read, its facts should be classified under each of these heads; and then the conceptual devices which are used to justify the decision should be studied.

1. THE VICTIM'S LOSS.

A judge once said "It is difficult to see why liability as such should depend on the nature of the damage." The difficulty is not apparent. Liability "as such" never exists; liability is always liability *for* something, and in tort it is liability for the harm caused. To cause harm means to have an adverse effect on something good. There are several good things in life, or "interests" as lawyers call them, such as life, liberty, bodily integrity, land, possessions, reputation and so on. These interests are all good, but they are not all *equally* good. This is evident when they come into conflict (one may jettison cargo to save passengers, but not vice versa, and one may detain a thing, but not a person, as security for a debt). Because these interests are not equally good, the protection afforded to them by the law is not equal: the law protects the better interests better. Accordingly, the better the interest invaded, the more readily does the law give compensation for the harm due to that invasion. In other words, whether you get the money you claim depends on what you are claiming it for. It would be surprising if it were otherwise.

The kinds of damage most frequently complained of are personal injury, property damage and financial loss, *i.e.* damage to three of the best things of life, namely, health, property and wealth.

As between health and wealth, the priority would seem to be clearly established: it is better to be well than wealthy. But people who are poorly soon become poor, because they cannot earn their living and have to buy medicaments: personal injury has economic consequences. May it not be *because* of those economic consequences that we protect people's bodies, regarding them as units of production and consumption rather than as sources of pleasure? If the question appears cynical, one should ponder the recommendation of the Pearson Commission that victims of personal injury should receive a full indemnity in tort for their lost earnings and extra expenses, but nothing for their pain and suffering for the first three months.

That people are more important than things has been said often enough. But are things more important than money? The question is topical, because the law of tort has recently started to extend to money interests the protection it has long given to property, and it is serious, for its answer may tell us something about the values of our society.

Things, unlike people, can be bought and sold, that is, they can be exchanged for money. Things are "money's worth." But there are valuables, *e.g.*, stocks and shares, which are not things. Things are defined as objects which can be touched: if it is invisible and intangible, it isn't a thing. Thus things appeal not only to economists but also to the human senses. The car which is merely an asset to the finance house which owns it is a positive pleasure to the hire-purchaser who drives it. The point is clearer with regard to immovables: a house has a human value to the family whose home it is but only an economic value to the building society which has lent money on it. It would therefore be entirely appropriate in a legal system which was concerned with human values to give greater protection to tangible property than to intangible wealth. This is what the law has done until recently: claims for property damage have been welcomed while claims for mere financial loss have been rejected; and the law has been much readier to grant a claim to the possessor of a chattel—the person who is enjoying it—than to the owner out of possession—the person who only profits from it. Of course there is one class of person, the artificial or legal person, to which this distinction between the thing and the mere asset can have no meaning whatever: that is because artificial persons have no senses. For companies it is immaterial whether there is one item less on the stock book or one item less on the credit side of the ledger. For people without senses, things are merely values, and a society without sensibility would so treat them. Our society is beginning to do so.

We have spoken thus far as if damage were requisite and as if the question whether there were damage or not was a pure question of fact. But suppose that I am locked up for five minutes. It would be difficult for me to show that this outrage had caused me any actual harm, unless I broke my leg trying to escape or missed an important engagement. Yet the person responsible should be made to pay. It is possible to hold him liable by saying that he has interfered with my right to liberty, and that my right to liberty is so important that to invade it is to cause me damage *ipso facto*. By using the concept of "right" we can conceal the fact that no damage need be proved. It might, however, be better to admit that in addition to its more obvious function of redressing harms the law of tort also vindicates rights: it has a constitutional as well as a compensatory function.

2. The Actor's Behaviour

(a) *The act*

Positive acts are a commoner ground of liability in tort than omissions to act. One is liable for stealing or damaging other people's goods, but not, in the absence of special circumstances, for not protecting them from theft or damage. The occupier must bestir himself for the safety of his visitors, and parents must try to save children from themselves and others, but generally at common law if you want someone to do something for you, you must pay him, and then if he doesn't do it you can sue him for breach of contract. Duties to act are not readily imposed by the common law. The legislature, however, is constantly imposing such duties on people, usually on public bodies. Those bodies do not always live up to their obligations, and it is one of the urgent questions of tort law how far they may be made liable for failing to do so. We have come a long way from the view that "not doing is no trespass," but it remains true that one is more likely to be liable for creating a danger than for failing to remove one.

Thus we can oppose acts to omissions. We can also oppose acts to activities. A Lord Justice of Appeal once said:" . . . our law of torts is concerned not with activities but with acts" (*Read* v. *Lyons* [1945] 1 K.B. 216, 228 (Scott L.J.)), and he was apparently right. So if a person is run down in the street, he cannot say to the driver: "When you started driving, you enhanced the risk of people being hurt; I have been hurt, so you must compensate me." The victim must show that the defendant drove badly, that in the activity of driving just before the impact the defendant did some particular act he ought not to have done. But although this is generally true, there are areas of the law where liability is imposed because the defendant was running an activity, and although he himself has acted quite properly. Suppose the careless driver was employed by a firm and was on the firm's business at the time of the collision. The victim can sue the firm if he establishes the fault of the driver. The firm responds for careless conduct in its activity, though the firm itself is otherwise free from fault (p. 221).

After deep scrutiny of our common and statutory law the Pearson Commission discerned an embryo principle which "can be broadly stated as one of strict liability for personal injury caused by dangerous things or activities." One of their proposals was to implement and expand this principle by having a statute which would lay down a framework of liability and a series of statutory instruments which would specify the activities and things to which it would apply. The proposal is unlikely to be adopted.

The behaviour of things, from which the acts of man can also be distinguished, is of importance to the tort lawyer because most people who are hurt are hurt by things, especially by metal things. The French Civil Code says: "A person is responsible not only for the damage caused by his own act, but also for the damage caused by the act of those for whom he is responsible, or of the things which he has in his control" (Art. 1384). There is no such general principle yet in the law of England, but there are circumstances where a thing involves liability. Thus if I am hurt by a thing under the control of the defendant, and the damage would not have occurred if the thing was properly controlled, then the behaviour of the thing, in the absence of explanation by the defendant, may bespeak carelessness on his part in looking after it. *Res ipsa loquitur* is the Latin form (p. 147). Again, if the defendant has brought an unusual thing on to his land, and it escapes and does damage to mine, he is liable as a matter of law (p. 369). If the defendant keeps a savage beast, and it gets out of control and bites me, then again, as a matter of law, the defendant is liable (p. 395). The rule is the same, in this regard, if the defendant's cattle escape and eat my tulips (p. 395).

Further, we can oppose acts to words. Lawyers have a tendency to confuse them (*Acts* of Parliament, *deeds* of individuals), but we must try to keep them distinct because they are quite different in origin, in quality and in mode of operation, even if they can both have harmful effects. First, speaking is an exercise of a specifically guaranteed freedom, in the way that driving a car, for example, is not; one must therefore be chary of unduly restraining communication by too ready an imposition of liability if something goes wrong. Secondly, it is technically rather easy to impose liability for words, because one can *prove* the falsehood of what was said whereas one can only *argue* for the wrongfulness of what was done: it is not easy to remember that being wrong is not necessarily doing wrong. Finally, acts commonly impinge directly on the person hurt, whereas words operate by indirection, by inducing him to hurt himself or inducing others to hurt him. The concept of reliance is used here.

It should be emphasised that we are not contrasting acts with omissions, activities, words and things in order to suggest that there is liability only for acts and not for these other variants: the suggestion is that one should be conscious which of them is involved in a particular situation, since it makes a difference, not necessarily by itself, but certainly in conjunction with other factors.

(b) *Quality of the act*

In most cases it is not enough to show simply that the defendant acted, and thereby caused the damage. His act must be legally qualified before liability follows. Here the prevalent test is whether the defendant acted *reasonably*. On the whole, a defendant who has acted reasonably is not going to have to pay damages. But there are exceptions, and it is very important to mark them when they occur. Sometimes the plaintiff's interest is so important that it is protected even against reasonable behaviour which infringes it. A person's land is protected against persons who reasonably but erroneously believe themselves entitled to enter it (p. 268); a person's liberty may be protected against officials acting bona fide but in excess of their powers (p. 329); a person's stolen chattels are protected against persons who reasonably buy or sell them in the normal channels of commerce (p. 416); a person's reputation is protected even against imputations unintended by the writer (p. 442). These are also the cases where no damage need be proved.

Sometimes a person is not liable for acting unreasonably even if he intended to bring about the damage complained of. This is because the activity being furthered by the defendant is regarded as very important. Trade competition and labour disputes qualify for protection here (p. 507); so also do public officials exercising a judicial capacity (p. 327). Judges, counsel and witnesses may say what they like in court, and Members of Parliament enjoy at least an equal immunity in Parliament. And since it is for the public good that suspected criminals be prosecuted, the person who prosecutes another is not liable merely for acting unreasonably; he must in addition be shown to have acted deviously (p. 520).

3. Relationship between Behaviour and Damage

A person is not in general responsible unless he has both caused damage and been to blame for it. "Cause" and "blame" are not synonymous except in vulgar language and Greek; they are the component elements of responsibility, but they are not easily dissociated. On the one hand, even a person who is blameworthy does not have to pay for damage if it would have occurred anyhow; a person is not liable unless he "caused" the damage (below, p. 175). On the other hand, a blameworthy person may not be liable for all the damage he can be said to have "caused."

What relationships can there be between an act and the damage complained of? The damage may be the *direct* result of the act; or it may be the *foreseeable* result of the act; or it may be the *typical* result of the act; or it may be that the act was *calculated* to produce that damage. All these devices have been used. But their use should not conceal the fact that underneath the apparent factuality of causal vocabulary lurk value-judgments. This can be seen from the fact that the more reprehensible behaviour is, the more causally potent it tends to be, whether it is the behaviour of the defendant, the plaintiff or of some third party.

4. Relationship between Plaintiff and Defendant

Whether you get the money you are claiming depends on whom you are claiming it from. In other words, the relationship between the plaintiff and the defendant is a material consideration in every tort suit. For example, suppose that the defendant is doing construction work under statutory powers in a main street, and that his crane is defective for want of repair. A load being lifted by it drops from a height on to a workman. Two people suffer shock at the sight of this tragedy, the craneman and a passer-by who has stopped to stare. It is probable that the craneman can sue and that the passer-by cannot (p. 77). Yet the behaviour of the defendant, the nature of the damage and the relationship between the damage and the behaviour are identical. The reason is that the defendant is in a protective relationship to the craneman, his employee, and is in no relationship with the pedestrian, save that constituted by physical proximity. Take another case. Suppose that A and B go out on a drinking party, and return very drunk in A's car. A carelessly collides with another car, and its driver C is injured as well as B. C can clearly recover, but B may have difficulties (p. 94). Again this is because the relationship between A and B is different from the relationship between A and C.

In order to accommodate these difficulties the law has the device of "special relationship" which may either heighten or lower the duty which is owed when the relationship is merely spatial. But in many cases where the concept of "special relationship" is not mentioned, the results can only be rationalised on the basis that one exists. If one takes as standard the relationship, miscalled "neighbourhood," which is said to exist merely because the defendant should have been thinking of the plaintiff as a possible victim of his carelessness, then there are some relationships which are very different. For example, the defendant may actually have been thinking of the plaintiff as the intended victim of his acts. This tends to make a difference. Or take the relationship (actual neighbourhood) existing between those who occupy adjoining flats or plots of land, a relationship characterised by continued physical proximity between people who did not choose each other. It would be impossible for a legal system to treat them as it treats those who pass each other on the highway; and the law has a special régime for real neighbours called "nuisance." Factual relationships differ widely, and the use of general terms should not conceal the fact. For example, plaintiff and defendant may be parties to a contract, and a contract is a very special relationship indeed.

In France the law of tort applies only in the absence of a contract; in other words, it applies only between strangers. The English law of tort applies between contractors, too, except in so far as it has been effectively excluded by the terms of the contract itself (effective exclusion now being difficult—see below p. 213. This concurrence of tort and contract leads to some difficulties. You bring the same action of trespass against the burglar as against the landlord who evicts you. You bring the same action against a thief as against the vendor who by mistake delivers to someone else the thing he sold to you.

Two factors at least distinguish the voluntary from the involuntary relationship. On the one hand, where persons have come together, they must know that they expose themselves to the risk of harm from each other. On the other hand, the coming together of the parties may throw on one of them a higher liability because he knows that the other party is relying on him; the best example of this is master and servant.

5. THE PLAINTIFF'S BEHAVIOUR

A person who "has only himself to blame" for an accident cannot claim from anyone else (except his insurer or social security). It would be monstrous if he could. Sometimes one feels that the plaintiff has only himself to blame even though the defendant is at fault in some way. One feels this mainly where the plaintiff's behaviour has been particularly unreasonable in comparison with that of the defendant. In such cases, the plaintiff's behaviour will be referable either to his relationship with the defendant, or to the relationship of the defendant's behaviour and the damage—one will say either "The defendant doesn't have to pay *him*" or "The defendant doesn't have to pay him for *that*." These points therefore can be dealt with in terms of duty or causation. If the plaintiff's behaviour was not very unreasonable, then the loss may be shared (below, p. 205).

While Western systems of law rather flatter themselves on paying no heed to the personal merits or demerits of claimants, it is really undeniable that good people get more and bad people less. Rescuers and other altruists are favoured by the law of tort (below, p. 77), burglars and other criminals disfavoured (below, p. 217).

These are aspects of the facts of all cases which cannot fail to be relevant to an acceptable decision; but the grounds of decision must be stated in terms of legal concepts, which may or may not reflect the differences in the facts. We have already seen how the concept of "right" may be used to conceal the fact that the plaintiff has really suffered no damage; it may also be used to make the defendant's act seem wrongful when it is really irreprehensible. Here it must suffice to deal briefly with the very important concept of "duty."

The word duty is used for two distinct purposes—to establish a relationship in law between the defendant and the plaintiff and to state the standard of behaviour which the law requires of the defendant in a question with that plaintiff. But in certain cases liability is so clear that we bypass the notion of duty. If A tells lies to B, we know that this is wrong, and do not take the intermediate step of saying "A was under a duty to be honest." People always are. So also we do not talk of a duty not to trespass, because it is elementary that trespassers are liable. It is when liability is not clear and when it is clear that there is no liability that we use the notion of "duty," either by stating it (p. 34) or denying it (p. 80).

For example, where the plaintiff has suffered damage as a consequence of the defendant's behaviour, and the courts are unwilling for one reason or another to impose liability on the defendant but are yet unable to deny that what the plaintiff is complaining of is "damage" or that the defendant acted unreasonably or that that unreasonable behaviour caused the damage, then they say that the defendant did not owe the plaintiff any duty to take care. Thus, although the defendant has acted without care, his act is not a breach of duty to the plaintiff, because that duty is said not to exist. This was one of the grounds on which the Court of Appeal recently dismissed the claim of a congenitally deformed child who, but for the defendant's negligence, would never have been born at all (*McKay* v. *Essex Area Health Authority* [1982] Q.B. 1166). This was the reason given for absolving a barrister whose negligent advocacy has allegedly led to his client's conviction (*Rondel* v. *Worsley* [1969] 1 A.C. 191). No other reason can be given for preventing a wife suing for her undoubted personal loss resulting from the negligent emasculation of her husband (*Best* v. *Samuel Fox* [1952] A.C. 716). Similarly, where the plaintiff is complaining of financial loss only, and the court is unwilling to shift the burden of that loss to a merely negligent defendant, the court may use the duty device to deny recovery by holding that no duty was owed (p. 80). The courts cannot say "This kind of damage cannot be compensated," because in other circumstances it can; nor can they say "such behaviour in a defendant does not involve him in liability," because in other circumstances it does; nor can the courts deny causation, because frequently all the tests of causation are satisfied (*e.g.*, the defendant negligently damages a car insured by the plaintiff).

Given that a duty exists, it must be a duty with a content. The duty fixes not only the relationship between the parties, but also the standard of behaviour to be required of the defendant. Here there is great flexibility. The flexibility can come either in the formulation of the duty or in its application to different sets of facts. Thus one can say that the person who hires out a ladder owes a duty to his contractor's employees to take reasonable care that it is not defective, whereas if they borrow a ladder from a neighbour, the neighbour's duty is only to disclose known defects. It is, however, just as satisfactory to say that both suppliers owe the same duty to take reasonable care, but that more extensive precautions are required to satisfy that duty in the one case than in the other. One expects both to take reasonable care, but one does not expect the housewife to test every rung; more is looked for in a business man than in a person doing a kindness. But this is satisfactory only so long as it is remembered that "reasonable care" means "reasonable care *in all the circumstances*." Otherwise one quickly goes wrong. (For a list of relevant circumstances, see Occupiers' Liability Act 1957, s. 2, below, p. 114). The present tendency of the common law is to state the duty generally as being the duty to take reasonable care; "gross negligence" is not required.

The "duty to take reasonable care" is a very satisfying one, because "duty" calls up a picture of a standard of behaviour, measured by the possible; we do not in private life stigmatise someone for breach of a duty unless it was within his power to fulfil it. But not all duties at common law are of a level such that a person acting reasonably satisfies them, and duties under statute usually are not. Cases will be found in this book where the courts say "The defendant's contractor was negligent, so the defendant's duty was not fulfilled." The defendant is accordingly in breach of his duty although he himself has done nothing wrong. The content of the duty, then, is not a pattern for behaviour, but a list of facts which must exist to exonerate the defendant. For example, when the legislature requires that dangerous parts of machinery be securely fenced (Factories Act 1961, s. 14), it is no excuse for a defendant, if a dangerous part is not securely fenced, that the machine could not be operated if it were. Thus there are duties which are broken only if the *defendant* was at fault (the duty owed by one user of the highway to another). There are duties which are broken only if *someone* was at fault—and the range of persons whose fault may involve a breach of duty by the defendant is infinitely extensible (*e.g.*, liability for independent contractors)—and there are duties which are broken although *no one* was at fault (*e.g.*, some statutory duties, and the vendor's liability to the purchaser of defective goods).

Dangers lurk, however, in the use of the word "duty." One such danger, recently made manifest, is the danger of supposing that tort liability *must* attach to behaviour which can be characterised as a breach of "duty." It is tempting but misleading to say "You ought to have done that, *i.e.*, you were under a duty to do it, so you must pay damages for not doing it." As Lord Edmund-Davies has observed: "In most situations it is better to be careful than careless, but it is quite another thing to elevate all carelessness into a tort. Liability has to be based on a legal duty not to be careless, and I can find none in this case." (*Moorgate Mercantile Co.* v. *Twitchings* [1977] A.C. 890, 919).

Thus if A has promised B to do something, A clearly "ought" to do it, and do it properly or carefully. His failure so to do it may injure C; but it does not follow that C should be able to sue A, though we may be misled into thinking that A is under some 'duty" to C just because there is a sense in which A "ought" to have done what he promised. Likewise, it is elementary that public officials "ought" to perform their functions properly: that is what they are there for and what they are paid for, and no one would deny that they have "duties" to perform. However, it is not at all clear that tort liability in damages is invariably the proper or sensible sanction for their failure to perform them. Here again it is dangerously easy to infer from the proposition that tort liability depends on breach of duty that every breach of duty must lead to tort liability. It does so only if the relationship between plaintiff and defendant is of a certain sort and if the damage is of a certain sort and is caused in a certain way.

PART I

NEGLIGENCE

CHAPTER 1

DUTY

(M'ALISTER or) DONOGHUE v. STEVENSON

House of Lords [1932] A.C. 562; 101 L.J.P.C. 119; 147 L.T. 281; 48 T.L.R. 494; 76 S.J. 396;
37 Com.Cas. 350; [1932] All E.R.Rep. 1

Action by consumer against manufacturer in respect of personal injury.

Mrs. Donoghue (*née* M'Alister) averred that a friend purchased a bottle of ginger-beer for her in Minchella's café in Paisley; that Minchella took the metal cap off the bottle, which was made of dark opaque glass, and poured some of the contents into a tumbler; that, having no reason to suspect that it was anything other than pure ginger-beer, she drank some of the contents; that when her friend refilled her glass from the bottle there floated out the decomposed remains of a snail; that she suffered from shock and severe gastro-enteritis as a result of the nauseating sight and of the impurities she had already consumed. She further averred that the ginger-beer was manufactured by the defender to be sold as a drink to the public (including herself), that it was bottled by him and labelled with a label bearing his name; and that the defender sealed the bottle with a metal cap. She also claimed that it was the duty of the defender to provide a system in his business which would prevent snails entering his ginger-beer bottles, and to provide an efficient system of inspection of bottles prior to their being filled with ginger-beer, and that his failure in both duties caused this accident.

The defender objected that the averments were irrelevant and insufficient (that is, that even if the pursuer established by proof all that she had averred, she would still not be entitled to judgment).

The Lord Ordinary overruled the defender's objection, and wanted to proceed with the evidence. The defender appealed to the Second Division of the Court of Session, who adhered to their judgment in *Mullen* v. *Barr & Co.*, 1929 S.C. 461, and allowed the appeal. The pursuer appealed to the House of Lords, who restored the interlocutor of the Lord Ordinary.

LORD ATKIN: My Lords, the sole question for determination in this case is legal: Do the averments made by the pursuer in her pleading, if true, disclose a cause of action? I need not restate the particular facts. The question is whether the manufacturer of an article of drink sold by him to a distributor, in circumstances which prevent the distributor or the ultimate purchaser or consumer from discovering by inspection any defect, is under any legal duty to the ultimate purchaser or consumer to take reasonable care that the article is free from defect likely to cause injury to health. I do not think a more important problem has occupied your Lordships in your judicial capacity: important both because of its bearing on public health and because of the practical test which it applies to the system under which it arises . . . The law . . . appears to be that in order to support an action for damages for negligence the complainant has to show that he has been injured by the breach of a duty owed to him in the circumstances by the defendant to take reasonable care to avoid such injury. In the present case we are not concerned with the breach of the duty; if a duty exists, that would be a question of fact which is sufficiently averred and for present purposes must be assumed. We are solely concerned with the question whether, as a matter of law in the circumstances alleged, the defender owed any duty to the pursuer to take care.

It is remarkable how difficult it is to find in the English authorities statements of general application defining the relations between parties that give rise to the duty. The Courts are concerned with the particular relations which come before them in actual litigation, and it is sufficient to say whether the duty exists in those circumstances. The result is that the Courts have been engaged upon an elaborate classification of duties as they exist in respect of property, whether real or personal, with further divisions as to ownership, occupation or control, and distinctions based on the particular relations of the one side or the other, whether manufacturer, salesman or landlord, customer, tenant, stranger, and so on. In this way it can be ascertained at any time whether the law recognizes a duty, but only where the case can be referred to some particular species which has been examined and classified. And yet the duty which in common to all the cases where liability is established must logically be based upon some element common to the cases where it is found to exist. To seek a complete logical definition of the general principle is probably to go beyond the function of the judge, for the more general the definition the more likely it is to omit essentials or to introduce non-essentials. The attempt was made by Brett M.R. in *Heaven* v. *Pender* ((1883) 11 Q.B.D. 503, 509), in a definition to which I will later refer. As framed, it was demonstrably too wide, though it appears to me, if properly limited, to be capable of affording a valuable practical guide.

At present I content myself with pointing out that in English law there must be, and is, some general conception of relations giving rise to a duty of care, of which the particular cases found in the books are but instances. The liability for negligence, whether you style it such or treat it as in other systems as a species of "culpa," is no doubt based upon a general public sentiment of moral wrongdoing for which the offender must pay. But acts or omissions which any moral code would censure cannot in a practical world be treated so as to give a right to every person injured by them to demand relief. In this way rules of law arise which limit the range of complaints and the extent of their remedy. The rule that you are to love your neighbour becomes in law, you must not injure your neighbour; and the lawyer's question, Who is my neighbour? receives a restricted reply. You must take reasonable care to avoid acts or omissions which you can reasonably foresee would be likely to injure your neighbour. Who, then, in law is my neighbour? The answer seems to be—persons who are so closely and directly affected by my act that I ought reasonably to have them in contemplation as being so affected when I am directing my mind to the acts or omissions which are called in question. This appears to me to be the doctrine of *Heaven* v. *Pender*, as laid down by Lord Esher (then Brett M.R.) when it is limited by the notion of proximity introduced by Lord Esher himself and A.L. Smith L.J. in *Le Lievre* v. *Gould* ([1893] 1 Q.B. 491, 497, 504). Lord Esher says: "That case established that, under certain circumstances, one man may owe a duty to another, even though there is no contract between them. If one man is near to another, or is near to the property of another, a duty lies upon him not to do that which may cause a personal injury to that other, or may injure his property." So A. L. Smith L.J.: "The decision of *Heaven* v. *Pender* was founded upon the principle, that a duty to take due care did arise when the person or property of one was in such proximity to the person or property of another that, if due care was not taken, damage might be done by the one to the other." I think that this sufficiently states the truth if proximity be not confined to mere physical proximity, but be used, as I think it was intended, to extend to such close and direct relations that the act complained of directly affects a person whom the person alleged to be bound to take care would know would be directly affected by his careless act. That this is the sense in which nearness or "proximity" was intended by Lord Esher is obvious from his own illustration in *Heaven* v. *Pender* of the application of his doctrine to the sale of goods. "This" (*i.e.*, the rule he has just formulated) "includes the case of goods, etc., supplied to be used immediately by a particular person or persons, or one of a class of persons, where it would be obvious to the person supplying, if he thought, that the goods would in all probability be used at once by such persons before a reasonable opportunity for discovering any defect which might exist, and where the thing supplied would be of such a nature that a neglect of ordinary care or skill as to its condition or the manner of supplying it would probably cause danger to the person or property of the person for whose use it was supplied, and who was about to use it. It would exclude a case in which the goods are supplied under circumstances in which it would be a chance by whom they would be used or whether they would be used or not, or whether they would be used before there would probably be means of observing any defect, or where the goods would be of such a nature that a want of care or skill as to their condition or the manner of supplying them would not probably produce danger of injury to person or property." I draw particular attention to the fact that Lord Esher emphasizes the necessity of goods having to be "used immediately" and "used at once before a reasonable opportunity of inspection." This is obviously to exclude the possibility of goods having their condition altered by lapse of time, and to call attention to the proximate relationship, which may be too remote where inspection even of the person using, certainly of an intermediate person, may reasonably be interposed. With this necessary qualification of proximate relationship as explained in *Le Lievre* v. *Gould*, I think the judgment of Lord Esher expresses the law of England; without the qualification, I think the majority of the Court in *Heaven* v. *Pender* were justified in thinking the principle was expressed in too general terms. There will no doubt arise cases where it will be difficult to determine whether the contemplated relationship is so close that the duty arises. But in the class of case now before the Court I cannot conceive any difficulty to arise. A manufacturer puts up an article of food in a container which he knows will be opened by the actual consumer. There can be no inspection by any purchaser and no reasonable preliminary inspection by the consumer. Negligently, in the course of preparation, he allows the contents to be mixed with poison. It is said that the law of England and Scotland is that the poisoned consumer has no remedy against the negligent manufacturer. If this were the result of the authorities I should consider the result a grave defect in the law, and so contrary to principle that I should hesitate long before following any decision to that effect which had not the authority of this House. I would point out that, in the assumed state of the authorities, not only would the consumer have no remedy against the manufacturer, he would have none against any one else, for in the circumstances alleged there would be no evidence of negligence against any one other than the manufacturer; and, except in the case of a consumer who was also a purchaser, no contract and no warranty of fitness, and in the case of the purchase of a specific article under its patent or trade name, which might well be the case in the purchase of some articles of food or drink, no warranty protecting even the purchase-consumer. There are other instances than of articles of food and drink where goods are sold intended to be used immediately by the consumer, such as many forms of goods sold for cleaning purposes, where the same liability must exist. The doctrine supported by the decision below would not only deny a remedy to the consumer who was injured by consuming bottled beer or chocolates poisoned by the negligence of the manufacturer, but also to the user of what should be a harmless proprietary medicine, an ointment, a soap, a cleaning fluid or cleaning powder. I confine myself to articles of common household use, where every one, including the manufacturer, knows that the articles will be used by other persons than the actual ultimate purchaser—namely, by members of his family and his servants, and in some cases his guests. I do not think so ill of our jurisprudence as to suppose that its principles are so remote from the ordinary needs of civilized society and the ordinary claims it makes upon its members as to deny a legal remedy where there is so obviously a social wrong.

It will be found, I think, on examination that there is no case in which the circumstances have been such as I have just suggested where the liability has been negatived. There are numerous cases, where the relations were much more remote, where the duty has been held not to exist . . .

My Lords, if your Lordships accept the view that this pleading discloses a relevant cause of action you will be affirming the proposition that by Scots and English law alike a manufacturer of products, which he sells in such a form as to show that he intends them to reach the ultimate consumer in the form in which they left him with no reasonable possibility of intermediate examination, and with the knowledge that the absence of reasonable care in the preparation or putting up the products will result in an injury to the consumer's life or property, owes a duty to the consumer to take that reasonable care.

It is a proposition which I venture to say no one in Scotland or England who was not a lawyer would for one moment doubt. It will be an advantage to make it clear that the law in this matter, as in most others, is in accordance with sound common sense. I think that this appeal should be allowed.

LORD MACMILLAN: . . . The law takes no cognizance of carelessness in the abstract. It concerns itself with carelessness only where there is a duty to take care and where failure in that duty has caused damage. In such circumstances carelessness assumes the legal quality of negligence and entails the consequences in law of negligence. What, then, are the circumstances which give rise to this duty to take care? In the daily contacts of social and business life human beings are thrown into, or place themselves in, an infinite variety of relations with their fellows; and the law can refer only to the standards of the reasonable man in order to determine whether any particular relation gives rise to a duty to take care as between those who stand in that relation to each other. The grounds of action may be as various and manifold as human errancy; and the conception of legal responsibility may develop in adaptation to altering social conditions and standards. The criterion of judgment must adjust and adapt itself to the changing circumstances of life. The categories of negligence are never closed. The cardinal principle of liability is that the party complained of should owe to the party complaining a duty to take care, and that the party complaining should be able to prove that he has suffered damage in consequence of a breach of that duty. Where there is room for diversity of view, it is in determining what circumstances will establish such a relationship between the parties as to give rise, on the one side, to a duty to take care, and on the other side to a right to have care taken.

To descend from these generalities to the circumstances of the present case, I do not think that any reasonable man or any twelve reasonable men would hesitate to hold that, if the appellant establishes her allegations, the respondent has exhibited carelessness in the conduct of his business. For a manufacturer of aerated water to store his empty bottles in a place where snails can get access to them, and to fill his bottles without taking any adequate precautions by inspection or otherwise to ensure that they contain no deleterious foreign matter, may reasonably be characterized as carelessness without applying too exacting a standard. But, as I have pointed out, it is not enough to prove the respondent to be careless in his process of manufacture. The question is: Does he owe a duty to take care, and to whom does he owe that duty? Now I have no hesitation in affirming that a person who for gain engages in the business of manufacturing articles of food and drink intended for consumption by members of the public in the form in which he issues them is under a duty to take care in the manufacture of these articles. That duty, in my opinion, he owes to those whom he intends to consume his products. He manufactures his commodities for human consumption; he intends and contemplates that they shall be consumed. By reason of that very fact he places himself in a relationship with all the potential consumers of his commodities, and that relationship which he assumes and desires for his own ends imposes upon him a duty to take care to avoid injuring them. He owes them a duty not to convert by his own carelessness an article which he issues to them as wholesome and innocent into an article which is dangerous to life and health. It is sometimes said that liability can only arise where a reasonable man would have foreseen and could have avoided the consequences of his act or omission. In the present case the respondent, when he manufactured his ginger-beer, had directly in contemplation that it would be consumed by members of the public. Can it be said that he could not be expected as a reasonable man to foresee that if he conducted his process of manufacture carelessly he might injure those whom he expected and desired to consume his ginger-beer? The possibility of injury so arising seems to me in no sense so remote as to excuse him from foreseeing it. Suppose that a baker, through carelessness, allows a large quantity of arsenic to be mixed with a batch of his bread, with the result that those who subsequently eat it are poisoned, could he be heard to say that he owed no duty to the consumers of his bread to take care that it was free from poison, and that, as he did not know that any poison had got into it, his only liability was for breach of warranty under his contract of sale to those who actually bought the poisoned bread from him? Observe that I have said "through carelessness," and thus excluded the case of pure accident such as may happen where every care is taken. I cannot believe, and I do not believe, that neither in the law of England nor in the law of Scotland is there redress for such a case. The state of facts I have figured might well give rise to a criminal charge, and the civil consequence of such carelessness can scarcely be less wide than its criminal consequences. Yet the principle of the decision appealed from is that the manufacturer of food products intended by him for human consumption does not owe to the consumers whom he has in view any duty of care, not even the duty to take care that he does not poison them . . .

I am anxious to emphasise that the principle of judgment which commends itself to me does not give rise to the sort of objection stated by Parke B. in *Longmeid* v. *Holliday* ((1851) 6 Exch. 761, 768; 155 E.R. 752), where he said: "But it would be going much too far to say, that so much care is required in the ordinary intercourse of life between one individual and another, that if a machine not in its nature dangerous—a carriage, for instance—but which might become so by a latent defect entirely unknown, although discoverable by the exercise of ordinary care, should be lent or given by one person, even by the person who manufactured it, to another, the former should be answerable to the latter for a subsequent damage accruing by the use of it." I read this passage rather as a note of warning that the standard of care exacted in human dealings must not be pitched too high than as giving any countenance to the view that negligence may be exhibited with impunity. It must always be a question of circumstances whether the carelessness amounts to negligence, and whether the injury is not too remote from the carelessness. I can readily conceive that where a manufacturer has parted with his product and it has passed into other hands it may well be exposed to vicissitudes which may render it defective or noxious, for which the manufacturer could not in any view be held to be to blame. It may be a good general rule to regard responsibility as ceasing when control ceases. So, also, where between the manufacturer and the user there is interposed a party who has the means and opportunity of examining the manufacturer's product before he re-issues it to the actual user. But where, as in the present case, the article of consumption is so prepared as to be intended to reach the consumer in the condition in which it leaves the manufacturer, and the manufacturer takes steps to ensure this by sealing or otherwise closing the container so that the contents cannot be tampered with, I regard his control as remaining effective until the article reaches the consumer and the container is opened by him. The intervention of any exterior agency is intended to be excluded, and was in fact in the present case excluded . . .

The burden of proof must always be upon the injured party to establish that the defect which caused the injury was present in the article when it left the hands of the party whom he sues, that the defect was occasioned by the carelessness of that party, and that the circumstances are such as to cast upon the defender a duty to take care not to injure the pursuer. There is no presumption of negligence in such a case as the present, nor is there any justification for applying the maxim, res ipsa loquitur. Negligence must be both averred and proved . . .

LORD THANKERTON: . . . A man cannot be charged with negligence if he has no obligation to exercise diligence . . . Unless the consumer can establish a special relationship with the manufacturer, it is clear, in my opinion, that neither the law of Scotland nor the law of England will hold that the manufacturer has any duty towards the consumer to exercise diligence . . . [But here there was a special relationship because the manufacturer] in placing his manufactured article of drink upon the market, has intentionally so excluded interference with, or examination of, the article by any intermediate handler of the goods between himself and the consumer that he has, of his own accord, brought himself into direct relationship with the consumer, with the result that the consumer is entitled to rely upon the exercise of diligence by the manufacturer to secure that the article shall not be harmful to the consumer . . .

LORD BUCKMASTER dissented on the ground that there were only two exceptions to the principle that "the breach of the defendant's contract with A. to use care and skill in and about the manufacture or repair of an article does not of itself give any cause of action to B. when he is injured by reason of the article proving to be defective" (*per* Lord Sumner in *Blacker* v. *Lake & Elliot Ltd.* (1912) 106 L.T. 533, 536), namely, where the article was dangerous in itself or had a defect known to the manufacturer. The majority decision was "simply to misapply to tort doctrine applicable to sale and purchase."

LORD TOMLIN also dissented.

Quotation

> "There may be in the cup
> A spider steep'd, and one may drink, depart,
> And yet partake no venom, for his knowledge
> It is not infected; but if one present
> The abhorr'd ingredient to his eye, make known
> How he hath drunk, he cracks his gorge, his sides
> With violent hefts. I have drunk, and seen the spider."

Shakespeare, *The Winter's Tale*, II.i.37.

Questions

1. Suppose that Mrs. Donoghue bought a bottle of Stevenson's ginger beer for 10p. and took it home; and that when she opened it, she saw a decomposed snail at the top of the bottle, and suffered shock at the thought of what she might have drunk. Could she recover from the manufacturer (a) damages for shock; (b) 10p.?

2. Suppose that Stevenson got his bottles from Louis, and that Mrs. Donoghue had been injured because of a defect in the bottle which Stevenson couldn't have discovered. Would Louis or Stevenson be liable, or both?

3. Suppose that the victim is not a regular consumer like Mrs. Donoghue but a shop-lifter or a tester for *Which*? Would you make the manufacturer liable? If not, would this be because he owed no duty or for some other reason?

Note:

Donoghue v. *Stevenson* is hardly the Last Word on the tort of negligence, since it was decided over 50 years ago, but it still deserves to come first in the book. Its importance lies not only in what it decided but also in how it was decided: it established, as its *ratio decidendi*, that a careless manufacturer of a dangerously defective product is liable to a consumer to whom it causes personal injury, but more importantly, it laid down in *obiter dicta* a general principle of liability for unintended harm, focussing on the duty of care.

The Manufacturer

Lord Thankerton spoke of the special relationship between manufacturer and consumer, *i.e.* the person whose appetite the manufacturer seeks to stimulate ("Don't be Vague: Ask for Stevenson's Ginger Beer"). There is such a special relationship, but in fact the manufacturer also owes a duty to the innocent bystander with whom he has no such relationship: the pedestrian injured by the defective car can sue just as well as its owner (*Lambert* v. *Lewis* [1982] A.C. 225). Everyone (or nearly everyone?) is entitled not to be maimed by defective goods carelessly made.

Lord Macmillan suggested that it was for the plaintiff to prove that the manufacturer was careless, but of course the victim can hardly know what went on in the factory. In *Grant* v. *Australian Knitting Mills* [1936] A.C. 85, the plaintiff complained of dermatitis resulting from the use of underpants manufactured by the defendant which contained excess sulphites. The defendant led evidence that he had manufactured 4,737,600 pairs of underpants with never a complaint. Yet the plaintiff succeeded. No one can reasonably say that a manufacturer with a failure rate of only one in a million is not a reasonably careful manufacturer; it is, indeed, an astonishing performance which should earn a prize. And one cannot say that he was not reasonably careful with the pants in question, since there was no evidence as to them, save their defect. He was in fact made to pay because the pants were defective when they left his factory. Thus the principal case, though it expresses the duty in terms of taking reasonable care, virtually results in a guarantor's liability. (See, for example, *Hill* v. *James Crowe* (*Cases*) *Ltd.* [1978] 1 All E.R. 812.)

Many goods are made abroad. It is tiresome to have to go abroad to sue the foreign manufacturer, yet the place of manufacture does seem to be the place of the tort. The courts can get round this by saying that the foreign manufacturer should have warned of the danger in the place where the thing was marketed (*Castree* v. *E.R. Squibb & Sons* [1980] 2 All E.R. 589).

Most things that are made are made to be sold, but there are many more sellers than makers. Even in this case the snail was sold not only by Stevenson (to Minchella) but also by Minchella (to Friend). Long before 1932 it was clear what the seller's duty was: his duty was to provide a good thing, not just to take care not to provide a bad one. The seller's liability was strict (*i.e.* not dependent on his carelessness) and it was triggered by the defect, even if the defect did not render the thing dangerous (*i.e.* apt to cause physical harm). Now Friend bought the ginger-beer for Mrs. Donoghue ("Please can I have a ginger-beer for my lady-friend here?"), and Mrs. Donoghue was very close to Minchella, perhaps physically just as close as Friend himself. In many systems of law Mrs. Donoghue would have been able to sue Minchella on the contract of sale, as its beneficiary. English law, however, does not allow a beneficiary to sue (*Beswick* v. *Beswick* [1968] A.C. 68), either to enforce the contract or to claim damages for its breach. The next following case shows how the law of tort can be used to make a contractor liable to a beneficiary, but in our case Mrs. Donoghue was suing Stevenson, not Minchella, and while Stevenson, like Minchella, was a seller, it is difficult to see Mrs. Donoghue as a beneficiary of the contract whereby Stevenson sold to Minchella. After all, if Stevenson had delivered 12 dozen bottles, that would make 144 beneficiaries, which is rather a lot for one contract.

In some countries, such as the United States, there is a special regime for manufacturers, and indeed distributors, of goods. This has not yet occurred in England, but many proposals are afoot. The Pearson Commission, which was itself set up because of the scandal arising from the defective drug thalidomide, recommended that the manufacturer should be strictly liable (*i.e.* liable without being at fault) for personal injury caused by a product which was defective in the sense that it was not, as presented, as safe as one had a right to expect. Essentially similar proposals have emanated from Strasbourg (for the Council of Europe) and from Brussels (for the EEC). It is likely that some such principle will be adopted. One difficulty is whether the manufacturer should bear the burden of "development risks," *i.e.* liability for damage done by things which only subsequent technology has shown to be defective. Note that the proposed strict liability would apply only where personal injury is caused, or perhaps also damage to personal (not commercial) property other than the thing itself.

The Principle

The decision did more than simply add manufacturer/consumer to the list of relationships which involved a duty to take care. It also laid down a principle much wider than the facts of the case required, *viz.* "You must take reasonable care to avoid causing foreseeable injury."

It is because this principle acts as a unifying force that *Donoghue* v. *Stevenson* is said to denote the birth of negligence as a tort.

There are two areas in respect of which the principle is wider than the rule required by the facts of the case:

(1) In the actual case, the harm allegedly suffered was physical, indeed internal, injury. The principle did not seem to be so limited. Was the principle extensible to purely psychical harm and to purely financial harm? See *McLoughlin* v. *O'Brian* (below, p. 68) and *Junior Books* (next case).

2. In the actual case Stevenson's conduct added a new danger to life. He positively caused the harm, he didn't just let it happen. Was the principle extensible to those who simply let the damage occur? See *Dorset Yacht* (below, p. 50) and *Anns* (below p. 56).

JUNIOR BOOKS LTD. v. VEITCHI CO. LTD.

House of Lords [1983] A.C. 520; [1982] 3 W.L.R. 477; [1982] 3 All E.R. 201

Action by employer-occupier against building sub-contractor for cost of replacing sub-standard work and business loss due thereto.

LORD BRANDON OF OAKBROOK (**dissenting**): My Lords, this appeal arises in an action in which Junior Books Ltd are the pursuers and Veitchi Co Ltd are the defenders. In that action, which purports to be founded in delict, the pursuers seek reparation from the defenders for loss and damage which they claim to have suffered by reason of the want of care of the defenders in laying flooring at the pursuer's factory in Grangemouth . . .

Avoiding all matters of detail, the averments contained in the condescendence can be summarised as follows. (I) In 1969–70 the pursuers had built for them by main contractors a factory in Grangemouth. (2) Earlier, in July 1968, the pursuers' architects had nominated the defenders as sub-contractors to lay flooring, consisting of a magnesium oxychloride composition, in the production area of the factory. (3) The pursuers' architects, in so nominating the defenders, had relied on the fact that the defenders were specialists in the laying of flooring. (4) The defenders had accepted the nomination and, after entering into a contract with the main contractors, laid flooring of the specified composition in the specified area. (5) It was the duty of the defenders to mix and lay the flooring with reasonable care. (6) The defenders were in breach of that duty in that they failed, in a number of respects, to mix and lay the flooring with reasonable care. (7) In consequence of that breach of duty by the defenders the flooring began to develop cracks in 1972 and had gone on cracking more and more ever since. (8) As a result of the cracking of the flooring the pursuers suffered the following items of damage or loss: necessary relaying or replacement of the flooring £50,000; storage of books during the carrying out of the work £1,000; removal of machinery to enable the work to be done, £2,000; loss of profits due to disturbance of business £45,000; wages of employees thrown away £90,000; overheads thrown away £16,000; investigation of necessary treatment of flooring £3,000. The total of these items was pleaded as £206,000; it is in fact, although the point is not material, £207,000.

For the purpose of considering the relevancy of the pursuers' averments of facts, it is necessary to make the assumption that all such averments are true. On the basis of that assumption, the dispute between the parties is not whether the defenders owed a duty of care to the pursuers in connection with the laying of the flooring; the existence of some duty arising from the proximity of the parties is, rightly in my view, admitted by the defenders. The dispute is rather concerned with the scope of that admitted duty of care.

For the defenders, on the one hand, it was contended that the duty was limited to a duty to exercise reasonable care so to mix and lay the flooring as to ensure that it was not a danger to persons or property, excluding for this purpose the property brought into being by the work and labour done, that is to say the flooring itself.

For the pursuers, on the other hand, it was contended that the duty was a duty to exercise reasonable care so to mix and lay the flooring as to ensure that it was free of any defects, whether dangerous to persons or property or not; alternatively, if the duty was in principle that put forward by the defenders, the relevant property, damage to which the defenders were under a duty to exercise reasonable care to avoid, included the property brought into being by the work and labour done, that is to say the flooring itself . . .

My Lords, it appears to me clear beyond doubt that, there being no contractual relationship between the pursuers and the defenders in the present case, the foundation, and the only foundation, for the existence of a duty of care owed by the defenders to the pursuers, is the principle laid down in the decision of your Lordships' House in *Donoghue* v. *Stevenson* [1932] A.C. 562. The actual decision in that case related only to the duty owed by a manufacturer of goods to their ultimate user or consumer, and can be summarised in this way: a person who manufactures goods which he intends to be used or consumed by others is under a duty to exercise such reasonable care in their manufacture as to ensure that they can be used or consumed in the manner intended without causing physical damage to persons or their property.

While that was the actual decision in *Donoghue* v. *Stevenson*, it was based on a much wider principle embodied in passages in the speech of Lord Atkin, which have been quoted so often that I do not find it necessary to quote them again here. Put shortly, that wider principle is that, when a person can or ought to appreciate that a careless act or omission on his part may result in physical injury to other persons or their property; he owes a duty to all such persons to exercise reasonable care to avoid such careless act or omission.

It is, however, of fundamental importance to observe that the duty of care laid down in *Donoghue* v. *Stevenson* was based on the existence of a danger of physical injury to persons or their property. That this is so clear from the observations made by Lord Atkin ([1932] A.C. 562, 581–2) with regard to the statements of law of Brett M.R. in *Heaven* v. *Pender* ((1883) 11 Q.B.D. 503, 509). It has further, until the present case, never been doubted, so far as I know, that the relevant property for the purpose of the wider principle on which the decision in *Donoghue* v. *Stevenson* was based was property other than the very property which gave rise to the danger of physical damage concerned.

My Lords, I have already indicated my opinion that the wider principle on which the decision in *Donoghue* v. *Stevenson* was based applies to the present case. The effect of its application is that the defenders owed a duty to the pursuers to exercise reasonable care so to mix and lay the flooring as to ensure that it did not, when completed and put to its contemplated use, constitute a danger of physical damage to persons or their property, other than the flooring itself.

The averments contained in the condescendence in the present case do not include any averment that the defects in the flooring complained of by the pursuers either constitute presently, or might reasonably be expected to constitute in the future, a danger of physical damage to persons or their property, other than the flooring itself. In the absence of any averment of that kind, I am of opinion that the averments contained in the condescendence disclose no cause of action in delict and are accordingly irrelevant.

My Lords, a good deal of the argument presented to your Lordships during the hearing of the appeal was directed to the question whether a person can recover, in an action founded on delict alone, purely pecuniary loss which is independent of any physical damage to persons or their property. If that were the question to be decided in the present case, I should have no hesitation in holding that, in principle and depending on the facts of a particular case, purely pecuniary loss may be recoverable in an action founded on delict alone. Two examples can be given of such cases. First, there is the type of case where a person suffers purely pecuniary loss as a result of relying on another person's negligent misstatements: see *Hedley*

Byrne & Co Ltd v. *Heller & Partners Ltd* [1964] A.C. 465. Second, there may be a type of case where a person, who has a cause or action based on *Donoghue* v. *Stevenson*, reasonably incurs pecuniary loss in order to prevent or mitigate imminent danger of damage to the persons or property exposed to that danger: see the dissenting judgment of Laskin J. in the Canadian Supreme Court case of *Rivtow Marine Ltd* v. *Washington Iron Works* [1974] S.C.R. 1189, referred to with approval in the speech of Lord Wilberforce in *Anns* v. *Merton London Borough* ([1978] A.C. 728, 760).

I do not, however, consider that the question of law for decision in this case is whether a person can, in an action founded in delict alone, recover for purely pecuniary loss. On the contrary, I adhere to the nature of the question of law to be decided which I formulated earlier, namely what is the scope of the duty of care owed by the defenders to the pursuers on the assumed facts of the present case?

My Lords, in support of their contentions, the pursuers placed reliance on the broad statements relating to liability in negligence contained in the speech of Lord Wilberforce in *Anns* v. *Merton London Borough* ([1978] A.C. 728, 751-2).

> "Through the trilogy of cases in this House, *Donoghue* v. *Stevenson* ([1932] A.C. 562), *Hedley Byrne & Co Ltd.* v. *Heller & Partners Ltd.* ([1964] A.C. 465) and *Home Office* v. *Dorset Yacht Co. Ltd.* ([1970] A.C. 1004), the position has now been reached that in order to establish that a duty of care arises in a particular situation, it is not necessary to bring the facts of that situation within those of previous situations in which a duty of care has been held to exist. Rather the question has to be approached in two stages. First one has to ask whether, as between the alleged wrongdoer and the person who has suffered damage there is a sufficient relationship of proximity or neighbour-hood such that, in the reasonable contemplation of the former, carelessness on his part may be likely to cause damage to the latter, in which case a prima facie duty of care arises. Secondly, if the first question is answered affirmatively, it is necessary to consider whether there are any considerations which ought to negative, or to reduce or limit the scope of the duty or the class of person to whom it is owed or the damages to which a breach of it may give rise . . . "

Applying that general statement of principle to the present case, it is, as I indicated earlier, common ground that the first question which Lord Wilberforce said one should ask oneself, namely whether there is sufficient proximity between the parties to give rise to the existence of a duty of care owed by the one to the other, falls to be answered in the affirmative. Indeed, it is difficult to imagine a greater degree of proximity, in the absence of a direct contractual relationship, than that which, under the modern type of building contract, exists between a building owner and a sub-contractor nominated by him or his architect.

That first question having been answered in the affirmative, however, it is necessary, according to the views expressed by Lord Wilberforce in the passage from his speech in *Anns* v. *Merton London Borough* quoted above, to ask oneself a second question, namely whether there are any considerations which ought, inter alia, to limit the scope of the duty which exists.

To that second question I would answer that there are two important considerations which ought to limit the scope of the duty of care which it is common ground was owed by the defenders to the pursuers on the assumed facts of the present case.

The first consideration is that, in *Donoghue* v. *Stevenson* itself and in all the numerous cases in which the principle of that decision has been applied to different but analogous factual situations, it has always been either stated expressly, or taken for granted, that an essential ingredient in the cause of action relied on was the existence of danger, or the threat of danger, of physical damage to persons or their property, excluding for this purpose the very piece of property from the defective condition of which such danger, or threat of danger, arises. To dispense with that essential ingredient in a cause of action of the kind concerned in the present case would, in my view, involve a radical departure from long-established authority.

The second consideration is that there is no sound policy reason for substituting the wider scope of the duty of care put forward for the pursuers for the more restricted scope of such duty put forward by the defenders. The effect of accepting the pursuers' contention with regard to the scope of the duty of care involved would be, in substance, to create, as between two persons who are not in any contractual relationships with each other, obligations of one of those two persons to the other, which are only really appropriate as between persons who do have such a relationship between them.

In the case of a manufacturer or distributor of goods, the position would be that he warranted to the ultimate user or consumer of such goods that they were as well designed, as merchantable and as fit for their contemplated purpose as the exercise of reasonable care could make them.

In the case of sub-contractors such as those concerned in the present case, the position would be that they warranted to the building owner that the flooring, when laid, would be as well designed, as free from defects of any kind and as fit for its contemplated purpose as the exercise of reasonable care could make it.

In my view, the imposition of warranties of this kind on one person in favour of another, when there is no contractual relationship between them, is contrary to any sound policy requirement.

It is, I think, just worth while to consider the difficulties which would arise if the wider scope of the duty of care put forward by the pursuers were accepted. In any case where complaint was made by an ultimate consumer that a product made by some persons with whom he himself had no contract was defective, by what standard or standards of quality would the question of defectiveness fall to be decided? In the case of goods bought from a retailer, it could hardly be the standard prescribed by the contract between the retailer and the wholesaler, or between the wholesaler and the distributor, or between the distributor and the manufacturer, for the terms of such contracts would not even be known to the ultimate buyer. In the case of sub-contractors such as the defenders in the present case, it could hardly be the standard prescribed by the contract between the sub-contractors and the main contractors, for, although the building owner would probably be aware of those terms, he could not, since he was not a party to such contract, rely on any standard prescribed in it. It follows that the question by what standard or standards alleged defects in a product complained of by its ultimate user or consumer are to be judged remains entirely at large and cannot be given any just or satisfactory answer.

If, contrary to the views expressed above, the relevant contract or contracts can be regarded in order to establish the standard or standards of quality by which the question of defectiveness falls to be judged, and if such contract or contracts happen to include provisions excluding or limiting liability for defective products or defective work, or for negligence generally, it seems that the party sued in delict should in justice be entitled to rely on such provisions. This illustrates with especial force the inherent difficulty of seeking to impose what are really contractual obligations by unprecedented and, as I think, wholly undesirable extensions of the existing law of delict.

By contrast, if the scope of the duty of care contended for by the defenders is accepted, the standard of defectiveness presents no problem at all. The sole question is whether the product is so defective that, when used or consumed in the way in which it was intended to be, it gives rise to a danger of physical damage to persons or their property, other than the product concerned itself.

My Lords, for the reasons which I have given, I would decide the question of relevancy in favour of the defenders and allow the appeal accordingly.

LORD ROSKILL: My Lords, there was much discussion before your Lordships' House as to the effect of the pleadings. I see no need to discuss them in detail. They seem to me clearly to contain no allegation that the flooring was in a dangerous state or that its condition was such as to cause danger to life or limb or to other property of other persons or that repairs were urgently or imminently required to avoid any such danger, or that any economic or financial loss had been, or would be, suffered save as would be consequential on the ultimate replacement of the flooring, the necessity of which was averred in condescendence VII. The essential feature of the respondents pleading was that it advanced a claim for the cost of remedying the alleged defects in the flooring itself by replacement together with resulting or economic or financial loss consequential on that replacement.

My Lords, it was because of that scope of the respondents' pleading and because that pleading was limited in this way that the appellants were able to mount their main attack on those pleadings and to contend that they were, at least in the absence of amendment, for which no leave has been sought at any stage, irrelevant since the law neither of Scotland nor of England made the appellants liable in delict or in negligence for the cost of replacing this flooring or for the economic or financial loss consequent on that replacement. It was strenuously argued for the appellants that for your Lordships' House now to hold that in those circumstances which I have just outlined the appellants were liable to the respondents would be to extend the duty of care owed by a manufacturer and others, to whom the principles first enunciated in *Donoghue* v. *Stevenson* have since been extended during the last half century, far beyond the limits to which the courts have hitherto extended them. The familiar "floodgates" argument was once again brought fully into play. My Lords, although it cannot be denied that policy considerations have from time to time been allowed to play their part in the last century and the present either in limiting or in extending the scope of the tort of negligence since it first developed as it were in its own right in the course of the last century, yet today I think its scope is best determined by considerations of principle rather than of policy. The "floodgates" argument is very familiar. It still may on occasion have its proper place but, if principle suggests that the law should develop along a particular route and if the adoption of that particular route will accord a remedy where that remedy has hitherto been denied, I see no reason why, if it be just that the law should henceforth accord that remedy, that remedy should be denied simply because it will, in consequence of this particular development, become available to many rather than to few.

My Lords, I think there is no doubt that *Donoghue* v. *Stevenson* by its insistence on proximity, in the sense in which Lord Atkin used that word, as the foundation of the duty of care which was there enunciated marked a great development in the law of delict and of negligence alike. In passing it should be noted that Lord Atkin emphasised that the laws of Scotland and of England were in that case, as is agreed in the present, identical (see [1932] A.C. 562, 579). But, that advance having been thus made in 1932, the doctrine then enunciated was at first confined by judicial decision within relatively narrow limits. The gradual developments of the law will be found discussed by the editor of *Salmond and Heuston on Torts* (18th ed, 1981) pp. 289 *et seq*. Though initially there is no doubt that, because of Lord Atkin's phraseology in *Donoghue* v. *Stevenson* ([1932] A.C. 562, 599), 'Injury to the consumer's life or property', it was thought that the duty of care did not extend beyond avoiding physical injury or physical damage to the person or the property of the person to whom the duty of care was owed, that limitation has long since ceased as Professor Heuston points out in the passage to which I have just referred.

My Lords, in discussion on the later developments of the law the decision of your Lordships' House (albeit by a majority) in *Morrison Steamship Co* v. *Greystoke Castle* (*cargo owners*) ([1947] A.C. 265) is sometimes overlooked. The facts were essentially simple. Two ships collided. For simplicity I will call them A and B. Both ships were to blame, albeit in unequal proportions. The owners of the cargo on ship

A became liable to contribution in general average to the owners of ship A. The cargo owners then sued ship B to recover the relevant proportion of that liability for general average contribution. They succeeded in that claim. My Lords, I shall not quote extensively from the speeches of either the majority or the minority. Suffice it to say that here the recovery of economic loss was allowed and I do not think that the decision is to be explained simply on some supposed esoteric mystery appertaining to the law regarding general average contribution. It is true that there seems to be little discussion in the speeches regarding the extent of the duty of care, but the very rejection by the majority of the views expressed by Lord Simonds in his dissenting speech that "nothing would justify me in holding that the cargo owner can recover damages from the wrong-doing ship, not because his cargo has suffered damage, but because he has been placed under an obligation to make a general average contribution" (see [1947] A.C. 265, 307), shows that Lord Simonds at least was appreciating the consequences of the step forward which the majority were then taking. The decision is indeed far from the previously limited application of the doctrine enunciated in *Donoghue* v. *Stevenson*.

Fifteen years later, in *Hedley Byrne & Co Ltd.* v. *Heller & Partners Ltd* ([1964] A.C. 465), your Lordships' House made plain that the duty of care was not limited in the manner for which the respondents in that appeal had contended. Your Lordships' House held without doubt that economic loss was recoverable without physical damage having been suffered provided that the relevant duty of care had existed and that the duty existed when the party to whom the allegedly negligent advice was given relied on the "judgment" or "skill" (I take those two words from the speech of Lord Morris ([1964] A.C. 465, 503 of him who gave the advice . . .) [His Lordship then quoted two passages from the speech of Lord Devlin in *Hedley Byrne* (below, pp. 38–39), one from Lord Reid's speech in *Dorset Yacht* (below p. 50) and the passage from the speech of Lord Wilberforce in *Anns* which Lord Brandon invoked in the present case (above p. 24)].

Applying those statements of general principle as your Lordships have been enjoined to do both by Lord Reid and by Lord Wilberforce rather than to ask whether the particular situation which has arisen does or does not resemble some earlier and different situation where a duty of care has been held or has not been held to exist, I look for the reasons why, it being conceded that the appellants owed a duty of care to others not to construct the flooring so that those others were in peril of suffering loss or damage to their persons or their property, that duty of care should not be equally owed to the respondents, who, though not in direct contractual relationship with the appellants, were as nominated sub-contractors in almost as close a commercial relationship with the appellants as it is possible to envisage short of privity of contract, so as not to expose the respondents to a possible liability to financial loss for repairing the flooring should it prove that the flooring had been negligently constructed. It is conceded that if the flooring had been so badly constructed that to avoid imminent danger the respondents had to expend money on renewing it the respondents could have recovered the cost of so doing. It seems curious that if the appellants' work had been so bad that to avoid imminent danger expenditure had been incurred the respondents could recover that expenditure but that if the work was less badly done so that remedial work could be postponed they cannot do so. Yet this is seemingly the result of the appellants' contentions.

My Lords, I have already said that there is no decided case which clearly points the way. But it is, I think, of assistance to see how far the various decisions have gone. I shall restrict my citation to the more important decisions both in this country and overseas. In *Dutton*, which . . . your Lordships' House expressly approved in *Anns*, the Court of Appeal held that the plaintiff, who bought the house in question long after it had been built and its foundations inadequately inspected by the defendants' staff, was entitled to recover from the defendants, *inter alia*, the estimated cost of repairing the house as well as other items of loss including diminution in value. There was in that case physical damage to the house. It was argued that the defendants were not liable for the cost of repairs or diminution in value. This argument was expressly rejected by Lord Denning M.R. and by Sachs L.J. (see [1972] 1 Q.B. 373, 396, 403–4). Stamp L.J. was however more sympathetic to this argument. He said ([1972] 1 Q.B. 373, 414–5):

> "It is pointed out that in the past a distinction has been drawn between constructing a dangerous article and constructing one which is defective or of inferior quality. I may be liable to one who purchases in the market a bottle of ginger beer which I have carelessly manufactured and which is dangerous and causes injury to person or property; but it is not the law that I am liable to him for the loss he suffers because what is found inside the bottle and for which he has paid money is not ginger beer but water. I do not warrant, except to an immediate purchaser and then by contract and not in tort, that the thing I manufacture is reasonably fit for its purpose. The submission is I think a formidable one and in my view raises the most difficult point for decision in this case. Nor can I see any valid distinction between the case of a builder who carelessly builds a house which, although not a source of danger to person or property, nevertheless owing to a concealed defect in its foundations starts to settle and crack and becomes valueless, and the case of a manufacturer who carelessly manufactures an article which, though not a source of danger to a subsequent owner or to his property, nevertheless owing to a hidden defect quickly disintegrates. To hold that either the builder or the manufacturer was liable, except in contract, would be to open up a new field of liability, the extent of which could not I think be logically controlled, and since it is not in my judgment necessary to do so for the purposes of this case, I do not, more particularly because of the absence of the builder, express an opinion whether the builder has a higher or lower duty than the manufacturer. But the distinction between the case of a manufacturer of a dangerous thing which causes damage and that of a thing which turns out to be defective and valueless lies I think not in the nature of the injury but in the character of the duty. I have a duty not carelessly to put out a dangerous thing which may cause damage to one who may purchase it, but the duty does not extend to putting out carelessly a defective or useless or valueless thing. So again one goes back to consider what was the character of the duty, if any, owed to the plaintiff, and one finds on authority that the injury which is one of the essential elements of the tort of negligence is not confined to physical damage to personal property but may embrace economic damage which the plaintiff suffers through buying a worthless thing, as is shown by the *Hedley Byrne* case."

Thus it was on the character of the duty that Stamp L.J. founded and was able to agree with the other members of the Court of Appeal in that case.

My Lords, a similar question arose some years later in *Batty* v. *Metropolitan Property Realizations Ltd.* ([1978] Q.B. 554). By the date of this decision the Court of Appeal had the benefit of the decision in your Lordships' House in *Anns*. Megaw L.J. (see [1978] Q.B. 554, 570) regarded the doubts raised by Stamp L.J as resolved by Lord Wilberforce's speech in *Anns*. Once again the argument based on absence of physical damage was advanced, as it had been in *Dutton*. Once again it was rejected, but on the basis that there was in the case as in *Dutton* the requisite degree of physical damage. . . .

My Lords, to my mind in the instant case there is no physical damage to the flooring in the sense in which that phrase was used in *Dutton, Batty* . . . and some of the other cases. As my noble and learned friend Lord Russell said during the argument, the question which your Lordships' House now has to decide is whether the relevant Scots and English law today extends the duty of care beyond a duty to prevent harm being done by faulty work to a duty to avoid such faults being present in the work itself. It was powerfully urged on behalf of the appellants that were your Lordships so to extend the law a pursuer in the position of the pursuer in *Donoghue* v. *Stevenson* could in addition to recovering for any personal injury suffered have also recovered for the diminished value of the offending bottle of ginger beer. Any remedy of that kind it was argued must lie in contract and not in delict or tort. My Lords, I seem to detect in that able argument reflections of the previous judicial approach to comparable problems before *Donoghue* v. *Stevenson* was decided. That approach usually resulted in the conclusion that in principle the proper remedy lay in contract and not outside it. But that approach and its concomitant philosophy ended in 1932 and for my part I should be reluctant to countenance its re-emergence some fifty years later in the instant case. I think today the proper control lies not in asking whether the proper remedy should lie in contract or instead in delict or tort, not in somewhat capricious judicial determination whether a particular case falls on one side of the line or the other, not in somewhat artificial distinctions between physical and economic or financial loss when the two sometimes go together and sometimes do not (it is sometimes overlooked that virtually all damage including physical damage is in one sense financial or economic for it is compensated by an award of damages) but in the first instance in establishing the relevant principles and then in deciding whether the particular case falls within or without those principles. To state this is to do no more than to restate what Lord Reid said in the *Dorset Yacht* case and Lord Wilberforce in *Anns*. Lord Wilberforce in the passage I have already quoted enunciated the two tests which have to be satisfied. The first is 'sufficient relationship of proximity', the second any considerations negativing, reducing or limiting the scope of the duty or the class of person to whom it is owed or the damages to which a breach of the duty may give rise. My Lords, it is I think in the application of those two principles that the ability to control the extent of liability in delict or in negligence lies. The history of the development of the law in the last fifty years shows that fears aroused by the 'floodgates' argument have been unfounded. . . .

Turning back to the present appeal I therefore ask first whether there was the requisite degree of proximity so as to give rise to the relevant duty of care relied on by the respondents. I regard the following facts as of crucial importance in requiring an affirmative answer to that question: (1) the appellants were nominated sub-contractors; (2) the appellants were specialists in flooring; (3) the appellants knew what products were required by [the respondents] and their main contractors and specialised in the production of those products; (4) the appellants alone were responsible for the composition and construction of the flooring; (5) the respondents relied on the appellants' skill and experience; (6) the appellants as nominated sub-contractors must have known that the respondents relied on their skill and experience; (7) the relationship between the parties was as close as it could be short of actual privity of contract; (8) the appellants must be taken to have known that if they did the work negligently (as it must be assumed that they did) the resulting defects would at some time require remedying by the respondents expending money on the remedial measures as a consequence of which the respondents would suffer financial or economic loss.

My Lords, . . . it seems to me that all the conditions existed which give rise to the relevant duty of care owed by the appellants to the respondents.

I then turn to Lord Wilberforce's second proposition. On the facts I have just stated, I see nothing whatever to restrict the duty of care arising from the proximity of which I have spoken. During the argument it was asked what the position would be in a case where there was a relevant exclusion clause in the main contract. My Lords, that question does not arise for decision in the instant appeal, but in principle I would venture the view that such a clause according to the manner in which it was worded might in some circumstances limit the duty of care just as in the *Hedley Byrne* case the plaintiffs were ultimately defeated by the defendants' disclaimer of responsibility. But in the present case the only suggested reason for limiting the damage (ex hypothesi economic or financial only) recoverable for the breach of the duty of care just enunciated is that hitherto the law has not allowed such recovery and therefore ought not in the future to do so. My Lords, with all respect to those who find this a sufficient answer I do not. I think this is the next logical step forward in the development of this branch of the law. I see no reason why what was called during the argument 'damage to the pocket' simpliciter should be disallowed when 'damage to the pocket' coupled with physical damage has hitherto always been allowed. I do not think that this development, if development it be, will lead to untoward consequences. The concept of proximity must always involve, at least in most cases, some degree of reliance; I have already mentioned the words 'skill' and 'judgment' in the speech of Lord Morris in *Hedley Byrne*. These words seem to me to be an echo, be it conscious or unconscious, of the language of s.14(1) of the Sale of Goods Act 1893. My Lords, though the analogy is not exact, I do not find it unhelpful for I think the concept of proximity of which I have spoken and the reasoning of Lord Devlin in the *Hedley Byrne* case involve factual considerations not unlike those involved in a claim under s 14(1); and as between an ultimate purchaser and a manufacturer would not easily be found to exist in the ordinary everyday transaction of purchasing chattels when it is obvious that in truth the real reliance was on the immediate vendor and not on the manufacturer.

My Lords, I have not thought it necessary to review all the cases cited in argument. If my conclusion be correct, certain of them can no longer be regarded as good law and others may have to be considered afresh hereafter, for example whether the decision of the majority of the Court of Appeal in *Spartan Steel and Alloys Ltd.* v. *Martin & Co. (Contractors) Ltd* ([1973] Q.B. 27; [below, p. 42]), is correct or whether the reasoning of Edmund-Davies L.J. in his dissenting judgment is to be preferred . . .

My Lords, for all these reasons I would dismiss this appeal and allow this action to proceed to proof before answer. . . .

LORD FRASER: . . . The floodgates argument was much discussed by the High Court of Australia in *Caltex Oil (Australia) Pty Ltd* v. *Dredge Willemstad* ((1976) 136 C.L.R. 529), where the majority of the court held that there was sufficient proximity between the parties to justify a claim for economic loss because the defendant knew (in the words of the headnote) 'that a particular person, not merely as a member of an unascertained class, [would] be likely to suffer economic loss as a consequence of his negligence'. Whether the defender's knowledge of the identity of the person likely to suffer from his negligence is relevant for the present purpose may with respect be doubted and it seems to be contrary to the views expressed in *Hedley Byrne & Co. Ltd.* v. *Heller & Partners Ltd.* ([1964] A.C. 465, 482, 494) by Lord Reid and by Lord Morris. But it is not necessary to decide the question in this appeal because the appellants certainly knew, or had the means of knowing, the identity of the respondents for whom the factory was being built. So, if knowledge of the respondents' identity is a relevant test, it is one that the appellant can satisfy. They can also satisfy most, if not all, of the other tests that have been suggested as safeguards against opening the floodgates. The proximity between the parties is extremely close, falling only just short of a direct contractual relationship. The injury to the respondents was a direct and foreseeable result of negligence by the appellants. The respondents, or their architects, nominated the appellants as specialist sub-contractors and they must therefore have relied on their skill and knowledge. It would surely be wrong to exclude from probation a claim which is so strongly based, merely because of anxiety about the possible effect of the decision on other cases where the proximity may be less strong. If and when such other cases arise they will have to be decided by applying sound principles to their particular facts. The present case seems to me to fall within limits already recognised in principle for this type of claim, and I would decide this appeal strictly on its own facts. I rely particularly on the very close proximity between the parties which in my view distinguishes this case from the case of producers of goods to be offered for sale to the public.

The second matter which might be thought to justify rejecting the respondents' claim as irrelevant is the difficulty of ascertaining the standard of duty owed by the appellants to the respondents. A manufacturer's duty to take care not to make a product that is dangerous sets a standard which is, in principle, easy to ascertain. The duty is owed to all who are his 'neighbours'. It is imposed on him by the general law and is in addition to his contractual duties to other parties to the contract. It cannot be discharged or escaped by pleading that it conflicts with his contractual duty. But a duty not to produce a *defective* article sets a standard which is less easily ascertained, because it has to be judged largely by reference to the contract. As Windeyer J. said in *Voli* v. *Inglewood Shire Council* ((1963) 110 C.L.R. 74, 85), if an architect undertakes to "design a stage to bear only some specified weight, he would not be liable for the consequences of someone thereafter negligently permitting a greater weight to be put upon it." Similarly a building constructed in fulfilment of a contract for a price of £100,000 might justly be regarded as defective, although the same building constructed in fulfilment of a contract for a price of £50,000 might not. Where a building is erected under a contract with a purchaser, then, provided the building, or part of it, is not dangerous to persons or to other property and subject to the law against misrepresentation, I see no reason why the builder should not be free to make with the purchaser whatever contractual arrangements about the quality of the product the purchaser wishes. However jerry-built the product, the purchaser would not be entitled to damages from the builder if it came up to the contractual standard. I do not think a subsequent owner could be in any better position, but in most cases he would not know the details of the contractual arrangements and, without such knowledge, he might well be unable to judge whether the product was defective or not. But in this case the respondents, although not a party to the contract with the appellants, had full knowledge of the appellants' contractual duties, and this difficulty does not arise. What the position might have been if the action had been brought by a subsequent owner is a matter which does not have to be decided now.

For the reasons given by my noble and learned friend Lord Roskill, and for the additional reasons which I have stated, I would dismiss this appeal.

LORD RUSSELL agreed with LORD FRASER and LORD ROSKILL

LORD KEITH OF KINKEL [held that as a duty to take reasonable care to avoid causing purely pecuniary harm had been recognised in *Hedley Byrne*, and *Dutton* and *Batty* had allowed the recovery of money expended to avert or counter harm due to breach of duty, the pursuers were entitled to sue for the cost of making good the purely pecuniary damage which resulted from the defects in the flooring, though not for the simple fact that the flooring was defective. Had the pursuers simply claimed that they 'had got a bad floor instead of a good one', his Lordship would have dismissed their claim, but he found that their pleadings implied that the defects in the floor would cause them some business loss, and accordingly allowed the claim for the cost of stemming such loss] . . .

Having thus reached a conclusion in favour of the respondents on the somewhat narrow ground which I have indicated, I do not consider this to be an appropriate case for seeking to advance the frontiers of the law of negligence on the lines favoured by certain of your Lordships. There are a number of reasons why such an extension would, in my view, be wrong in principle. In the first place, I am unable to regard the deterioration of the flooring which is alleged in this case as being damage to the respondents' property such as to give rise to a liability falling directly within the principle of *Donoghue* v. *Stevenson*. The flooring had an inherent defect in it from the start. The appellants did not, in any sense consistent with the ordinary use of language or contemplated by the majority in *Donoghue* v. *Stevenson*, damage the respondents' property. They supplied them with a defective floor. Such an act can, in accordance with the views I have expressed above, give rise to liability in negligence in certain circumstances. But it does not do so merely because the flooring is defective or valueless or useless and requires to be replaced. So to hold would raise very difficult and delicate issues of principle having a wide potential application. I think it would necessarily follow that any manufacturer of products would become liable to the ultimate purchaser if the product, owing to negligence in manufacture, was, without being harmful in any way, useless or worthless or defective in quality so that the purchaser wasted the money he spent on it. One instance mentioned in argument and adverted to by Stamp L.J. in *Dutton* v. *Bognor Regis United Building Co. Ltd.* ([1972] 1 Q.B. 373, 414) was a product purchased as ginger beer which turned out to be only water, and many others may be figured. To introduce a general liability covering such situations would be disruptive of commercial practice, under which manufacturers of products commonly provide the ultimate purchaser with limited guarantees, usually undertaking only to replace parts exhibiting defective workmanship and excluding any consequential loss. There being no contractual relationship between manufacturer and ultimate consumer, no room would exist, if the suggested principle were accepted, for limiting the manufacturer's liability. The policy considerations which would be involved in introducing such a state of affairs appear to me to be such as a court of law cannot properly assess, and the question whether or not it would be in the interests of commerce and the public generally is, in my view, much better left for the legislature. The purchaser of a defective product normally can proceed for breach of contract against the seller who can bring his own supplier into the proceedings by third party procedure, so it cannot be said that the present state of the law is unsatisfactory from the point of view of available remedies. I refer to *Young & Marten Ltd.* v. *McManus Childs Ltd.* ([1967] 1 A.C. 454). In the second place, I can foresee that very considerable difficulties might arise in assessing the standards of quality by which the allegedly defective product is to be judged. This aspect is more fully developed in the speech . . . delivered by my noble and learned friend Lord Brandon, with whose views on the matter I respectfully agree.

My Lords, for the reasons which I have given I would concur in the dismissal of the appeal.

Questions
1. Could Mrs. Donoghue now get damages from Stevenson if the ginger beer, instead of being poisonous, were simply flat?

2. Do you agree with Lord Roskill that a purchaser normally relies on the vendor rather than on the manufacturer of the goods he buys? Did Mrs. Donoghue rely on Minchella's skill or on Stevenson's?

3. Can you support Lord Keith's distinction between the money wasted on a poor floor and the money lost because the floor is poor?

4. Can you support Lord Brandon's distinction between a product which is dangerously defective and one which is defective without being dangerous? Why does our language (and every other) have the word "dangerous" as well as the word "harmful"?

5. The pursuers claimed £90,000 for employees' wages thrown away. If they suspended their employees, would the employees have a claim against the defenders for their loss of wages? Is what is a foreseeable loss to Junior Books an unforeseeable one to their employees?

6. Suppose that the defenders negligently *delayed* the laying of the floor, so that the construction work was held up and money lost in consequence. Could the pursuers claim?

7. Main contractors have often been held liable for defective work by sub-contractors (see *Young & Marten* v. *McManus Childs* [1969] 1 A.C. 454). Is this necessary, or desirable, any longer?

9. Does the pursuers' right to sue the defenders depend on whether the main contractors, had they suffered loss, could have sued the defenders?

10. Suppose that in the contract between the main contractors and the defenders there was (a) a clause limiting the defenders' liability to twice the price of the floor, except in respect of

actual physical harm due to defects in it; (b) a clause providing that no claim would lie in respect of defects which had not manifested themselves within 12 months of the completion of the contract; (c) a clause whereby any dispute arising out of the work must be submitted to arbitration rather than taken to court; (d) a clause that no one save the main contractors should be able to sue on the contract. Would or should the pursuers have been affected by any of these clauses?

11. Could the pursuers have recovered damages under the Defective Premises Act 1972, s.1 (below, p. 64)? If not, why not? Why do you think the statute has this effect?

12. In this case the floor was defective because Veitchi Co.'s employees mixed the ingredients improperly. Would those employees be liable to Junior Books? Would Veitchi Co.'s managing director be liable for failing to keep an eye on them? Would the main contractor's clerk of works be liable?

13. Lord Fraser said "I would decide this appeal strictly on its own facts." Whatever does that mean? Is he not applying a rule of some kind? If so, what rule?

14. In what sense, if any, is it more arbitrary and illogical to distinguish between purely economic harm and physical damage on the one hand than between those who are close enough and those who are not close enough on the other?

15. Do any changes in (a) the commercial environment, (b) public sensibility justify the extension of liability in this case?

Note:

Stevenson was careless. So was Veitchi Co. That is a common factor. Stevenson's carelessness was a breach of his contract with Minchella. Veitchi Co.'s carelessness was a breach of its contract with Ogilvie (the main contractor). That is another common factor. But Stevenson's conduct caused actual bodily harm to an individual, whereas Veitchi Co. just caused economic loss to a company. Stevenson's conduct was dangerous and Veitchi Co.'s was not. Thus the nature of the harm complained of in the two cases was very different; and the defendants' conduct in the two cases was comparable only in mode, not in propensity. Accordingly there is no real sense in which this decision *follows* from *Donoghue* v. *Stevenson*. Their Lordships must therefore have supposed that the common features were more important than the different features. That is rather surprising, especially as Mrs. Donoghue had no one to sue unless she could sue Stevenson, whereas Junior Books had a perfectly good claim against Ogilvie (the main contractor) whom, after all, they had chosen to be responsible for the whole works.

Is the decision a fair one? Let us see. Junior Books got a poor floor, and it was Veitchi Co.'s fault, for Veitchi Co. was supposed to provide a good floor and be paid for it. But it was not Junior Books who was to pay them, even if they provided the best of all possible floors. Veitchi Co. can claim payment only from Ogilvie, the main contractor, and their claim is not even a very special one at law (see *Modern Engineering (Bristol) Ltd.* v. *Gilbert-Ash (Northern) Ltd.* [1974] A.C. 689, or, indeed, *Veitchi Co.* v. *Crowley Russell & Co.* [1972] S.C. 225 (O.H.)). Now if Veitchi Co. has no right to payment for a good floor from Junior Books, is it entirely fair that Junior Books should have a right to payment from Veitchi Co. for a poor floor? Does *justice* demand the result in this case? It does not. Nor (for a wonder) did their Lordships, or any of them, suggest that it did.

Did *authority* demand the result? Far from it. Lord Fraser's observation that "The present case seems . . . to fall well within limits already recognised in principle for this type of claim" caused some surprise, since the only well-known and relevant decision was *Ross* v. *Caunters* [1980] Ch. 297, which was cited to, but not by, the House. However Lord Fraser (alone of the *Junior Books* panel) had sat in the House of Lords in May 1980 when it decided *I.B.A.* v. *E.M.I. and British Insulated Callender's Construction Co.* (reported only at 14 Building L.R. 9). In that case an experimental television transmission aerial designed by the second defendant sub-contractor had collapsed, destroying nothing but itself, and the sub-contractor was held liable in negligence. This might seem like an authority, but it is not, because the sub-contractor *conceded* that it owed a duty to the site-owner and did not contest the adequacy of the damage: the only issue discussed and decided was whether the sub-contractor had in fact been careless or not. Now why did the sub-contractor in that case make the concessions which Veitchi Co. refused to make? Because in that case the main contractor was also being sued. The main contractor would certainly be held liable to the plaintiff if the sub-contractor had been careless, and if he were held liable to the plaintiff he would unquestionably have had an unanswerable claim against the sub-contractor for a complete indemnity. If that sounds complicated, it should be remembered that building law *is* very complicated, so complicated that it may not be greatly simplified by muttering Lord Atkin's spells and waving his golden metwand.

Then is the decision a convenient one? It is not. The judgments allude to the difficulty that will arise in determining whether or not a defendant who is under a duty to take care to provide a proper thing and not just a safe one was in breach of his duty, since the test of reasonable safety is absolute whereas fitness depends on what the thing was for. There is, however, a further problem, the very problem to which *Donoghue* v. *Stevenson* was directed, namely, who can sue? Now undoubtedly if Veitchi Co.'s men had been asked for whom they were laying the floor, they would have answered "Junior Books," whose premises they were on at the time, though the company accountant, being scrupulously careful, would probably have added "Under contract with Ogilvie." So there is no doubt that in a legal system which admits that the beneficiary of a contract can sue on it Junior Books would qualify as such a beneficiary and be allowed to sue on the contract. This is a convenient procedure in its way: the contract which determines whether the defendant's conduct was faulty or not also determines who can sue, for it is not enough that the plaintiff be *foreseeable* or even foreseen, he must be the person for whom the thing or service was *intended* by the contractor being sued. Now English law has decided to deploy the law of tort here, to move it, as it were, from the Department of Public Safety to the Ministry of Works. The trouble is that the traditional concepts of tort law will make it extremely difficult to contain this new liability. It is all very well to say that the victim must be "sufficiently proximate" (legal for "close enough"), but we all know that the test of sufficient proximity is reasonable foreseeability, because Lord Atkin said so. In any case we can test it. Would the *Junior Books* court allow Mrs. Donoghue to sue Stevenson for the cost of replacing a dud ginger-beer? Apparently not. But *why* not? The reasons given, especially by Lord Roskill, are incoherent. But there must be a reason. Surely it lies in the distinction drawn above (p. 21), namely that while Mrs. Donoghue was a beneficiary of the contract of sale from Minchella to Friend, she was not a beneficiary of the contract of sale from Stevenson (whom she was suing) to Minchella. However, this distinction simply does not mesh with the traditional concepts of tort law, as one can infer from the fact that Lord Roskill invoked *The Greystoke Castle* and questioned *Spartan Steel* (below, p. 42), cases which have nothing remotely to do with contractual misbehaviour.

HEDLEY BYRNE & CO. v. HELLER & PARTNERS LTD.

House of Lords [1964] A.C. 465; [1963] 3 W.L.R. 101; 107 S.J. 454; [1963] 2 All E.R. 575; [1963] 1 Lloyd's Rep. 485

Action against gratuitous informant in respect of financial loss.

The plaintiffs, advertising agents, had booked space and time on behalf of a customer, Easipower Ltd., under contracts making them personally liable. They then had doubts about Easipower's financial position, and asked their bankers to obtain from the defendants, merchant bankers with whom Easipower Ltd. had their account, a statement on Easipower's standing. This was done in the first instance by telephone, when the defendants said: "We believe that the company would not undertake any commitments they were unable to fulfil." Three months later the plaintiffs, through their bankers, asked whether Easipower were trustworthy to the extent of £100,000 per year. The defendants replied, in a letter headed "For your private use and without responsibility on the part of this bank or its officials," that Easipower Ltd. were a " . . . respectably constituted company, considered good for its ordinary business engagements" and that "Your figures are larger than we are accustomed to see." In reliance upon their view of what these statements meant the plaintiffs refrained from cancelling the advertising contracts, and when Easipower Ltd. went into liquidation lost sums calculated at £17,661 18s. 6d.

The plaintiffs abandoned an allegation of fraud, but maintained that the defendants' replies were given in breach of their duty of care. McNair J. held that the defendants were careless but that they owed no duty. The Court of Appeal affirmed judgment for the defendants on the same ground [1962] 1 Q.B. 396. The House of Lords affirmed the judgment on different grounds.

Lord Reid: My Lords, this case raises the important question whether and in what circumstances a person can recover damages for loss suffered by reason of his having relied on an innocent but negligent misrepresentation . . .

Before coming to the main question of law, it may be well to dispose of an argument that there was no sufficiently close relationship between these parties to give rise to any duty. It is said that the respondents did not know the precise purpose of the inquiries and did not even know whether the National Provincial Bank wanted the information for its own use or for the use of a customer: they knew nothing of the appellants. I would reject that argument. They knew that the inquiry was in connection with an advertising contract, and it was at least probable that the information was wanted by the advertising contractors. It seems to me quite immaterial that they did not know who these contractors were: there is no suggestion of any speciality which could have influenced them in deciding whether to give information or in what form to give it. I shall therefore treat this as if it were a case where a negligent misrepresentation is made directly to the person seeking information, opinion or advice, and I shall not attempt to decide what kind or degree of proximity is necessary before there can be a duty owed by the defendant to the plaintiff.

The appellants' first argument was based on *Donoghue* v. *Stevenson* ([1932] A.C. 562). That is a very important decision, but I do not think that it has any direct bearing on this case. That decision may encourage us to develop existing lines of authority, but it cannot entitle us to disregard them. Apart altogether from authority, I would think that the law must treat negligent words differently from negligent acts. The law ought so far as possible to reflect the standards of the reasonable man, and that is what *Donoghue* v. *Stevenson* sets out to do. The most obvious difference between negligent words and negligent acts is this. Quite careful people often express definite opinions on social or informal occasions even when they see that others are likely to be influenced by them; and they often do that without taking that care which they would take if asked for their opinion professionally or in a business connection. The appellant agrees that there can be no duty of care on such occasions, and we are referred to American and South African authorities where that is recognised, although their law appears to have gone much further than ours has yet done. But it is at least unusual casually to put into circulation negligently made articles which are dangerous. A man might give a friend a negligently prepared bottle of home-made wine and his friend's guests might drink it with dire results. But it is by no means clear that those guests would have no action against the negligent manufacturer.

Another obvious difference is that a negligently made article will only cause one accident, and so it is not very difficult to find the necessary degree of proximity or neighbourhood between the negligent manufacturer and the person injured. But words can be broadcast with or without the consent or the foresight of the speaker or writer. It would be one thing to say that the speaker owes a duty to a limited class, but it would be going very far to say that he owes a duty to every ultimate "consumer" who acts on those words to his detriment. It would be no use to say that a speaker or writer owes a duty but can disclaim responsibility if he wants to. He, like the manufacturer, could make it part of a contract that he is not to be liable for his negligence: but that contract would not protect him in a question with a third party, at least if the third party was unaware of it.

So it seems to me that there is good sense behind our present law that in general an innocent but negligent misrepresentation gives no cause of action. There must be something more than the mere misstatement. I therefore turn to the authorities to see what more is required. The most natural requirement would be that expressly or by implication from the circumstances the speaker or writer has undertaken some responsibility, and that appears to me not to conflict with any authority which is binding on this House. Where there is a contract there is no difficulty as regards the contracting parties: the question is whether there is a warranty. The refusal of English law to recognise any *jus quaesitum tertio* causes some difficulties, but they are not relevant here. Then there are cases where a person does not merely make a statement but performs a gratuitous service. I do not intend to examine the cases about that, but at least they show that in some cases that person owes a duty of care apart from any contract, and to that extent they pave the way to holding that there can be a duty of care in making a statement of fact or opinion which is independent of contract.

[Lord Reid considered *Derry* v. *Peek* (1889) 14 App.Cas. 337, which had erroneously been supposed to have decided that "To found an action for damages there must be a contract and breach, or fraud" (*per* Lord Bramwell at 347), quoted the view of Lord Haldane in *Nocton* v. *Lord Ashburton* [1914] A.C. 932, 947, and *Robinson* v. *National Bank of Scotland* 1916 S.C. (H.L.) 154, 157 and proceeded:]

This passage makes it clear that Lord Haldane did not think that a duty to take care must be limited to cases of fiduciary relationship in the narrow sense of relationships which had been recognised by the Court of Chancery as being of a fiduciary character. He speaks of other special relationships, and I can see no logical stopping place short of all those relationships where it is plain that the party seeking information or advice was trusting the other to exercise such a degree of care as the circumstances required, where it was reasonable for him to do that, and where the other gave the information or advice when he knew or ought to have known that the inquirer was relying on him. I say "ought to have known" because in questions of negligence we now apply the objective standard of what the reasonable man would have done.

A reasonable man, knowing that he was being trusted or that his skill and judgment were being relied on, would, I think, have three courses open to him. He could keep silent or decline to give the information or advice sought: or he could give an answer with a clear qualification that he accepted no responsibility for it or that it was given without that reflection or inquiry which a careful answer would require: or he could simply answer without any such qualification. If he chooses to adopt the last course he must, I think, be held to have accepted some responsibility for his answer being given carefully, or to have accepted a relationship with the inquirer which requires him to exercise such care as the circumstances require.

If that is right, then it must follow that *Candler* v. *Crane, Christmas & Co.* ([1951] 2 K.B. 164) was wrongly decided. There the plaintiff wanted to see the accounts of a company before deciding to invest in it. The defendants were the company's accountants, and they were told by the company to complete the company's accounts as soon as possible because they were to be shown to the plaintiff who was a potential investor in the company. At the company's request the defendants showed the completed accounts to the plaintiff, discussed them with him, and allowed him to take a copy. The accounts had been carelessly prepared and gave a wholly misleading picture. It was obvious to the defendants that the plaintiff was relying on their skill and judgment and on their having exercised that care which by contract they owed to the company, and I think that any reasonable man in the plaintiff's shoes would have relied on that. This seems to me to be a typical case of agreeing to assume a responsibility: they knew why the plaintiff wanted to see the accounts and why their employers, the company, wanted them to be shown to him, and agreed to show them to him without even a suggestion that he should not rely on them.

The majority of the Court of Appeal held that they were bound by *Le Lievre* v. *Gould* ([1893] 1 Q.B. 491) and that *Donoghue* v. *Stevenson* had no application. . . .

In *Le Lievre* v. *Gould* a surveyor, Gould, gave certificates to a builder who employed him. The plaintiffs were mortgagees of the builder's interest and Gould knew nothing about them or the terms of their mortgage; but the builder, without Gould's authority, chose to show them Gould's report. I have said that I do not intend to decide anything about the degree of proximity necessary to establish a relationship giving rise to a duty of care, but it would seem difficult to find such proximity in this case, and the actual decision in *Le Lievre* v. *Gould* may therefore be correct. But the decision was not put on that ground: if it had been, *Cann* v. *Willson* ((1883) 39 Ch.D. 39) would not have been overruled.

Lord Esher M.R. held that there was no contract between the plaintiffs and the defendant and that this House in *Derry* v. *Peek* had "restated the old law that, in the absence of contract, an action for negligence cannot be maintained when there is no fraud" ([1893] 1 Q.B. 491, 498). Bowen L.J. gave a similar reason; he said (at 501): "Then *Derry* v. *Peek* decided this further point—*viz.*, that in cases like the present (of which *Derry* v. *Peek* was itself an instance) there is no duty enforceable in law to be careful"; and he added that the law of England "does not consider that what a man writes on paper is like a gun or other dangerous instrument, and, unless he intended to deceive, the law does not, in the absence of contract, hold him responsible for drawing his certificate carelessly." So both he and Lord Esher held that *Cann* v. *Willson* was wrong in deciding that there was a duty to take care. We now know on the authority of *Donoghue* v. *Stevenson* that Bowen L.J. was wrong in limiting duty of care to guns or other dangerous instruments, and I think that, for reasons which I have already given, he was also wrong in limiting the duty of care with regard to statements to cases where there is a contract. On both points Bowen L.J. was expressing what was then generally believed to be the law, but later statements in this House have gone far to remove those limitations. I would therefore hold that the ratio in *Le Lievre* v. *Gould* was wrong and that *Cann* v. *Willson* ought not to have been overruled.

Now I must try to apply these principles to the present case. What the appellants complain of is not negligence in the ordinary sense of carelessness, but rather misjudgment, in that Mr. Heller, while honestly seeking to give a fair assessment, in fact made a statement which gave a false and misleading impression of his customer's credit. It appears that bankers now commonly give references with regard to their customers as part of their business. I do not know how far their customers generally permit them to disclose their affairs, but, even with permission, it cannot always be easy for a banker to reconcile his duty to his customer with his desire to give a fairly balanced reply to an inquiry. And inquirers can hardly expect a full and objective statement of opinion or accurate factual information such as skilled men would be expected to give in reply to other kinds of inquiry. So it seems to me to be unusually difficult to determine just what duty beyond a duty to be honest a banker would be held to have undertaken if he gave a reply without an adequate disclaimer of responsibility or other warning . . .

But here the appellants' bank, who were their agents in making the inquiry, began by saying that "they wanted to know in confidence and without responsibility on our part," that is, on the part of the respondents. So I cannot see how the appellants can now be entitled to disregard that and maintain that the respondents did incur a responsibility to them.

The appellants founded on a number of cases in contract where very clear words were required to exclude the duty of care which would otherwise have flowed from the contract. To that argument there are, I think, two answers. In the case of a contract it is necessary to exclude liability for negligence, but in this case the question is whether an undertaking to assume a duty to take care can be inferred: and that is a very different matter. And, secondly, even in cases of contract general words may be sufficient if there was no other kind of liability to be excluded except liability for negligence: the general rule is that a party is not exempted from liability for negligence "unless adequate words are used"—*per* Scrutton L.J. in *Rutter* v. *Palmer* ([1932] 2 K.B. 87, 92). It being admitted that there was here a duty to give an honest reply, I do not see what further liability there could be to exclude except liability for negligence: there being no contract there was no question of warranty.

I am therefore of opinion that it is clear that the respondents never undertook any duty to exercise care in giving their replies. The appellants cannot succeed unless there was such a duty and therefore in my judgment this appeal must be dismissed.

LORD MORRIS OF BORTH-Y-GEST: . . . My Lords, I consider that it follows and that it should now be regarded as settled that if someone possessed of a special skill undertakes, quite irrespective of contract, to apply that skill for the assistance of another person who relies upon such skill, a duty of care will arise. The fact that the service is to be given by means of or by the instrumentality of words can make no difference. Furthermore, if in a sphere in which a person is so placed that others could reasonably rely upon his judgment or his skill or upon his ability to make careful inquiry, a person takes it upon himself to give information or advice to, or allows his information or advice to be passed on to, another person who, as he knows or should know, will place reliance upon it, then a duty of care will arise . . .

LORD DEVLIN: . . . I think, therefore, that there is ample authority to justify your Lordships in saying now that the categories of special relationships which may give rise to a duty to take care in word as well as in deed are not limited to contractual relationships or to relationships of fiduciary duty, but include also relationships which in the words of Lord Shaw in *Nocton* v. *Lord Ashburton* are "equivalent to contract," that is, where there is an assumption of responsibility in circumstances in which, but for the absence of consideration, there would be a contract. Where there is an express undertaking, an express warranty as distinct from mere representation, there can be little difficulty. The difficulty arises in discerning those cases in which the undertaking is to be implied. In this respect the absence of consideration is not irrelevant. Payment for information or advice is very good evidence that it is being relied upon and that the informer or adviser knows that it is. Where there is no consideration, it will be necessary to exercise greater care in distinguishing between social and professional relationships and between those which are of a contractual character and those which are not. It may often be material to consider whether the adviser is acting purely out of good nature or whether he is getting his reward in some indirect form. The service that a bank performs in giving a reference is not done simply out of a desire to assist commerce. It would discourage the customers of the bank if their deals fell through because the bank had refused to testify to their credit when it was good.

I have had the advantage of reading all the opinions prepared by your Lordships and of studying the terms which your Lordships have framed by way of definition of the sort of relationship which gives rise to a responsibility towards those who act upon information or advice and so creates a duty of care towards them. I do not understand any of your Lordships to hold that it is a responsibility imposed by law upon certain types of persons or in certain sorts of situations. It is a responsibility that is voluntarily accepted or undertaken, either generally where a general relationship, such as that of solicitor and client or banker and customer, is created, or specifically in relation to a particular transaction. In the present case the appellants were not, as in *Woods* v. *Martins Bank Ltd.* ([1959] 1 Q.B. 55), the customers or potential customers of the bank. Responsibility can attach only to the single act, that is, the giving of the reference, and only if the doing of that act implied a voluntary undertaking to assume responsibility. This is a point of great importance because it is, as I understand it, the foundation for the ground on which in the end of the House dismisses the appeal. I do not think it is possible to formulate with exactitude all the conditions under which the law will in a specific case imply a voluntary undertaking any more than it is possible to formulate those in which the law will imply a contract. But in so far as your Lordships describe the circumstances in which an implication will ordinarily be drawn, I am prepared to adopt any one of your Lordships' statements as showing the general rule; and I pay the same respect to the statement by Denning L.J. in his dissenting judgment in

Candler v. *Crane, Christmas & Co.* about the circumstances in which he says a duty to use care in making a statement exists.

I do not go further than this for two reasons. The first is that I have found in the speech of Lord Shaw in *Nocton* v. *Lord Ashburton* and in the idea of a relationship that is equivalent to contract all that is necessary to cover the situation that arises in this case. Mr. Gardiner does not claim to succeed unless he can establish that the reference was intended by the respondents to be communicated by the National Provincial Bank to some unnamed customer of theirs, whose identity was immaterial to the respondents, for that customer's use. All that was lacking was formal consideration. The case is well within the authorities I have already cited and of which *Wilkinson* v. *Coverdale* ((1793) 1 Esp. 75; 170 E.R. 284) is the most apposite example.

I shall therefore content myself with the proposition that wherever there is a relationship equivalent to contract, there is a duty of care. Such a relationship may be either general or particular. Examples of a general relationship are those of solicitor and client and of banker and customer. For the former *Nocton* v. *Lord Ashburton* has long stood as the authority and for the latter there is the decision of Salmon J. in *Woods* v. *Martin Bank Ltd.* which I respectfully approve. There may well be others yet to be established. Where there is a general relationship of this sort, it is unnecessary to do more than prove its existence and the duty follows. Where, as in the present case, what is relied on is a particular relationship created *ad hoc*, it will be necessary to examine the particular facts to see whether there is an express or implied undertaking of responsibility . . .

I regard this proposition as an application of the general conception of proximity. Cases may arise in the future in which a new and wider proposition, quite independent of any notion of contract, will be needed. There may, for example, be cases in which a statement is not supplied for the use of any particular person, any more than in *Donoghue* v. *Stevenson* the ginger beer was supplied for consumption by any particular person; and it will then be necessary to return to the general conception of proximity and to see whether there can be evolved from it, as was done in *Donoghue* v. *Stevenson*, a specific proposition to fit the case. When that has to be done, the speeches of your Lordships today as well as the judgment of Denning L.J. to which I have referred—and also, I may add, the proposition in the *American Restatement of the Law of Torts,* Vol. III, p. 122, para. 552, and the cases which exemplify it—will afford good guidance as to what ought to be said. I prefer to see what shape such cases take before committing myself to any formulation, for I bear in mind Lord Atkin's warning, which I have quoted, against unnecessary restrictions on the adaptability of English law. I have, I hope, made it clear that I take quite literally the dictum of Lord Macmillan, so often quoted from the same case, that "the categories of negligence are never closed." English law is wide enough to embrace any new category or proposition that exemplifies the principle of proximity.

I have another reason for caution. Since the essence of the matter in the present case and in others of the same type is the acceptance of responsibility, I should like to guard against the imposition of restrictive terms notwithstanding that the essential condition is fulfilled. If a defendant says to a plaintiff: "Let me do this for you; do not waste your money in employing a professional, I will do it for nothing and you can rely on me," I do not think he could escape liability simply because he belonged to no profession or calling, had no qualifications or special skill and did not hold himself out as having any. The relevance of these factors is to show the unlikelihood of a defendant in such circumstances assuming a legal responsibility, and as such they may often be decisive. But they are not theoretically conclusive and so cannot be the subject of definition. It would be unfortunate if they were . . .

Questions
   1. At whose risk does a business man lay out money on credit in the hope of profit?

2. If you had been so suspicious as to make repeated inquiries about Easipower's financial standing, how would you have understood the statement made by the defendant in this case? In what precise respects was the defendant negligent?

3. Suppose that the plaintiff had in his files, but had forgotten it, information suggesting that the defendant could not have meant what he appeared to be saying; would you allow the plaintiff to recover part of his loss on the ground that both were negligent? For the terms of the Law Reform (Contributory Negligence) Act 1945, see below, p. 205, and see Lord Reid at [1971] A.C. 793, 811.

4. The disclaimer of responsibility apart, do you think the plaintiff should have recovered only what he had lost, or also his loss of profit on the transaction in question?

5. In these cases the debtor (here Easipower) will probably go into liquidation or bankruptcy, and it may be some time before it is clear what portion of their claims the creditors will receive. At what time may the plaintiff issue his writ against the defendant?

6. Are you amused that the leading case on misrepresentation should involve an advertising agent—as *plaintiff*?

7. During the War it was announced on posters that "Careless Talk Costs Lives." What does careless talk in peacetime typically cost? (For the legal aspects of Pope's line "At ev'ry word a reputation dies" see the Chapter on Defamation below, p. 433).

8. If the Unfair Contract Terms Act 1977 (see below, p. 213) had been in force at the time, would the defendant's disclaimer of responsibility have been efficacious?

Notes:

1. This case may not seem very striking in the light of *Junior Books*, but it was decided 18 years earlier, and it was the first great case where a merely negligent person was, in principle, held liable to a non-contractor for causing him merely pecuniary loss. It was thought by some to herald a general liability in negligence for causing foreseeable financial harm, but the next case shows that it has not quite had that effect.

There was no question in this case of any danger. Dangerous misstatement ("Come on, it's perfectly safe" . . . *Crash!*) had led to liability before, but here the only possible harm was financial: the situation was commercial not collisional.

For some years plaintiffs sought to characterise defendants' conduct as misrepresentation so as to be able to invoke *Hedley Byrne*. Indeed in *I.B.A.* v. *E.M.I.* (above, p. 33) much play was made of the sub-contractor's statement to the plaintiffs "We are satisfied that the structure will not oscillate dangerously." The trial judge held that if the sub-contractors had been negligent in designing the structure, that automatically made their statement a negligent one, and the House of Lords agreed that liability could be based on the statement as well as on the negligent conduct. After *Junior Books*, however, we can concentrate on conduct again and give up hunting for obscure misrepresentations. Even before *Junior Books*, in which it was not cited, Megarry V-C. founded on *Donoghue* v. *Stevenson* rather than on *Hedley Byrne* in order to impose liability on a solicitor who, having been instructed by the testator to prepare a will whereunder the plaintiff was to receive a handsome bequest, carelessly caused the plaintiff to lose the bequest by allowing the will to be witnessed by her husband (*Ross* v. *Caunters* [1980] Ch. 297).

Hedley Byrne can then be seen as having been historically necessary for the development of liability, within a special relationship, for pecuniary harm negligently caused, but it is not now necessary as a matter of authority except in cases where the defendant did nothing but speak; for the differences between speech and action are irreducible.

2. The reason that *Hedley Byrne* is a "tort" case and not a "contract" case is that the plaintiff didn't pay the defendant anything for the information, and there cannot be a contract in England unless there is *consideration*. (See, for instance, *Charnock* v. *Liverpool Corp.* [1968] 1 W.L.R. 1498; in what terms would it be decided nowadays ?). As *Hedley Byrne* shows, however, the law can impose a duty to take care if one chooses to speak without being paid, but consideration still retains a role, since it generates the duty to speak in the first place. Another requirement of contract in England is *privity*, that extreme proximity, that cheek-by-jowlness which exists between parties to a deal and only between them. On Lord Reid's view, such privity existed on the facts of *Hedley Byrne*. but there was no privity in *Junior Books* (though there was proximity and consideration), and we have seen that that, too, makes little difference. A third requirement for contractual liability in England is "intention to enter legal relations." The tort equivalent is "in a business context," "not on a purely social occasion," etc.

The nature of this requirement was in issue in *Mutual Life* v. *Evatt* [1971] A.C. 793 which occasioned dissension as well as dissent in the Privy Council. An investor had asked his insurance company about his investments and got bad advice. He lost his claim on the ground that it was not the defendant's business to give such advice. Quite right, too. However, the High Court of Australia has rejected this limitation on the 'principle' of *Hedley Byrne* (*L. Shaddock & Associates* v. *Parramatta* [1981] 36 A.L.R. 385), and *Evatt's* case will probably not be followed in England. Lord Denning has propounded a more flexible test, *viz.* was it clear in all the circumstances that the inquiry was directed to obtaining considered advice rather than a quick answer? (*Howard Marine* v. *Ogden & Sons* [1978] Q.B. 574, 591).

3. When parties are negotiating a contract, the *Hedley Byrne* duty may perfectly well exist (*Esso* v. *Mardon* [1976] Q.B. 801): if a contract between them actually results, the Misrepresentation Act 1967 will also apply: "In the course of negotiations leading to a contract the Statute imposes an absolute obligation not to state facts which the representor cannot prove he had reasonable ground to believe" (*Howard Marine* v. *Ogden & Sons* [1978] Q.B. 574, 596, *per* Bridge L.J.).

4. If a relationship "equivalent to contract" engenders a legal duty to take care of another's financial interests, such a duty must surely arise where the relationship is actually contractual. Nor need the duty be limited to care in the making of statements. It has been so held by Oliver J. in *Midland Bank Trust Co.* v. *Hett, Stubbs & Kemp* [1978] 3 All E.R. 571. This may lead to perplexing results unless one remembers that it is reasonable for a contractor to look after his own interests as well as, perhaps in preference to, his contractor's. It is, however, unlikely that we shall have to throw away the contract books. Judges have for over a century been "implying" tort duties into contracts (see *The Moorcock* (1889) 14 P.D. 64), and this device is unproblematical, *pace* the Unfair Contract Terms Act 1977, since traditionally a duty cannot be implied when the express terms of the contract are in conflict with it.

5. Professionals such as judges, arbitrators, valuers and architects, who decide how much people are to pay or be paid, are naturally very apt to cause financial loss by their decisions. Now that they may be sued by a party who did not employ them, the question of their liability has become very acute. That judges are immune from liability is well established (*Sirros* v. *Moore* [1975] Q.B. 118). That arbitrators are also immune was conceded by counsel in a recent case, though two of their Lordships doubted it (*Arenson* v. *Casson, Beckman Rutley & Co.* [1977] A.C. 405); the same case, following a decision about an architect's interim certificate of what was due to a builder (*Sutcliffe* v. *Thackrah* [1974] A.C. 727), held that mutual valuers have no immunity unless, perhaps, they are actually resolving a formulated dispute between the parties.

6. Here are some of the questions which have been raised since *Hedley Byrne*.

Does the bank on which a cheque is drawn owe a duty to the payee to take care in honouring their customer's cheque? No, *per* Kerr J. in *National Westminster Bank* v. *Barclay's Bank International* [1975] Q.B. 654.

Does a member of the organisation which receives, records and divulges information about the hire-purchase contracts affecting members' motor-cars owe a duty to fellow members to take care to supply relevant information? A bare majority of the House of Lords in *Moorgate Mercantile* v. *Twitchings* [1977] A.C. 890 thought not.

When a landlord had arranged insurance on tenanted premises did his successor owe a duty to the tenant to tell him that the insurance was not being continued? No, *per* Croom-Johnson J. in *Argy Trading* v. *Lapid Developments* [1977] 3 All E.R. 785 (*sed quaere*.)

Do the directors of a company owe a duty to the shareholders (as opposed to the company itself) to take care of the company's assets? No, *per* Templeman J. in *Daniels* v. *Daniels* [1978] Ch. 406 (though they may be liable if they profit from their negligence).

A house is surveyed at the instance of a building society. The surveyor negligently reports that the house is worth £25,000. The building society offers to lend £25,000 for the purchase of the house, which is worth much less. Can the purchaser sue the surveyor? Yes: *Yianni* v. *Edwin Evans & Sons* [1982] Q.B. 438.

X lends money to a company, taking a debenture. Y guarantees the company's debt. The company breaks, and X appoints Z as receiver to realise its assets. The less Z gets for those assets, the more Y will have to pay X. Does Z owe Y a duty to take care? Yes. *Standard Chartered Bank* v. *Walker* [1982] 3 All E.R. 938 (C.A.).

7. *Reliance*. The notion of reliance is not an easy one. It can be used in a very extensive sense (we rely on oncoming drivers not to cross the median of the highway) or in a narrower sense (I rely on the accuracy of what you tell me). It is in the latter sense that reliance is used in the *Hedley Byrne* cases. (See Lord Denning in *Dutton* [1972] 1 Q.B. 373, 395). It is used to describe the mechanism whereby a person who is misinformed typically suffers harm as a result: a person who credits a falsehood automatically and *ipso facto* makes a mistake, and if he takes action which he believes beneficial when that belief is mistaken, he is apt to be

disappointed when the truth emerges. This is what happened to the plaintiff misrepresentee in *Hedley Byrne*.

But harm may be suffered by others than the person taking action in reliance on the truth of what was said. For example, if I carelessly say to X that a certain course of conduct will not hurt Y and in that belief he engages in it, then it may be Y who is hurt. Yet Y has not relied on what I said. This case is different from *Hedley Byrne*, which does not of itself help us to solve it. Traditionally more than mere carelessness is required to make the speaker liable to Y (see below, p. 510).

Harm may be caused by a statement though no one relies on it at all. This is because some statements are constitutive of legal rights and liabilities. Such a case, an odd one, but well worth reading, is *Ministry of Housing and Local Government* v. *Sharp* [1970] 2 Q.B. 223 (C.A.).

In one case the defendant accountants had prepared rather misleading accounts for a company. The plaintiffs, who took over that company, had studied the accounts, and Woolf J. held that in deciding to make the take-over, which proved unprofitable, they had relied on them. Nevertheless he held that the misrepresentation did not contribute to the plaintiffs' loss, because they would have proceeded with the take-over even if the accounts had been accurate where they were not. (*J.E.B. Fasteners* v. *Marks & Bloom* [1981] 3 All E.R. 289, affirmed [1983] 1 All E.R. 583). The notion of reliance may need some refinement now that it is to be used where defendants have been merely negligent, since in all prior cases in which it was employed, the defendants had been fraudulent: and bad people are made to pay more.

SPARTAN STEEL AND ALLOYS LTD. v. MARTIN & CO. (CONTRACTORS) LTD.

Court of Appeal [1973] 1 Q.B. 27; [1972] 3 W.L.R. 502; 116 S.J. 648; [1972] 3 All E.R. 557

Action by industrialist against highway contractor in respect of lost profits.

Excavating with a mechanical shovel, the defendant carelessly damaged a cable and interrupted the supply of electricity to the plaintiff's factory 400 yards away. In order to prevent damage to their furnace the plaintiffs had to damage its contents (on which they would have made a profit of £400) by £368, and they were prevented by the absence of electric current from processing four more "melts" which would have netted them £1,767.

Faulks J. held that the plaintiffs were entitled to all three sums; the Court of Appeal (Edmund Davies L.J. dissenting) held that they were entitled to the first two sums only.

Lord Denning M.R.: . . . At bottom I think the question of recovering economic loss is one of policy. Whenever the courts draw a line to mark out the bounds of *duty*, they do it as matter of policy so as to limit the responsibility of the defendant. Whenever the courts set bounds to the *damages* recoverable—saying that they are, or are not, too remote—they do it as matter of policy so as to limit the liability of the defendant.

In many of the cases where economic loss had been held not to be recoverable, it has been put on the ground that the defendant was under no *duty* to the plaintiff. Thus where a person is injured in a road accident by the negligence of another, the negligent driver owes a duty to the injured man himself, but he owes no duty to the servant of the injured man—see *Best* v. *Samuel Fox & Co. Ltd.* ([1952] A.C. 716, 731): nor to the master of the injured man—*Inland Revenue Commissioners* v. *Hambrook* ([1956] 2 Q.B. 641, 660): nor to anyone else who suffers loss because he had a contract with the injured man—see *Simpson & Co.* v. *Thomson* ((1887) 3 App.Cas. 279, 289): nor indeed to anyone who only suffers economic loss on account of the accident: see *Kirkham* v. *Boughey* ([1958] 2 Q.B. 338, 341). Likewise, when property is damaged by the negligence of another, the negligent tortfeasor owes a duty to the owner or possessor of the chattel, but not to one who suffers loss only because he had a contract entitling him to use the chattel or giving him a right to receive it at some later date: see *Elliott Steam Tug Co. Ltd.* v. *Shipping Controller* ([1922] 1 K.B. 127, 139) and *Margarine Union GmbH* v. *Cambay Prince Steamship Co. Ltd.* ([1969] 1 Q.B. 219, 251–252).

In other cases, however, the defendant seems clearly to have been under a duty to the plaintiff, but the economic loss has not been recovered because it is *too remote*. Take the illustration given by Blackburn J. in *Cattle* v. *Stockton Waterworks Co.* ((1875) L.R. 10 Q.B. 453, 457), when water escapes from a reservoir and floods a coal mine where many men are working. Those who had their tools or clothes destroyed could recover: but those who only lost their wages could not. Similarly, when the defendants' ship negligently sank a ship which was being towed by a tug, the owner of the tug lost his remuneration, but he could not recover it from the negligent ship: though the same duty (of navigation with reasonable care) was owed to both tug and tow: see *Société Anonyme de Remorquage à Hélice* v. *Bennetts* ([1911] 1 K.B. 243, 248). In such cases if the plaintiff or his property had been physically injured, he would have recovered: but, as he only suffered economic loss, he is held not entitled to recover. This is, I should think, because the loss is regarded by the law as too remote: see *King* v. *Phillips* ([1953] 1 Q.B. 429, 439–440).

On the other hand, in the cases where economic loss by itself had been held to be recoverable, it is plain that there was a duty to the plaintiff and the loss was not too remote. Such as when one ship negligently runs down another ship, and damages it, with the result that the cargo has to be discharged and reloaded. The negligent ship was already under a duty to the cargo owners: and they can recover the cost of discharging and reloading it, as it is not too remote: see *Morrison Steamship Co. Ltd.* v. *Greystoke Castle (Cargo Owners)* ([1947] A.C. 265). Likewise, when a banker negligently gives a reference to one who acts on it, the duty is plain and the damage is not too remote: see *Hedley Byrne & Co. Ltd.* v. *Heller & Partners Ltd.* ([1964] A.C. 465).

The more I think about these cases, the more difficult I find it to put each into its proper pigeon-hole. Sometimes I say "There was no duty." In others I say: "The damage was too remote." So much so that I think the time has come to discard those tests which have proved so elusive. It seems to me better to consider the particular relationship in hand, and see whether or not, as a matter of policy, economic loss should be recoverable, or not. Thus in *Weller & Co.* v. *Foot and Mouth Disease Research Institute* ([1966] 1 Q.B. 569) it was plain that the loss suffered by the auctioneers was not recoverable, no matter whether it is put on the ground that there was no duty or that the damage was too remote. Again in *Electrochrome Ltd.* v. *Welsh Plastics Ltd.* ([1968] 2 All E.R. 205), it is plain that the economic loss suffered by the plantiffs' factory (due to the damage to the fire hydrant) was not recoverable, whether because there was no duty or that it was too remote.

So I turn to the relationship in the present case. It is of common occurrence. The parties concerned are: the electricity board who are under a statutory duty to maintain supplies of electricity in their district; the inhabitants of the district, including this factory, who are entitled by statute to a continuous supply of electricity for their use; and the contractors who dig up the road. Similar relationships occur with other statutory bodies, such as gas and water undertakings. The cable may be damaged by the negligence of the statutory undertaker, or by the negligence of the contractor, or by accident without any negligence by anyone: and the power may have to be cut off whilst the cable is repaired. Or the power may be cut off owing to a short-circuit in the power house: and so forth. If the cutting off of the supply causes economic loss to the consumers, should it as matter of policy by recoverable? And against whom?

The first consideration is the position of the statutory undertakers. If the board do not keep up the voltage or pressure of electricity, gas or water—or, likewise, if they shut it off for repairs—and thereby cause economic loss to their consumers, they are not liable in damages, not even if the cause of it is due to their own negligence. The only remedy (which is hardly ever pursued) is to prosecute the board before the magistrates. Such is the result of many cases starting with a water board—*Atkinson* v. *Newcastle and Gateshead Waterworks Co.* ((1887) 2 Ex.D. 441); going on to a gas board—*Clegg, Parkinson & Co.* v. *Earby Gas Co* ([1896] 1 Q.B. 592); and then to an electricity company—*Stevens* v. *Aldershot Gas, Water & District Lighting Co. Ltd.* (best reported in (1932) 31 L.G.R. 48; also in 102 L.J.K.B. 12). In those cases the courts, looking at the legislative enactments, held that Parliament did not intend to expose the board to liability for damages to the inhabitants en masse: see what Lord Cairns L.C. said in *Atkinson* v. *Newcastle and Gateshead Waterworks Co.* (2 Ex.D. 441, 445) and Wills J. in *Clegg, Parkinson & Co.* v. *Earby Gas Co.* ([1896] 1 Q.B. 592, 595). In those cases there was *indirect* damage to the plaintiffs, but it was not recoverable. There is another group of cases which go to show that, if the board, by their negligence in the conduct of their supply, cause direct physical damage or injury to person or property, they are liable: see *Milnes* v. *Huddersfield Corporation* ((1886) 11 App.Cas. 511, 530) by Lord Blackburn; *Midwood & Co. Ltd.* v. *Manchester Corporation* ([1905] 2 K.B. 597); *Heard* v. *Brymbo Steel Co. Ltd.* ([1947] 2 K.B. 692) and *Hartley* v. *Mayoh & Co.* ([1954] 1 Q.B. 383). But one thing is clear: the statutory undertakers have never been held liable for economic loss only. If such be the policy of the legislature in regard to electricity boards, it would seem right for the common law to adopt a similar policy in regard to contractors. If the electricity boards are not liable for economic loss due to negligence which results in the cutting off the supply, nor should a contractor be liable.

The second consideration is the nature of the hazard, namely, the cutting of the supply of electricity. This is a hazard which we all run. It may be due to a short circuit, to a flash of lightning, to a tree falling on the wires, to an accidental cutting of the cable, or even to the negligence of someone or other. And when it does happen, it affects a multitude of persons: not as a rule by way of physical damage to them or their property, but by putting them to inconvenience, and sometimes to economic loss. The supply is usually restored in a few hours, so the economic loss is not very large. Such a hazard is regarded by most people as a thing they must put up with—without seeking compensation from anyone. Some there are who install a stand-by system. Others seek refuge by taking out an insurance policy against breakdown in the supply. But most people are content to take the risk on themselves. When the supply is cut off, they do not go running round to their solicitor. They do not try to find out whether it was anyone's fault. They just put up with it. They try to make up the economic loss by doing more work next day. This is a healthy attitude which the law should encourage.

The third consideration is this: if claims for economic loss were permitted for this particular hazard, there would be no end of claims. Some might be genuine, but many might be inflated, or even false. A machine might not have been in use anyway, but it would be easy to put it down to the cut in supply. It would be well-nigh impossible to check the claims. If there was economic loss on one day, did the claimant do his best to mitigate it by working harder next day? And so forth. Rather than expose claimants to such temptation and defendants to such hard labour—on comparatively small claims—it is better to disallow economic loss altogether, at any rate when it stands alone, independent of any physical damage.

The fourth consideration is that, in such a hazard as this, the risk of economic loss should be suffered by the whole community who suffer the losses—usually many but comparatively small losses—rather than on the one pair of shoulders, that is, on the contractor on whom the total of them, all added together, might be very heavy.

The fifth consideration is that the law provides for deserving cases. If the defendant is guilty of negligence which cuts off the electricity supply and causes actual physical damage to person or property, that physical damage can be recovered: see *Baker* v. *Crow Carrying Co. Ltd.* ((unreported) February 1, 1960; Bar Library Transcript No. 45), referred to by Buckley L.J. in *S.C.M. (United Kingdom) Ltd.* v. *W.J. Whittall & Son Ltd.* ([1971] 1 Q.B. 337, 356); and also any economic loss truly consequential on the material damage: see *British Celanese Ltd.* v. *A.H. Hunt (Capacitors) Ltd.* ([1969] 1 W.L.R. 959) and *S.C.M. (United Kingdom) Ltd.* v. *W.J. Whittall & Son Ltd.* ([1971] 1 Q.B. 337). Such cases will be comparatively few. They will be readily capable of proof and will be easily checked. They should be and are admitted.

These considerations lead me to the conclusion that the plaintiffs should recover for the physical damage to the one melt (£368), and the loss of profit on that melt consequent thereon (£400): but not for the loss of profit on the four melts (£1,767), because that was economic loss independent of the physical damage. I would, therefore, allow the appeal and reduce the damages to £768.

EDMUND DAVIES L.J. (dissenting): . . . The facts giving rise to this appeal have already been set out . . . Their very simplicity serves to highlight a problem regarding which differing judicial and academic views have been expressed and which it is high time should be finally solved. The problem may be thus stated: Where a defendant who owes a duty of care to the plaintiff breaches that duty and, as both a direct and a reasonably foreseeable result of that injury, the plaintiff suffers only economic loss, is he entitled to recover damages for that loss?

In expressing in this way the question which now arises for determination, I have sought to strip away those accretions which would otherwise obscure the basic issue involved. Let me explain. We are not here concerned to inquire whether the defendants owed a duty of care to the plaintiffs or whether they breached it, for these matters are admitted. Nor need we delay to consider whether as a direct and reasonably foreseeable result of the defendants' negligence any harm was sustained by the plaintiffs, for a "melt" valued at £368 was admittedly ruined and the defendants concede their liability to make that loss good. But what *is* in issue is whether the defendants must make good (a) the £400 loss of profit resulting from that material being spoilt and (b) the £1,767 further loss of profit caused by the inability to put four more "melts" through the furnace before power was restored. As to (a), the defendants, while making no unqualified admission, virtually accept their liability, on the ground that the £400 loss was a *direct* consequence of the physical damage caused to the material in the furnace. But they reject liability in respect of (b), not because it was any the less *direct* and reasonably foreseeable consequence of the defendants' negligence than was the £400, but on the ground that it was unrelated to any physical damage and that economic loss not anchored to and resulting from physical harm to person or property is not recoverable under our law as damages for negligence.

In my respectful judgment, however it may formerly have been regarded, the law is today otherwise. I am conscious of the boldness involved in expressing this view, particularly after studying such learned dissertations as that of Professor Atiyah on *Negligence and Economic Loss* ((1967) 83 L.Q.R. 243), where the relevant cases are cited. I recognise that proof of the necessary linkage between negligent acts and purely economic consequences may be hard to forge. I accept, too, that if economic loss of itself confers a right of action this may spell disaster for the negligent party. But this may equally be the outcome where physical damage alone is sustained, or where physical damage leads directly to economic loss. Nevertheless, when this occurs it was accepted in *S.C.M. (United Kingdom) Ltd.* v. *W.J. Whittall & Son Ltd.* ([1971] 1 Q.B. 337) that compensation is recoverable for both types of damage. It follows that this must be regardless of whether the injury (physical or economic, or a mixture of both) is immense or puny, diffused over a wide area or narrowly localised, provided only that the requirements as to foreseeability and directness are fulfilled. I therefore find myself unable to accept as factors determinant of legal principle those considerations of policy canvassed in the concluding passages of the judgment just delivered by Lord Denning M.R. . . .

For my part, I cannot see why the £400 loss of profit here sustained should be recoverable and not the £1,767. It is common ground that both types of loss were equally foreseeable and equally direct consequences of the defendants' admitted negligence and the only distinction drawn is that the former figure represents the profit lost as a result of the physical damage done to the material in the furnace at the time when power was cut off. But what has that purely fortuitous fact to do with legal principle? In my judgment, nothing . . .

Despite the frequency with which *Cattle* v. *Stockton Waterworks Co.* is cited as authority for the proposition that pecuniary loss, without more, can never sustain an action for negligence, I respectfully venture to think that Blackburn J. was there laying down no such rule. Had he intended to do so when, two years later as Lord Blackburn, he was a party to the decision in *Simpson & Co.* v. *Thomson* ((1877) 3 App.Cas. 279), this fact would surely have emerged when he concurred (at pp. 292 *et seq*), in the dismissal of underwriters' claim for recoupment of the sum they had paid for a total loss. . . .

In *Hedley Byrne & Co. Ltd.* v. *Heller & Partners Ltd.* ([1964] A.C. 465), one of those "exceptional cases" referred to by Lord Denning M.R. in *S.C.M.* (*United Kingdom*) *Ltd.* v. *W.J. Whittall & Son Ltd.* and a landmark in the branch of the law with which we are here concerned, Lord Devlin, referring to *Morrison Steamship Co. Ltd.* v. *Greystoke Castle* (*Cargo Owners*), said (at p. 518): "Their Lordships did not in that case lay down any general principle about liability for financial loss in the absence of physical damage; but the case itself makes it impossible to argue that there is any general rule showing that such loss is of its nature irrecoverable." This is increasingly recognised as being the legal position, and ample illustrations of this are available. Thus in *Ministry of Housing* v. *Sharp* ([1970] 2 Q.B. 238), Salmon L.J. said (at p. 278): "So far, however, as the law of negligence relating to civil actions is concerned, the existence of a duty to take reasonable care no longer depends upon whether it is physical injury or financial loss which can reasonably be foreseen as a result of a failure to take such care." And in *Dutton* v. *Bognor Regis Urban District Council* ([1972] 1 Q.B. 372, 404) Sachs L.J. said that " . . . to pose the question: 'Is it physical damage or economic damage?' is to adopt a fallacious approach."

Having considered the intrinsic nature of the problem presented in this appeal, and having consulted the relevant authorities, my conclusion, as already indicated, is that an action lies in negligence for damages in respect of purely economic loss, provided that it was a reasonably foreseeable and direct consequence of failure in a duty of care. The application of such a rule can undoubtedly give rise to difficulties in certain sets of circumstances, but so can the suggested rule that economic loss may be recovered *provided* it is directly consequential upon physical damage. Many alarming situations were conjured up in the course of counsel's arguments before us. In their way, they were reminiscent of those formerly advanced against awarding damages for nervous shock; for example, the risk of fictitious claims and expensive litigation, the difficulty of disproving the alleged cause and effect, and the impossibility of expressing such a claim in financial terms. But I suspect that they (like the illustrations furnished by Lord Penzance in *Simpson & Co.* v. *Thomson* ((1877) 3 App.Cas. 279, 289 *et seq*.)) would for the most part be resolved either on the ground that no duty of care was owed to the injured party or that the damages sued for were irrecoverable *not* because they were simply financial but because they were too remote . . .

I should perhaps again stress that we are here dealing with economic loss which was both reasonably foreseeable and a direct consequence of the defendants' negligent act. What the position should or would be were the latter feature lacking (as in *Weller & Co.* v. *Foot and Mouth Disease Research Institute* ([1966] 1 Q.B. 569)) is not our present concern. By stressing this point one is not reviving the distinction between direct and indirect consequences which is generally thought to have been laid at rest by *The Wagon Mound* ([1961] A.C. 388), for, in the words of Professor Atiyah, *Negligence and Economic Loss* (83 L.Q.R. 263), that case "was solely concerned with the question whether the directness of the damage is a *sufficient* test of liability, . . . In other words, *The Wagon Mound* merely decides that a plaintiff cannot recover for unforeseeable consequences even if they are direct; it does not decide that a plaintiff can always recover for foreseeable consequences even if they are indirect." Both directness and foreseeability being here established, it follows that I regard Faulks J. as having rightly awarded the sum of £2,535.

LAWTON L.J.: This appeal raises neatly a question which has been asked from time to time since Blackburn J. delivered his well-known judgment in *Cattle v. Stockton Waterworks Co.* ((1875) L.R. 10 Q.B. 453) and more frequently since the decision in *Hedley Byrne & Co. Ltd.* v. *Heller & Partners Ltd.* ([1964] A.C. 465), namely, whether a plaintiff can recover from a defendant, proved or admitted to have been negligent, foreseeable financial damage which is not consequential upon foreseeable physical injury or damage to property. Any doubts there may have been about the recovery of such consequential financial damage were settled by this court in *S.C.M. (United Kingdom) Ltd.* v. *W.J. Whittall & Son Ltd.* ([1971] 1 Q.B. 337). In my judgment the answer to this question is that such financial damage cannot be recovered save when it is the immediate consequence of a breach of duty to safeguard the plaintiff from that kind of loss.

This is not the first time a negligent workman has cut an electric supply cable nor the first claim for damages arising out of such an incident. When in practice at the Bar I myself advised in a number of such cases. Most practitioners acting for insurers under the so-called "public liability" types of policy will have had similar professional experiences; if not with electrical supply, with gas and water mains. Negligent interference with such services is one of the facts of life and can cause a lot of damage, both physical and financial. Water conduits have been with us for centuries; gas mains for nearly a century and a half; electricity supply cables for about three-quarters of a century; but there is not a single case in the English law reports which is an authority for the proposition that mere financial loss resulting from negligent interruption of such services is recoverable. Why?

Many lawyers would be likely to answer that ever since *Cattle v. Stockton Waterworks Co.* (L.R. 10 Q.B. 453), such damages have been irrecoverable. Edmund Davies L.J. has just stated that he doubts whether Blackburn J. laid down any such rule. Knowing that he had these doubts, I have re-read *Cattle v. Stockton Waterworks Co.* The claim was in negligence. The declaration was as follows: "that defendants, being a water company, so negligently laid down under a certain turnpike road their pipes for supplying water to a district, and so negligently kept and maintained the pipes in such insufficient repair, and in such imperfect and leaky condition, that, while plaintiff was lawfully constructing for reward to the plaintiff a tunnel across the turnpike road, and was lawfully using the road for such purpose, the pipes leaked, and large quantities of water flowed into the road, and upon the plaintiff's workings, and flooded them, and the plantiff was hindered and delayed in the work, and suffered great loss." The declaration raised precisely the problem which has to be solved in this case; Blackburn J.'s answer was in these words, at p. 458: "In the present case there is no pretence for saying that the defendants were malicious or had any intention to injure anyone. They were, at most, guilty of a neglect of duty which occasioned injury to the property of Knight, but which did not injure any property of the plaintiff. The plaintiff's claim is to recover the damage which he has sustained by his contract with Knight becoming less profitable, or, it may be, a losing contract, in consequence of this injury to Knight's property. We think this does not give him any right of action."

Earlier in his judgment he had said (at p. 457): "No authority in favour of the plaintiff's right to sue was cited, and, as far as our knowledge goes, there was none that could have been cited." There is still no authority directly in point today. Blackburn J.'s judgment has been cited with approval and followed many times: the judgment of Hamilton J. in *Société Anonyme de Remorquage à Hélice* v. *Bennetts* ([1911] 1 K.B. 243, 248) and of Widgery J. in *Weller & Co.* v. *Foot and Mouth Disease Research Institute* ([1966] 1 Q.B. 569, 588) are instances. For nearly 100 years now contractors and insurers have negotiated policies and premiums have been calculated on the assumption that the judgment of Blackburn J. is a correct statement of the law; and those affected financially by the acts of negligent contractors have been advised time and time again that mere financial loss is irrecoverable.

It was argued that the law has developed since 1875, albeit the development was unnoticed by Hamilton J. and Widgery J. Has it? . . .

. . . If, in the *Greystoke Castle* case, the House of Lords overruled *Cattle* v. *Stockton Waterworks Co.* (L.R. 10 Q.B. 453), it did so by an unobserved flanking movement, not by a direct assault. The two leading counsel, Sir William McNair K.C. and Sir Robert Aske K.C. do not seem to have appreciated that a bastion of the common law was in danger of falling, as neither seems to have cited *Cattle* v. *Stockton Waterworks Co.* The only one of the Law Lords who did was Lord Simonds, who clearly did so with respect and approval: his speech, however, was a dissenting one. Lord Roche commented upon the judgment of Hamilton J. in *Société Anonyme de Remorquage à Hélice* v. *Bennetts* ([1911] 1 K.B. 243). He sought to explain it on the ground that the unsuccessful plaintiff had not proved a breach of duty. Had he intended to disapprove a long-standing judgment of such an eminent common lawyer as Blackburn J., I would have expected him to have done so in terms. The House did, however, by a majority, adjudge that the cargo owners had a direct claim against the owners of the colliding ship for a proportion of the general average contribution. The case was argued and speeches delivered on the basis that the House was considering a problem of maritime law. I would not have the temerity to express any opinion as to the extent to which maritime law and the common law differ as to the kinds of damage which are recoverable; but having regard to their differing historical developments it would not surprise me if there were divergencies. The policies governing their developments may well have been different. What I am satisfied about is that the House of Lords in the *Greystoke Castle* case ([1947] A.C. 265) cannot be said to have overruled *Cattle* v. *Stockton Waterworks Co.* (L.R. 10 Q.B. 453).

The differences which undoubtedly exist between what damage can be recovered in one type of case and what in another cannot be reconciled on any logical basis. I agree with Lord Denning M.R. that such differences have arisen because of the policy of the law. Maybe there should be one policy for all cases; the enunciation of such a policy is not, in my judgment, a task for this court . . . In my judgment the rule enunciated in 1875 by Blackburn J. is the correct one to apply in negligence cases.

When this principle is applied to the facts of this case it produces the result referred to by Lord Denning M.R. in his judgment. I too would allow the appeal and reduce the damages to £768.

Questions

1. If a company loses profits, its shareholders may lose dividends and its employees some wages. If the company is permitted to recover, do the shareholders or the employees benefit? Could the shareholders or employees themselves sue? If not, why not? (See *Prudential Assurance Co.* v. *Newman Industries* (*No.* 2) [1982] 1 All E.R. 354, 366–7).

2. An articulated lorry jack-knifes on the motorway. The following car collides with it, and the driver is injured. No one else suffers physical harm, but the motorway is closed for two hours, and many people miss valuable appointments. Do you think it would be reasonable to distinguish between the different types of harm caused by a single incident?

3. What class of litigants will bring an action for lost profits if such an action is allowed? What class of litigants can bring an action for personal injuries?

4. Does a proper sense of social responsibility require one to bear in mind the financial well-being of trading companies with limited liability?

5. Suppose that the defendant had been operating, with the plaintiff's permission, on the plaintiff's land. Would the result be the same?

6. The old idea that the law of tort should be determined by a moral view of the demands of social responsibility is being challenged by the theory that the law of tort should be determined by its function as a loss-distributing device. Might the results of the two views diverge in the present case?

Note:

A person's chances of obtaining the money he is claiming depend on what he is claiming it for and who he is claiming it from: in other words, both the type of injury he has suffered and the nature of his relationship with the defendant are material, perhaps vital, considerations.

Since *Donoghue* v. *Stevenson* people who act dangerously may have to pay even a complete stranger to whom they cause physical harm. *Junior Books* and *Hedley Byrne*, where there was no danger at all, afforded a remedy for purely financial harm, but only to those in an especially close relationship with the defendant. Here in *Spartan Steel* the plaintiff recovered for the physical harm, but not for the purely financial harm which was an equally foreseeable consequence of a stranger's dangerous conduct. There is no conflict at all between the cases.

The plaintiff in *Spartan Steel* suffered economic loss because the defendant damaged the electricity cable which belonged to a third party. Where property has been damaged by carelessness the courts long held that only those with a proprietary or possessory interest in the property may bring an action. There are masses of cases: courts have rejected claims by the insurer who had to pay out on his policy (*Simpson* v. *Thomson* (1877) 3 App.Cas. 179), the salvor whose reward was at stake (*Société Anonyme de Remorquage à Hélice* v. *Bennetts* [1911] 1 K.B. 243), the person who would have bought the chattel at a profit (*Margarine Union GmbH* v. *Cambay Prince S.S. Co.* [1969] 1 Q.B. 219), or sold it on commission (*Weller & Co.* v. *Foot and Mouth Disease Research Institute* [1966] 1 Q.B. 569), or used it profitably under a charter (*The World Harmony* [1967] P. 341). How the law could have taken a clearer position it is difficult to see.

The position adopted is also right and convenient. It is right to distinguish property damage from financial loss because things, being capable of gratifying the senses, are more significant than wealth, just as people are more significant than things. It would also be inconvenient not to distinguish property damage from financial loss because whereas property damage is always limited in extent (thanks to the physical laws of inertia), the incidence of financial loss knows no bounds, and the courts would have a fearful time trying to set them.

But estimable though the position of the majority in *Spartan Steel* is, it is now unstable. Lord Roskill expressly questioned it in *Junior Books* (above p. 30) and his own excellent judgment in *Margarine Union* has been disapproved, with a blitheness and inconsequentiality bordering on flippancy, by Lloyd J., whose argument as counsel Roskill J. had refused to accept (*The Irene's Success* [1982] Q.B. 481). Lloyd J. did not dissent from *Weller*, but held that a purchaser of goods who had accepted the risk without acquiring the property in them could sue the person who negligently damaged them and thereby made his good bargain bad. Since such a contract of sale is indistinguishable, so far as the passing of risk without property goes, from the contract of insurance, it will be interesting to see how this holding can be reconciled with *Simpson* v. *Thomson* which Lloyd J. described as "an unshakeable authority" as indeed, being a House of Lords decision, it is. The next step will doubtless be to allow the charterer of a ship, who (unlike the hirer of a car which he himself drives) has only a contractual right to its use, to sue the person who negligently collides with it. *The World Harmony* will thus be sunk by *The Greystoke Castle*, rather submerged until Lord Roskill raised it again in *Junior Books*, and by *The Willemstad* (1977) 51 A.J.L.R. 270, 11 A.L.R. 227, much praised by Megarry V-C. in *Ross* v. *Caunters* [1980] Ch. 297.

Once again a critical case has arisen in Scotland. The pursuer was one of a consortium of firms engaged on a huge construction project in the Firth of Forth. The project depended on the availability of a crane-barge. This was hired by another member of the consortium, who procured wire slings from the defender. One day while a concrete pile belonging to the pursuer was being raised, the sling snapped. The pile sank and the crane-barge was badly damaged. The pursuer naturally recovered for the loss of its pile, but not for the great expense it suffered because the crane-barge was put out of commission for eight weeks and the construction work delayed. *Wimpey Construction Co. (U.K.) Ltd.* v. *Martin Black & Co.*, 1982 S.L.T. 239. A conflict between *Spartan Steel* and *Junior Books* seems inevitable.

HOME OFFICE v. DORSET YACHT CO.

House of Lords [1970] A.C. 1004; [1970] 2 W.L.R. 1140; [1970] 2 All E.R. 294; [1970] 1
Lloyd's Rep. 453; 114 S.J. 375

*Action by owner against Home Office in respect of property damage done by
runaway Borstal boys.*

Seven Borstal boys, five of whom had escaped before, were on a training exercise
on Brownsea Island in Poole Harbour, and ran away one night when the three
officers in charge of them were, contrary to instructions, all in bed. They boarded
one of the many vessels in the harbour, started it and collided with the plaintiff's
yacht, which they then boarded and damaged further.

To the preliminary question of law, whether on the facts as pleaded any duty of
care capable of giving rise to a liability in damages was owed to the plaintiff by the
defendant, their servants or agents, an affirmative answer was given by Thesiger J.,
by the Court of Appeal [1969] 2 Q.B. 412, and by the House of Lords (Viscount
Dilhorne dissenting).

LORD REID: . . . The case for the Home Office is that under no circumstances can
Borstal officers owe any duty to any member of the public to take care to prevent
trainees under their control or supervision from injuring him or his property. If that
is the law, then inquiry into the facts of this case would be a waste of time and
money because whatever the facts may be the respondents must lose. That case is
based on three main arguments. First it is said that there is virtually no authority
for imposing a duty of this kind. Secondly, it is said that no person can be liable for a
wrong done by another who is of full age and capacity and who is not the servant or
acting on behalf of that person. And thirdly it is said that public policy (or the
policy of the relevant legislation) requires that these officers should be immune
from any such liability.

The first would at one time have been a strong argument. About the beginning of
this century most eminent lawyers thought that there were a number of separate
torts involving negligence, each with its own rules, and they were most unwilling to
add more. They were of course aware from a number of leading cases that in the
past the courts had from time to time recognised new duties and new grounds of
action. But the heroic age was over; it was time to cultivate certainty and security in
the law; the categories of negligence were virtually closed. The Attorney-General
invited us to return to those halcyon days, but, attractive though it may be, I cannot
accede to his invitation.

In later years there has been a steady trend towards regarding the law of
negligence as depending on principle so that, when a new point emerges, one
should ask not whether it is covered by authority but whether recognised principles
apply to it. *Donoghue* v. *Stevenson* ([1932] A.C. 562) may be regarded as a
milestone, and the well-known passage in Lord Atkin's speech should I think be
regarded as a statement of principle. It is not to be treated as if it were a statutory
definition. It will require qualification in new circumstances. But I think that the
time has come when we can and should say that it ought to apply unless there is
some justification or valid explanation for its exclusion. For example, causing
economic loss is a different matter; for one thing, it is often caused by deliberate
action. Competition involves traders being entitled to damage their rivals' interests
by promoting their own, and there is a long chapter of the law determining in what
circumstances owners of land can and in what circumstances they may not use their
proprietary rights so as to injure their neighbours. But where negligence is involved
the tendency has been to apply principles analogous to those stated by Lord Atkin:
cf. Hedley Byrne & Co. Ltd. v. *Heller & Partners Ltd.* ([1964] A.C. 465). And
when a person has done nothing to put himself in any relationship with another
person in distress or with his property mere accidental propinquity does not require

him to go to that person's assistance. There may be a moral duty to do so, but it is not practicable to make it a legal duty. And then there are cases, *e.g.* with regard to landlord and tenant, where the law was settled long ago and neither Parliament nor this House sitting judicially has made any move to alter it. But I can see nothing to prevent our approaching the present case with Lord Atkin's principles in mind.

Even so, it is said that the respondents must fail because there is a general principle that no person can be responsible for the acts of another who is not his servant or acting on his behalf. But here the ground of liability is not responsibility for the acts of the escaping trainees; it is liability for damage caused by the carelessness of these officers in the knowledge that their carelessness would probably result in the trainees causing damage of this kind. So the question is really one of remoteness of damage . . .

If the carelessness of the Borstal officers was the cause of the plaintiff's loss, what justification is there for holding that they had no duty to take care? The first argument was that their right and power to control the trainees was purely statutory and that any duty to exercise that right and power was only a statutory duty owed to the Crown. I would agree, but there is a good authority for the proposition that if a person performs a statutory duty carelessly so that he causes damage to a member of the public which would not have happened if he had performed his duty properly he may be liable. In *Geddis* v. *Proprietors of Bann Reservoir* ((1873) 3 App.Cas 430) Lord Blackburn said (at pp. 455–456): "For I take it, without citing cases, that it is now thoroughly well established that no action will lie for doing that which the legislature has authorised, if it be done without negligence, although it does occasion damage to anyone; but an action does lie for doing that which the legislature has authorised, if it be done negligently." The reason for this is, I think, that Parliament deems it to be in the public interest that things otherwise unjustifiable should be done, and that those who do such things with due care should be immune from liability to persons who may suffer thereby. But Parliament cannot reasonably be supposed to have licensed those who do such things to act negligently in disregard of the interests of others so as to cause them needless damage.

Where Parliament confers a discretion the position is not the same. Then there may, and almost certainly will, be errors of judgment in exercising such a discretion and Parliament cannot have intended that members of the public should be entitled to sue in respect of such errors. But there must come a stage when the discretion is exercised so carelessly or unreasonably that there has been no real exercise of the discretion which Parliament has conferred. The person purporting to exercise his discretion has acted in abuse or excess of his power. Parliament cannot be supposed to have granted immunity to persons who do that. The present case does not raise this issue because no discretion was given to these Borstal officers. They were given orders which they negligently failed to carry out. But the county court case of *Greenwell* v. *Prison Commissioners* ((1951) 101 L.J. 486) was relied on and I must deal with it.

Some 290 trainees were held in custody in an open Borstal institution. During the previous year there had been no less than 172 escapes. Two trainees escaped and took and damaged the plaintiff's motor truck; one of these trainees had escaped on three previous occasions from this institution. For three months since his past escape the question of his removal to a more secure institution had been under consideration but no decision has been reached. The learned judge held that the authorities there had been negligent. In my view, this decision could only be upheld if it could be said that the failure of those authorities to deal with the situation was so unreasonable as to show that they had been guilty of a breach of their statutory duty and that that had caused the loss suffered by the plaintiff.

Governors of these institutions and other responsible authorities have a difficult and delicate task. There was some argument as to whether the present system was fully authorised by the relevant statutes, but I shall assume that it is. This system is based on the belief that it assists the rehabilitation of trainees to give them as much freedom and responsibility as possible. So the responsible authorities must weigh on the one hand the public interest of protecting neighbours and their property from the depredations of escaping trainees and on the other hand the public interest of promoting rehabilitation. Obviously there is much room here for differences of opinion and errors of judgment. In my view there can be no liability if the discretion is exercised with due care. There could only be liability if the person entrusted with discretion either unreasonably failed to carry out his duty to consider the matter or reached a conclusion so unreasonable as again to show failure to do his duty.

It was suggested that these trainees might have been deliberately released at the time when they escaped and that then there could have been no liability. I do not agree. Presumably when trainees are released either temporarily or permanently some care is taken to see that there is no need for them to resort to crime to get food or transport. I could not imagine any more unreasonable exercise of discretion than to release trainees on an island in the middle of the night without making any provision for their future welfare.

We were also referred to *Holgate* v. *Lancashire Mental Hospitals Board* ([1937] 4 All E.R. 19), where the alleged fault was in releasing a mental patient. For similar reasons I think that this decision could only be supported if it could be said that the release was authorised so carelessly that there had been no real exercise of discretion.

If the appellants were right in saying that there can never be a right in a private individual to complain of negligent exercise of a duty to keep a prisoner under control, I do not see how *Ellis* v. *Home Office* ([1953] 2 All E.R. 149) can be correct. The plaintiff was in prison, and on one occasion, as he alleged, owing to inadequate control by warders another prisoner assaulted and injured him. It was assumed that he had a right of action, and the Attorney-General did not challenge this. But when the other prisoner assaulted Ellis he was not in fact under control or he would not have been permitted to carry out the assault. It would be very odd if the only persons entitled to complain of negligent performance of the statutory duty to control prisoners were other prisoners. If the main argument for the appellants were right I think that it would necessarily involve holding that *Ellis* was wrong.

It was suggested that a decision against the Home Office would have very far-reaching effects; it was, indeed, suggested in the Court of Appeal that it would make the Home Office liable for the loss occasioned by a burglary committed by a trainee on parole or a prisoner permitted to go out to attend a funeral. But there are two reasons why in the vast majority of cases that would not be so. In the first place it would have to be shown that the decision to allow any such release was so unreasonable that it could not be regarded as a real exercise of discretion by the responsible officer who authorised the release. And secondly it would have to be shown that the commission of the offence was the natural and probable, as distinct from merely a foreseeable, result of the release—that there was no novus actus interveniens. *Greenwell's* case (101 L.J. 486) received a good deal of publicity at the time; it was commented on in the *Law Quarterly Review*, Vol. 68 (1952), p. 18. But it has not been followed by a series of claims. I think that the fears of the appellants are unfounded: I cannot believe that negligence or dereliction of duty is widespread among prison or Borstal officers.

Finally I must deal with public policy. It is argued that it would be contrary to public policy to hold the Home Office or its officers liable to a member of the public for this carelessness—or, indeed, any failure of duty on their part. The basic question is: who shall bear the loss caused by that carelessness—the innocent respondents or the Home Office, who are vicariously liable for the conduct of their careless officers? I do not think that the argument for the Home Office can be put better than it was put by the Court of Appeals of New York in *Williams* v. *State of*

New York ((1955) 127 N.E. 2d 545, 550): " . . . public policy also requires that the State be not held liable. To hold otherwise would impose a heavy responsibility upon the State, or dissuade the wardens and principal keepers of our prison systems from continued experimentation with 'minimum security' work details—which provide a means for encouraging better-risk prisoners to exercise their senses of responsibility and honour and so prepare themselves for their eventual return to society. Since 1917, the legislature has expressly provided for out-of-prison work, Correction Law, § 182, and its intention should be respected without fostering the reluctance of prison officials to assign eligible men to minimum security work, lest they thereby give rise to costly claims against the State, or indeed inducing the State itself to terminate this 'salutary procedure' looking toward rehabilitation.' It may be that public servants of the State of New York are so apprehensive, easily dissuaded from doing their duty and intent on preserving public funds from costly claims that they could be influenced in this way. But my experience leads me to believe that Her Majesty's servants are made of sterner stuff. So I have no hesitation in rejecting this argument. I can see good ground in public policy for giving this immunity to a government department. I would dismiss this appeal.

VISCOUNT DILHORNE (dissenting): . . . If, applying Lord Atkin's test, it be held that a duty of care existed in this case, I do not think that such a duty can be limited to being owed only to those in the immediate proximity of the place from which the escape is made. In *Donoghue* v. *Stevenson* the duty was held to be owed to consumers wherever they might be. If there be such a duty, it must, in my view, be owed to all those who it can reasonably be foreseen are likely to suffer damage as a result of the escape. Surely it is reasonably foreseeable that those who escape may take a succession of vehicles, perhaps many miles from the place from which they escaped, to make their getaway. Surely it is reasonably foreseeable that those who escape from prisons, Borstals and other places of confinement will, while they are on the run, seek to steal food for their sustenance and money and are likely to break into premises for that purpose.

If the foreseeability test is applied to determine to whom the duty is owed, I am at a loss to perceive any logical ground for excluding liability to persons who suffer injury or loss, no matter how far they or their property may be from the place of escape, if the loss or injury was of a character reasonably foreseeable as the consequence of failure to take proper care to prevent the escape.

Lord Atkin's answer to the question "Who, then, in law is my neighbour?" while very relevant to determine to whom a duty of care is owed, cannot determine, in my opinion, the question whether a duty of care exists.

I find support for this view in the observations of du Parcq L.J. in *Deyong* v. *Shenburn* ([1946] K.B. 227). There the plaintiff has been employed in a theatre by the defendant. Some of his clothing had been stolen from his dressing room due, it was alleged, to the negligence of the defendant.

du Parcq L.J. said (at p. 233): "It is said that this is a case of tort, and we were reminded of observations which are very familiar to lawyers in *Heaven* v. *Pender* ((1883) 11 Q.B.D. 503) and *Donoghue* v. *Stevenson*. I do not think that I need cite them in terms. There are well known words of Lord Atkin in *Donoghue* v. *Stevenson* as to the duty towards one's neighbour and the method of ascertaining who is one's neighbour. It has been pointed out (and this only shows the difficulty of stating a general proposition which is not too wide) that unless one somewhat narrows the term of the proposition as it has been stated, one would be including in it something which the law does not support. It is not true to say that wherever a man finds himself in such a position that unless he does a certain act another person may suffer, or that if he does something another person will suffer, then it is his duty in the one case to be careful to do the act and in the other case to be careful not to do the act. Any such proposition is much too wide. There has to be a breach of a duty which the law recognises, and to ascertain what the law recognises regard must be had to the decisions of the courts. There has never been a decision that a master must, merely because of the relationship which exists between master and servant, take reasonable care for the safety of his servant's belongings in the sense that he must take steps to ensure, so far as he can, that no wicked person shall have an opportunity of stealing the servant's goods. That is the duty contended for here, and there is not a shred of authority to suggest that any such duty exists or ever has existed."

This was cited and followed by my learned and noble friends Lord Hodson and Lord Morris of Borth-y-Gest in *Edwards* v. *West Herts. Group Hospital Management Committee* ([1957] 1 W.L.R. 415, 420, 422).

In *Commissioner for Railways* v. *Quinlan* ([1964] A.C. 1054) the question was considered whether on the facts of that case and on the principle of *Donoghue* v. *Stevenson* [above, p. 15] a general duty of care and liability in negligence for its breach existed in relation to a trespasser. Viscount Radcliffe, delivering the judgment of the board, said (at p. 1070): " . . . such a duty, it was suggested, might be founded on a general principle derived from the House of Lords decision in *Donoghue* v. *Stevenson*. Their Lordships think this view mistaken. They cannot see that there is any general principle to be deduced from that decision which throws any particular light upon the legal rights and duties that arise when a trespasser is injured on a railway level crossing where he has no right to be . . . " Later he said (at p. 1084): " . . . passages occur in one or two of the other judgments that suggest that a trespasser can somehow become the occupier's 'neighbour,' within the meaning of the somewhat overworked shorthand of *Donoghue* v. *Stevenson* . . . " In the light of those passages I think that it is clear that the *Donoghue* v. *Stevenson* principle cannot be regarded as an infallible test of the existence of a duty of care, nor do I think that, if that test is satisfied, there arises any presumption of the existence of such a duty. . . .

Apart from [*Greenwell* v. *Prison Commissioners*] in which *Donoghue* v. *Stevenson* was applied, no shred of authority can be found to support the view that a duty of care, breach of which gives rise to liability in damages, is under the common law owed by the custodians of persons lawfully in custody to anyone who suffers damage or loss at the hands of persons who have escaped from custody.

Lord Denning M.R. in the course of his judgment in this case ([1969] 2 Q.B. 412, 424) said that he thought that the absence of authority was "because, until recently, no lawyer ever thought such an action would lie" on one of two grounds, first, that the damage was far too remote, the chain of causation being broken by the act of the person who had escaped; and, secondly, that the only duty owed was to the Crown.

Whatever be the reasons for the absence of authority, the significant fact is its absence and this leads me to the conclusion, despite the disclaimer of Mr. Fox-Andrews for the respondents of any such intention, that we are being asked to create in reliance on Lord Atkin's words an entirely new and novel duty and one which does not arise out of any novel situation.

I, of course, recognise that the common law develops by the application of well-established principles to new circumstances but I cannot accept that the application of Lord Atkin's words, which, though they applied in *Deyong* v. *Shenburn* ([1946] K.B. 227), and might have applied in *Commissioner for Railways* v. *Quinlan* ([1964] A.C. 1054), were not held to impose a new duty on a master to his servant or on an occupier to a trespasser, suffices to impose a new duty on the Home Office and on others in charge of persons in lawful custody of the kind suggested.

No doubt very powerful arguments can be advanced that there should be such a duty. It can be argued that it is wrong that those who suffer loss or damage at the hands of those who have escaped from custody as a result of negligence on the part of the custodians should have no redress save against the persons who inflicted the loss or damage who are unlikely to be able to pay; that they should not have to bear the loss themselves, whereas, if there is such a duty, liability might fall on the Home Office and the burden on the general body of taxpayers.

However this may be, we are concerned not with what the law should be but with what it is. The absence of authority shows that no such duty now exists. If there should be one, that is, in my view, a matter for the legislature and not for the courts . . .

Questions

1. Is there any difference between a duty to take care that your ginger-beer doesn't hurt people and the duty to take care that other people don't?

2. Should it be the judges who decide whether a penal system has been (a) wisely instituted, (b) properly run?

3. Why is it "not negligence to keep an open Borstal" (*per* Lord Denning M.R.) if it is one of the risks of the system that boys will sometimes escape and do damage?

4. Is this case an instance of conflict between property and liberty?

5. As between the state and the plaintiff's insurance company (who have been paid to take the risk of damage to the yacht) "on whom should the risk of negligence fall"?

6. Why do you think that the Criminal Injuries Compensation Board, which disburses public funds, pays only the victims of *personal injury* directly attributable to a crime of violence?

7. Would the police be liable to anyone for incompetently failing to catch (a) an escaped convict, (b) a suspected criminal?

8. Who caused the damage—the Home Office, the warders or the boys? Why is this the wrong question?

9. After having twelve double whiskies in X's pub, A drove to Y's roadhouse; Y refused to serve him since he was obviously drunk but made no effort to stop him driving away. A collided with B, a pedestrian. Can B sue X or Y or both?

10. If warders carelessly allow a confidence trickster and a burglar to escape from prison, would a person duped by the former or raped by the latter be able to sue the Home Office?

11. There are two major grounds of distinction between the principal case and *Ellis* v. *Home Office* (above, p. 52). What are they?

Note:

Considering that an employer has been held liable to an apprentice for letting another employee brutalise him in *Hudson* v. *Ridge Manufacturing Co.* [1957] 2 Q.B. 348, and that an education authority has been held liable to a truck-driver who ran into a tree in order to avoid killing a child which it had carelessly allowed to run on to the highway in *Carmarthenshire C.C.* v. *Lewis* [1955] A.C. 549, it is perhaps not surprising that the House of Lords should combine the two principles and hold an occupier liable for the property damage which adults who were carelessly allowed to escape were likely to cause. Only a very tiresome critic would seek to draw a distinction between, on the one hand, a young apprentice blown up with compressed air by a bully or a truck-driver sacrificing himself to save a toddler and, on the other hand, an insured yacht, doubly symbolic of capitalist excess, damaged by predictably incompetent outcasts.

If it's the principle that counts (or the structure, as it's called nowadays), then the striking thing about *Dorset Yacht* is that the defendants were held liable to total strangers for not protecting them from the ravages of the boys: the yachts anchored in the harbour were just like cars parked on the road outside a borstal (except that walking is a bit easier than swimming). An occupier has been held liable to his neighbour (in the strict sense of the "person next door") for the escape of natural hazards (see *Leakey* v. *National Trust*, below, p. 355), but it is doubtful if a mere passer-by could have sued. Of course, the Home Office didn't just fail to prevent the borstal boys escaping, it brought them to the island in the first place . . .

The judgment of Lord Diplock, too integrated for excerption and too long for inclusion, should be read with care. He emphasised that the duty in question, namely to detain the Borstal boys, was very different from the duty to control one's property or one's own activities. He also emphasised that the power to detain the boys came from statute, and that the principal legal device for controlling the exercise of that power was the doctrine of *vires*; if, however, what the officers had done was *ultra vires*, as it would be if it were in breach of instructions or wholly unreasonable, the private law doctrine of negligence might enter, in favour of those immediately in the vicinity. His conclusion was that "any duty of a borstal officer to use reasonable care to prevent a borstal trainee from escaping from his custody was owed only to persons whom he could reasonably forsee had property situate in the vicinity of the place of detention of the detainee which the detainee was likely to steal or to appropriate and damage in the course of eluding immediate pursuit and recapture."

Viscount Dilhorne was certainly right to say that it will be very difficult to limit this duty to those in the immediate vicinity. In the shock cases, as we shall see, there was a well-established rule that only those *on the spot* could claim. That convenient limitation has now been discarded with scorn and derision, since it is incompatible with the 'foreseeability' formula, as is the holding in this case (*McLoughlin* v. *O'Brian*, below p. 68).

Under *Donoghue* v. *Stevenson*, it was observed above that (p. 22) there were two respects in which Lord Atkin's principle was wider than the facts of the case. We have seen the extension from liability for causing physical harm to liability for causing economic harm. Now we see the extension from liability for causing harm to liability for letting others cause harm, in this case physical harm.

Now one can only be liable for letting someone cause harm if one has the power to prevent him. While it is true that some private people have certain powers of control (occupiers of premises, parents, employers), most of the powers to stop people doing things are vested in the government. It is amazing how many things the government can stop people doing, or conversely let them do if it chooses to license them. That is the next case. But the next case, unlike this one, involved merely financial harm, which is exactly the kind of harm most likely to be caused by governmental decisions. So we are immediately caught up in a vast extension of governmental liability in the field of private law. The number of people entitled as of right (for tort claims can be brought as of right) to harass the government, especially local government, has vastly increased as a result of these decisions. The courts now realise what they have let loose and have decided that if one is questioning a decision of a governmental body in the area of public law, one must use the special procedure for such matters (R.S.C. Order 53) rather than an ordinary action. The special procedure permits an award of damages but allows the court much greater control and considerable discretion. (*Cocks* v. *Thanet D.C.* [1982] 3 W.L.R. 1121, [1982] 3 All E.R. 1135 (H.L.)).

In *Smith* v. *Scott* [1973] Ch. 314 the local authority installed a notoriously unruly and anti-social family in a house next the plaintiff's. The lease forbade the Scotts to cause a nuisance, but of course they did and the plaintiffs had to move out of their own house. The local authority was held to have committed no wrong to the plaintiffs: *Donoghue* v. *Stevenson* did not apply. The trial judge quoted the end of the third paragraph of Lord Reid's speech in *Dorset Yacht* as excerpted above p. 50).

ANNS v. MERTON LONDON BOROUGH COUNCIL

House of Lords [1978] A.C. 728; [1977] 2 W.L.R. 1024; 121 S.J. 377; [1977] 2 All E.R. 492

Action by householders against builder and local authority in respect of building defects.

The plaintiffs were leaseholders of flats in a block built by Walcroft in 1962. In 1970 the wall began to crack and the floors started to tilt. According to the plaintiffs, this settlement was attributable to the inadequacy of the foundations. In 1972 they issued a writ against Walcroft, claiming damages for breach of contract and of the undertakings implied by section 6 of the Housing Act 1957; they also issued a writ against the local authority, claiming damages for negligent failure to inspect the foundations or to detect, on inspection, that they were shallower than was required by bye-laws or was indicated on the approved plans.

On the preliminary point whether the claim was time-barred the local authority appealed without success from an adverse decision of the Court of Appeal.

LORD WILBERFORCE: . . . before the appeal to this House came on, the council presented a petition, asking for leave to argue the question whether the council was under any duty of care to the plaintiffs at all.

The question had not been considered by Judge Fay, or by the Court of Appeal, because it was thought, rightly in my opinion, that it was concluded by *Dutton's* case ([1972] 1 Q.B. 373). Thus the council wished to challenge the correctness of the latter decision. In that case the defendant council of Bognor Regis was held liable for damages in negligence (*viz.* negligent inspection by one of its officers), consisting of a breach of a duty at common law to take reasonable care to see that the byelaws were complied with. On 21st October 1976 this House acceded to the petition. The council thus have leave to argue that in the circumstances they owed no duty of care to the plaintiffs.

This being a preliminary point of law, as was the argument on limitation, it has to be decided on the assumption that the facts are as pleaded. There is some difference between those facts and those on which *Dutton's* case was based, and in the present case the plaintiffs rely not only on negligent inspection but, in the alternative, on a failure to make any inspections.

In these circumstances I take the questions in this appeal to be: (1) whether the council were under: (a) a duty of care to the plaintiffs to carry out an inspection of the foundations (which did not arise in *Dutton's* case); (b) a duty, if any inspection was made, to take reasonable care to see that the byelaws were complied with (as held in *Dutton's* case); (c) any other duty including a duty to ensure that the building was constructed in accordance with the plans, or not to allow the builder to construct the dwelling-house on foundations which were only two feet six inches deep instead of three feet or deeper (as pleaded); (2) if the council was under any such duty as alleged, and committed a breach of it, resulting in damage, at what date the cause of action of the plaintiffs arose for the purposes of the Limitation Act 1939. No question arises directly as this stage as to the damages which the plaintiffs can recover and no doubt there will be issues at the trial as to causation and quantum which we cannot anticipate. But it will be necessary to give some general consideration to the kind of damages to which, if they succeed, the plaintiffs may become entitled. This matter was discussed in *Dutton's* case and is closely connected with that of the duty which may be owed and with the arising of the cause of action.

The duty of care

Through the trilogy of cases in this House, *Donoghue* v. *Stevenson* [above, p. 15], *Hedley Byrne & Co. Ltd.* v. *Heller & Partners Ltd.* [above, p. 34], and *Home Office* v. *Dorset Yacht Co. Ltd.* [above, p. 50], the position has now been reached that in order to establish that a duty of care arises in a particular situation, it is not necessary to bring the facts of that situation within those of previous situations in which a duty of care has been held to exist. Rather the question has to be approached in two stages. First one has to ask whether, as between the alleged wrongdoer and the person who has suffered damage there is a sufficient relationship of proximity or neighbourhood such that, in the reasonable contemplation of the former, carelessness on his part may be likely to cause damage to the latter, in which case a prima facie duty of care arises. Secondly, if the first question is answered affirmatively, it is necessary to consider whether there are any considerations which ought to negative, or to reduce or limit the scope of the duty or the class of person to whom it is owed or the damages to which a breach of it may give rise (see the *Dorset Yacht* case, *per* Lord Reid). Examples of this are *Hedley Byrne & Co. Ltd.* v. *Heller & Partners Ltd.* where the class of potential plaintiffs was reduced to those known to have relied on the correctness of statements made, and *Weller & Co.* v. *Foot and Mouth Disease Research Institute* ([1966] 1 Q.B. 569) and (I cite these merely as illustrations, without discussion) cases about "economic loss" where, a duty having been held to exist, the nature of the recoverable damages was limited (see *SCM (United Kingdom) Ltd.* v. *W.J. Whittall & Son Ltd.* ([1971] 1 Q.B. 337), *Spartan Steel and Alloys Ltd.* v. *Martin & Co. (Contractors) Ltd.* [above, p. 42].

The factual relationship between the council and owners and occupiers of new dwellings constructed in their area must be considered in the relevant statutory setting, under which the council acts. That was the Public Health Act 1936. I must refer to the relevant provisions . . . [His Lordship did so] . . .

To summarise the statutory position. The Public Health Act 1936, in particular Part II, was enacted in order to provide for the health and safety of owners and occupiers of buildings, including dwelling houses, by, *inter alia*, setting standards to be complied with in construction, and by enabling local authorities, through building byelaws, to supervise and control the operations of builders. One of the particular matters within the area of local authority supervision is the foundations of buildings, clearly a matter of vital importance, particularly because this part of the building comes to be covered up as building proceeds. Thus any weakness or inadequacy will create a hidden defect which whoever acquires the building has no means of discovering: in legal parlance there is no opportunity for intermediate inspection. So, by the byelaws, a definite standard is set for foundation work (see byelaw 18 (1) (*b*) [that the foundations of every building shall be taken down to such a depth, or be so designed and constructed as to safeguard the building against damage by swelling or shrinking of the subsoil]); the builder is under a statutory (*sc.* byelaw) duty to notify the local authority before covering up the foundations; the local authority has at this stage the right to inspect and to insist on any correction necessary to bring the work into conformity with the byelaws. It must be in the reasonable contemplation not only of the builder but also of the local authority that failure to comply with the byelaws' requirement as to foundations may give rise to a hidden defect which in the future may cause damage to the building affecting the safety and health of owners and occupiers. And as the building is intended to last, the class of owners and occupiers likely to be affected cannot be limited to those who go in immediately after construction.

What then is the extent of the local authority's duty towards these persons? Although, as I have suggested, a situation of "proximity" existed between the council and owners and occupiers of the houses, I do not think that a description of the council's duty can be based on the "neighbourhood" principle alone or on merely any such factual relationship as "control" as suggested by the Court of Appeal. So to base it would be to neglect an essential factor which is that the local authority is a public body, discharging functions under statute: its powers and duties are definable in terms of public not private law. The problem which this type of action creates, is to define the circumstances in which the law should impose, over and above, or perhaps alongside, these public law powers and duties, a duty in private law towards individuals such that they may sue for damages in a civil court. It is in this context that the distinction sought to be drawn between duties and mere powers has to be examined.

Most, indeed probably all, statutes relating to public authorities or public bodies, contain in them a large area of policy. The courts call this "discretion", meaning that the decision is one for the authority or body to make, and not for the courts. Many statutes also prescribe or at least presuppose the practical execution of policy decisions: a convenient description of this is to say that in addition to the area of policy or discretion, there is an operational area. Although this distinction between the policy area and the operational area is convenient, and illuminating, it is probably a distinction of degree; many "operational" powers or duties have in them some element of "discretion". It can safely be said that the more "operational" a power or duty may be, the easier it is to superimpose on it a common law duty of care.

I do not think that it is right to limit this to a duty to avoid causing extra or additional damage beyond what must be expected to arise from the exercise of the power or duty. That may be correct when the act done under the statute *inherently* must adversely *affect* the interest of individuals. But many other acts can be done without causing any harm to anyone—indeed may be directed to preventing harm from occurring. In these cases the duty is the normal one of taking care to avoid harm to those likely to be affected.

Let us examine the Public Health Act 1936 in the light of this. Undoubtedly it lays out a wide area of policy. It is for the local authority, a public and elected body, to decide on the scale of resources which it can make available in order to carry out its functions under Part II of the Act—how many inspectors, with what expert qualifications, it should recruit, how often inspections are to be made, what tests are to be carried out, must be for its decision. It is no accident that the Act is drafted in terms of functions and powers rather than in terms of positive duty. As was well said, public authorities have to strike a balance between the claims of efficiency and thrift (du Parcq L.J. in *Kent and Porter* v. *East Suffolk Rivers Catchment Board* ([1940] 1 K.B. 319, 338)): whether they get the balance right can only be decided through the ballot box, not in the courts. It is said (there are reflections of this in the judgments in *Dutton's* case) that the local authority is under no duty to inspect, and this is used as the foundation for an argument, also found in some of the cases, that if it need not inspect at all, it cannot be liable for negligent inspection: if it were to be held so liable, so it is said, councils would simply decide against inspections. I think that this is too crude an argument. It overlooks the fact that local authorities are public bodies operating under statute with a clear responsibility for public health in their area. They must, and in fact do, make their discretionary decisions responsibly and for reasons which accord with the statutory purpose; *cf. Ayr Harbour Trustees* v. *Oswald, per* Lord Watson ((1883) 8 App.Cas. 623, 639):

> . . . the powers which [s. 10] confers are discretionary . . . But it is the plain import of the clause that the harbour trustees . . . shall be vested with, and shall avail themselves of, these discretionary powers, whenever and as often as they may be of opinion that the public interest will be promoted by their exercise.

If they do not exercise their discretion in this way they can be challenged in the courts. Thus, to say that councils are under no duty to inspect, is not a sufficient statement of the position. They are under a duty to give proper consideration to the question whether they should inspect or not. Their immunity from attack, in the event of failure to inspect, in other words, though great is not absolute. And because it is not absolute, the necessary premise for the proposition "if no duty to inspect, then no duty to take care in inspection" vanishes.

Passing then to the duty as regards inspection, if made. On principle there must surely be a duty to exercise reasonable care. The standard of care must be related to the duty to be performed, namely to ensure compliance with the byelaws. It must be related to the fact that the person responsible for construction in accordance with the byelaws is the builder, and that the inspector's function is supervisory. It must be related to the fact that once the inspector has passed the foundations they will be covered up, with no subsequent opportunity for inspection. But this duty, heavily operational though it may be, is still a duty arising under the statute. There may be a discretionary element in its exercise, discretionary as to the time and manner of inspection, and the techniques to be used. A plaintiff complaining of negligence must prove, the burden being on him, that action taken was not within the limits of a discretion bona fide exercised, before he can begin to rely on a common law duty of care. But if he can do this, he should, in principle, be able to sue.

Is there, then, authority against the existence of any such duty or any reason to restrict it? It is said that there is an absolute distinction in the law between statutory duty and statutory power—the former giving rise to possible liability, the latter not; or at least not doing so unless the exercise of the power involves some positive act creating some fresh or additional damage.

My Lords, I do not believe that any such absolute rule exists: or perhaps, more accurately, that such rules as exist in relation to powers and duties existing under particular statutes, provide sufficient definition of the rights of individuals affected by their exercise, or indeed their non-exercise, unless they take account of the possibility that, parallel with public law duties there may coexist those duties which persons, private or public, are under at common law to avoid causing damage to others in sufficient proximity to them. This is, I think, the key to understanding of the main authority relied on by the council, *East Suffolk Rivers Catchment Board* v. *Kent* ([1941] A.C. 74) . . .

. . . the law, as stated in some of the speeches in the *East Suffolk* case, but not in those of Lord Atkin or Lord Thankerton, requires at the present time to be understood and applied with the recognition that, quite apart from such consequences as may flow from an examination of the duties laid down by the particular statute, there may be room, once one is outside the area of legitimate discretion or policy, for a duty of care at common law. It is irrelevant to the existence of this duty of care whether what is created by the statute is a duty or a power: the duty of care may exist in either case. The difference between the two lies in this, that, in the case of a power, liability cannot exist unless the act complained of lies outside the ambit of the power. In *Home Office* v. *Dorset Yacht Co. Ltd.* the officers may (on the assumed facts) have acted outside any discretion delegated to them and having disregarded their instructions as to the precautions which they should take to prevent the trainees from escaping (see *per* Lord Diplock ([1970] A.C. 1004, 1069)). So in the present case, the allegations made are consistent with the council or its inspector having acted outside any delegated discretion either as to the making of an inspection, or as to the manner in which an inspection was made. Whether they did so must be determined at the trial. In the event of a positive determination, and only so, can a duty of care arise. I respectfully think that Lord Denning M.R. in *Dutton's* case ([1972] 1 Q.B. 373, 392) put the duty too high.

To whom the duty is owed. There is, in my opinion, no difficulty about this. A reasonable man in the position of the inspector must realise that if the foundations are covered in without adequate depth or strength as required by the byelaws, injury to safety or health may be suffered by owners or occupiers of the house. The duty is owed to them, not of course to a negligent building owner, the source of his own loss. I would leave open the case of users, who might themselves have a remedy against the occupier under the Occupiers' Liability Act 1957. A right of action can only be conferred on an owner or occupier, who is such when the damage occurs (see below). This disposes of the possible objection that an endless, indeterminate class of potential plaintiffs may be called into existence.

The nature of the duty. This must be related closely to the purpose for which powers of inspection are granted, namely to secure compliance with the byelaws. The duty is to take reasonable care, no more, no less, to secure that the builder does not cover in foundations which do not comply with byelaw requirements. The allegations in the statements of claim, in so far as they are based on non-compliance with the plans, are misconceived.

The position of the builder. I agree with the majority in the Court of Appeal in thinking that it would be unreasonable to impose liability in respect of defective foundations on the council, if the builder, whose primary fault it was, should be immune from liability. So it is necessary to consider this point, although it does not directly arise in the present appeal. If there was at one time a supposed rule that the doctrine of *Donoghue* v. *Stevenson* did not apply to realty, there is no doubt under modern authority that a builder of defective premises may be liable in negligence to persons who thereby suffer injury: see *Gallagher* v. *N. McDowell Ltd.* ([1961] N.I. 26), *per* Lord MacDermott C.J., a case of personal injury. Similar decisions have been given in regard to architects (*Clayton* v. *Woodman & Son (Builders) Ltd.* ([1962] 2 Q.B. 533), *Clay* v. *A.J. Crump & Sons Ltd.* ([1964] 1 Q.B. 533)). *Gallagher's* case expressly leaves open the question whether the immunity against action of builder-owners, established by older authorities (*e.g., Bottomley* v. *Bannister* ([1932] 1 K.B. 458)) still survives.

That immunity, as I understand it, rests partly on a distinction being made between chattels and real property, partly on the principle of 'caveat emptor' or, in the case where the owner leases the property, on the proposition that (fraud apart) there is no law against letting a "tumbledown house" (*Robbins* v. *Jones* ((1863) 15 C.B.N.S. 221, 143 E.R. 768), *per* Erle C.J.). But leaving aside such cases as arise between contracting parties, when the terms of the contract have to be considered (see *Voli* v. *Inglewood Shire Council* ((1963) 110 C.L.R. 74, 85), *per* Windeyer J.), I am unable to understand why this principle or proposition should prevent recovery in a suitable case by a person, who has subsequently acquired the house, on the principle of *Donoghue* v. *Stevenson*: the same rules should apply to all careless acts of a builder: whether he happens also to own the land or not. I agree generally with the conclusions of Lord Denning M.R. on this point (*Dutton's* case). In the alternative, since it is the duty of the builder (owner or not) to comply with the byelaws, I would be of opinion that an action could be brought against him, in effect, for breach of statutory duty by any person for whose benefit or protection the byelaw was made. So I do not think that there is any basis here for arguing from a supposed immunity of the builder to immunity of the council.

Nature of the damages recoverable and arising out of the cause of action. There are many questions here which do not directly arise at this stage and which may never arise if the actions are tried. But some conclusions are necessary if we are to deal with the issue as to limitation. The damages recoverable include all those which foreseeably arise from the breach of the duty of care which, as regards the council, I have held to be a duty to take reasonable care to secure compliance with the byelaws. Subject always to adequate proof of causation, these damages may include damages for personal injury and damages to property. In my opinion they may also include damage to the dwelling-house itself; for the whole purpose of the byelaws in requiring foundations to be of certain standard is to prevent damage arising from weakness of the foundations which is certain to endanger the health or safety of occupants.

To allow recovery for such damage to the house follows, in my opinion, from normal principle. If classification is required, the relevant damage is in my opinion material, physical damage, and what is recoverable is the amount of expenditure necessary to restore the dwelling to a condition in which it is no longer a danger to the health or safety of persons occupying and possibly (depending on the circumstances) expenses arising from necessary displacement . . .

When does the cause of action arise? We can leave aside cases of personal injury or damage to other property as presenting no difficulty. It is only the damage for the house which required consideration. In my respectful opinion the Court of Appeal was right when, in *Sparham-Souter* v. *Town and Country Developments (Essex) Ltd.* [1976] Q.B. 858, it abjured the view that the cause of action arose immediately on delivery, i.e. conveyance of the defective house. It can only arise when the state of the building is such that there is present or imminent danger to the health or safety of persons occupying it. We are not concerned at this stage with any issue relating to remedial action nor are we called on to decide on what the measure of the damages should be; such questions, possibly very difficult in some cases, will be for the court to decide. It is sufficient to say that a cause of action arises at the point I have indicated.

The Limitation Act 1939. If the fact that defects to the maisonettes first appeared in 1970, then, since the writs were issued in 1972, the consequence must be that none of the present actions are barred by the Act.

Conclusion. I would hold: (1) that *Dutton* v. *Bognor Regis United Building Co. Ltd.* was in the result rightly decided; the correct legal basis for the decision must be taken to be that established by your Lordships in this appeal; (2) that the question whether the council by itself or its officers came under a duty of care toward the plaintiffs must be considered in relation to the powers, duties and discretions arising under the Public Health Act 1936; (3) that the council would not be guilty of a breach of duty in not carrying out inspection of the foundations of the block unless it were shown (a) not properly to have exercised its discretion as to the making of inspections, and (b) to have failed to exercise reasonable care in its acts or omissions to secure that the byelaws applicable to the foundations of the block were complied with; (4) that the council would be liable to the plaintiffs for breach of duty if it were proved that its inspector, having assumed the duty of inspecting the foundations, and acting otherwise than in the bona fide exercise of any discretion under the Act, did not exercise reasonable care to ensure that the byelaws applicable to the foundations were complied with; (5) that on the facts as pleaded none of the actions is barred by the Limitation Act 1939. And consequently that the appeal should be dismissed with costs.

LORD DIPLOCK, LORD SIMON OF GLAISDALE AND LORD RUSSELL OF KILLOWEN agreed with LORD WILBERFORCE. LORD SALMON delivered a concurring opinion.

Questions

1. Suppose that the builder is bankrupt. Who ultimately pays the money that successful plaintiffs in such cases recover?

2. Suppose that Anns was aware of the condition of the house but nevertheless stayed in it until the house fell on his head. Could he claim damages for the concussion? If not, in what sense is the house dangerous?

3. Local authorities are empowered to prevent the construction of buildings with inadequate foundations. Is this in order to see that citizens do not waste their money on bad housing?

4. Could Mrs. Donoghue now recover from Stevenson the cost of a ginger beer which is (a) poisonous, (b) flat?

Note:

Did Stevenson damage Mrs. Donoghue's ginger beer? No, he didn't. The ginger beer he made was certainly disgusting, and it damaged her, but the kind of damage it caused her was personal injury: she was well and was made ill. If she had thrown up over her clothes, that would have been property damage because her clothes would have been made worse than they had been, and the fact that the measure of damages would be the amount of the dry-cleaning bill, *i.e.*, what she spent to repair the damage, would not alter that fact.

Just as Stevenson did not damage Mrs. Donoghue's ginger beer (though he damaged her), so Walcroft the builder did not damage Mr. Anns's house (though he damaged him). Walcroft made a bad house and it damaged Mr. Anns. The kind of damage it caused him was pecuniary or purely economic: he was out of pocket because he paid too much for the house, too much by the amount it would cost him to put it right. He might have suffered personal injury if the house had fallen on him, and he might have suffered property damage if the house had fallen on his car or his pet or even on his carpet. None of these things happened. His loss was purely economic. No property of his was damaged. By making a bad thing you do not damage it: you damage a thing by making it worse than it was. It is idle for Lord Wilberforce to say that there was material, physical damage. You do not turn a horse into a cow by calling it a cow, as you will quickly discover when you try to milk it. This misdescription of the damage in issue as material rather than financial has led to appalling chaos on the question of limitation.

Victims of wrongs must sue within a certain period of time—three years for personal injuries, six years for other damage. For contract claims the period starts to run when the contract is broken, in tort when the cause of action accrues, normally when the damage occurs. (This very fact shows the importance of *Hedley Byrne* and *Junior Books* in allowing the victim of a breach of contract to sue in tort: the same period will start later, at any rate if, as often happens, the damage occurs after the breach).

But when does the period start to run in cases like *Anns*? Let us consider. The house is bad as soon as it is built, though the defect is latent, subterranean. Then X buys it. Has he suffered harm already? Well, he has wasted his money, though he doesn't know it. Of course if he sells soon enough, he will get his money back, but the fact that he has made a bad bargain is unaffected by the consideration that he may yet make a good one: the person who buys a thing which is not worth what he paid for it suffers economic harm at the time of the purchase. In *Anns*, however, Lord Wilberforce held that time did not start to run then: after all, he had just held that the damage was material. Indeed, it would be inconvenient to hold that time ran from the purchase, for then time would start running afresh with every new purchase, and the local authority would never escape: but that just shows that the decision is substantially unsound.

Now what have the courts said? In *Dutton* Lord Denning said that the damage was done when the foundations were badly built; that, however, is the time the house started being bad, not the time the purchaser suffered loss. In *Sparham-Souter* [1976] Q.B. 858 he "recanted" and held that time started to run when the physical defects might reasonably have been detected: that was consistent with his stated (but not actually held) view that the damage was physical. The House of Lords in *Anns* seemed to have upheld *Sparham-Souter*, but now they have disapproved it, holding that time starts to run when the damage manifests itself, whether or not it was reasonably discoverable than (*Pirelli General Cable Works* v. *Oscar Faber & Partners* [1983] 1 All E.R. 65: cracks occurred at the top of a tall chimney in 1970, were not reasonably discoverable until 1972, and were not actually discovered until 1977). The House also held that once time started to run, it ran against all subsequent purchasers as well—a view which Roskill L.J. had mercilessly derided in *Sparham-Souter*. This deliberate back-tracking by the House of Lords is very welcome, since it will prevent claims like that in *Dennis* v. *Charnwood* B.C. [1982] 3 All E.R. 486, where the Court of Appeal held that the defendant liable although the house had been built 27 years previously under a different authority, and cracks had appeared five years later.

If the courts have had trouble with this creature of theirs, the local authorities have, of course, had much more. Indeed the courts which decided *Dutton* and *Anns* seem to have been lacking in reasonable foresight as well as reasonable care. "It will be very rarely that the council will be sued or found liable," per Lord Denning in *Dutton*, [1972] 1 Q.B. 373, 398. "I do not think that there is any danger that the responsibility which . . . lies on the council is likely to lead to any flood of litigation," per Lord Salmon in *Anns*, [1978] A.C. 728, 767. "His optimism is not . . . the experience of some local authorities," per Lawton L.J. in *Dennis* [1982] 3 All E.R. 486, 495. " . . . all authorities engaged in supervising compliance with the Building Regulations . . . adopt a much more stringent approach than they adopted before the *Anns* decision declared what the responsibilities of inspectors in relation to these matters were" (*Worlock* v. *SAWS*, June 19, 1981 per Woolf J.).

Nor, as the last-mentioned decision shows, is the local authority liable only for failure to inspect the foundations properly: it is liable if it unreasonably passes plans which are not in accordance with the bye-laws, or indeed if it fails to make inquiries when the building is built otherwise than in accordance with the plans as approved. And if the scope of the duty is being extended, so also is the list of those entitled to invoke it. One might have supposed from Lord Wilberforce's emphasis on health and safety (remember his suggestion that time started to run only when they were imperilled?) that the duty was owed only to human beings such as Mrs. Dutton and Mr. Anns and the Dennises. Not a bit of it. Eames London Estates Ltd. is not a human being, but in 1980 it got damages for an industrial building erected on an unsuitable site in 1964 (*Eames London Estates Ltd.* v. *North Herts C.C.* (1980) 259 E.G. 491). And even in respect of dwellings it is not only the human occupier or personal owner who can sue. The Court of Appeal has been pleased to hold that the *developer* of a site (*i.e.* a money-grubbing financier lurking behind a corporate facade) can sue the local authority (*i.e.* honest citizens who pay rates) if the inspector did not go quite far enough in correcting the incompetence of the developer's own architect (*Acrecrest* v. *W.S. Hattrell & Partners*, [1983] 1 All E.R. 17). It is hardly necessary to observe that this is arrant foolishness which puts up the cost of building as well as the rates and which—since Parliament has provided a proper remedy for proper cases (below p. 64)—profits only lawyers.

Well-intentioned though the decision in *Anns* doubtless was, the damage it has done to society and the law is immense. It is not, however, easy to see how that damage can be stemmed. Of course Parliament should enact a law which grants to local authorities immunity from liability arising out of the exercise of their powers to oversee Building Regulations, but that in itself would not be enough, for in our crazy legal system judicial decisions outlast legislative reversal except within the precise purview of the reversing statute. The House of Lords needs to use its powers under the 1966 declaration to admit its error, to abandon this disastrous line of jurisprudence and to hold that in the absence of a very special relationship no one owes anyone else a duty to stop a third party causing him to waste his money.

To sum up, the importance of this case lies in the ambiguous nature of the damage involved. If the damage in *Anns* is really physical damage, then it goes little further than *Dorset Yacht*. If the harm is purely economic, then it goes further than *Junior Books*, since the relationship between the parties in *Anns* was much less close than that in *Junior Books*. That is why *Anns* points to a liability which the House of Lords in *Junior Books* was reluctant to admit, namely the liability of the careless manufacturer of goods to compensate the ultimate consumer for their worthlessness.

Linking passage:

"As it happened, whilst the courts were thus developing the common law, the Law Commission were busy recommending changes by means of statute." (*per* Lord Denning M.R. in *Sparham-Souter* v. *Town and Country Developments* (*Essex*) *Ltd*. [1976] Q.B. 858, 869). Most of those recommendations were embodied in the

DEFECTIVE PREMISES ACT 1972

1.—(1) A person taking on work for or in connection with the provision of a dwelling (whether the dwelling is provided by the erection or by the conversion or enlargement of a building) owes a duty—

    (*a*) if the dwelling is provided to the order of any person, to that person; and

    (*b*) without prejudice to paragraph (*a*) above, to every person who acquires an interest (whether legal or equitable) in the dwelling;

to see that the work which he takes on is done in a workmanlike or, as the case may be, professional manner, with proper materials and so that as regards that work the dwelling will be fit for habitation when completed.

(2) A person who takes on any such work for another on terms that he is to do it in accordance with instructions given by or on behalf of that other shall, to the extent to which he does it properly in accordance with those instructions, be treated for the purposes of this section as discharging the duty imposed on him by subsection (1) above except where he owes a duty to that other to warn him of any defects in the instructions and fails to discharge that duty.

(3) A person shall not be treated for the purposes of subsection (2) above as having given instructions for the doing of work merely because he has agreed to the work being done in a specified manner, with specified materials or to a specified design.

(4) A person who—

    (*a*) in the course of a business which consists of or includes providing or arranging for the provision of dwellings or installations in dwellings; or

    (*b*) in the exercise of a power of making such provision or arrangements conferred by or by virtue of any enactment;

arranges for another to take on work for or in connection with the provision of a dwelling shall be treated for the purposes of this section as included among the persons who have taken on the work.

(5) Any cause of action in respect of a breach of the duty imposed by this section shall be deemed, for the purposes of the Limitation Act 1939, the Law Reform (Limitation of Actions, etc.) Act 1954 and the Limitation Act 1963, to have accrued at the time when the dwelling was completed, but if after that time a person who has done work for or in connection with the provision of the dwelling does further work to rectify the work he has already done, any such cause of action in respect of that further work shall be deemed for those purposes to have accrued at the time when the further work was finished.

    . . .

Note:

Like the judges in *Anns*, Parliament in this section was seeking to help the person who buys a poorly built house. The builder is the obvious defendant, but as builders tend to go bankrupt, especially if they build bad houses, both the legislature and the judiciary have given the plaintiff someone else to sue as well. The Act imposes liability on whoever *procures* the builder to build (the developer in the case of private housing and the council in respect of council housing), while the judges, as we have seen, impose liability on the local authority which carelessly *permits* the builder to build badly.

There are other differences between the legislative and the judicial rules:

(1) The Act covers only dwellings, that is, homes for people: the common law rule must apply to all buildings, even offices and factories, if not to all manufactured products as well.

(2) The builder is liable under the Act even if the defect in the house is not his fault: at common law he will be liable only if he was to blame for it, or perhaps if he deviated from building regulations.

(3) Liability under the Act arises if the house is unfit for habitation: liability at common law may depend on its being unsafe.

(4) Once the house is six years old, the builder is freed from the statutory liability: he remains liable at common law for six years after the defects have manifested themselves.

(5) The Act applies only to houses built after its enactment: the common law rule is retrospective.

Question

Before formulating its proposals for the solution of any particular problem, the Law Commission consults all the bodies which may have an interest in the matter, and considers in the most extensive way the possible social and economic effects of the different solutions. The eventual proposals are passed in review by the House of Commons, which contains representatives of almost everyone affected, and by the House of Lords, which is adorned by the most distinguished judges in the land. The rules of common law, by contrast, are laid down (1) by handful of unelected persons, not wholly reflective in their social origins or personal value-judgments of the wide variety of denizens of our island home, (2) in response to argument limited in its scope by rules of evidence and conventions of forensic propriety, and (3) based on the possibly emotive facts of an individual case to which, however, the eventual rule cannot be limited.

Which method of lawmaking do you think better adapted to the solution of specific problems like that of the disappointed purchaser of a defective house? Which of the rules produced by the judiciary and legislature respectively do you favour? Does either have unfortunate or unforeseen side-effects?

CIVIL LIABILITY (CONTRIBUTION) ACT 1978

Preliminary Note

Both in the Defective Premises Act 1972 and in the decision in *Anns* the lawmakers were eager to give the house-purchaser someone to sue, over and above the actual builder. To have two people to sue is substantially advantageous to the plaintiff if one of the possible defendants is bankrupt, but even if they are both perfectly solvent he may sue them both, concurrently or consecutively, and obtain judgment against them both for the full amount of his compensable loss. Neither defendant is helped in the very least by the argument that the other is liable as well: a person who is liable for harm is liable for all of it, regardless of how many other people are liable too. Naturally the victim may only recover up to the amount of his loss: once he has been paid, all possible defendants are released from liability to him. Then arises the question whether the loss may be split between the defendants. Until 1935 the loss had to lie where the victim had cast it, since no tortfeasor who was at fault could claim contribution from anyone else. The 1978 Act, set out in part below, is an expanded and improved version of the Law Reform (Married Women and Tortfeasors) Act 1935 which introduced the claim to contribution and, by making for fairness between tortfeasors, induced the judges to increase their number.

A good instance of multiple liability is provided by *Clay* v. *Crump* [1964] 1 Q.B. 533 (C.A.). When an old building was being demolished prior to the erection of a new one, the site-owner asked the architect if one of its walls could be left standing. The architect unwisely agreed, and the demolition contractor, who should have known better, proceeded to demolish the walls which supported it. The building contractor then sent his men on to the site without checking it for safety, and one of them was injured when the remaining wall fell on him. The victim sued the site-owner, the architect, the demolition contractor and his employer. The site-owner was let off because it was reasonable for him, as an amateur, to trust the professionals, but the demolition contractor was held liable because he should have known that he was making the wall unsafe, the building contractor was held liable for sending his men to a place he should have known to be dangerous, and the architect was held liable because he failed to show the professional skill the others were relying on him to display. The plaintiff obtained judgment in full against all the defendants who were held liable, and was entitled to collect from them as he pleased. As between themselves, the defendants were liable in the following proportions: architect 42 per cent.; demolition contractor 38 per cent.; building contractor/employer 20 per cent.

CIVIL LIABILITY (CONTRIBUTION) ACT 1978

1.—(1) Subject to the following provisions of this section, any person liable in respect of any damage suffered by another person may recover contribution from any other person liable in respect of the same damage (whether jointly with him or otherwise).

(2) A person shall be entitled to recover contribution by virtue of subsection (1) above notwithstanding that he has ceased to be liable in respect of the damage in question since the time when the damage occurred, provided that he was so liable immediately before he made or was ordered or agreed to make the payment in respect of which the contribution is sought.

(3) A person shall be liable to make contribution by virtue of subsection (1) above notwithstanding that he has ceased to be liable in respect of the damage in question since the time when the damage occurred, unless he ceased to be liable by virtue of the expiry of a period of limitation or prescription which extinguished the right on which the claim against him in respect of the damage was based.

(4) A person who has made or agreed to make any payment in bona fide settlement or compromise of any claim made against him in respect of any damage (including a payment into court which has been accepted) shall be entitled to recover contribution in accordance with this section without regard to whether or not he himself is or ever was liable in respect of the damage, provided, however, that he would have been liable assuming that the factual basis of the claim against him could be established.

(5) A judgment given in any action brought in any part of the United Kingdom by or on behalf of the person who suffered the damage in question against any person from whom contribution is sought under this section shall be conclusive in the proceedings for contributions as to any issue determined by that judgment in favour of the person from whom the contribution is sought.

(6) References in this section to a person's liability in respect of any damage are references to any such liability which has been or could be established in an action brought against him in England and Wales by or on behalf of the person who suffered the damage; but it is immaterial whether any issue arising in any such action was or would be determined (in accordance with the rules of private international law) by reference to the law of a country outside England and Wales.

2.—(1) Subject to subsection (3) below, in any proceedings for contribution under section 1 above the amount of the contribution recoverable from any person shall be such as may be found by the court to be just and equitable having regard to the extent of that person's responsibility for the damage in question.

(2) Subject to subsection (3) below, the court shall have power in any such proceedings to exempt any person from liability to make contribution, or to direct that the contribution to be recovered from any person shall amount to a complete indemnity.

(3) Where the amount of the damages which have or might have been awarded in respect of the damage in question in any action brought in England and Wales by or on behalf of the person who suffered it against the person from whom the contribution is sought was or would have been subject to—

(a) any limit imposed by or under any enactment or by any agreement made before the damage occurred;
(b) any reduction by virtue of section 1 of the Law Reform (Contributory Negligence) Act 1945 or section 5 of the Fatal Accidents Act 1976; or
(c) any corresponding limit or reduction under the law of a country outside England and Wales;

the person from whom the contribution is sought shall not by virtue of any contribution awarded under section 1 above be required to pay in respect of the damage a greater amount than the amount of those damages as so limited or reduced.

3. A judgment recovered against any person liable in respect of any debt or damage shall not be a bar to an action, or to the continuance of an action, against any other person who is (apart from any such bar) jointly liable with him in respect of the same debt or damage.

4. If more than one action is brought in respect of any damage by or on behalf of the person by whom it was suffered against persons liable in respect of the damage (whether jointly or otherwise) the plaintiff shall not be entitled to costs in any of those actions, other than that in which judgment is first given, unless the court is of the opinion that there was reasonable ground for bringing the action.

. . .

6.—(1) A person is liable in respect of any damage for the purposes of this Act if the person who suffered it (or anyone representing his estate or dependants) is entitled to recover compensation from him in respect of that damage (whatever the legal basis of his liability, whether tort, breach of contract, breach of trust or otherwise).

(2) References in this Act to an action brought by or on behalf of the person who suffered any damage include references to an action brought for the benefit of his estate or dependants.

. . .

Note:

In *Anns* Lord Wilberforce observed that the local authority's duty was owed to owners and occupiers of the defective building, "not of course to the negligent building owner, the source of his own loss." Very right and proper. But note what happens under this Act. The occupier sues both builder and local authority. He obtains judgment against both for the whole sum. He naturally collects from the local authority, rich from the rates of other home-owners and, indeed, council tenants. The local authority has to pay, and seeks to collect from the builder, fortunately solvent. But will it get a full indemnity? No, indeed. The normal practice is to let the council collect only 75 per cent. There is not the slightest justification for this practice, of which one judge, who helped to establish it, coyly observed that "the blameworthiness of the policeman who fails to detect the crime is less than that of the criminal himself." (*Eames London Estates*, 259 E.G. 491, 498 (1980)). Indeed it is. It is, relatively, zero, not 25 per cent. Are we to suppose that the Home Office would recover from the borstal boys only 75 per cent. of what it paid the Dorset Yacht Co., supposing that the borstal boys had won the pools?

McLOUGHLIN v. O'BRIAN

House of Lords [1983] A.C. 410; [1982] 2 W.L.R. 982; [1982] 2 All E.R. 298; [1982]
R.T.R. 209

Action by mother against driver for shock at family's injuries.

The plaintiff stayed at home one autumn afternoon while her husband was out in the car with three of the children, the eldest being at the wheel. About 5 p.m. a friend arrived with the grim news that an hour beforehand the car had been involved in a very bad accident about two miles away. He drove her to the hospital. There she found her husband and sons screaming, bloody and bemused, and learnt that her eldest daughter was dead.

These events, due to the defendants' negligence, were such as to cause her severe shock, organic depression and a change of personality, it being assumed that she was a person of normal fortitude.

LORD WILBERFORCE: . . . On these facts, or assumed facts, the trial judge, Boreham J., gave judgment for the respondents holding, in a most careful judgment reviewing the authorities, that the respondents owed no duty of care to the appellant because the possibility of her suffering injury by nervous shock, in the circumstances, was not reasonably foreseeable.

On appeal by the appellant, the judgment of Boreham J. was upheld, but not on the same ground ([1981] Q.B. 599). Stephenson L.J. took the view that the possibility of injury to the appellant by nervous shock *was* reasonably foreseeable and that the respondents owed the appellant a duty of care. However, he held that considerations of policy prevented the appellant from recovering. Griffiths L.J. held that injury by nervous shock to the appellant was 'readily foreseeable' but that the respondents owed no duty of care to the appellant. The duty was limited to those on the road nearby. Cumming-Bruce L.J. agreed with both judgments. The appellant now appeals to this House. The critical question to be decided is whether a person in the position of the appellant, i.e. one who was not present at the scene of grievous injuries to her family but who comes on those injuries at an interval of time and space, can recover damages for nervous shock.

Although we continue to use the hallowed expression 'nervous shock', English law, and common understanding, have moved some distance since recognition was given to this symptom as a basis for liability. Whatever is unknown about the mind-body relationship (and the area of ignorance seems to expand with that of knowledge), it is now accepted by medical science that recognisable and severe physical damage to the human body and system may be caused by the impact, through the senses, of external events on the mind. There may thus be produced what is as identifiable an illness as any that may be caused by direct physical impact. It is safe that this, in general terms, is understood by the ordinary man or woman who is hypothesised by the courts in situations where claims for negligence are made. Although in the only case which has reached this House (*Bourhill* v. *Young* [1943] A.C. 92) a claim for damages in respect of 'nervous shock' was rejected on its facts, the House gave clear recognition to the legitimacy, in principle, of claims of that character. As the result of that and other cases, assuming that they are accepted as correct, the following position has been reached:

1. While damages cannot, at common law, be awarded for grief and sorrow, a claim for damages for 'nervous shock' caused by negligence can be made without the necessity of showing direct impact or fear of immediate personal injuries for oneself. The reservation made by Kennedy J. in *Dulieu* v. *White & Sons* ([1901] 2 K.B. 669), though taken up by Sargant L.J. in *Hambrook* v. *Stokes Bros* ([1925] 1 K.B. 141), has not gained acceptance, and although the respondents, in the courts below, reserved their right to revive it, they did not do so in argument. I think that

it is now too late to do so. The arguments on this issue were fully and admirably stated by the Supreme Court of California in *Dillon* v. *Legg* ((1968) 29 A.L.R. 3d 1316).

2. A plaintiff may recover damages for 'nervous shock' brought on by injury caused not to him or herself but to a near relative, or by the fear of such injury. So far (subject to 5 below), the cases do not extend beyond the spouse or children of the plaintiff (*Hambrook* v. *Stokes Bros., Boardman* v. *Sanderson* ([1964] 1 W.L.R. 1317), *Hinz* v. *Berry* [1970] 2 Q.B. 40 including foster children (where liability was assumed), and see *King* v. *Phillips* ([1953] 1 Q.B. 429).

3. Subject to the next paragraph, there is no English case in which a plaintiff has been able to recover nervous shock damages where the injury to the near relative occurred out of sight and earshot of the plaintiffs. In *Hambrook* v. *Stokes Bros* an express distinction was made between shock caused by what the mother saw with her own eyes and what she might have been told by bystanders, liability being excluded in the latter case.

4. An exception from, or I would prefer to call it an extension of, the latter case has been made where the plaintiff does not see or hear the incident but comes on its immediate aftermath. In *Boardman* v. *Sanderson* the father was within earshot of the accident to his child and likely to come on the scene; he did so and suffered damage from what he then saw. In *Marshall* v. *Lionel Enterprises* ((1971) 25 D.L.R. (3d) 141) the wife came immediately to the badly injured body of her husband. And in *Benson* v. *Lee* ([1972] V.R. 879), a situation existed with some similarity to the present case. The mother was in her home 100 yards away, and, on communication by a third party, ran out to the scene of the accident and there suffered shock. Your Lordships have to decide whether or not to validate these extensions.

5. A remedy on account of nervous shock has been given to a man who came on a serious accident involving people immediately thereafter and acted as a rescuer of those involved (*Chadwick* v. *British Transport Commission* ([1967] 1 W.L.R. 912)). 'Shock' was caused neither by fear for himself nor by fear or horror on account of a near relative. The principle of 'rescuer' cases was not challenged by the respondents and ought, in my opinion, to be accepted. But we have to consider whether, and how far, it can be applied to such cases as the present.

Throughout these developments, as can be seen, the courts have proceeded in the traditional manner of the common law from case to case, on a basis of logical necessity. If a mother, with or without accompanying children, could recover on account of fear for herself, how can she be denied recovery on account of fear for her accompanying children? If a father could recover had he seen his child run over by a backing car, how can he be denied recovery if he is in the immediate vicinity and runs to the child's assistance? If a wife and mother could recover if she had witnessed a serious accident to her husband and children, does she fail because she was a short distance away and immediately rushes to the scene? (*cf Benson* v. *Lee*). I think that, unless the law is to draw an arbitrary line at the point of direct sight and sound, these arguments require acceptance of the extension mentioned above under principle 4 in the interests of justice.

If one continues to follow the process of logical progression, it is hard to see why the present plaintiff also should not succeed. She was not present at the accident, but she came very soon after on its aftermath. If, from a distance of some 100 yards (*cf Benson* v. *Lee*), she had found her family by the roadside, she would have come within principle 4 above. Can it make any difference that she comes on them in an ambulance, or, as here, in a nearby hospital, when, as the evidence shows, they were in the same condition, covered with oil and mud, and distraught with pain? If Mr. Chadwick can recover when, acting in accordance with normal and irresistible human instinct, and indeed moral compulsion, he goes to the scene of an accident, may not a mother recover if, acting under the same motives, she goes to where her family can be found?

I could agree that a line can be drawn above her case with less hardship than would have been apparent in *Boardman's* and *Hinz's* cases, but so to draw it would not appeal to most people's sense of justice. To allow her claim may be, I think it is, on the margin of what the process of logical progression would allow. But where the facts are strong and exceptional, and, as I think, fairly analogous, her case ought, prima facie, to be assimilated to those which have passed the test.

To argue from one factual situation to another and to decide by analogy is a natural tendency of the human and legal mind. But the lawyer still has to inquire whether, in so doing, he has crossed some critical line behind which he ought to stop. That is said to be the present case. The reasoning by which the Lords Justices decided not to grant relief to the plaintiff is instructive. Both Stephenson and Griffiths L.JJ. accepted that the 'shock' to the plaintiff was foreseeable; but from this, at least in presentation, they diverge. Stephenson L.J. considered that the defendants owed a duty of care to the plaintiff, but that for reasons of policy the law should stop short of giving her damages: it should limit relief to those on or near the highway at or near the time of the accident caused by the defendants' negligence. He was influenced by the fact that the courts of this country, and of other common law jurisdictions, had stopped at this point: it was indicated by the barrier of commercial sense and practical convenience. Griffiths L.J. took the view that, although the injury to the plaintiff was foreseeable, there was no duty of care. The duty of care of drivers of motor vehicles was, according to decided cases, limited to persons and owners of property on the road or near to it who might be directly affected. The line should be drawn at this point. It was not even in the interest of those suffering from shock as a class to extend the scope of the defendants' liability: to do so would quite likely delay their recovery by immersing them in the anxiety of litigation.

I am deeply impressed by both of these arguments, which I have only briefly summarised. Though differing in expression, in the end, in my opinion, the two presentations rest on a common principle, namely that, at the margin, the boundaries of a man's responsibility for acts of negligence have to be fixed as a matter of policy. Whatever is the correct jurisprudential analysis, it does not make any essential difference whether one says, with Stephenson L.J., that there is a duty but, as a matter of policy, the consequences of breach of it ought to be limited at a certain point, or whether, with Griffiths L.J., one says that the fact that consequences may be foreseeable does not automatically impose a duty of care, does not do so in fact where policy indicates the contrary. This is an approach which one can see very clearly from the way in which Lord Atkin stated the neighbour principle in *Donoghue* v. *Stevenson* ([1932] A.C. 562, 580): ' . . . persons who are so closely and directly affected by my act that I ought reasonably to have them in contemplation as being so affected . . . '

This is saying that foreseeability must be accompanied and limited by the law's judgment as to persons who ought, according to its standards of value or justice, to have been in contemplation. Foreseeability, which involves a hypothetical person, looking with hindsight at an event which has occurred, is a formula adopted by English law, not merely for defining, but also for limiting the persons to whom duty may be owed, and the consequences for which an actor may be held responsible. It is not merely an issue of fact to be left to be found as such. When it is said to result in a duty of care being owed to a person or a class, the statement that there is a 'duty of care' denotes a conclusion into the forming of which considerations of policy have entered. That foreseeability does not of itself, and automatically, lead to a duty of care is, I think, clear. I gave some examples in *Anns* v. *Merton London Borough* [above p. 57], *Anns* itself being one. I may add what Lord Reid said in *McKew* v. *Holland & Hannen & Cubitts (Scotland) Ltd.* [below pp. 201–2]: 'A defender is not liable for a consequence of a kind which is not foreseeable. But it does not follow that he is liable for every consequence which a reasonable man could foresee.'

We must then consider the policy arguments. In doing so we must bear in mind that cases of 'nervous shock' and the possibility of claiming damages for it are not necessarily confined to those arising out of accidents in public roads. To state, therefore, a rule that recoverable damages must be confined to persons on or near the highway is to state not a principle in itself but only an example of a more general rule that recoverable damages must be confined to those within sight and sound of an event caused by negligence or, at least, to those in close, or very close, proximity to such a situation.

The policy arguments against a wider extension can be stated under four heads. First, it may be said that such extension may lead to a proliferation of claims, and possibly fraudulent claims, to the establishment of an industry of lawyers and psychiatrists who will formulate a claim for nervous shock damages, including what in America is called the customary miscarriage, for all, or many, road accidents and industrial accidents. Second, it may be claimed that an extension of liability would be unfair to defendants, as imposing damages out of proportion to the negligent conduct complained of. In so far as such defendants are insured, a large additional burden will be placed on insurers, and ultimately on the class of persons insured: road users or employers. Third, to extend liability beyond the most direct and plain cases would greatly increase evidentiary difficulties and tend to lengthen litigation. Fourth, it may be said (and the Court of Appeal agreed with this) that an extension of the scope of liability ought only to be made by the legislature, after careful research. This is the course which has been taken in New South Wales and the Australian Capital Territory.

The whole argument has been well summed up by Dean Prosser in *The Law of Torts* (4th edn, 1971) p 256:

'The reluctance of courts to enter this zone even where the mental injury is clearly foreseeable, and the frequent mention of the difficulties of proof, the facility of fraud and the problem of finding a place to stop and draw the line, suggest that here it is the nature of the interest invaded and the type of damages which is the real obstacle.'

Since he wrote, the type of damage has, in this country at least, become familiar and less deterrent to recovery. And some of the arguments are susceptible of answer. Fraudulent claims can be contained by the courts, which, also, can cope with evidentiary difficulties. The scarcity of cases which have occurred in the past, and the modest sums recovered, give some indication that fears of a flood of litigation may be exaggerated: experience in other fields suggests that such fears usually are. If some increase does occur, that may only reveal existence of a genuine social need; that legislation has been found necessary in Australia may indicate the same thing.

But, these discounts accepted, there remains, in my opinion, just because 'shock' in its nature is capable of affecting so wide a range of people, a real need for the law to place some limitation on the extent of admissible claims. It is necessary to consider three elements inherent in any claim: the class of persons whose claims should be recognised; the proximity of such persons to the accident; and the means by which the shock is caused. As regards the class of persons, the possible range is between the closest of family ties, of parent and child, or husband and wife, and the ordinary bystander. Existing law recognises the claims of the first; it denies that of the second, either on the basis that such persons must be assumed to be possessed of fortitude sufficient to enable them to endure the calamities of modern life or that defendants cannot be expected to compensate the world at large. In my opinion, these positions are justifiable, and since the present case falls within the first class it is strictly unnecessary to say more. I think, however, that it should follow that other cases involving less close relationships must be very carefully scrutinised. I cannot say that they should never be admitted. The closer the tie (not merely in relationship, but in care) the greater the claim for consideration. The claim, in any case, has to be judged in the light of the other factors, such as proximity to the scene in time and place, and the nature of the accident.

As regards proximity to the accident, it is obvious that this must be close in both time and space. It is after all, the fact and consequence of the defendant's negligence that must be proved to have caused the 'nervous shock'. Experience has shown that to insist on direct and immediate sight or hearing would be impractical and unjust and that under what may be called the 'aftermath' doctrine, one who, from close proximity comes very soon on the scene, should not be excluded. In my opinion, the result in *Benson* v. *Lee* ([1972] V.R. 879) was correct and indeed inescapable. It was based, soundly, on 'direct perception of some of the events which go to make up the accident as an entire event, and this includes . . . the immediate aftermath'. The High Court of Australia's majority decision in *Chester* v. *Waverley Municipal Council* ((1939) 62 C.L.R. 1), where a child's body was found floating in a trench after a prolonged search, may perhaps be placed on the other side of a recognisable line (Evatt J. in a powerful dissent placed it on the same side), but in addition, I find the conclusion of Lush J. in *Benson* v. *Lee* to reflect developments in the law.

Finally, and by way of reinforcement of 'aftermath' cases, I would accept, by analogy with 'rescue' situations, that a person of whom it could be said that one could expect nothing else than he or she would come immediately to the scene (normally a parent or a spouse) could be regarded as being within the scope of foresight and duty. Where there is not immediate presence, account must be taken of the possibility of alterations in the circumstances, for which the defendant should be responsible.

Subject only to these qualifications, I think that a strict test of proximity by sight or hearing should be applied by the courts.

Lastly, as regards communication, there is no case in which the law has compensated shock brought about by communication by a third party. In *Hambrook* v. *Stokes Bros* ([1925] 1 K.B. 141), indeed, it was said that liability would not arise in such a case, and this is surely right. It was so decided in *Abramzik* v. *Brenner* ((1967) 65 D.L.R. (2d) 651). The shock must come through sight or hearing of the event or of its immediate aftermath. Whether some equivalent of sight or hearing, e.g. through simultaneous television, would suffice may have to be considered.

My Lords, I believe that these indications, imperfectly sketched, and certainly to be applied with common sense to individual situations in their entirety, represent either the existing law, or the existing law with only such circumstantial extension as the common law process may legitimately make. They do not introduce a new principle. Nor do I see any reason why the law should retreat behind the lines already drawn. I find on this appeal that the appellant's case falls within the boundaries of the law so drawn. I would allow her appeal.

Lord Russell of Killowen: My Lords, I make two comments at the outset. First, we are not concerned with any problem that might have been posed had the accident been not wholly attributable to the negligence of the defendants, but partly attributable to negligent driving by the injured son of the plaintiff. Second, the plaintiff is to be regarded as of normal disposition or phlegm; we are therefore not concerned to investigate the applicability of the 'thin skull' cases to this type of case. . . .

[His Lordship then stated that he could see no policy consideration which was sufficient to deprive "this plaintiff of just compensation for the reasonably foreseeable damage done to her."]

Lord Edmund-Davies, agreeing with Lord Wilberforce, objected to the application, in nervous shock cases, of physical limitations on what was reasonably foreseeable; he was prepared to treat the mother's visit to hospital as an act of rescue, he rejected the "floodgates" argument, and then very strongly objected to the view of Lord Bridge and Lord Scarman that "public policy" could not be invoked by a court in order to deprive of compensation a person who had suffered reasonably foreseeable harm. He agreed with Griffiths L.J. that "The test of foreseeability is not a universal touchstone to determine the extent of liability for the consequences of wrongdoing" ([1981] Q.B. 599, 618), but held that in this case there were no public policy considerations which would justify debarring the plaintiff.

LORD BRIDGE: . . . In approaching the question whether the law should, as a matter of policy, define the criterion of liability in negligence for causing psychiatric illness by reference to some test other than that of reasonable foreseeability it is well to remember that we are concerned only with the question of liability of a defendant who is, ex hypothesi, guilty of fault in causing the death, injury or danger which has in turn triggered the psychiatric illness. A policy which is to be relied on to narrow the scope of the negligent tortfeasor's duty must be justified by cogent and readily intelligible considerations, and must be capable of defining the appropriate limits of liability by reference to factors which are not purely arbitrary. A number of policy considerations which have been suggested as satisfying these requirements appear to me, with respect, to be wholly insufficient. I can see no ground whatever for suggesting that to make the defendant liable for reasonably foreseeable psychiatric illness caused by his negligence would be to impose a crushing burden on him out of proportion to his moral responsibility. However liberally the criterion of reasonable foreseeability is interpreted, both the number of successful claims in this field and the quantum of damages they will attract are likely to be moderate. I cannot accept as relevant the well-known phenomenon that litigation may delay recovery from a psychiatric illness. If this were a valid policy consideration, it would lead to the conclusion that psychiatric illness should be excluded altogether from the heads of damage which the law will recognise. It cannot justify limiting the cases in which damages will be awarded for psychiatric illness by reference to the circumstances of its causation. To attempt to draw a line at the furthest point which any of the decided cases happen to have reached, and to say that it is for the legislature, not the courts, to extend the limits of liability any further, would be, to my mind, an unwarranted abdication of the court's function of developing and adapting principles of the common law to changing conditions, in a particular corner of the common law which exemplifies, par excellence, the important and indeed necessary part which that function has to play. In the end I believe that the policy question depends on weighing against each other two conflicting considerations. On the one hand, if the criterion of liability is to be reasonable foreseeability simpliciter, this must, precisely because questions of causation in psychiatric medicine give rise to difficulty and uncertainty, introduce an element of uncertainty into the law and open the way to a number of arguable claims which a more precisely fixed criterion of liability would exclude. I accept that the element of uncertainty is an important factor. I believe that the 'floodgates' argument, however, is, as it always has been, greatly exaggerated. On the other hand, it seems to me inescapable that any attempt to define the limit of liability by requiring, in addition to reasonable foreseeability, that the plaintiff claiming damages for psychiatric illness should have witnessed the relevant accident, should have been present at or near the place where it happened, should have come on its aftermath and thus have some direct perception of it, as opposed to merely learning of it after the event, should be related in some particular degree to the accident victim—to draw a line by reference to any of those criteria must impose a largely arbitrary limit of liability. I accept, of course, the importance of the factors indicated in the guidelines suggested by Tobriner J. in *Dillon* v. *Legg* ((1968) 68 Cal. 2d 728, 441 P. 2d 912) as bearing on the *degree* of foreseeability of the plaintiff's psychiatric illness. But let me give two examples to illustrate what injustice would be wrought by any such hard and fast lines of policy as have been suggested. First, consider the plaintiff who learned after the event of the relevant accident. Take the case of a mother who knows that her husband and children are staying in a certain hotel. She reads in her morning newspaper that it has been the scene of a disastrous fire. She sees in the paper a photograph of unidentifiable victims trapped on the top floor waving for help from the windows. She learns shortly afterwards that all her family have perished. She suffers an acute psychiatric illness. That her illness in these circumstances was a reasonably foreseeable consequence of the events resulting from the fire is undeniable. Yet, is the law to deny her damages as against a defendant whose negligence was responsible for the fire simply on the ground that an important link in the chain of causation of her psychiatric illness was supplied by her imagination of the agonies of mind and body in which her family died, rather than by direct perception of the event? Second, consider the plaintiff who is unrelated to the victims of the relevant accident. If rigidly applied, an exclusion of liability to him would have defeated the plaintiff's claim in *Chadwick* v. *British Transport Commission*. The Court of Appeal treated that case as in a special category because Mr Chadwick was a rescuer. Now, the special duty owed to a rescuer who voluntarily places himself in physical danger to save others is well understood, and is illustrated by *Haynes* v. *Harwood* ([1935] K.B. 146), the case of the constable injured in stopping a runaway horse in a crowded street. But, in relation to the psychiatric consequences of witnessing such terrible carnage as must have resulted from the Lewisham train disaster, I would find it difficult to distinguish in principle the position of a rescuer, like Mr Chadwick, from a mere spectator, as, for example, an uninjured or only slightly injured passenger in the train, who took no part in the rescue operations but was present at the scene after the accident for some time, perforce observing the rescue operations while he waited for transport to take him home.

My Lords, I have no doubt that this is an area of the law of negligence where we should resist the temptation to try yet once more to freeze the law in a rigid posture which would deny justice to some who, in the application of the classic principles of negligence derived from *Donoghue* v. *Stevenson* ought to succeed, in the interests of certainty, where the very subject matter is uncertain and continuously developing, or in the interests of saving defendants and their insurers from the burden of having sometimes to resist doubtful claims. I find myself in complete agreement with Tobriner J. that the defendant's duty must depend on reasonable foreseeability and—

> 'must necessarily be adjudicated only upon a case-by-case basis. We cannot now predetermine defendant's obligation in every situation by a fixed category; no immutable rule can establish the extent of that obligation for every circumstance of the future.'

To put the matter in another way, if asked where the thing is to stop, I should answer, in an adaptation of the language of Lord Wright and Stephenson L.J., 'Where in the particular case the good sense of the judge, enlightened by progressive awareness of mental illness, decides.'

My Lords, I would accordingly allow the appeal.

LORD SCARMAN: My Lords, I have had the advantage of reading in draft the speech of my noble and learned friend Lord Bridge. It cannot be strengthened or improved by any words of mine. I accept his approach to the law and the conclusion he reaches. But I also share the anxieties of the Court of Appeal. I differ, however, from the Court of Appeal in that I am persuaded that in this branch of the law it is not for the courts but for the legislature to set limits, if any be needed, to the law's development.

The appeal raises directly a question as to the balance in our law between the functions of judge and legislature. The common law, which in a constitutional context includes judicially developed equity, covers everything which is not covered by statute. It knows no gaps: there can be no casus omissus. The function of the court is to decide the case before it, even though the decision may require the extension or adaptation of a principle or in some cases the creation of new law to meet the justice of the case. But, whatever the court decides to do, it starts from a baseline of existing principle and seeks a solution consistent with or analogous to a principle or principles already recognised.

The distinguishing feature of the common law is this judicial development and formulation of principle. Policy considerations will have to be weighed; but the objective of the judges is the formulation of principle. And, if principle inexorably requires a decision which entails a degree of policy risk, the court's function is to adjudicate according to principle, leaving policy curtailment to the judgment of Parliament. Here lies the true role of the two law-making institutions in our constitution. By concentrating on principle the judges can keep the common law alive, flexible and consistent, and can keep the legal system clear of policy problems which neither they, nor the forensic process which it is their duty to operate, are equipped to resolve. If principle leads to results which are thought to be socially unacceptable, Parliament can legislate to draw a line or map out a new path.

The real risk to the common law is not its movement to cover new situations and new knowledge but lest it should stand still, halted by a conservative judicial approach. If that should happen, and since the 1966 practice direction of the House (see *Note* [1966] 1 W.L.R. 1234) it has become less likely, there would be a danger of the law becoming irrelevant to the consideration, and inept in its treatment, of modern social problems. Justice would be defeated. The common law has, however, avoided this catastrophe by the flexibility given it by generations of judges. Flexibility carries with it, or course, certain risks, notably a degree of uncertainty in the law and the 'floodgates' risk which so impressed the Court of Appeal in the present case.

The importance to be attached to certainty and the size of the 'floodgates' risk vary from one branch of the law to another. What is required of the law in its approach to a commercial transaction will be very different from the approach appropriate to problems of tortious liability for personal injuries. In some branches of the law, notably that now under consideration, the search for certainty can obstruct the law's pursuit of justice, and can become the enemy of the good.

The present case is a good illustration. Certainty could have been achieved by leaving the law as it was left by *Victorian Rlys Comrs* v. *Coultas* ((1883) 13 App.Cas. 222), or again, by holding the line drawn in 1901 by *Dulieu* v. *White & Sons* ([1901] 1 K.B. 669) or today by confining the law to what was regarded by Lord Denning M.R. in *Hinz* v. *Berry* ([1970] 2 Q.B. 40, 42) as 'settled law', namely that 'damages can be given for nervous shock caused by the sight of an accident, at any rate to a close relative'.

But at each landmark stage common law principle, when considered in the context of developing medical science, has beckoned the judges on. And now, as has been made clear by Evatt J, dissenting in *Chester* v. *Waverley Municipal Council* ((1939) 62 C.L.R. 1) in the High Court of Australia, by Tobriner J., giving the majority judgment in the Californian case of *Dillon* v. *Legg* ((1968) 68 Cal. 2d 728), and by my noble and learned friend in this case, common law principle requires the judges to follow the logic of the 'reasonably forseeable test' so as, in circumstances where it is appropriate, to apply it untrammelled by spatial, physical or temporal limits. Space, time, distance, the nature of the injuries sustained and the relationship of the plaintiff to the immediate victim of the accident are factors to be weighed, but not legal limitations, when the test or reasonable foreseeability is to be applied.

But I am by no means sure that the result is socially desirable. The 'floodgates' argument may be exaggerated. Time alone will tell; but I foresee social and financial problems if damages for 'nervous shock' should be made available to persons other than parents and children who without seeing or hearing the accident, or being present in the immediate aftermath, suffer nervous shock in consequence of it. There is, I think, a powerful case for legislation such as has been enacted in New South Wales and the Australian Capital Territory.

Why then should not the courts draw the line, as the Court of Appeal manfully tried to do in this case? Simply, because the policy issue where to draw the line is not justiciable. The problem is one of social, economic, and financial policy. The considerations relevant to a decision are not such as to be capable of being handled within the limits of the forensic process.

My Lords, I would allow the appeal for the reasons developed by my noble and learned friend Lord Bridge, while putting on record my view that there is here a case for legislation.

Questions

1. What is the majority holding in this case?

2. Is it (a) easier, (b) much easier, to tell whether the plaintiff was (i) at the scene of the accident, (ii) a reasonably foreseeable victim of shock? Does the ease of application of a rule affect the number of claims and settlements respectively?

3. What is wrong with rules of thumb? Are judicial-foot-rules any better?

4. Is it true, as Lord Bridge asseverates, that the reason for uncertainty in the application of the foreseeability test is because the causation of psychical harm is obscure? Is the application of the foreseeability test easy when causation is clear, *e.g. The Wagon Mound (nos.* 1 *and* 2) below p. 180?

5. Would a policeman, fireman or doctor who suffered shock at a nasty accident occasioned by the defendant's negligence be likely to recover damages for his shock?

6. A train-driver was shocked to see a headless corpse on the railway line. He obtained an award from the Criminal Injuries Compensation Board(!). Could he have sued the suicide's estate?

7. Why do women form such a high proportion of the plaintiffs in these cases?

8. Would either Lord Wilberforce or Lord Bridge grant recovery in the following cases?

(i) Agatha has a fit when she sees her cat run over by a drunk driver who could easily, had he been sober, have avoided it;

(ii) Fred's car is involved in a collision solely because of a manufacturing defect. Fred's passenger is killed, and Fred, who is himself unhurt, is horrified at the thought that he has killed his friend;

(iii) Martha, holidaying in Majorca, receives a telegram "Father involved in bad accident. Come soonest." She is unable to effect telephonic communication and has great difficulty obtaining a flight. When she gets home, she is in a terrible condition and her father is dead. (Note: a child cannot sue for emotional harm occasioned by the death of a parent: see Fatal Accidents Act 1976 s.1A below p. 78).

9. Suppose that a mother is riding in a car being driven for his own purposes by her son, and that she suffers actual physical injury in a collision with an oncoming car carelessly driven. It is clear law that her claim against the oncoming driver is not affected by the fact (a) that her son was also to blame for the collision (below p. 206) and (b) that she was especially susceptible to injury. In the light of this, what do you make of Lord Russell's preliminary observations?

10. Distinctions are sometimes drawn between fear, shock and grief. If the distinction is between the emotional reactions to what may happen, what is happening and what has happened, which was involved in the present case?

11. Consider the application to the facts of this case of s.1A Fatal Accidents Act 1976 (introduced in 1982). Should the defendant now have to pay Mrs. McLoughlin extra for not killing the rest of her family?

Notes

1. *Shock.* There is no doubt that it is *harm* to be rendered unfit to cope with the daily exigencies of life, to have one's merriment turned to misery, to feel one's peace of mind shattered by a shocking occurrence. So, too, it is harm to lose a limb and have to hobble about. But there is equally no doubt that the public—crass and ignorant as it may be—draws a distinction between the neurotic and the cripple, between the man who loses his concentration and the man who loses his leg. It is widely felt that being frightened is less than being struck, that trauma to the mind is less than lesion to the body. Many people would

consequently say that the duty to avoid injuring strangers is greater than the duty not to upset them. The law has reflected this distinction as one would expect, not only by refusing damages for grief altogether, but by granting recovery for other psychical harm only late and grudgingly, and then only in very clear cases. In tort, clear means close—close to the victim, close to the accident, close to the defendant.

The principal case involved a plaintiff who was close to the victims (mother/family), not very close to the accident in time or place, and a complete stranger to the defendant truck-drivers. In other cases the plaintiff is close to the defendant, and, as one would expect, that can make a big difference. Thus in *Dooley* v. *Cammell Laird* [1951] 1 Lloyd's Rep. 271 a crane-driver sued his employer for his shock when a defect in the crane caused the load which he was lifting to fall into the hold where his mates were working. Of course the plaintiff recovered damages: an employer owes a duty to his workmen regarding their peace of mind as well as their physical integrity. Similarly one can expect that occupiers will fairly readily be held liable to shocked visitors (airline/passengers), and doctors, even psychiatrists, to their patients for brutal treatment. But what about husbands to wives, given the frequency of mental cruelty in days of yore?

It is because of the closeness of the parties that "In a proper case damages for mental distress can be recovered in contract, just as damages for shock can be recovered in tort", per Lord Denning M.R. in *Jarvis* v. *Swans Tours* [1973] Q.B. 233, 237–238. Jarvis got damages for pique when his Alpine holiday was less fun than promised by the tour operator. Mrs. Heywood got £150 from solicitors who negligently failed to stop a man harassing her (*Heywood* v. *Wellers* [1976] 1 All E.R. 300), and a man called Cox who suffered "vexation, frustration and distress" on being demoted got £500 from his employers (*Cox* v. *Philips Industries* [1976] 3 All E.R. 161). So, too, the surveyor of a house has had to pay for the distress suffered by the purchaser in discovering, and living with, unreported defects (*Perry* v. *Sidney Phillips & Son* [1982] 3 All E.R. 705).

The sums awarded are quite small, but they have a considerable nuisance value. Even in proper shock cases the damages awarded are meagre as compared with the damages for loss of amenity resulting from physical harm (see *Hinz* v. *Berry* [1970] 2 Q.B. 40). As you would expect.

2. *Rescue.* In *Chadwick* the plaintiff, who lived nearby, nobly assisted the victims of the terrible train disaster at Lewisham in 1957, and the horror of it marked him for life. British Rail had to pay him, on the principle that a person who negligently causes an accident may be liable to those who come to help the victims and get injured themselves. The injury is usually physical. The three defences which the negligent party may seek to raise in such a case are unlikely to succeed: (i) "You weren't endangered; you came on the scene voluntarily, so I didn't owe you any duty"; (ii) "You weren't taking proper care of your own safety"; (iii) "Your intervention, not my negligence, was the cause of your injuries." Just as bad people pay more, so good people get more. (See *Baker* v. *Hopkins* (*T.E.*) *& Sons* [1959] 1 W.L.R. 966, [1959] 3 All E.R. 225 (C.A.)).

If the rescuer can sue A who negligently endangers B (regardless of whether B himself was negligent), can the rescuer equally sue B who negligently puts himself in apparent need of rescue? In *Harrison* v. *British Railways Board* [1981] 3 All E.R. 679 a railway employee, leaving work early, tried to leap on to a train already in motion. He was held liable to the guard on the train who tried to help him aboard and was himself pulled off.

In early 1983 the following sea-side tragedy occurred. A young man who was a strong swimmer was walking along the Blackpool promenade one very stormy day with his Jack Russell terrier and threw a ball for the dog to retrieve. The ball went over the sea-wall and the dog went after it. The young man followed his dog and got into difficulties in the high seas. Four police officers tried to save him and three of them were drowned. Analyse the situation in legal terms.

FATAL ACCIDENTS ACT 1976 (as amended)

1.—(1) If death is caused by any wrongful act, neglect or default which is such as would (if death had not ensued) have entitled the person injured to maintain an action and recover damages in respect thereof, the person who would have been liable if death had not ensued shall be liable to an action for damages, notwithstanding the death of the person injured.

(2) Subject to section 1A(2) below, every such action shall be for the benefit of the dependants of the person ("the deceased") whose death has been so caused.

(3) In this Act "dependant" means—

(*a*) the wife or husband or former wife or husband of the deceased;
(*b*) any person who—

(i) was living with the deceased in the same household immediately before the date of the death; and
(ii) had been living with the deceased in the same household for at least two years before that date; and
(iii) was living during the whole of that period as the husband or wife of the deceased;

(*c*) any parent or other ascendant of the deceased;
(*d*) any person who was treated by the deceased as his parent;
(*e*) any child or other descendant of the deceased;
(*f*) any person (not being a child of the deceased) who, in the case of any marriage to which the deceased was at any time a party, was treated by the deceased as a child of the family in relation to that marriage;
(*g*) any person who is, or is the issue of, a brother, sister, uncle or aunt of the deceased.

(4) The reference to the former wife or husband of the deceased in subsection (3)(*a*) above includes a reference to a person whose marriage to the deceased has been annulled or declared void as well as a person whose marriage to the deceased has been dissolved.

(5) In deducing any relationship for the purposes of subsection (3) above—

(*a*) any relationship by affinity shall be treated as a relationship by consanguinity, any relationship of the half blood as a relationship of the whole blood, and the stepchild of any person as his child, and
(*b*) an illegitimate person shall be treated as the legitimate child of his mother and reputed father.

(6) Any reference in this Act to injury includes any disease and any impairment of a person's physical or mental condition.

1A.—(1) An action under this Act may consist of or include a claim for damages for bereavement.

(2) A claim for damages for bereavement shall only be for the benefit—

(*a*) of the wife or husband of the deceased; and
(*b*) where the deceased was a minor who was never married—

(i) of his parents, if he was legitimate; and
(ii) of his mother, if he was illegitimate.

(3) Subject to subsection (5) below, the sum to be awarded as damages under this section shall be £3,500.

(4) Where there is a claim for damages under this section for the benefit of both the parents of the deceased, the sum awarded shall be divided equally between them (subject to any deduction falling to be made in respect of costs not recovered from the defendant).

(5) The Lord Chancellor may by order made by statutory instrument, subject to annulment in pursuance of a resolution of either House of Parliament, amend this section by varying the sum for the time being specified in subsection (3) above.

2.—(1) The action shall be brought by and in the name of the executor or administrator of the deceased.

(2) If—

(*a*) there is no executor or administrator of the deceased, or
(*b*) no action is brought within six months after the death by and in the name of an executor or administrator of the deceased,

the action may be brought by and in the name of all or any of the persons for whose benefit an executor or administrator could have brought it.

(3) Not more than one action shall lie for and in respect of the same subject matter of complaint.

(4) The plaintiff in the action shall be required to deliver to the defendant or his solicitor full particulars of the persons for whom and on whose behalf the action is brought and of the nature of the claim in respect of which damages are sought to be recovered.

3.—(1) In the action such damages, other than damages for bereavement, may be awarded as are proportioned to the injury resulting from the death to the dependants respectively.

(2) After deducting the costs not recovered from the defendant any amount recovered otherwise than as damages for bereavement shall be divided among the dependants in such shares as may be directed.

(3) In an action under this Act where there fall to be assessed damages payable to a widow in respect of the death of her husband there shall not be taken account the re-marriage of the widow or her prospects of re-marriage.

(4) In an action under this Act where there fall to be assessed damages payable to a person who is a dependant by virtue of section 1(3)(b) above in respect of the death of the person with whom the dependant was living as husband or wife there shall be taken into account (together with any other matter that appears to the court to be relevant to the action) the fact that the dependants had no enforceable right to financial support by the deceased as a result of their living together.

(5) If the dependants have incurred funeral expenses in respect of the deceased, damages may be awarded in respect of those expenses.

(6) Money paid into court in satisfaction of a cause of action under this Act may be in one sum without specifying any person's share.

4. In assessing damages in respect of a person's death in an action under this Act, benefits which have accrued or will or may accrue to any person from his estate or otherwise as a result of his death shall be disregarded.".

5. Where any person dies as the result partly of his own fault and partly of the fault of any other person or persons, and accordingly if an action were brought for the benefit of the estate under the Law Reform (Miscellaneous Provisions) Act 1934 the damages recoverable would be reduced under section 1 (1) of the Law Reform (Contributory Negligence) Act 1945, any damages recoverable in an action under this Act shall be reduced to a proportionate extent.

Note:

We have already seen how reluctant the common law was to compensate A for financial harm consequent on damage to the property of B (above p. 49). It was reluctant, too, to compensate A for harm consequent on personal injury to B, fatal or not.

Those affected by a person's *death* had, and have, no claim at common law at all. Any claim they may now have must stem from statute. The original Fatal Accidents Act was passed in 1846 when the other Stephenson's invention came of age. As amended in 1959, consolidated in 1976 and re-amended in 1982, it provides the leading example of liability in tort for negligently causing financial harm. It does not lay down that the tortfeasor owes a duty towards his victim's dependants: it simply enables them to sue the tortfeasor if the deceased could have done so when he died. Thus if the primary victim has settled with the tortfeasor or sued him to judgment or let his claim become time-barred, the dependants have no claim.

Only the persons specified in the statute, including now the ex-wife and the live-in lover, may sue. Many other people may suffer loss, such as the employer, the partner, the insurance company or the donee who becomes liable to tax. None of these may sue; indeed, a person cannot sue for the loss of his business partner even if he was married to her (*Burgess* v. *Florence Nightingale Hospital* ([1955] 1 Q.B. 349 (*sed quaere*)).

The claim for bereavement is new. Until 1982 only financial loss was recoverable under the Act: no damages at all could be awarded for grief. This was particularly hard in the case where a small child was killed, for then there was no financial loss—indeed, rather a saving—and the appalling human loss went quite unalleviated. But the provision is odd in some respects. Why should a child not be able to sue when bereft of its mother? (Actually, it can sue, but for lost services rather than bereavement). And why did the legislator lay down a fixed sum rather than a ceiling? Under this rule Niobe could collect £49,000 from Apollo and Artemis.

Some of the problems in determining the amount of the award are discussed below at p. 541.

But the family may be affected by *non-fatal* injuries to one of its members. Here the very strong tendency is to allow only the primary victim to claim, and to dress up the loss to others as being the primary victim's loss. Thus if the husband is emasculated, the wife will clearly suffer; she cannot sue, however, for he will be paid for the pleasure he can neither receive nor give (*Best* v. *Samuel Fox* ([1952] A.C. 716). Again, the wage-earner who will shortly die because of the injury can hardly be said to have lost the wages he will not be on earth to earn; he is, however, treated as having a present interest in providing for his survivors (*Pickett* v. *British Rail Engineering* ([1980] A.C. 136). If the mother is incapacitated the family loses her services; she can sue for their value, though she doesn't seem to have lost anything except trouble, and her husband, who has, cannot (*Daly* v. *General Steam Navigation Co.* ([1980] 3 All E.R. 696; Administration of Justice Act 1982, s.2). If the mother is rendered permanently unconscious, it is only the family that suffers (pointless visits to hospital, the near corpse in the upstairs room); they cannot sue, and the immense sum payable to the mother, which she can never use, seems to reflect the fact (*West* v. *Shephard* (below p. 532)). If a child is injured, the mother may give up her job to nurse him; the child can sue for the value of the free services received, often equal to the wages given up (*Donnelly* v. *Joyce* [1974] Q.B. 454).

Note the impact on general propositions of negligence law of the fact that victims of such ricochet damage, whether financial or human, are generally unable to sue, although the harm to them is eminently foreseeable. It is true that in 1976 Lord Kilbrandon said "The law now treats the employer as knowing that nearly all the men and many of the women he employs have dependants who are maintained out of the wages he pays and that those dependants will suffer grief as well as patrimonial loss if he, by neglect of his duty of care, occasions his employees physical harm. Those dependants are therefore persons to whom he owes that duty." (*Dick* v. *Burgh of Falkirk* ((1976) S.L.T. 21, 25 (H.L.)). But this "revolutionary" observation was sternly denounced and disavowed by all the members of the House of Lords in *Robertson* v. *Turnbull* ((1982) S.L.T. 96). The law thus is that you do not owe a person any duty not to maim or kill his nearest and dearest unless you do it in his presence or nearly (per Lord Wilberforce in *McLoughlin*, above p. 72), or (per Lord Bridge), if it is foreseeable that he or she may be shocked.

CONGENITAL DISABILITIES (CIVIL LIABILITY) ACT 1976

1.—(1) If a child is born disabled as the result of such an occurrence before its birth as is mentioned in subsection (2) below, and a person (other than the child's own mother) is under this section answerable to the child in respect of the occurrence, the child's disabilities are to be regarded as damage resulting from the wrongful act of that person and actionable accordingly at the suit of the child.

(2) An occurrence to which this section applies is one which—

(a) affected either parent of the child in his or her ability to have a normal, healthy child; or
(b) affected the mother during her pregnancy, or affected her or the child in the course of its birth, so that the child is born with disabilities which would not otherwise have been present.

(3) Subject to the following subsections, a person (here referred to as "the defendant") is answerable to the child if he was liable in tort to the parent or would, if sued in due time, have been so; and it is no answer that there could not have been such liability because the parent suffered no actionable injury, if there was a breach of legal duty which, accompanied by injury, would have given rise to the liability.

(4) In the case of an occurrence preceding the time of conception, the defendant is not answerable to the child if at the time either or both of the parents knew the risk of their child being born disabled (that is to say, the particular risk created by the

occurrence); but should it be the child's father who is the defendant, this subsection does not apply if he knew of the risk and the mother did not.

(5) The defendant is not answerable to the child, for anything he did or omitted to do when responsible in a professional capacity for treating or advising the parent, if he took reasonable care having due regard to then received professional opinion applicable to the particular class of case; but this does not mean that he is answerable only because he departed from received opinion.

(6) Liability to the child under this section may be treated as having been excluded or limited by contract made with the parent affected, to the same extent and subject to the same restrictions as liability in the parent's own case; and a contract term which could have been set up by the defendant in an action by the parent, so as to exclude or limit his liability to him or her, operates in the defendant's favour to the same, but no greater, extent in an action under this section by the child.

(7) If in the child's action under this section it is shown that the parent affected shared the responsibility for the child being born disabled, the damages are to be reduced to such extent as the court thinks just and equitable having regard to the extent of the parent's responsibility.

2. A woman driving a motor vehicle when she knows (or ought reasonably to know) herself to be pregnant is to be regarded as being under the same duty to take care for the safety of her unborn child as the law imposes on her with respect to the safety of other people; and if in consequence of her breach of that duty her child is born with disabilities which would not otherwise have been present, those disabilities are to be regarded as damage resulting from her wrongful act and actionable accordingly at the suit of the child. . . .

Note:

In *McKay* v. *Essex Area Health Authority* ([1982] Q.B. 1166) the allegations were that the defendant doctor had negligently failed (a) to diagnose rubella in the pregnant mother, (b) to recommend an abortion, and (c) to take steps which might have reduced the disabilities with which the infant plaintiff was born. The Court of Appeal held that while the mother could sue for the pain and expense of having a disabled child, and while the infant could sue on the ground that its disabilities were greater than they would have been if the doctor had treated the mother properly, the infant could not claim damages on the ground that the doctor had negligently prevented her being aborted. Stephenson L.J. said " . . . neither defendant was under any duty to the child to give the child's mother an opportunity to terminate the child's life. That duty may be owed to the mother, but it cannot be owed to the child." (at 1180). What would Lord Scarman (above p. 75) have said to that? *McKay* was decided under the common law which was abrogated by the above statute. What would the position be under the statute today?

WHEAT v. E. LACON & CO

House of Lords [1966] A.C. 552; [1966] 2 W.L.R. 581; 110 S.J. 149; [1966] 1 All E.R. 582

Action against occupier in respect of visitor's death.

On the facts stated below, Winn J. held that Lacons, as occupier, owed the deceased a duty to take care, but that their breach did not cause his death. In the Court of Appeal a majority held that Lacons owed the deceased no duty as occupier ([1966] 1 Q.B. 335). The plaintiff's appeal to the House of Lords was dismissed on the grounds that, although Lacons owed an occupier's duty to the deceased, the duty was not broken.

LORD DENNING: My Lords, The "Golfers Arms" at Great Yarmouth is owned by the brewery company, E. Lacon & Co. Ltd. The ground floor was run as a public-house by Mr. Richardson as manager for the brewery company. The first floor was used by Mr. and Mrs. Richardson as their private dwelling. In the summer Mrs. Richardson took in guests for her private profit. Mr. and Mrs. Wheat and their family were summer guests of Mrs. Richardson. About 9 p.m. one evening, when it was getting dark, Mr. Wheat fell down the back staircase in the private portion and was killed. Winn J. held that there were two causes: (i) the handrail was too short because it did not stretch to the foot of the stairs; (ii) someone had taken the bulb out of the light at the top of the stairs.

The case raises this point of law: did the brewery company owe any duty to Mr. Wheat to see that the handrail was safe to use or to see that the stairs were properly lighted? That depends on whether the brewery company was "an occupier" of the private portion of the "Golfers Arms," and Mr. Wheat its "visitor" within the Occupiers' Liability Act 1957: for, if so, the brewery company owed him the "common duty of care." . . .

In the Occupiers' Liability Act 1957, the word "occupier" is used in the same sense as it was used in the common law cases on occupiers' liability for dangerous premises. It was simply a convenient word to denote a person who had a sufficient degree of control over premises to put him under a duty of care towards those who came lawfully on to the premises . . . This duty is simply a particular instance of the general duty of care which each man owes to his "neighbour." When Lord Esher first essayed a definition of this general duty, he used the occupiers' liability as an instance of it: see *Heaven* v. *Pender* ((1883) 11 Q.B.D. 503, 508–509); and when Lord Atkin eventually formulated the general duty in acceptable terms, he, too, used occupiers' liability as an illustration: see *Donoghue* v. *Stevenson* (above p. 15), and particularly his reference to *Grote* v. *Chester Railway Company* ((1848) 2 Ex. 251, 154 E.R. 485). Translating this general principle into its particular application to dangerous premises, it becomes simply this: wherever a person has a sufficient degree of control over premises that he ought to realise that any failure on his part to use care may result in injury to a person coming lawfully there, then he is an "occupier" and the person coming lawfully there is his "visitor" : and the "occupier" is under a duty to his "visitor" to use reasonable care. In order to be an "occupier" it is not necessary for a person to have entire control over the premises. He need not have exclusive occupation. Suffice it that he has some degree of control. He may share the control with others. Two or more may be "occupiers." And whenever this happens, each is under a duty to use care towards persons coming lawfully on to the premises, dependent on his degree of control. If each fails in his duty, each is liable to a visitor who is injured in consequence of his failure, but each may have a claim to contribution from the other.

In *Salmond on Torts*, 14th ed. (1965), p. 372, it is said that an "occupier" is "he who has the immediate supervision and control and the power of permitting or prohibiting the entry of other persons." . . . There is no doubt that a person who fulfils that test is an "occupier." He is the person who says "come in." But I think that test is too narrow by far. There are other people who are "occupiers," even though they do not say "come in." If a person has any degree of control over the state of the premises it is enough. The position is best shown by examining the cases in four groups.

First, where a landlord let premises by demise to a tenant, he was regarded as parting with all control over them. He did not retain any degree of control, even though he had undertaken to repair the structure. Accordingly, he was held to be under no duty to any person coming lawfully on to the premises, save only to the tenant under the agreement to repair. In *Cavalier* v. *Pope* ([1906] A.C. 428) it was argued that the premises were under the control of the landlord because of his agreement to repair: but the House of Lords rejected that argument. That case has now been overruled by section 4 of the Act of 1957 to the extent therein mentioned.

Secondly, where an owner let floors or flats in a building to tenants, but did not demise the common staircase or the roof or some other parts, he was regarded as having retained control of all parts not demised by him. Accordingly, he was held to be under a duty in respect of those retained parts to all persons coming lawfully on to the premises. So he was held liable for a defective staircase in *Miller* v. *Hancock* ([1893] 2 Q.B. 177); for the gutters in the roof of *Hargroves, Aronson & Co.* v. *Hartopp* ([1905] 1 K.B. 472); and for the private balcony in *Sutcliffe* v. *Clients Investment Co. Ltd.* ([1924] 2 K.B. 746). . . . the extent of the duty is now simply the common duty of care. But the old cases still apply so as to show that the landlord is responsible for all parts not demised by him, on the ground that he is regarded as being sufficiently in control of them to impose on him a duty of care to all persons coming lawfully on to the premises.

Thirdly, where an owner did not let premises to a tenant but only licensed a person to occupy them on terms which did not amount to a demise, the owner still having the right to do repairs, he was regarded as being sufficiently in control of the structure to impose on him a duty towards all persons coming lawfully on to the premises. So he was held liable for a visitor who fell on the defective step to the front door in *Hawkins* v. *Coulsdon and Purley U.D.C.* ([1954] 1 Q.B. 319); and to the occupier's wife for the defective ceiling which fell on her in *Greene* v. *Chelsea Borough Council* ([1954] 2 Q.B. 127) . . .

Fourthly, where an owner employed an independent contractor to do work on premises or a structure, the owner was usually still regarded as sufficiently in control of the place as to be under a duty towards all those who might lawfully come there. In some cases he might fulfil that duty by entrusting the work to the independent contractor: see *Haseldine* v. *C.A. Daw & Son* ([1941] 2 K.B. 343) and section 2 (4) of the Act of 1957. In other cases he might only be able to fulfil it by exercising proper supervision himself over the contractor's work, using due diligence himself to prevent damage from unusual danger: see *Thomson* v. *Cremin* ([1956] 1 W.L.R. 103n.), as explained by Lord Reid in *Davie* v. *New Merton Board Mills Ltd.* ([1959] A.C. 604). But in addition to the owner, the courts regarded the independent contractor as himself being sufficiently in control of the place where he worked as to owe a duty of care towards all persons coming lawfully there. He was then said to be an "occupier" also: see *Hartwell's* case ([1947] K.B. 901); but this is only a particular instance of his general duty of care: see *Billings (A.C.) & Sons Ltd.* v. *Riden* ([1958] A.C. 240), *per* Lord Reid.

In the light of these cases, I ask myself whether the brewery company had a sufficient degree of control over the premises to put them under a duty to a visitor. Obviously they had complete control over the ground floor and were "occupiers" of it. But I think that they had also sufficient control over the private portion. They had not let it out to Mr. Richardson by a demise. They had only granted him a licence to occupy it, having a right themselves to do repairs. That left them with a residuary degree of control which was equivalent to that retained by the Chelsea Corporation in *Greene's* case. They were in my opinion "an occupier" within the Act of 1957. Mr. Richardson, who had a licence to occupy, had also a considerable degree of control. So had Mrs. Richardson, who catered for summer guests. All three of them were, in my opinion, "occupiers" of the private portion of the "Golfers Arms." There is no difficulty in having more than one occupier at one and the same time, each of whom is under a duty of care to visitors. The Court of Appeal so held in the recent case of *Crockfords Club* ([1965] 1 W.L.R. 1093) . . .

LORD PEARCE: . . . I agree . . . that the respondents were under a duty of care to the deceased under the Occupiers' Liability Act 1957. But that Act may impose a duty of care on more than one person. And in my opinion the Richardsons were also under a duty of care. The safety of premises may depend on the acts or omissions of more than one person, each of whom may have a different right to cause or continue the state of affairs which creates the danger and on each a duty of care may lie. But where separate persons are each under a duty of care the acts or omissions which would constitute a breach of that duty may vary very greatly. That which would be negligent in one may well be free from blame in the other. If the Richardsons had a dangerous hole in the carpet which they chose to put down in their sitting-room that would be negligent in them towards a visitor who was injured by it. But the respondents could fairly say that they took no interest in the Richardson's private furnishings and that no reasonable person in their position would have noticed or known of or taken any steps with regard to the dangerous defect. If the construction of the staircase was unsafe that would be negligence on the respondents' part. Whether the Richardsons would also be negligent in not warning their visitors or taking steps to reveal the danger would depend on whether a reasonable person in their position would have done so. Once the duty of care is imposed, the question whether a defendant failed in that duty becomes a question of fact in all the circumstances. In the present case the respondents are not shown to have failed in their duty of care . . .

I would dismiss the appeal.

Note:

The manufacturer is responsible for the condition of the ginger-beer; the occupier is responsible for the state of the premises; both are under a duty to take reasonable care. This equation is delusive, however, since the duties differ in their basis and in their extent. The manufacturer is responsible because he *does* make the thing dangerous, whereas the occupier is responsible because he *can* make the thing safe; the manufacturer's duty arises from his action, the occupier's from his capacity to act (he must because he can). And the extent of the duties differs. Unlike the manufacturer, the occupier is not just under a duty not to cause harm to people; he must prevent harm to them; he must mend the premises and tend the visitor. For example, he must protect the visitor against other visitors. Those other visitors of course owe a duty to everyone present or probably present, but that duty is only the standard one of not hurting them; they are not responsible save in so far as they make the place dangerous; the occupier must make it reasonably safe.

The occupier's duty extends also to goods on his premises with his permission; he must protect them from damage, but he need not, unless he is a hotelier, protect them from theft. The distinction is sensible; thieves are not dangerous. The duty to protect goods from theft comes not from *being* in charge of the place where they are but *taking* charge of the goods themselves, *assuming* control of them; the bailee's duty arises not from his capacity to protect the goods but from his undertaking to do so. Indeed, there may be an assumption of responsibility sufficient to give rise to a duty to take positive steps to protect the goods even if there is no proper bailment or contract (*Fairline Shipping Co.* v. *Adamson* [1975] Q.B. 180). Liability for failure to take such positive steps is somewhat easier to exclude than liability for damage caused by positive negligence (*Johnson Matthey* v. *Constantine Terminals* [1976] 2 Lloyd's Rep. 215).

Thus we have three different sources of duties in tort; the manufacturer's stems from his act, the occupier's from his power to act and the bailee's from his undertaking to act. They are all (need it be said?) under a duty to take reasonable care; but that simplistic formula masks the difference between the obligation not to act unreasonably and the obligation to act reasonably.

DEFECTIVE PREMISES ACT 1972

4. Landlord's duty of care in virtue of obligation or right to repair premises demised

(1) Where premises are let under a tenancy which puts on the landlord an obligation to the tenant for the maintenance or repair of the premises, the landlord owes to all persons who might reasonably be expected to be affected by defects in the state of the premises a duty to take such care as is reasonable in all the circumstances to see that they are reasonably safe from personal injury or from damage to their property caused by a relevant defect.

(2) The said duty is owed if the landlord knows (whether as the result of being notified by the tenant or otherwise) or if he ought in all the circumstances to have known of the relevant defect.

(3) In this section "relevant defect" means a defect in the state of the premises existing at or after the material time and arising from, or continuing because of, an act or omission by the landlord which constitutes or would if he had had notice of the defect, have constituted a failure by him to carry out his obligation to the tenant for the maintenance or repair of the premises; and for the purposes of the foregoing provision "the material time" means—

(*a*) where the tenancy commenced before this Act, the commencement of this Act; and

(*b*) in all other cases, the earliest of the following times, that is to say—

(i) the time when the tenancy commences;

(ii) the time when the tenancy agreement is entered into;

(iii) the time when possession is taken of the premises in contemplation of the letting.

(4) Where premises are let under a tenancy which expressly or impliedly gives the landlord the right to enter the premises to carry out any description of maintenance or repair of the premises, then, as from the time when he first is, or by notice or otherwise can put himself, in a position to exercise the right and so long as he is or can put himself in that position, he shall be treated for the purposes of subsections (1) to (3) above (but for no other purpose) as if he were under an obligation to the tenant for that description of maintenance or repair of the premises; but the landlord shall not owe the tenant any duty by virtue of this subsection in respect of any defect in the state of the premises arising from, or continuing because of, a failure to carry out an obligation expressly imposed on the tenant by the tenancy.

(5) For the purposes of this section obligations imposed or rights given by any enactment in virtue of a tenancy shall be treated or imposed or given by the tenancy.

(6) This section applies to a right of occupation given by contract or any enactment and not amounting to a tenancy as if the right were a tenancy, and "tenancy" and cognate expressions shall be construed accordingly.

Note:

Since the very reason one pays rent is in order to occupy the premises one is paying it for, it is, as Lord Denning explained in *Wheat* v. *Lacon*, the tenant rather than the landlord who is under the occupier's duty to take steps to see that visitors are reasonably safe. But tenants who pay very low rents probably cannot afford to do repairs, and short-term tenants cannot be expected to do substantial work, so section 6 of the Housing Act 1957 requires the landlord of low-rent housing to keep it fit for human habitation and section 32 of the Housing Act 1961 (below) specifies the matters which the landlord must attend to in leases of up to seven years. These provisions only affect the contract between the landlord and the tenant. It is section 4 of the Defective Premises Act 1972 which imposes on the landlord a duty to save third parties from physical harm by taking reasonable steps to discover and remedy defects in the premises which are his responsibility rather than that of the tenant-occupier.

HOUSING ACT 1961

32.—(1) In any lease of a dwelling-house, being a lease to which this section applies, there shall be implied a covenant by the lessor—

(*a*) to keep in repair the structure and exterior of the dwelling-house (including drains, gutters and external pipes); and

(*b*) to keep in repair and proper working order the installations in the dwelling-house—

(i) for the supply of water, gas and electricity, and for sanitation (including basins, sinks, baths and sanitary conveniences but not, except as aforesaid, fixtures and appliances for making use of the supply of water, gas or electricity), and

(ii) for space heating or heating water,

and any covenant by the lessee for the repair of the premises (including any covenant to put in repair or deliver up in repair, to paint, point or render or to pay money in lieu of repairs by the lessee or on account of repairs by the lessor) shall be of no effect so far as it relates to the matters mentioned in paragraphs (*a*) and (*b*) of this subsection.

(2) The covenant implied by this section (hereinafter referred to as the lessor's repairing covenant) shall not be construed as requiring the lessor—

(*a*) to carry out any works or repairs for which the lessee is liable by virtue of his duty to use the premises in a tenant-like manner, or would be so liable apart from any express covenant on his part;

(*b*) to rebuild or reinstate the premises in the case of destruction or damage by fire, or by tempest, flood, or other inevitable accident; or

(*c*) to keep in repair or maintain anything which the lessee is entitled to remove from the dwelling-house;

and subsection (1) of this section shall not avoid any covenant by the lessee so far as it imposes on the lessee any of the requirements mentioned in paragraph (*a*) or paragraph (*c*) of this subsection.

(3) In determining the standard of repair required by the lessor's repairing covenant, regard shall be had to the age, character and prospective life of the dwelling-house and the locality in which it is situated.

(4) In any lease in which the lessor's repairing covenant is implied, there shall also be implied a covenant by the lessee that the lessor, or any person authorised by him in writing, may at reasonable times of the day, on giving twenty-four hours' notice in writing to the occupier, enter the premises comprised in the lease for the purpose of viewing their conditions and state of repair.

(5) In this and the next following section the following expressions have the meanings hereby respectively assigned to them, that is to say:—

"lease" includes an underlease, an agreement for a lease or underlease, and any other tenancy, but does not include a mortgage, and "covenant", "demise" and "term" shall be construed accordingly;

"lease of a dwelling-house" means a lease whereby a building or part of a building is let wholly or mainly as a private dwelling, and "the dwelling-house" means that building or part of a building;

"lessee" and "lessor" means respectively the person for the time being entitled to the term of a lease and to the reversion expectant thereon.

33.—(1) Section thirty-two of this Act applies, subject to the provisions of this section, to any lease of a dwelling-house granted after the passing of this Act, being a lease for a term of less than seven years.

BRITISH RAILWAYS BOARD v. HERRINGTON

House of Lords [1972] A.C. 877; [1972] 2 W.L.R. 537; 116 S.J. 178; [1972] 1 All E.R. 749

Action by child trespasser against occupier in respect of personal injuries

The defendant's electrified railway line ran between two National Trust properties where the children of Mitcham played. There was a fence alongside the railway line and a footbridge over it. For some time it had been possible to cross the railway line without using the bridge because at the very point where the path turned along the fence to reach the bridge the fence had got out of repair: the mesh had come away from the uprights and had been flattened. Railway staff had seen children on the line at this point. One Whit Monday the plaintiff, a boy of six, strayed from his companions, went over the dilapidated fence and was severely burnt on the electrified rail.

Cairns J. gave judgment for the plaintiff, which was affirmed by the Court of Appeal on the ground that the defendant, though not reckless, was in breach of his duty to the plaintiff.

LORD PEARSON: My Lords, in relation to an occupier of premises the position of a trespasser must be radically different from that of a lawful visitor. The broad effect of section 2 of the Occupiers' Liability Act 1957 is that an occupier of premises owes to his lawful visitors, *i.e.* the persons who come on the premises at his invitation or with his permission, the common duty of care; and that is a duty to take such care as in all the circumstances of the case is reasonable to see that the visitor will be reasonably safe in using the premises for the purposes for which he is invited or permitted to be there. In my opinion, the occupier of premises does not owe any such duty to a trespasser: he does *not* owe to the trespasser a duty to take such care as in all the circumstances of the case is reasonable to see that the trespasser will be reasonably safe in using the premises for the purposes for which he is trespassing. That seems to me to be the fundamental distinction, and it should be fully preserved.

It does not follow that the occupier never owes any duty to the trespasser. If the presence of the trespasser is known to or reasonably to be anticipated by the occupier, then the occupier has a duty to the trespasser, but it is a lower and less onerous duty than the one which the occupier owes to a lawful visitor. Very broadly stated, it is a duty to treat the trespasser with ordinary humanity . . . But this is a vague phrase. What is the content of the duty to treat the trespasser with ordinary humanity? The authoritative formulation of the duty, as given in *Robert Addie & Sons (Colleries) Ltd.* v. *Dumbreck* ([1929] A.C. 358) is severely restrictive and is, I think, now inadequate. Subject to the difficulty created by that formulation, I think one can deduce from decided cases that, normally at any rate, the occupier is not at fault, he has done as much as is required of him, if he has taken reasonable steps to deter the trespasser from entering or remaining on the premises, or the part of the premises, in which he will encounter a dangerous situation. In simple language, it is normally sufficient for the occupier to make reasonable endeavours to keep out or chase off the potential or actual intruder who is likely to be or is in a dangerous situation. The erection and maintenance of suitable notice boards or fencing or both, or the giving of suitable oral warning, or a practice of chasing away trespassing children will usually constitute reasonable endeavours for this purpose . . . If the trespasser, in spite of the occupier's reasonable endeavours to deter him, insists on trespassing or continuing his trespass, he must take the condition of the land and the operations on the land as he finds them and cannot normally hold the occupier of the land or anyone but himself responsible for injuries resulting from the trespass, which is his own wrongdoing. But that statement is subject to this proviso: if the occupier knows or as good as knows that some emergency has arisen whereby the trespasser has been placed in a position of imminent peril, ordinary humanity requires further steps to be taken: the very obvious example is that, if the driver of a train sees a trespasser fallen on the line in front of him, he must try to stop the train. The variety of possible situations is so great that one cannot safely try to formulate for all cases what steps an occupier is required to take for the protection or rescue of a trespasser, but the decided cases show what is required in typical situations, and that I have endeavoured to summarise. In *Commissioner for Railways (N.S.W.)* v. *Cardy* ((1960) 104 C.L.R. 274, 286), Dixon C.J. said: "The duty is measured by the nature of the danger or peril but it may, according to circumstances, be sufficiently discharged by warning of the danger, by taking steps to exclude the intruder or by removal or reduction of the danger." In the case of the poisonous berries in the public park (*Glasgow*

Corporation v. *Taylor* [1922] 1 A.C. 44) the simplest and cheapest and most effective way of protecting children who might be tempted to eat them would have been, not the erection of a fence or warning notices, but to dig up and remove the tree or shrub on which the poisonous berries grew. But as an illustration of the duty to trespassers normally being sufficiently discharged by reasonable measures designed to exclude them from the situation of danger, I will cite a passage from the judgment of Windeyer J. in *Munnings* v. *Hydro-Electric Commission* ((1971) 45 A.L.J.R. 378, 389). He said: " . . . the duty of care that the commission owed to the plaintiff was not a duty to have its pole safe for trespassers. It was a duty which arose from the very fact that it was dangerous to trespassers. High voltage electricity is a highly dangerous thing. To bring such a dangerous thing to a locality frequented by members of the public imposed a duty of care. That duty could be discharged by putting live wires beyond easy reach and not enabling unauthorised persons to come to them." There are several reasons why an occupier should not have imposed upon him onerous obligations to a trespasser—

(1) There is the unpredictability of the possible trespasser both as to whether he will come on the land at all and also as to where he will go and what he will do if he does come on the land. I enlarged on this point in *Videan* v. *British Transport Commission* ([1963] 2 Q.B. 650, 679), and I will only summarise it shortly here. As the trespasser's presence and movements are unpredictable, he is not within the zone of reasonable contemplation (*Bourhill* v. *Young* ([1943] A.C. 92) and he is not a "neighbour" (*Donoghue* v. *Stevenson*) to the occupier, and the occupier cannot reasonably be required to take precautions for his safety. Occupiers are entitled to farm lands, operate quarries and factories, run express trains at full speed through stations, fell trees and fire shots without regard to the mere general possibility that there might happen to be in the vicinity a trespasser who might be injured. The occupiers do not have to cease or restrict their activities in view of that possibility, which is too remote to be taken into account and could not fairly be allowed to curtail their freedom of action.

(2) Even when his presence is known or reasonably to be anticipated, so that he becomes a neighbour, the trespasser is rightly to be regarded as an under-privileged neighbour. The reason for this appears, I think, most clearly from a consideration of the analogous position of a lawful visitor who exceeds his authority, going outside the scope of his licence or permission. In *Hillen and Pettigrew* v. *I.C.I. (Akali) Ltd.* ([1936] A.C. 65, 69–70) Lord Atkin said: " . . . this duty to an invitee only extends so long as and so far as the invitee is making what can reasonably be contemplated as an ordinary and reasonable use of the premises by the invitee for the purposes for which he has been invited. He is not invited to use any part of the premises for purposes which he knows are wrongfully dangerous and constitute an improper use. Scrutton L.J. has pointedly said: 'When you invite a person into your house to use the staircase you do not invite him to slide down the banisters.' (*The Calgarth* [1926] P. 93, 110.) So far as he sets foot on so much of the premises as lie outside the invitation or uses them for purposes which are alien to the invitation he is not an invitee but a trespasser, and his rights must be determined accordingly. In the present case the stevedores knew that they ought not to use the covered hatch in order to load cargo from it; for them for such a purpose it was out of bounds; they were trespassers. The defendants had no reason to contemplate such a use; they had no duty to take any care that the hatch when covered was safe for such a use; they had no duty to warn anyone that it was not fit for such use." . . .

(3) It would in many, if not most, cases be impracticable to take effective steps to prevent (instead of merely endeavouring to deter) trespassers from going into or remaining in situations of danger. The cost of erecting and maintaining an impenetrable and unclimbable or, as it has been put, "boy-proof" fence would be prohibitive, if it could be done at all . . . As Lord Goddard said in *Edwards* v. *Railway Executive* ([1952] A.C. 737, 747), referring to the Railway Executive: "Had they to provide watchmen to guard every place on the railways of the

Southern Region where children may and do get on to embankments and lines, railway fares would be a great deal higher than they are already."

(4) There is also a moral aspect. Apart from trespasses which are inadvertent or more or less excusable, trespassing is a form of misbehaviour, showing lack of consideration for the rights of others. It would be unfair if trespassers could by their misbehaviour impose onerous obligations on others. One can take the case of a farmer. He may know well from past experience that persons are likely to trespass on his land for the purpose of tearing up his primroses and bluebells, or picking his mushrooms or stealing his turkeys, or for the purpose of taking country walks in the course of which they will tread down his grass and leave gates open and watch their dogs chasing the farmer's cattle and sheep. It would be intolerable if a farmer had to take expensive precautions for the protection of such persons in such activities.

I have said that an occupier does not owe to a trespasser the "common duty of care," which is now the relevant statutory expression for the occupier's duty to lawful visitors. It can also be said that the occupier does not owe to the trespasser any general duty of care. This question was fully considered and decided in the case of *Commissioner for Railways* v. *Quinlan* ([1964] A.C. 1054). . . .

There is economy of doctrine, simplicity of principle, in having one exclusive and comprehensive formula defining the duty of occupier to trespasser. But the formula itself has created difficulties and aroused criticism, and I think it is not now adequate or defensible as applying to modern conditions. Before coming to the formula, I will attempt a summary of the principles so far dealt with.

It seems to me that there is rational justification for the common law attitude towards trespassers, in so far as it has recognised that—(a) in relation to an occupier the position of a trespasser is radically different from that of a lawful visitor; (b) the unknown and merely possible trespasser is not a "neighbour" in the sense in which that word "neighbour" was used by Lord Atkin in *Donoghue* v. *Stevenson*, and the occupier owes to such a trespasser no duty to take precautions for his safety; and (c) if the presence of the trespasser is known to or reasonably to be anticipated by the occupier, then the occupier—(i) does not owe to the trespasser the common duty of care (which is the single statutory substitute for the different duties formerly owing to invitees and licensees); (ii) does not owe to the trespasser a general duty of care; but (iii) does owe to the trespasser a lower and less onerous duty, which has been described as a duty to treat him with ordinary humanity.

So far so good. In so far as those are the rules of the common law on this subject, they seem to be fully acceptable. The difficulty, however, arises from the narrow formulation of the duty to trespassers in *Robert Addie & Sons (Colleries) Ltd.* v. *Dumbreck* ([1929] A.C. 358) . . . The formulation is too narrow and inadequate in at least three respects. *First*, it appears to hold the occupier liable only for positive acts and not in respect of omissions. Suppose that the occupier is running an electrified railway, with an exposed live rail, in the vicinity of a public playground, and that he has not provided any warning notice or fence to deter children from straying on to the railway, and in consequence a child strays on to the live rail and is seriously injured. Surely common sense and justice require that the occupier must be held liable in such a case for his nonfeasance. I doubt, however, whether it was intended to confine liability to positive acts. Perhaps the words "act" and "acting" in *Addie's* case can be interpreted as including omissions.

Secondly, the formulation appears to say that the occupier has no duty to do anything for the protection of trespassers until there is a trespasser actually on the land and the occupier knows he is there. But again the case of a child straying on the live rail of an electrified railway shows that there must be a duty on the occupier to take some steps in advance to deter children from trespassing on the railway.

Thirdly, the formulation makes the occupier liable only in respect of deliberate or reckless acts. I think the word "reckless" in the context does not mean grossly negligent but means that there must be a conscious disregard of the consequences—

in effect deciding not to bother about the consequences. Thus a subjective, mental element, a sort of mens rea is required as a condition of liability. Mere negligence would not be enough to create liability according to the formulation. There would be no duty to take care, but only a duty to abstain from deliberately or recklessly causing injury. That is plainly inadequate . . .

In my opinion the *Addie* v. *Dumbreck* formulation of the duty of occupier to trespasser is plainly inadequate for modern conditions, and its rigid and restrictive character has impeded the proper development of the common law in this field. It has become an anomaly and should be discarded. But in my opinion the duty of occupier to trespasser should remain limited in the ways that I have endeavoured to indicate.

I need not lengthen this already long opinion by describing again the facts of the present case which have been described by my noble and learned friends. The railway board in the circumstances had a duty to take reasonable steps to deter children from straying from the public space on to the electrified railway line. Obviously, reasonable steps for this purpose included proper maintenance of the fence. But the railway board failed to repair the broken down fence even after they had been notified that children had been seen on the line. There was a clear breach of the duty.

I would dismiss the appeal.

LORD REID, LORD MORRIS, LORD WILBERFORCE and LORD DIPLOCK delivered opinions concurring in the result.

Questions
1. What has happened since 1929 to render *Addie's* case an anomaly? Have children become more adventurous, has electricity become more dangerous, have fences become stronger or have employees become more reliable? Is it that disregard of other people's property is more acceptable now? Or is it that there has developed a general principle of liability for carelessly causing or permitting physical harm such that every exception seems anomalous?
2. Do landlords owe trespassers a duty under section 4 of the Defective Premises Act 1972 (above, p. 84).
3. Is it because children are innocent of wrongdoing or ignorant of danger that they deserve special protection as compared with adult trespassers?

Note:
1. Only since 1966 has the House of Lords been free to depart from *Addie's* case, which at any rate laid down a clear rule. So unclear was the law after *Herrington* that the Lord Chancellor immediately referred the matter to the Law Commission. The Law Commission produced the following draft clause, which has received the approval of the Pearson Commission:

(1) An occupier of premises owes a duty to an uninvited entrant upon the premises in respect of a danger if, but only if, the danger is one against which, in all the circumstances of the case, the occupier can reasonably be expected to offer him some protection.
(2) The duty owed by an occupier in accordance with subsection (1) above is a duty to take such care as is reasonable in all the circumstances of the case to see that the entrant does not suffer personal injury or death by reason of the danger.

(2) The House of Lords has held that a plaintiff's damages cannot be reduced under the Contributory Negligence Act (below, p. 205) on the mere ground that he was a trespasser (*Westwood* v. *Post Office* [1974] A.C. 1). This is rather a pity, since it seems odd to give full damages, if any, to a person who ought not to have been where he was even if he did not know that it was unsafe to be there.
3. A trespasser savaged by an animal has to prove the occupier's negligence, at least. Other visitors usually need not. See Animals Act 1971, s.5(3), below, p. 396).
4. It is a very safe bet that *Herrington* will not survive, and that *Donoghue* v. *Stevenson* will be extended to benefit the trespasser. The only difficulty in extending to the trespasser the "common duty of care" owed to lawful visitors is that it imposes positive duties on the occupier, and that seems a little excessive when the victim shouldn't have been there at all.

But perhaps we should make the world safe for children, and debar the wicked trespasser, the burglar, the peeping Tom and so on by the defence of unlawfulness (below, p. 217). This blend of sentimentality and moralism would be quite characteristic of our age.

WOOLDRIDGE v. SUMNER

Court of Appeal [1963] 2 Q.B. 43; [1962] 3 W.L.R. 616; 106 S.J. 489; [1962] 2 All E.R. 978

Action by spectator against participant in respect of personal injury.

During a competition for heavyweight hunters at the National Horse Show the plaintiff was taking photographs from between some potted shrubs on the edge of the arena. One of the horses competing was "Work of Art," owned by the first defendant and ridden by Ronald Holladay. It came down the far side of the course, rounded the bend at great speed, and then galloped furiously and apparently out of control down the line of shrubs to where the plaintiff was standing. In fright, the plaintiff tried to pull another spectator out of the way, but fell back into the horse's path and was seriously hurt. The horse returned and won.

Barry J. held that the rider had been negligent in allowing the horse to go so fast, and in attempting to bring it back on course when there were people in the way. He gave judgment for the plaintiff for £6,500. The defendant's appeal was allowed.

DIPLOCK L.J.: . . . It is a remarkable thing that in a nation where during the present century so many have spent so much of their leisure in watching other people take part in sports and pastimes there is an almost complete dearth of judicial authority as to the duty of care owed by the actual participants to the spectators. In *Cleghorn* v. *Oldham* ((1927) 43 T.L.R. 465) the act relied on as constituting negligence by a golfer was not done in the actual course of play and the case, which was tried by a jury and only very briefly reported, throws little light upon the extent of the duty of care. So, too, in the Canadian case of *Payne & Payne* v. *Maple Leaf Gardens Ltd.* ([1949] 1 D.L.R. 369) the negligent act was not committed in the course of play but in the course of a private fight between two players over the possession of an ice hockey stick at the opposite side of the arena to that in which the game was going on at the relevant time. There have been other cases—*Hall* v. *Brooklands Auto Racing Club* ([1933] 1 K.B. 205) itself is one of them—in which the actual participants in the game or competition have been sued as well as the occupiers of the premises on which it took place, but juries have acquitted the participants of negligence and the cases are reported only upon the duty owed by an occupier of premises to invitees. Such duty is not based upon negligence simpliciter but flows from a consensual relationship between the occupier and the invitee; there is thus no conceptual difficulty in implying a term in that consensual relationship (which in the reported cases has in fact been a contractual relationship) that the occupier need take no precautions to protect the invitee from all or from particular kinds of risks incidental to the game or competition which the spectator has come upon the premises to watch.

In the case of a participant, however, any duty of care which he owed to the spectator is not based upon any consensual relationship between them but upon mere "proximity," if I may use that word as a compendious expression of what makes one person a "neighbour" of another in the sense of Lord Atkin's definition in *Donoghue* v. *Stevenson* as expanded in *Hay* (*or Bourhill*) v. *Young*. Nevertheless, some assistance is to be gathered from the invitee cases, for the term as to the duty of the occupier to take precautions to prevent damage being sustained upon the premises by his invitee, which was implied at common law, was closely analogous to the duty a breach of which constitutes negligence simpliciter, namely, "to use reasonable care to ensure safety" (*Hall* v. *Brooklands Auto Racing Club, per* Scrutton L.J.), "that reasonable skill and care have been used to make [the premises] safe" (*per* Greer L.J.).

To treat Lord Atkin's statement: "You must take reasonable care to avoid acts or omissions which you can reasonably foresee would be likely to injure your neighbour," as a complete exposition of the law of negligence is to mistake aphorism for exegesis. It does not purport to define what is reasonable care and was directed to identifying the persons to whom the duty to take reasonable care is owed. What is reasonable care in a particular circumstance is a jury question and where, as in a case like this, there is no direct guidance or hindrance from authority it may be answered by inquiring whether the ordinary reasonable man would say that in all the circumstances the defendant's conduct was blameworthy.

The matter has to be looked at from the point of view of the reasonable spectator as well as the reasonable participant; not because of the maxim volenti non fit injuria, but because what a reasonable spectator would expect a participant to do without regarding it as blameworthy is as relevant to what is reasonable care as what a reasonable participant would think was blameworthy conduct in himself. The same idea was expressed by Scrutton L.J. in *Hall* v. *Brooklands:* "What is reasonable care would depend upon the perils which might be reasonably expected to occur, *and the extent to which the ordinary spectator might be expected to appreciate and take the risk of such perils.*"

A reasonable spectator attending voluntarily to witness any game or competition knows and presumably desires that a reasonable participant will concentrate his attention upon winning, and if the game or competition is a fast-moving one, will have to exercise his judgment and attempt to exert his skill in what, in the analogous context of contributory negligence, is sometimes called "the agony of the moment." If the participant does so concentrate his attention and consequently does exercise his judgment and attempt to exert his skill in circumstances of this kind which are inherent in the game or competition in which he is taking part, the question whether any mistake he makes amounts to a breach of duty to take reasonable care must take account of those circumstances.

The law of negligence has always recognised that the standard of care which a reasonable man will exercise depends upon the conditions under which the decision to avoid the act or omission relied upon as negligence has to be taken. The case of the workmen engaged on repetitive work in the noise and bustle of the factory is a familiar example. More apposite for present purposes are the collision cases, where a decision has to be made upon the spur of the moment. "A's negligence makes collision so threatening that though by the appropriate measure B could avoid it, B has not really time to think and by mistake takes the wrong measure. B is not to be held guilty of any negligence and A wholly fails" (*Admiralty Commissioners* v. *S.S. Volute* [1922] 1 A.C. 129, 136). A fails not because of his own negligence; there never has been any contributory negligence rule in Admiralty. He fails because B has exercised such care as is reasonable in circumstances in which he has not really time to think. No doubt if he has got into those circumstances as a result of a breach of duty of care which he owes to A, A can succeed upon this antecedent negligence; but a participant in a game or competition gets into the circumstances in which he has no time or very little time to think by his decision to take part in the game or competition at all. It cannot be suggested that the participant, at any rate if he has some modicum of skill is, by the mere act of participating, in breach of his duty of care to a spectator who is present for the very purpose of watching him do so. If, therefore, in the course of the game or competition, at a moment when he really has not time to think, a participant by mistake takes a wrong measure, he is not, in my view, to be held guilty of any negligence.

Furthermore, the duty which he owes is a duty of care, not a duty of skill. Save where a consensual relationship exists between a plaintiff and a defendant by which the defendant impliedly warrants his skill, a man owes no duty to his neighbour to exercise any special skill beyond that which an ordinary reasonable man would acquire before indulging in the activity in which he is engaged at the relevant time. It may well be that a participant in a game or competition would be guilty of negligence to a spectator if he took part in it when he knew or ought to have known that his lack of skill was such that even if he exerted it to the utmost he was likely to cause injury to a spectator watching him. No question of this arises in the present case. It was common ground that Mr. Holladay was an exceptionally skilful and experienced horseman.

The practical result of this analysis of the application of the common law of negligence to participant and spectator would, I think, be expressed by the common man in some such terms as these: "A person attending a game or competition takes the risk of any damage caused to him by any act of a participant done in the course of and for the purposes of the game or competition notwithstanding that such act may involve an error of judgment or a lapse of skill, unless the participant's conduct is such as to evince a reckless disregard of the spectator's safety." . . .

Beyond saying that the question is one of degree, the judge has not expressly stated in his judgment anything which would indicate the considerations which he had in mind in determining that Mr. Holladay was in breach of the duty of care owed by a participant in a competition of this character to a spectator who had chosen to watch the event in the arena in which it was taking place. There is, however, no reference in his judgment to the fact, which is, in my view, of the utmost relevance, that Mr. Holladay's decisions as to what he should do once the signal for the gallop has been given had to be made in circumstances in which he had no time to exercise an unhurried judgment. It is, I think, clear that if the trial judge gave any weight to this factor he did not make proper allowance for it.

As regards the speed at which Mr. Holladay went round the bandstand end of the arena, I doubt whether his error of judgment would have amounted to negligence even if one were to ignore completely the fact that his judgment had to be exercised rapidly in the excitement of the contest although not at a moment of intense crisis. For it does not seem to me that any miscalculation of the speed at which "Work of Art" could take the corner could be reasonably foreseen to be likely to injure any spectator sitting on or standing by the benches twenty to thirty yards from the point at which a horse taking the corner at too great a speed would cross the line demarcated by the shrubs . . . The horse was deflected from its course before it reached the benches and no spectator would have been injured had not the plaintiff, in a moment of panic, stepped or stumbled back out of his proper and safe place among the other spectators in the line of benches into the path of the horse. Such panic in the case of a person ignorant of equine behaviour and, as the judge found, paying little or no attention to what was going on, is understandable and excusable, but, in my view, a reasonable competitor would be entitled to assume that spectators actually in the arena would be paying attention to what was happening, would be knowledgeable about horses, and would take such steps for their own safety as any reasonably attentive and knowledgeable spectator might be expected to take.

When due allowance is made for the circumstances in which Mr. Holladay had in fact to exercise his judgment as to the speed at which to take the corner, his conduct in taking the corner too fast could not, in my view, amount to negligence.

As regards the second respect in which the judge found Mr. Holladay to be negligent, namely, in his attempt to bring back the horse into the arena after it had come into contact with the first shrub, I have already stated the reasons why I am unable to accept the judge's inference of fact that the course taken by the horse along the line of shrubs was due to Mr. Holladay's attempt to bring it back into the arena instead of letting it run out on to the cinder track. But even if the judge's inference of fact be accepted, here was a classic case where Mr. Holladay's decision what to do had to be taken in the "agony of the moment," when he had no time to think, and if he took the wrong decision that could not in law amount to negligence.

The most that can be said against Mr. Holladay is that in the course of and for the purposes of the competition he was guilty of an error or errors of judgment or a lapse of skill. That is not enough to constitute a breach of the duty of reasonable care which a participant owes to a spectator. In such circumstances something in the nature of a reckless disregard of the spectator's safety must be proved, and of this there is no suggestion in the evidence. I, too, would allow this appeal.

NETTLESHIP v. WESTON

Court of Appeal [1971] 2 Q.B. 691; [1971] 3 W.L.R. 370; 115 S.J. 624; [1971] 3 All E.R. 581

Action in respect of personal injuries by driving instructor against learner driver

The defendant asked the plaintiff, who was a friend and not a professional driving instructor, to teach her to drive her husband's car. On being assured that there was fully comprehensive insurance cover, he agreed to do so. During the third lesson the defendant stopped at a junction prior to turning left. The plaintiff engaged first gear for her, and she started to turn slowly to the left. Her grip on the steering wheel tightened implacably, and despite the plaintiff's advice and efforts, the car followed a perfect curve, mounted the nearside pavement and struck a lamp post with sufficient impact to fracture the plaintiff's knee.

The trial judge dismissed the plaintiff's claim on the ground that the defendant's only duty to him was to do her best, and this she had done, poor though it was. The Court of Appeal allowed the plaintiff's appeal, subject (Megaw L.J. dissenting) to a reduction of the damages by 50 per cent. in respect of his contributory negligence.

LORD DENNING M.R. delivered a judgment allowing the plaintiff's appeal.

SALMON L.J.: I need not recite the facts which have been so lucidly stated by Lord Denning M.R. I entirely agree with all he says about the responsibility of a learner driver in criminal law. I also agree that a learner driver is responsible and owes a duty in civil law towards persons on or near the highway to drive with the same degree of skill and care as that of the reasonably competent and experienced driver. The duty in civil law springs from the relationship which the driver, by driving on the highway, has created between himself and persons likely to suffer damage by his bad driving. This is not a special relationship. Nor, in my respectful view, is it affected by whether or not the driver is insured. On grounds of public policy, neither the criminal nor civil responsibility is affected by the fact that the driver in question may be a learner, infirm or drunk. The onus, of course, lies on anyone claiming damages to establish a breach of duty and that it has caused the damage which he claims.

Any driver normally owes exactly the same duty to a passenger in his car as he does to the general public, namely, to drive with reasonable care and skill in all the relevant circumstances. As a rule, the driver's personal idiosyncrasy is not a relevant circumstance. In the absence of a special relationship what is reasonable care and skill is measured by the standard of competence usually achieved by the ordinary driver. In my judgment, however, there may be special facts creating a special relationship which displaces this standard or even negatives any duty, although the onus would certainly be upon the driver to establish such facts. With minor reservations I respectfully agree with and adopt the reasoning and conclusions of Sir Owen Dixon in his judgment in *The Insurance Commissioner* v. *Joyce* ((1948) 77 C.L.R. 39). I do not agree that the mere fact that the driver has, to the knowledge of his passenger, lost a limb or an eye or is deaf can affect the duty which he owes the passenger to drive safely. It is well known that many drivers suffering from such disabilities drive with no less skill and competence than the ordinary man. The position, however, is totally different when, to the knowledge of the passenger, the driver is so drunk as to be incapable of driving safely. Quite apart from being negligent, a passenger who accepts a lift in such circumstances clearly cannot expect the driver to drive other than dangerously.

The duty of care springs from relationship. The special relationship which the passenger has created by accepting a lift in the circumstances postulated surely cannot entitle him to expect the driver to discharge a duty of care or skill which *ex hypothesi* the passenger knows the driver is incapable of discharging. Accordingly, in such circumstances, no duty is owed by the driver to the passenger to drive safely, and therefore no question of *volenti non fit injuria* can arise.

The alternative view is that if there is a duty owed to the passenger to drive safely, the passenger by accepting a lift has clearly assumed the risk of the driver failing to discharge that duty. What the passenger has done goes far beyond establishing mere "scienter." If it does not establish "volens," it is perhaps difficult to imagine what can.

Such a case seems to me to be quite different from *Smith* v. *Baker & Sons* ([1891] A.C. 325) and *Slater* v. *Clay Cross Co. Ltd.* ([1956] 2 Q.B. 264). Like Sir Owen Dixon, I prefer to rest on the special relationship between the parties displacing the prima facie duty on the driver to drive safely rather than on the ground of *volenti non fit injuria*. Whichever view is preferable, it follows that, in spite of the very great respect I have for any judgment of Lord Asquith, I do not accept that *Dann* v. *Hamilton* ([1939] 1 K.B. 509) was correctly decided. Although Sir Owen Dixon's judgment was delivered in 1948, I cannot think of anything which has happened since which makes it any less convincing now than it was then.

I should like to make it plain that I am not suggesting that whenever a passenger accepts a lift knowing that the driver has had a few drinks, this displaces the prima facie duty ordinarily resting on a driver, let alone that it establishes *volenti non fit injuria*. Indeed, Sir Owen Dixon dissented in *Joyce's* case, because he did not agree that the evidence was capable of establishing that the plaintiff passenger knew that the driver was so drunk as to be incapable of exercising ordinary care and skill. In practice it would be rare indeed that such a defence could be established.

There are no authorities which bear directly on the duty owed by a learner driver to his instructor. I have dwelt upon the authorities concerning the relationship between a drunken driver and his passenger because to some extent there is an analogy between those two classes of case. But the analogy is by no means exact. The drunken driver is in sole charge of the car. His condition may be such that the passenger knows that it is impossible for him to drive with any care or skill. On the other hand, the learner driver and his instructor are jointly in charge of the car. The instructor is entitled to expect the learner to pay attention to what he is told, perhaps to take exceptional care, and certainly to do his best. The instructor, in most cases such as the present, knows, however, that the learner has practically no driving experience or skill and that, for the lack of this experience and skill the learner will almost certainly make mistakes which may well injure the instructor unless he takes adequate steps to correct them. To my mind, therefore, the relationship is usually such that the beginner does not owe the instructor a duty to drive with the skill and competence to be expected of an experienced driver. The instructor knows that the learner does not possess such skill and competence. The alternative way of putting the case is that the instructor voluntarily agrees to run the risk of injury resulting from the learner's lack of skill and experience.

The point may be tested in this way: suppose that the instructor is paid for the lessons he gives and there is a contract governing the relationship between the parties, but the contract is silent about the duty owed by the learner to the instructor. It is well settled that the law will not imply any term into such a contract unless it is necessary to do so for the purpose of giving to the contract ordinary business efficacy. Could it really be said that in order to give this contract ordinary business efficacy, it is necessary to imply a term that the learner owed the instructor a duty to drive with the degree of skill and competence which both parties know that he does not possess? If the law were to imply such a term, far from it giving the contract efficacy, it would, in my view, only make itself and the contract look absurd.

Nor can I think that even when there is no payment and no contract, the special relationship between the parties can as a rule impose any such duty upon the learner. Indeed such a duty is excluded by that relationship.

If, however, the learner, for example, refuses to obey instructions or suddenly accelerates to a high speed or pays no attention to what he is doing and as a result the instructor is injured, then, in my view, the learner is in breach of duty and liable to the instructor in damages. The duty is still the duty to use reasonable care and skill in all the relevant circumstances. What is reasonable depends, however, on the special relationship existing between the learner and his instructor. This relationship, in my view, makes the learner's known lack of skill and experience a highly relevant circumstance.

I do not think that the learner is usually liable to his instructor if an accident occurs as a result of some mistake which any prudent beginner doing his best can be expected to make. I recognise that on this view, cases in which a driving instructor is injured while his pupil is driving may raise difficult questions of fact and degree. Equally difficult questions of fact and degree are, however, being assessed and decided in our courts every day. The law lays down principles but not a rule of thumb for deciding issues arising out of any special relationship between the parties. A rule of thumb, if it existed, might no doubt remove difficulties, but could hardly produce justice either in practice or in theory.

It does not appear to me to be incongruous that a learner is responsible for acts or omissions in criminal law and indeed to the public at large in civil law and yet not necessarily responsible for such acts or omissions to his instructor. The learner has no special relationship with the public. The learner is certainly not liable to his instructor if his responsibility is excluded by contract. I can see no reason why, in the absence of contract, the same result should not follow from the special relationship between the parties.

For the reasons I have stated, I would, but for one factor agree with the judge's decision in favour of the defendant. I have, however, come to the conclusion, not without doubt, that this appeal should be allowed. Mr. Nettleship when he gave evidence was asked: "Q. Was there any mention made of what the position would be if you were involved in an accident? A. I had checked with Mr. and Mrs. Weston regarding insurance, and I was assured that they had fully comprehensive insurance which covered me as a passenger in the event of an accident." Mrs. Weston agreed, when she gave evidence, that this assurance had been given before Mr. Nettleship undertook to teach her. In my view this evidence completely disposes of any possible defence of *volenti non fit injuria.* Moreover, this assurance seems to me to be an integral part of the relationship between the parties. In *Hedley Byrne & Co. Ltd.* v. *Heller & Partners Ltd.* ([1964] A.C. 465), the House of Lords decided that the relationship which there existed between the parties would have imposed a duty of care upon the defendants in giving the plaintiffs information but for the fact that the defendants gave the information "without responsibility." This disclaimer of responsibility was held to colour the whole relationship between the parties by negativing any duty of care on the part of the defendants.

Much the same result followed when a passenger accepted a lift in a car which exhibited a notice stating: "Warning. Passengers travelling in this vehicle do so *at their own risk*": *Bennett* v. *Tugwell* ([1971] 2 Q.B. 267). The present case is perhaps the converse of the cases of *Hedley Byrne* and *Bennett* v. *Tugwell.*

On the whole, I consider, although with some doubt, that the assurance given to Mr. Nettleship altered the nature of the relationship which would have existed between the parties but for the assurance. The assurance resulted in a relationship under which Mrs. Weston accepted responsibility for any injury which Mr. Nettleship might suffer as a result of any failure on her part to exercise the ordinary driver's standards of reasonable care and skill . . .

MEGAW L.J.: . . . The important question of principle which arises is whether, because of Mr. Nettleship's knowledge that Mrs. Weston was not an experienced driver, the standard of care which was owed to him by her was lower than would otherwise have been the case.

In *The Insurance Commissioner* v. *Joyce* ((1948) 77 C.L.R. 39, 56–60), Dixon J. stated persuasively the view that there is, or may be, a "particular relation" between the driver of a vehicle and his passenger resulting in a variation of the standard of duty owed by the driver. He said (at p. 56): "The case of a passenger in a car differs from that of a pedestrian not in the kind or degree of danger which may come from any want of care or skill in driving but in the fact that the former has come into a more particular relation with the driver of the car. It is because that relation may vary that the standard of duty or of care is not necessarily the same in every case . . . the gratuitous passenger may expect prima facie the same care and skill on the part of the driver as is ordinarily demanded in the management of a car. Unusual conditions may exist which are apparent to him or of which he may be informed and they may affect the application of the standard of care that is due. If a man accepts a lift from a car driver whom he knows to have lost a limb or an eye or to be deaf, he cannot complain if he does not exhibit the skill and competence of a driver who suffers from no defect." He summarised the same principle in these words (at p. 59): "It appears to me that the circumstances in which the defendant accepts the plaintiff as a passenger and in which the plaintiff accepts the accommodation in the conveyance should determine the measure of duty . . . " Theoretically, the principle as thus expounded is attractive. But, with very great respect, I venture to think that the theoretical attraction should yield to practical considerations.

As I see it, if this doctrine of varying standards were to be accepted as part of the law on these facts, it could not logically be confined to the duty of care owed by learner drivers. There is no reason in logic why it should not operate in a much wider sphere. The disadvantages of the resulting unpredictability, uncertainty and, indeed, impossibility of arriving at fair and consistent decisions outweigh the advantages. The certainty of a general standard is preferable to the vagaries of a fluctuating standard.

As a first example of what is involved, consider the converse case: the standard of care (including skill) owed, not by the driver to the passenger, but by the passenger instructor to the learner driver. Surely the same principle of varying standards, if it is a good principle, must be available also to the instructor, if he is sued by the driver for alleged breach of the duty of care in supervising the learner driver. On this doctrine, the standard of care, or skill, owed by the instructor, vis-à-vis the driver, may vary according to the knowledge which the learner driver had, at some moment of time, as to the skill and experience of the particular instructor. Indeed, if logic is to prevail, it would not necessarily be the knowledge of the driver which would be the criterion. It would be the expectation which the driver reasonably entertained of the instructor's skill and experience, if that reasonable expectation were greater than the actuality. Thus, if the learner driver knew that the instructor had never tried his hand previously even at amateur instructing, or if, as may be the present case, the driver knew that the instructor's experience was confined to two cases of amateur instructing some years previously, there would, under this doctrine, surely be a lower standard than if the driver knew or reasonably supposed that the instructor was a professional or that he had had substantial experience in the recent past. But what that standard would be, and how it would or should be assessed, I know not. For one has thus cut oneself adrift from the standard of the competent and experienced instructor, which up to now the law has acquired without regard to the particular personal skill, experience, physical characteristics or temperament of the individual instructor, and without regard to a third party's knowledge or assessment of those qualities or characteristics.

Again, when one considers the requisite standard of care of the learner driver, if this doctrine were to apply, would not logic irresistibly demand that there should be something more than a mere single, conventional, standard applicable to anyone who falls into the category of learner driver: that is, of anyone who has not yet qualified for (or perhaps obtained) a full licence? That standard itself would necessarily vary over a wide range, not merely with the actual progress of the learner, but also with the passenger's knowledge of that progress: or, rather, if the passenger has in fact over-estimated the driver's progress, it would vary with the passenger's reasonable assessment of that progress at the relevant time. The relevant time would not necessarily be the moment of the accident.

The question, what is the relevant time, would itself have to be resolved by reference to some principle. The instructor's reasonable assessment of the skill and competence of the driver (and also the driver's assessment of the instructor's skill and competence) might alter drastically between the start of the first lesson and the start of a later lesson, or even in the course of one particular spell of driving. I suppose the principle would have to be that the relevant time is the last moment when the plaintiff (whether instructor or driver) could reasonably have refused to continue as passenger or driver in the light of his then knowledge. That factor in itself would introduce yet another element of difficulty, uncertainty and, I believe, serious anomaly.

I, for my part, with all respect, do not think that our legal process could successfully or satisfactorily cope with the task of fairly assessing or applying to the facts of a particular case such varying standards, depending on such complex and elusive factors, including the assessment by the court, not merely of a particular person's actual skill or experience, but also of another person's knowledge or assessment of that skill or experience at a particular moment of time.

Again, if the principle of varying standards is to be accepted, why should it operate, in the field of driving motor vehicles, only up to the stage of the driver qualifying for a full licence? And why should it be limited to the quality of inexperience? If the passenger knows that his driver suffers from some relevant defect, physical or temperamental, which could reasonably be expected to affect the quality of his driving, why should not the same doctrine of varying standards apply? Dixon J. thought it should apply. Logically there can be no distinction. If the passenger knows that his driver, though holding a full driving licence, is blind in one eye or has the habit of taking corners too fast, and if an accident happens which is attributable wholly or partly to that physical or that temperamental defect, why should not some lower standard apply, vis-à-vis the fully informed passenger, if standards are to vary?

Why should the doctrine, if it be part of the law, be limited to cases involving the driving of motor cars? Suppose that to the knowledge of the patient a young surgeon, whom the patient has chosen to operate on him, has only just qualified. If the operation goes wrong because of the surgeon's inexperience, is there a defence on the basis that the standard of skill and care is lower than the standard of a competent and experienced surgeon? Does the young newly qualified solicitor owe a lower standard of skill and care when the client chooses to instruct him with the knowledge of his experience?

True, these last two examples may fall within the sphere of contract; and a contract may have express terms which deal with the question, or it may have implied terms. But in relationships such as are involved in this case, I see no good reason why a different term should be implied where there is a contract from the term which the law should attach where there is, or may be, no contract. Of course, there may be a difference—not because of any technical distinction between cases which fall within the law of tort and those which fall within the law of contract—but because the very factor or factors which create the contractual relationship may be relevant to the question of the implication of terms. Thus, if it is a contract because of consideration consisting of the promise of payment, that very fact may be relevant. I do not say that it is relevant. I do say that it may be relevant. Or the amount or the circumstances of the payment may be relevant. That is not a question which arises here, and I think that it would be unwise to consider it hypothetically.

In my judgment, in cases such as the present it is preferable that there should be a reasonably certain and reasonably ascertainable standard of care, even if on occasion that may appear to work hardly against an inexperienced driver or his insurers. The standard of care required by the law is the standard of the competent and experienced driver: and this is so, as defining the driver's duty towards a passenger who knows of his inexperience, as much as towards a member of the public outside the car; and as much in civil as in criminal proceedings.

It is not a valid argument against such a principle that it attributes tortious liability to one who may not be morally blameworthy. For tortious liability has in many cases ceased to be based on moral blameworthiness. For example, there is no doubt whatever that if Mrs. Weston had knocked down a pedestrian on the pavement when the accident occurred, she would have been liable to the pedestrian. Yet so far as any moral blame is concerned, no different considerations would apply in respect of the pedestrian from those which apply in respect of Mr. Nettleship.

In criminal law also, the inexperience of the driver is wholly irrelevant. In the phrase commonly used in directions to juries in charges of causing death by dangerous driving, the driver may be guilty even though the jury think that he was "doing his incompetent best": see *Reg.* v. *Evans* ([1963] 1 Q.B. 412, 418) and *Reg.* v. *Scammell* ((1967) 51 Cr.App.R. 398). There can be no doubt that in criminal law, further, it is no answer to a charge of driving without due care and attention that the driver was inexperienced or lacking in skill: see *McCrone* v. *Riding* ([1938] 1 All E.R. 157). In the present case, indeed, there was a conviction for that offence.

If the criminal law demands of an inexperienced driver the standard of care and competence of an experienced driver, why should it be wrong or unjust or impolitic for the civil law to require that standard, even vis-à-vis an injured passenger who knew of the driver's inexperience?

Different considerations may, indeed, exist when a passenger has accepted a lift from a driver whom the passenger knows to be likely, through drink or drugs, to drive unsafely. There may in such cases sometimes be an element of aiding and abetting a criminal offence; or, if the facts fall short of aiding and abetting, the passenger's mere assent to benefit from the commission of a criminal offence may involve questions of *turpis causa*. For myself, with great respect, I doubt the correctness on its facts of the decision in *Dann* v. *Hamilton* ([1939] 1 K.B. 509). But the present case involves no such problem . . .

Questions

1. Suppose that the lessons had been given in the plaintiff's car and he sued in respect of damage suffered by it. Same result?

2. Would the result have been the same if the means of harm had been a motorised lawn-mower in the use of which the plaintiff was giving the defendant instruction on the defendant's premises? Suppose Albert was teaching Bella how to play Frisbee in a public park and, owing to her lack of deftness, he is struck in the eye by it.

3. Why must learner drivers carry visible "L" plates on the car?

4. Personal factors, irrelevant to criminal guilt, may be taken into account in sentencing. If personal factors are made irrelevant to civil liability, can or should they be taken into account in assessing damages? Were they taken into account in this case?

5. What is the duty of a driving examiner? And what is the duty of the candidate towards him? The answers are in a case involving a collision between two candidates: *British School of Motoring* v. *Simms* [1971] 1 All E.R. 317.

Note:

One's only purpose in asking whether a driver's duty is to do his best or to do as well as others do is to find out whether his actual driving constituted a breach of duty, the subject-matter of the next chapter.

Take *Roberts* v. *Ramsbottom*, for example ([1980] 1 All E.R. 7). One morning a 73-year old accountant was about to drive his wife to the office some 2 1/2 miles away when he suffered a quite unheralded stroke which impaired his consciousness considerably. He forgot all about his wife and drove off. He managed to negotiate a few corners but then struck a parked van. He told the van-driver he felt all right and continued his progress. Next he knocked a boy off his bike and finally rammed the plaintiff's stationary car and injured the family by it. He was held liable despite his curious condition since it fell short of automatism and complete loss of consciousness, and because after striking the van he should have realised (though he could not) that he was unfit to continue driving. "An impairment of judgment does not provide a defence." In *Waugh* v. *James K. Allen* ((1964) S.L.T. 269 (H.L.)) by contrast, the man at the wheel could not be said to be driving at all, as he had suffered a total black-out, and he was not liable for remaining at the wheel since there was no premonition of the heart-attack.

CHAPTER 2

BREACH

Section 1.—Specific or General?

QUALCAST (WOLVERHAMPTON) LTD. v. HAYNES

House of Lords [1959] A.C. 743; [1959] 2 W.L.R. 510; 103 S.J. 310; [1959] 2 All E.R. 38

Action by employee against employer in respect of personal injury.

The plaintiff was an experienced metal moulder, employed by the defendants; he burnt his left foot when the ladle of molten metal he was holding slipped from his grasp. He was wearing ordinary leather boots at the time. His employers had a stock of protective spats for the asking and of reinforced boots at a price, but they had never urged the plaintiff to wear them. The county court judge felt bound by authority to hold that the employers were under a duty to urge the plaintiff to wear protective clothing, and gave judgment for the plaintiff, subject to 75 per cent. contributory negligence. He also said: "I think he knew of all the risks involved and quite voluntarily decided to wear the boots which he was wearing, and I believe that since the accident and since his return to work as a moulder he has not worn any protective clothing."

The Court of Appeal affirmed the judgment for the plaintiff [1958] 1 W.L.R. 225. The defendants appealed to the House of Lords, and their appeal was allowed.

LORD SOMERVELL OF HARROW: My Lords, I also would allow the appeal. In the present case the county court judge, after having found the facts, had to decide whether there was, in relation to this plaintiff, a failure by the defendants to take reasonable care for his safety. It is, I think, clear from the passage cited by my noble and learned friend that he would have found for the defendants but for some principle laid down, as he thought, by the authorities, to which he referred.

I hope it may be worth while to make one or two general observations on the effect on the precedent system of the virtual abolition of juries in negligence actions. Whether a duty of reasonable care is owed by A to B is a question of law. In a special relationship such as that of employer to employee the law may go further and define the heads and scope of the duty. There are cases in your Lordships' House which have covered this ground, I would have thought by now, exhaustively (*Wilson's and Clyde Coal Co. Ltd. v. English* ([1938] A.C. 57); *Latimer v. A.E.C. Ltd.* ([1953] A.C. 643); *General Cleaning Contractors Ltd. v. Christmas* [below p. 104] and there are, of course, others). There would seem to be little, if anything, that can be added to the law. Its application in borderline cases may, of course, still come before appellate tribunals. When negligence cases were tried with juries the judge would direct them as to the law as above. The question whether on the facts in that particular case there was or was not a failure to take reasonable care was a question for the jury. There was not, and could not be, complete uniformity of standard. One jury would attribute to the reasonable man a greater degree of prescience than would another. The jury's decision did not become part of our law citable as a precedent. In those days it would only be in very exceptional circumstances that a judge's direction would be reported or be citable. So far as the law is concerned they would all be the same. Now that negligence

101

cases are mostly tried without juries, the distinction between the functions of judge and jury is blurred. A judge naturally gives reasons for the conclusion formerly arrived at by a jury without reasons. It may sometimes be difficult to draw the line, but if the reasons given by a judge for arriving at the conclusion previously reached by a jury are to be treated as "law" and citable, the precedent system will die from a surfeit of authorities. In *Woods* v. *Durable Suites Ltd.* ([1953] 1 W.L.R. 857) counsel for the plaintiff was seeking to rely on a previous decision in a negligence action. Singleton L.J. said this: "That was a case of the same nature as that which is now under appeal. It is of the greatest importance that it should be borne in mind that though the nature of the illness and the nature of the work are the same, the facts were quite different. Mr. Doughty claims that the decision of this court in *Clifford* v. *Charles H. Challen & Son Ltd.* ([1951] 1 K.B. 495) lays down a standard to be adopted in a case of this nature. In other words, he seeks to treat that decision as deciding a question of law rather than as being a decision on the facts of that particular case."

In the present case, and I am not criticising him, the learned county court judge felt himself bound by certain observations in different cases which were not, I think, probably intended by the learned judges to enunciate any new principles or gloss on the familiar standard of reasonable care. It must be a question on the evidence in each case whether, assuming a duty to provide some safety equipment, there is a duty to advise everyone, whether experienced or inexperienced, as to its use. . . .

I have come to the conclusion that the learned judge's first impulse was the right conclusion on the facts as he found them, and for the reasons which he gives. I will not elaborate these reasons or someone might cite my observations as part of the law of negligence.

LORD DENNING: My Lords, in 1944 du Parcq L.J. gave a warning which is worth repeating today: "There is danger, particularly in these days when few cases are tried with juries, of exalting to the status of propositions of law what really are particular applications to special facts of propositions of ordinary good sense"; see *Easson* v. *London & North Eastern Railway Co.* ([1944] K.B. 421, 426).

In the present case the only proposition of law that was relevant was the well-known proposition—with its threefold sub-division—that it is the duty of a master to take reasonable care for the safety of his workmen. No question arose on that proposition. The question that did arise was this: What did reasonable care demand of the employers in this particular case? That is not a question of law at all but a question of fact. To solve it the tribunal of fact—be it judge or jury—can take into account any proposition of good sense that is relevant in the circumstances, but it must beware not to treat it as a proposition of law. I may perhaps draw an analogy from the Highway Code. It contains many propositions of good sense which may be taken into account in considering whether reasonable care has been taken, but it would be a mistake to elevate them into propositions of law.

Applying this to the present case: You start with the fact that, when a moulder in an iron foundry carries a ladle full of hot molten metal and pours it into the moulding box, there is a danger that the hot metal may splash over onto his feet. In order to safeguard him from injury, the employers ought, I should have thought, to provide protective footwear for him. But in saying so, I speak as a juryman, for it is not a proposition of law at all, but only a proposition of good sense. If the employers fail to provide protective footwear, the tribunal of fact can take it into account in deciding whether the employers took reasonable care for the safety of their men.

But the question here is not whether the employers ought to provide protective footwear for the men—for they clearly did so. The question is whether, having provided spats and boots, they ought to go further and *urge* the men to wear them. Here too I should have thought that the employers ought to advise and encourage the men to wear protective footwear. But again I speak as a juryman and not as a judge: because it is not a proposition of law at all, but a proposition of good sense. And that is the very point where the county court judge fell into error. He treated it as matter of strict law. He thought that, as this man "was never told that they must be worn," he was *bound by authority* to find that the employers were negligent. He treated it almost as on a par with a statutory regulation: whereas it was nothing of the kind. The distinction was taken by Lord Wright twenty-five years ago: "Whereas at the ordinary law the standard of duty must be fixed by the verdict of a jury, the statutory duty is conclusively fixed by the statute"; see *Lochgelly Iron & Coal Co. Ltd.* v. *M'Mullan* ([1934] A.C. 1). So here, this being a case governed by the common law and not by any statute or regulation, the standard of care must be fixed by the judge as if he were a jury, without being rigidly bound by authorities. What is "a proper system of work" is a matter for evidence, not for law books. It changes as the conditions of work change. The standard goes up as men become wiser. It does not stand still as the law sometimes does.

I can well see how it came about that the county court judge made this mistake. He was presented with a number of cases in which judges of the High Court had given reasons for coming to their conclusions of fact. And those reasons seemed to him to be so expressed as to be rulings in point of law: whereas they were in truth nothing more than propositions of good sense. This is not the first time this sort of thing has happened. Take accidents on the road. I remember well that in several cases Scrutton L.J. said that "if a person rides in the dark he must ride at such a pace that he can pull up within the limits of his vision" (*Baker* v. *E. Longhurst & Sons Ltd.* ([1933] 2 K.B. 461, 468)). That was treated as a proposition of law until the Court of Appeal firmly ruled that it was not (*Tidy* v. *Battman* ([1934] 1 K.B. 319); *Morris* v. *Luton Corporation* ([1946] K.B. 114)). So also with accidents in factories. I myself once said that an employer must, by his foreman, "do his best to keep [the men] up to the mark" (*Clifford* v. *Charles H. Challen & Son Ltd.* ([1951] 1 K.B. 495)). Someone shortly afterwards sought to treat me as having laid down a new proposition of law, but the Court of Appeal, I am glad to say, corrected the error (*Woods* v. *Durable Suites Ltd.* ([1953] 1 W.L.R. 857)). Such cases all serve to bear out the warning which has been given in this House before. " . . . we ought to beware of allowing tests or guides which have been suggested by the court in one set of circumstances, or in one class of cases, to be applied to other surroundings," and thus by degrees to turn that which is at bottom a question of fact into a proposition of law. That is what happened in the cases under the Workmen's Compensation Act and it led to a "wagon-load of cases"; see *Harris* v. *Associated Portland Cement Manufacturers Ltd.* ([1939] A.C. 71, 78) by Lord Atkin. Let not the same thing happen to the common law, lest we be crushed under the weight of our own reports.

Seeing, then, that the county court judge fell into error, what should the Court of Appeal have done? The answer seems to me this: the Court of Appeal should have done as the judge would have done if he had not felt bound by authority. He would have found that the employers had not been guilty of negligence. . . . In this case I would not myself be prepared to differ from the judge's view that there was no negligence on the part of the employers in regard to this particular workman. He knew all there was to know, without being told; and he voluntarily decided to wear his own boots, which he had bought for the purpose.

Only one word more. It is on causation. Even if it had been the duty of the employers to urge this workman to wear spats, I do not think their omission should be taken to be one of the causes of the accident. It is often said that a person who omits to do his duty "cannot be heard to say" that it would have made no difference even if he had done it: see *Roberts* v. *Dorman Long & Co. Ltd.* ([1953] 1 W.L.R. 942, 946). But this is an overstatement. The judge *may* infer the omission to be a cause, but he is not bound to do so. If, at the end of the day, he thinks that, whether the duty was omitted or fulfilled, the result would have been the same, he is at liberty to say so. So here, this workman, after he recovered from the injury, went back to work and did the same as before. He never wore spats. If the warning given by the accident made no difference, we may safely infer that no advice beforehand would have had any effect.

I would allow the appeal.

Question

If this case says, as it seems to, that all fact situations are as a matter of law distinguishable, what becomes of the principle of *stare decisis,* if that principle is based on the view that like cases should be treated alike?

Note:

This simple case has two important effects. Its first effect is to emphasise that the proper form of question, when one is dealing with breach of duty, is "Did the defendant take reasonable care?" One must not pick on some feature of the defendant's acts and say: "Was he under a duty not to do that?" (see also *A. C. Billings & Sons* v. *Riden* [1958] A.C. 240, 264, *per* Lord Somervell of Harrow). Of course, the plaintiff must normally identify what it was in the defendant's behaviour that he finds objectionable—*e.g.,* that he omitted to give a signal before turning right on the highway. But the question remains "Did the defendant drive with reasonable care, considering that he gave no signal?" and does not become "Was the defendant under a duty to give a signal?" Matters of detail are to be treated as part of the question of breach, not as raising sub-duties with a specific content.

The second effect is to deter counsel from citing decisions on breach as authority for subsequent cases. For the student, this means that he ought not to seek out cases on the principle used by the housewife in the haberdashery to find a matching thread; if he wants to, there is nothing better than Bingham, *The Modern Cases on Negligence* (3rd ed., 1978). He should, however, exercise his judgment as if he were twelve other people; but he may well have to read a lot of cases in order to gain vicariously the experience which lies at the root of sound judgment. Despite the best efforts of higher courts, however, counsel (who are paid by the day) continue to cite enormous numbers of cases (see *Lambert* v. *Lewis* [1982] A.C. 225), and county court judges (who are paid to use their judgment) continue to apply decisions on breach as if they were cases which laid down rules to be applied (*Worsfold* v. *Howe* [1980] 1 All E.R. 1028—"inching forward into traffic isn't negligence").

The puzzling distinction between questions of fact and questions of law used to be important in two principal connections. The first was that questions of law belonged to the judge and questions of fact to the jury; the jury has now virtually disappeared in actions for negligence. The second was that no appeal lay from the answer given by a county court judge to a question of fact; the County Courts Act 1959, s.109, now allows such an appeal where the damage exceeds £200.

GENERAL CLEANING CONTRACTORS LTD. v. CHRISTMAS

House of Lords [1953] A.C. 180; [1953] 2 W.L.R. 6; 97 S.J. 7; [1952] 2 All E.R. 1110; 51 L.G.R. 109

Action by employee against employer in respect of personal injury.

The plaintiff was cleaning the library windows of the Caledonian Club on the instructions of his employers for whom he had worked for twenty years. After cleaning the inside, he went outside on to the sill, which was 6¼ inches wide and 27 feet above the ground. He cleaned the outside top sash and pushed it up, leaving the bottom sash slightly open so as to afford himself a grip on the underside of the top sash. Then the bottom sash suddenly fell as such sashes were known to do; it dislodged the plaintiff's fingers and caused him to fall.

He sued both the occupiers and his employers, and succeeded against both at first instance [1951] W.N. 294. The Court of Appeal reversed the decision against the Club (and there was no appeal against that reversal), but affirmed the judgment against the employers [1952] 1 K.B. 141. The employers appealed to the House of Lords, and their appeal was dismissed.

LORD REID: My Lords, it appears that it has for long been the general practice of window cleaners to clean the outsides of ordinary two-sash windows while standing on the window sill outside the window. When the sill is narrow, as it often is, the window cleaner must have something to hold on to, and it is unusual for there to be anything for the cleaner to grasp except part of the window itself. If the window is completely closed there is nothing to grasp, but if either the top or bottom sash is even slightly open there is room for the cleaner to insert his fingers between the wooden bar which forms the bottom of the top sash and the panes of glass in the lower sash. It might seem that, even with this hold, the cleaner's position is precarious and unsafe, but the evidence in this case is not to that effect. A window cleaner with this hold does not appear to be in greater danger than men who work in many other trades in exposed places high above the ground with apparently little to assist them to keep their balance. But a peculiar danger in window cleaning arises from the fact that sometimes a sash moves down unexpectedly so as to deprive the man of his hold, and the evidence shows that it is not very uncommon for this to happen and to cause a serious accident. The respondent in this case was severely injured by an accident of this kind.

The main case made for the respondent in his pleadings and at the trial was that this method of cleaning windows is in itself so unsafe that a master who requires his servants to adopt it is in breach of his duty to provide a safe system of working. Two other methods of doing this kind of work were advocated. In the first place it was said that it could be done by men standing on ladders. It was proved that it would have been practicable and reasonably safe to use this method to clean the outside of the window where this accident happened: this window was on the first floor. But there was no evidence about the general applicability of this method, and it seems fairly obvious that it would not be practicable in a large number of cases. The main objection to using it where it is practicable is that it takes longer and is more expensive to clean windows in this way than by standing on the sill. The other method advocated is to support the man on the sill by a safety belt. Such a belt must be attached to two hooks—one on either side of the window—and these hooks must be firmly attached to the building so as to support his whole weight if he slips. It was not disputed that, to get sufficient strength, the shaft of the hook must be driven right through the wall of the building from the outside and then anchored in some way on the inside of the wall. No evidence was led about the cost or difficulty of doing this, but it is plainly an operation which could not be carried out by a window cleaner, and, if this is to be the only alternative to using ladders, I think that I must assume that vast numbers of these hooks would be needed: the evidence shows that such hooks have only been provided in a very small proportion of existing buildings. The evidence is that even where hooks are available the men generally do not use them.

A plaintiff who seeks to have condemned as unsafe a system of work which has been generally used for a long time in an important trade undertakes a heavy onus: if he is right it means that all, or practically all, the numerous employers in the trade have been habitually neglecting their duty to their men. The evidence in this case appears to me to be quite inadequate to establish either that the window sill method is so inherently dangerous that it cannot be made reasonably safe by taking proper precautions, or that the ladder method or the safety belt method are as a general rule reasonably practicable alternatives.

That brings me to what I have found to be the most difficult part of the case. The evidence does prove that the window sill method is often dangerous if no precautions are taken, and in this case no precautions were taken; and if the respondent is to succeed it must, I think, be on the ground that it was the duty of the appellants to devise for the window sill method a proper system of precautions and instruct their servants to follow that system, and that, if they had done so and their orders had been obeyed, this accident would, or at least would probably, have been prevented. No such case is made in the pleadings and no attempt was made to prove it at the trial. The best that can be said is that the pleadings can perhaps be read so as not to exclude it, and there are a number of bits of evidence which, if eked out with common knowledge, lend support to it. I would not think it proper or fair to the appellants to consider this case were it not for the fact that the appellants' counsel in effect asked us to treat the case as a test case and enlighten employers in the trade as to their duty. In the circumstances I think that I can properly consider this case on such evidence as there is to support it.

The need to provide against the danger of a sash moving unexpectedly appears to me to be so obvious that, even if it were proved that it is the general practice to neglect this danger, I would hold that it ought not to be neglected and that precautions should be taken. It is at this point that lack of evidence causes difficulty, for there is no evidence as to what would be reasonably practicable or effective precautions. But I cannot believe that there would be any great difficulty in devising a simple method of preventing the lower sash from closing. I do not know what the best method would be. Generally the plaintiff ought to put forward some method which can be tested by evidence. But in this case I am assisted by the fact that the appellants in their defence allege negligence against the respondent " . . . (b) if he knew of the said defect, [the tendency of this window to move easily] in taking no or no adequate steps to wedge or secure the said window; (c) if he did not know of the said defect, in taking no or no adequate steps to ascertain whether it was safe to rely on the sashes of the said window for handhold." This is in line with the impression which I get from the evidence, that a simple test would show whether a sash is loose or not and that if it moved at all easily it could be wedged or something could be placed across the window sill which would prevent the sash from closing fully. It does appear from the evidence that very simple tests after the accident showed that this sash was loose and ran down very easily. I think that this ought to have been discovered before the accident, and I think that I am entitled to assume that if it had been discovered some simple and effective precaution could have been taken. But I must confess that even in this case I make this assumption with some reluctance in the absence of evidence and I would not be prepared to do so in a less clear case.

The question then is whether it is the duty of the appellants to instruct their servants what precautions they ought to take and to take reasonable steps to see that those instructions are carried out. On that matter the appellants say that their men are skilled men who are well aware of the dangers involved and as well able as the appellants to devise and take any necessary precautions. That may be so but, in my opinion, it is not a sufficient answer. Where the problem varies from job to job it may be reasonable to leave a great deal to the man in charge, but the danger in this case is one which is constantly found, and it calls for a system to meet it. Where a practice of ignoring an obvious danger has grown up I do not think that it is reasonable to expect an individual workman to take the initiative in devising and using precautions. It is the duty of the employer to consider the situation, to devise a suitable system, to instruct his men what they must do and to supply any implements that may be required such as, in this case, wedges or objects to be put on the window sill to prevent the window from closing. No doubt he cannot be certain that his men will do as they are told when they are working alone. But if he does all that is reasonable to ensure that his safety system is operated he will have done what he is bound to do. In this case the appellants do not appear to have done anything as they thought they were entitled to leave the taking of precautions to the discretion of each of their men. In this I think that they were in fault, and I think that this accident need not have happened if the appellants had done as I hold they ought to have done. I therefore agree that the appeal should be dismissed.

Question
If the plaintiff had been employed cleaning windows for twenty years, did he or his employer know more about the risks of cleaning windows?

Note:

Here we have the backside of the point made in *Qualcast* v. *Haynes* (above, p. 101). The employers wanted to be told authoritatively exactly what they must do to comply with the requirement of the common law that they take reasonable care of their employees. They didn't learn much from their appeal to the House of Lords; they were told that they must do what was reasonable; and they knew that before.

This illustrates something about the common law of torts. It says after the event whether something was done badly or not; it does not give instructions about how to act well. That is for the legislature to do; and we shall see shortly (below, p. 163) how the judges react when the legislature has done so.

In the Court of Appeal [1952] 1 K.B. 141, 149, Denning L.J. said: "If employers employ men on this dangerous work for their own profit, they must take proper steps to protect them, even if they are expensive. If they cannot afford to provide adequate safeguards, then they should not ask them to do it at all. It is not worth the risk." Is it worth the risk that, in a country without full employment, the employee's family should have a weekly pay packet rather than unemployment benefit only? An employee has even brought an action against an employer on the ground that it was careless of the employer to give the employee a job she had asked for. The action failed only on appeal (*Withers* v. *Perry Chain Co.* [1961] 1 W.L.R. 1314). In Scotland a man with no sight in one eye and defective vision in the other has successfully alleged that his employer was negligent in letting him do outside work (*Porteous* v. *National Coal Board*, 1967 S.L.T. 117).

Contrast the attitude of Lord Bramwell, whose sense of the dignity of man, as expressed through his will, made him decline to save man from himself: "It is a rule of good sense that if a man voluntarily undertakes a risk for a reward which is adequate to induce him, he shall not, if he suffers from the risk, have a compensation for which he did not stipulate. He can, if he chooses, say, 'I will undertake the risk for so much, and if hurt, you must give me so much more, or an equivalent for the hurt.' But drop the maxim [sc. *volenti non fit injuria*]. Treat it as a question of bargain. The plaintiff here thought the pay worth the risk, and did not bargain for a compensation if hurt. . . . Suppose he had said, 'If I am to run this risk, you must give me 6s. a day and not 5s.' and the master agreed, would he in reason have a claim if he got hurt? Clearly not. What difference is there if the master says, 'No; I will only give the 5s.'? None. I am ashamed to argue it." *Smith* v. *Baker* [1891] A.C. 325, 344. In the same speech Lord Bramwell welcomed the idea of compensation from the state. That now exists, and it should not be forgotten.

Note that the occupier of the premises which had the defective window-sash was held not liable. This result is now endorsed by Occupiers' Liability Act 1957, s.2(3)(*b*), (below, p. 114).

Both the previous cases have been concerned with the question whether the defendant's conduct was reasonable. There are two types of case in which attention may be diverted from this question, which is the right one. In cases of misrepresentation, there is a tendency to concentrate on whether the statement was right or wrong, not on whether it was wrong of the defendant to make it. And in cases of defective products, attention may be focussed on the question whether they were faulty rather than whether the defendant's conduct was. *Junior Books* makes this risk particularly clear.

Section 2.—What is Reasonable?

BOLTON v. STONE

House of Lords [1951] A.C. 850; [1951] 1 T.L.R. 977; [1951] 1 All E.R. 1078; 50 L.G.R. 32; 95 S.J. 333

Action by pedestrian against occupier of land adjoining the highway in respect of personal injury.

On August 9, 1947, Miss Stone was standing on the highway outside her home and was struck by a cricket ball hit by a visiting batsman from the grounds of the Cheetham Cricket Club which adjoined the highway. She sued the committee and members of the Club, not including the batsman in question.

The ground had been used for cricket since 1864, long before the surrounding houses were built. Balls were only rarely hit over the fence during a match, and committee members could not recall an accident. A nearer neighbour said that balls had been hit into his yard. This particular ball had travelled seventy-eight yards before passing over the fence (the top of which was seven feet above the highway and seventeen feet above the pitch) and about twenty-five yards further before striking Miss Stone.

The plaintiff claimed damages on the ground of negligence and nuisance. The particulars of negligence alleged were that the defendants "(a) pitched the cricket pitch too near to the said road; (b) failed to erect a . . . fence . . . of sufficient height to prevent balls being struck into the said road; (c) failed to ensure that cricket balls would not be hit into the said road."

Oliver J. gave judgment for the defendants [1949] 1 All E.R. 237. The Court of Appeal, by a majority, allowed the plaintiff's appeal, on the grounds that the defendants were guilty of negligence [1950] 1 K.B. 201. The defendants' appeal to the House of Lords was allowed.

LORD RADCLIFFE: My Lords, I agree that this appeal must be allowed. I agree with regret, because I have much sympathy with the decision that commended itself to the majority of the members of the Court of Appeal. I can see nothing unfair in the appellants being required to compensate the respondent for the serious injury that she has received as a result of the sport that they have organised on their cricket ground at Cheetham Hill. But the law of negligence is concerned less with what is fair than with what is culpable, and I cannot persuade myself that the appellants have been guilty of any culpable act or omission in this case.

I think that the case is in some respects a peculiar one, not easily related to the general rules that govern liability for negligence. If the test whether there has been a breach of duty were to depend merely on the answer to the question whether this accident was a reasonably foreseeable risk, I think that there would have been a breach of duty, for that such an accident might take place some time or other might very reasonably have been present to the minds of the appellants. It was quite foreseeable, and there would have been nothing unreasonable in allowing the imagination to dwell on the possibility of its occurring. But there was only a remote, perhaps I ought to say only a very remote, chance of the accident taking place at any particular time, for, if it was to happen, not only had a ball to carry the fence round the ground but it had also to coincide in its arrival with the presence of some person on what does not look like a crowded thoroughfare and actually to strike that person in some way that would cause sensible injury.

Those being the facts, a breach of duty has taken place if they show the appellants guilty of a failure to take reasonable care to prevent the accident. One may phrase it as "reasonable care" or "ordinary care" or "proper care"—all these phrases are to be found in decisions of authority—but the fact remains that, unless there has been something which a reasonable man would blame as falling beneath the standard of conduct that he would set for himself and require of his neighbour, there has been no breach of legal duty. And here, I think, the respondent's case breaks down. It seems to me that a reasonable man, taking account of the chances against an accident happening, would not have felt himself called upon either to abandon the use of the ground for cricket or to increase the height of his surrounding fences. He would have done what the appellants did: in other words, he would have done nothing. Whether, if the unlikely event of an accident did occur and his play turn to another's hurt, he would have thought it equally proper to offer no more consolation to his victim than the reflection that a social being is not immune from social risks, I do not say, for I do not think that that is a consideration which is relevant to legal liability.

I agree with the others of your Lordships that if the respondent cannot succeed in negligence she cannot succeed on any other head of claim.

Questions
    1. Would the defendants be liable if a similar accident occurred today?

2. Would the result have been the same if Miss Stone had been sitting in her garden at the time the ball struck her?

3. Suppose that the ball had been struck during practice at the nets rather than during a match. Same result?

4. Suppose that Miss Stone had been (a) a spectator or (b) the tea-lady in the pavilion. In what terms would one decide her suit against (a) the cricket club and (b) the batsman? (See *Wooldridge* v. *Sumner*, above, p. 91).

Note:

The reason for selecting this speech (rather than Lord Reid's, for example) is that Viscount Radcliffe makes it quite clear that the ultimate and vital question is "Was the conduct unreasonable?" and not "Was the harm foreseeable?" Of course if behaviour is apparently innocuous, *i.e.*, such that no one would foresee any harm resulting from it, and unpredictably does cause some freak damage, we would not make the defendant pay. If behaviour is dangerous, on the other hand, *i.e.* such that one could foresee harm resulting from it, we are tempted to castigate it. But it is not *all* dangerous conduct which renders a person liable, it is only *unreasonably* dangerous conduct, conduct which, in the light (*inter alia*) of the recognisable danger, is *unreasonable*.

Sixteen years later Lord Reid was still in some perplexity over this case. In *The Wagon Mound* (*No.* 2) [1967] 1 A.C. 617, he said this:

"*Bolton* v. *Stone* posed a new problem. There a member of a visiting team drove a cricket ball out of the ground on to an unfrequented adjacent public road and it struck and severely injured a lady who happened to be standing in the road. That it might happen that a ball would be driven on to this road could not have been said to be a fantastic or far-fetched possibility: according to the evidence it had happened about six times in twenty-eight years. Moreover it could not have been said to be a far-fetched or fantastic possibility that such a ball would strike someone in the road: people did pass along the road from time to time. So it could not have been said that, on any ordinary meaning of the words, the fact that a ball might strike a person in the road was not foreseeable or reasonably foreseeable. It was plainly foreseeable; but the chance of its happening in the foreseeable future was infinitesimal. A mathematician given the data could have worked out that it was only likely to happen once in so many thousand years. The House of Lords held that the risk was so small that in the circumstances a reasonable man would have been justified in disregarding it and taking no steps to eliminate it.

It does not follow that, no matter what the circumstances may be, it is justifiable to neglect a risk of such a small magnitude. A reasonable man would only neglect such a risk if he had some valid reason for doing so: *e.g.*, that it would involve considerable expense to eliminate the risk. He would weigh the risk against the difficulty of eliminating it. If the activity which caused the injury to Miss Stone had been an unlawful activity there can be little doubt but that *Bolton* v. *Stone* would have been decided differently. In their lordships' judgment *Bolton* v. *Stone* did not alter the general principle that a person must be regarded as negligent if he does not take steps to eliminate a risk which he knows or ought to know is a real risk and not a mere possibility which would never influence the mind of a reasonable man. What that decision did was to recognise and give effect to the qualification that it is justifiable not to take steps to eliminate a real risk if it is small and if the circumstances are such that a reasonable man, careful of the safety of his neighbour, would think it right to neglect it.

In the present case there was no justification whatever for discharging the oil into Sydney Harbour. Not only was it an offence to do so, but also it involved considerable loss financially. If the ship's engineer had thought about the matter there could have been no question of balancing the advantages and disadvantages. From every point of view it was both his duty and his interest to stop the discharge immediately."

Cricket has given more trouble recently. In *Miller* v. *Jackson* [1977] Q.B. 966 a couple who had bought a new house on the edge of a small village cricket ground sought to have the cricket stopped and claimed damages. Contrast the views of Lord Denning M.R. and Geoffrey Lane L.J.:

LORD DENNING M.R.: "The club were entitled to use this ground for cricket in the accustomed way. It was not a nuisance, nor was it negligence of them so to run it. Nor was the batsman negligent when he hit the ball for six. All were doing simply what they were entitled to do. So if the club had put it to the test, I would have dismissed the claim for damages also."

GEOFFREY LANE L.J.: "The evidence . . . makes it clear that the risk of injury to property at least was both foreseeable and foreseen. It is obvious that such injury is going to take place so long as cricket is being played on this field. It is the duty of the cricketers so to conduct their operations as not to harm people they can or ought reasonably to foresee may be affected . . . The risk of injury to persons and property is so great that on each occasion when a ball comes over the fence and causes damage to the plaintiffs, the defendants are guilty of negligence."

CUMMING-BRUCE L.J. agreed with Geoffrey Lane L.J. in holding the cricket club liable in damages for negligence, but agreed with Lord Denning that the cricket should be allowed to continue: "So on the facts of this case a court of equity must seek to strike a fair balance between the right of the plaintiffs to have quiet enjoyment of their house and garden without exposure to cricket balls occasionally falling like thunderbolts from the heavens, and the opportunity of the inhabitants of the village in which they live to continue to enjoy the manly sport which constitutes a summer recreation for adults and young persons . . . "

But can the common law of negligence itself not "seek to strike a fair balance"? Surely the test of what is reasonable in all the circumstances (unlike the question whether harm was foreseeable) is an apt one for the purpose. Safety first equal?

So important is it to see that the question here is "was the conduct unreasonable?" rather than "was the harm foreseeable?" that at the risk of labouring the point we cite a glaring example of judicial confusion. *Smith* v. *Blackburn* [1974] R.T.R. 533 involved a head-on collision. Since the plaintiff was driving impeccably and the defendant was driving like a madman, the only question was whether the plaintiff's damages should be reduced on the ground that his failure to wear a seat-belt constituted contributory negligence. The judge said this:

> "The accident happened in an unusual place, the Bushey Road Flyover. Here was a one-way road going up to a rise to a crest and along that road Mr. Smith was driving his car absolutely normally. He was doing nothing wrong at all, and yet it was really suggested that he should have foreseen that a madman would drive up the flyover in the wrong direction, travelling along a one-way street in the opposite direction to that which he should have been, and at high speed, so that when he did meet somebody minding his own business, they collided head on.
>
> To start with in my judgment the law does not require a person in the position of Mr. Smith in the place where he was to foresee that that kind of accident will occur. He may foresee that he may come upon a broken-down vehicle or all sorts of things, but I see no ground for assuming that the law required Mr. Smith to foresee that.
>
> If the law does not require him to foresee it, why should the law be said to require him to take precautions against the possible event?"

Even if the accident was unforeseeable by Mr. Smith it was unreasonable of him not be wearing a seat-belt: seat-belts are no trouble to put on and they do in fact reduce the incidence of serious injury, so reasonable people wear them. Whether Mr. Smith's injuries would actually have been reduced by a seat-belt is a quite different question, but pointing to the improbability of the collision which took place does not help us to answer it.

Take another case. A man was employed to stamp the initials "CA" on steel tyres. The way everyone does this is to hold the stamp and hit it firmly with a heavy hammer. One day, after many many days of doing this more than 100 times a day, the plaintiff mishit the stamp and broke his thumb. The judge held that the accident was foreseeable (which no one who has used a hammer could deny) and that *therefore* the employer was negligent. The Court of Appeal reversed, because the judge "did not ask the proper and right question". *Pindall* v. *British Steel Corp.* (March 7, 1980).

WATT v. HERTFORDSHIRE COUNTY COUNCIL

Court of Appeal [1954] 1 W.L.R. 835; 118 J.P. 377; 98 S.J. 372; [1954] 2 All E.R. 368; 52 L.G.R. 383

Action by employee against employer in respect of personal injury.

The plaintiff had for twelve years been a fireman at the Watford Fire Station. He was on duty on July 27, 1951, when an emergency call was received; a woman was trapped under a heavy vehicle only 200 or 300 yards away. The sub-officer in charge left the station immediately after giving instructions that the plaintiff's team should follow in a Fordson lorry and bring a large jack for lifting heavy weights. The jack, which stood on four small wheels and weighed two or three hundredweights, put on the back of the lorry, where the plaintiff with two others steadied it. There was no mechanical means of securing the jack, since the lorry had a smooth floor and there was nothing to which the jack could be lashed. The driver had to brake suddenly. The three men in the back were thrown off balance, and the jack slewed forward, catching the plaintiff's ankle and causing him serious injuries. The fire station normally had a vehicle suitable for carrying the jack safely, but it was not in the station at the time. When that vehicle was not available and the jack was needed, it was the practice to notify another fire station; to follow that practice in this case would have involved a delay of at least ten minutes.

The plaintiff failed before Barry J. [1954] 1 W.L.R. 208. The Court of Appeal, in unreserved judgments, dismissed his appeal.

SINGLETON L.J.: I am in complete agreement with the judgment of Barry J. but it is right that I should state my reasons for having formed that opinion.

The fire service is a service which must always involve risk for those who are employed in it, and, as Mr. Baker on behalf of the plaintiff pointed out, they are entitled to expect that their equipment shall be as good as reasonable care can secure. An emergency arose, as often happens. The sub-officer who had given the order, was asked in re-examination: "From your point of view you thought it was a piece of luck, with this unfortunate woman under the bus, that the Fordson was available and you could use it? (A.) Yes. It is recognised in the service that we use our initiative at all times, and in doing so any reasonable step you take is considered satisfactory if it is a question of saving life. You have to make a sudden decision."

It is not alleged that there was negligence on the part of any particular individual, nor that the driver was negligent in driving too fast, nor that the sub-officer was negligent in giving the order which he did. The case put forward in this court is that as the defendants had a jack, it was their duty to have a vehicle fitted in all respects to carry that jack, from which it follows, I suppose, that it is said that there must be a vehicle kept at the station at all times, or that if there is not one the lifting jack must not be taken out; indeed, Mr. Baker claimed that in the case of a happening such as this, if there was not a vehicle fitted to carry the jack the sub-officer ought to have telephoned to the fire station at St. Albans and arranged that they should attend to the emergency. St. Albans is some seven miles away, and it was said that an extra ten minutes or so would have elapsed if that had been done. I cannot think that that is the right way to approach the matter. There was a real emergency; the woman was under a heavy vehicle; these men in the fire service thought that they ought to go promptly and to take a lifting jack, and they did so. Most unfortunately this accident happened.

What is the duty owed by employers? It has been stated often, and never more clearly than it was by Lord Herschell in *Smith* v. *Baker & Sons* ([1891] A.C. 325, 362), in these words: "It is quite clear that the contract between employer and employed involves on the part of the former the duty of taking reasonable care to provide proper appliances, and to maintain them in a proper condition, and so to carry on his operations as not to subject those employed by him to unnecessary risk."

The employee in this case was a member of the fire service, who always undertake some risk—but, said Mr. Baker, not this risk. Is it to be said that if an emergency call reaches a fire station the one in charge has to ponder on the matter in this way: "Must I send out my men with the lifting jack in these circumstances, or must I telephone to St. Albans, seven miles away, to ask them to undertake the task?" I suppose he must think about his duty; but what would a reasonable man do, faced as he was? Would the reasonably careful head of the station have done anything other than that which the sub-officer did? I think not. Can it be said, then, that there is a duty on the employers here to have a vehicle built and fitted to carry this jack at all times, or if they have not, not to use the jack for a short journey of 200 or 300 yards? I do not think that that will do.

Asquith L.J., in *Daborn* v. *Bath Tramways Motor Co. Ltd.* said ([1946] 2 All E.R. 333, 336): "In determining whether a party is negligent, the standard of reasonable care is that which is reasonably to be demanded in the circumstances. A relevant circumstance to take into account may be the importance of the end to be served by behaving in this way or in that. As has often been pointed out, if all the trains in this country were restricted to a speed of five miles an hour, there would be fewer accidents, but our national life would be intolerably slowed down. The purpose to be served, if sufficiently important, justifies the assumption of abnormal risk."

The purpose to be served in this case was the saving of life. The men were prepared to take that risk. They were not, in my view, called on to take any risk other than that which normally might be encountered in this service. I agree with Barry J. that on the whole of the evidence it would not be right to find that the employers were guilty of any failure of the duty which they owed to their workmen. In my opinion the appeal should be dismissed.

DENNING L.J.: It is well settled that in measuring due care you must balance the risk against the measures necessary to eliminate the risk. To that proposition there ought to be added this: you must balance the risk against the end to be achieved. If this accident had occurred in a commercial enterprise without any emergency there could be no doubt that the servant would succeed. But the commercial end to make profit is very different from the human end to save life or limb. The saving of life or limb justifies taking considerable risk, and I am glad to say that there have never been wanting in this country men of courage ready to take those risks, notably in the fire service.

In this case the risk involved in sending out the lorry was not so great as to prohibit the attempt to save life. I quite agree that fire engines, ambulances and doctors' cars should not shoot past the traffic lights when they show a red light. That is because the risk is too great to warrant the incurring of the danger. It is always a question of balancing the risk against the end. I agree that this appeal should be dismissed.

Questions

1. Suppose the plaintiff had been a pedestrian run over by the driver in his haste to reach the scene of the emergency. Would his case have been stronger or weaker than that of the present plaintiff?

2. Could Watt recover from the person who carelessly provoked the emergency?

3. Would the answer have been any different if the cause of the injury had been a defective wheel on the jack?

4. Do you think that the pension schemes of local fire services take account of the risks of the calling?

WARD v. HERTFORDSHIRE COUNTY COUNCIL

Court of Appeal [1970] 1 W.L.R. 356; 114 S.J. 87; 68 L.G.R. 151; [1970] 1 All E.R. 535

Action for personal injuries by pupil against school.

LORD DENNING M.R. On 29th April 1966, Mrs. Ward took her two small children to the junior primary school at Sarratt in Hertfordshire. Timothy (the infant plaintiff) was about eight years of age, and Sarah five. She left them at the school at about 8.50 a.m. The school started at about 8.55 a.m. After she left them there, the infant plaintiff played with the other boys in the playground until school was ready. They decided to have a race up and down the playground. As the infant plaintiff was running, he tumbled. He tripped and fell against a wall at one side of the playground.

The wall was of a common type. It was built about 100 years ago. It had brick pillars and in between flints set in mortar. Just an ordinary flint wall. It was quite a low wall, 3 feet to 3 feet 6 inches high. The flints only came up to about 2 feet 3 inches above the ground, and there was a brick coping above. The infant plaintiff fell headlong, almost as it were diving into the wall. His head hit one of the flints. It must have had rather a sharp edge. He was seriously injured. Fortunately, he has made a remarkably good recovery. He had to have a plate put into his head, but he is now nearly normal. He can do most of the things a boy likes to do, except that he must not dive in the swimming bath, and he must not head the ball, and so forth. Naturally, the infant plaintiff's parents were very upset at this accident. They felt that the wall was dangerous; and, further, that there had not been proper supervision. So they brought this action against the local education authority for negligence and breach of duty.

The judge found ([1969] 1 W.L.R. 790, 794) that the playground "with its flint walls and sharp and jagged flints protruding, was inherently dangerous"; and that the local education authority was wrong in allowing it to be in that condition. He said that it ought to have rendered the wall or put up some railings or netting, or something of that kind, to prevent a child falling against it. Furthermore, he held that one of the teachers ought to have been in the playground supervising from the time when the children came in. The local education authority appeals to this court.

I must say, reviewing all the evidence, that I do not think that this wall was dangerous. One has only to look at the pictures to see that it is a wall of the commonest type. It is an ordinary flint wall. It was built in the days when flints were picked off the ground and used to make walls. One-third of this Hertfordshire village has flint walls like this; 16 of the schools in Hertfordshire have; and goodness knows how many in the country at large. At that time all the church schools were made in this way. These flint walls have, of course, their angles and sharp edges. But that does not mean that they are dangerous. We have lived with them long enough to know.

The infant plaintiff's parents sought to rely on previous accidents; but, when examined, they come to nothing. They happened to boys who were at the school some years ago, but have now grown up to be men. Each hurt himself against the wall. Mr. Bidderstaff was there over 30 years ago. He had been playing a game of football, and hit his head on the top of the wall, not on the flints. He had a bruise about the size of an egg. Mr. Parker was there 14 years ago. He was rushing across to see his father. He ran into the wall and hurt his knee, and the teacher bandaged it up. Mr. Styles was there 14 or 15 years ago. He tripped and fell into the wall and lost his front teeth. He said he hit against the flints, but he did not say that it was against the sharp edge. Those three incidents are just the ordinary sort of thing which happens in any playground. They do not show that the wall was dangerous.

I may add that the infant plaintiff's mother herself said that it never occurred to her to think that the wall was dangerous before the accident, and she was quite happy about it. I cannot see any evidence that the wall was dangerous.

The judge also held that there should have been supervision over the children in the playground. But I do not think that that was established. The headmaster said that the teachers took charge of the children from the moment they were due to be in school at 8.55 a.m. until the time when they were let out. Before the school began the staff were indoors preparing for the day's work. They cannot be expected to be in the playground, too. He said that even if he had been in the playground, he would not have stopped the children playing. It often happens that children run from one side of the playground to the other. It is impossible so to supervise them that they never fall down and hurt themselves. I cannot think that this accident shows any lack of supervision by the local education authority.

Great as is the respect which I have for the judge, I am afraid on this occasion I cannot go with him. It is a case where a small boy playing at school hurt himself badly, but the local education authority is not liable for it. . . .

SALMON L.J. delivered a concurring opinion.

CROSS L.J. This wall is undoubtedly somewhat less suitable as a boundary wall to a school playground than the ordinary brick wall would be, because in unusual circumstances, such as most unfortunately arose in this case, a child falling against it may suffer much more serious injury than he would suffer from falling against an ordinary brick wall; but although I naturally hesitate to differ from a judge whose experience in this field is so much greater than my own, I cannot bring myself to think that this wall, which has stood in the school playground since 1862, has been such a source of danger that those in charge of the school were guilty of negligence in not having it rendered with a smooth surface or masked by a wooden fence or wire netting. I agree with Salmon L.J. that increased supervision would have been useless because it would be unreasonable for any supervisor to prevent or attempt to prevent children from running races between the walls. In the course of his judgment the judge said that—"a prudent parent of a large family would have realised that this playground, with its flint walls and sharp and jagged flints protruding, was inherently dangerous." But, as my Lords have pointed out, the parents of the children in this village seem not to have so regarded it, for they have never represented to the local education authority that this wall was a source of danger. With reluctance I agree that this appeal should be allowed.

Note:
Things have come to a pretty pass when it can solemnly be argued that a local authority should put a fence round a wall, but the trial judge had "no hesitation at all in finding . . . that the defendant was guilty of a breach of its common law duty."

OCCUPIERS' LIABILITY ACT 1957

2.—(1) An occupier of premises owes the same duty, the "common duty of care," to all his visitors, except in so far as he is free to and does extend, restrict, modify or exclude his duty to any visitor or visitors by agreement or otherwise.

(2) The common duty of care is a duty to take such care as in all the circumstances of the case is reasonable to see that the visitor will be reasonably safe in using the premises for the purposes for which he is invited or permitted by the occupier to be there.

(3) The circumstances relevant for the present purpose include the degree of care, and of want of care, which would ordinarily be looked for in such a visitor, so that (for example) in proper cases—

(a) an occupier must be prepared for children to be less careful than adults; and
(b) an occupier may expect that a person, in the exercise of his calling, will appreciate and guard against any special risks ordinarily incident to it, so far as the occupier leaves him free to do so.

(4) In determining whether the occupier of premises has discharged the common duty of care to a visitor, regard is to be had to all the circumstances, so that (for example)—

(a) where damage is caused to a visitor by a danger of which he had been warned by the occupier, the warning is not to be treated without more as absolving the occupier from liability, unless in all the circumstances it was enough to enable the visitor to be reasonably safe; and
(b) where damage is caused to a visitor by a danger due to the faulty execution of any work of construction, maintenance or repair by an independent contractor employed by the occupier, the occupier is not to be treated without more as answerable for the danger if in all the circumstances he had acted reasonably in entrusting the work to an independent contractor and had taken such steps (if any) as he reasonably ought in order to satisfy

himself that the contractor was competent and that the work had been properly done.

(5) The common duty of care does not impose on an occupier any obligation to a visitor in respect of risks willingly accepted as his by the visitor (the question whether a risk was so accepted to be decided on the same principles as in other cases in which one person owes a duty of care to another).

(6) For the purposes of this section, persons who enter premises for any purpose in the exercise of a right conferred by law are to be treated as permitted by the occupier to be there for that purpose, whether they in fact have his permission or not.

THE HIGHWAYS (MISCELLANEOUS PROVISIONS) ACT 1961

1.—(1) The rule of law exempting the inhabitants at large and any other persons as their successors from liability for non-repair of highways is hereby abrogated.

(2) In an action against a highway authority in respect of damage resulting from their failure to maintain a highway maintainable at the public expense, it shall be a defence (without prejudice to any other defence or the application of the law relating to contributory negligence) to prove that the authority had taken such care as in all the circumstances was reasonably required to secure that the part of the highway to which the action relates was not dangerous for traffic.

(3) For the purposes of a defence under the last foregoing subsection, the court shall in particular have regard to the following matters, that is to say—

(a) the character of the highway, and the traffic which was reasonably to be expected to use it;

(b) the standard of maintenance appropriate for a highway of that character and used by such traffic;

(c) the state of repair in which a reasonable person would have expected to find the highway;

(d) whether the highway authority knew, or could reasonably have been expected to know, that the condition of the part of the highway to which the action relates was likely to cause danger to users of the highway;

(e) where the highway authority could not reasonably have been expected to repair that part of the highway before the cause of action arose, what warning notices of its condition had been displayed;

but for the purposes of such a defence it shall not be relevant to prove that the highway authority had arranged for a competent person to carry out or supervise the maintenance of the part of the highway to which the action relates unless it is also proved that the authority had given him proper instructions with regard to the maintenance of the highway and that he had carried out the instructions.

Note:

Before this enactment a highway authority, though liable if it made the highway worse, was not liable if it failed to keep it good or make it better. The authority was certainly under a duty to maintain its highways, but there was no liability in damages for breach of it—a good example of a public duty giving rise to no private action. The duty was restated in the Highways Act 1959, s.44(1), and the immunity was removed by the 1961 Act, which provided a defence instead. In the result, if a person using the highway is injured by its condition, he establishes a breach of the authority's duty simply by showing that the highway was not reasonably safe, though the mere fact of injury does not by itself show that the highway was not reasonably safe (*Meggs* v. *Liverpool Corp.* [1968] 1 All E.R. 1137). It is then for the authority to exculpate itself by proving that it took the care specified in section 1(2) above. Whether the liability attaches only to failure to repair a structural condition or extends also to failure to remove obstructions on it has been the subject of dispute (*Haydon* v. *Kent C.C.* [1978] Q.B. 343).

GLASGOW CORPORATION v. MUIR

House of Lords [1943] A.C. 448; 112 L.J.P.C. 1; 169 L.T. 53; 107 J.P. 140; 59 T.L.R. 266; 87
S.J. 182; 41 L.G.R. 173; [1943] 2 All E.R. 44

Action by visitor against occupier in respect of personal injury.

On a Saturday afternoon in June 1940, rain frustrated the plans of a party of
thirty or forty persons from the Milton Street Free Church to picnic in the grounds
of King's Park, Glasgow. Their leader, McDonald, therefore asked Mrs.
Alexander, the manageress of the defender's tearooms there, if they might eat their
food in the tearooms. To this Mrs. Alexander agreed, for a charge of 12s. 6d.; she
then went back to serving a group of children at a sweet counter in the hall.
McDonald and a boy of his party accordingly brought the urn of tea down to the
building. As they entered the hall, the children at the sweet counter were about five
feet away from them, and Mrs. Alexander had her back to the scene as she was
scooping ice-cream from the freezer. McDonald suddenly lost his grip on the back
handle of the urn and six children, including the pursuer, were scalded by its
contents. No one knew why McDonald lost his grip on the urn, since the pursuer
did not call him as a witness. The urn itself was a perfectly ordinary metal one with
a lid, about sixteen inches high, fifteen inches in diameter, and weighing, when full,
not more than 100 pounds.

After the evidence, the Lord Ordinary dismissed the action; the First Division of
the Court of Session (the Lord President dissenting) allowed the pursuer's appeal,
1942 S.C. 126. The Corporation appealed to the House of Lords, who allowed the
appeal.

LORD MACMILLAN: My Lords, the degree of care for the safety of others which
the law requires human beings to observe in the conduct of their affairs varies
according to the circumstances. There is no absolute standard, but it may be said
generally that the degree of care required varies directly with the risk involved.
Those who engage in operations inherently dangerous must take precautions which
are not required of persons engaged in the ordinary routine of daily life. It is, no
doubt, true that in every act which an individual performs there is present a
potentiality of injury to others. All things are possible, and, indeed, it has become
proverbial that the unexpected always happens, but, while the precept *alterum non
laedere* requires us to abstain from intentionally injuring others, it does not impose
liability for every injury which our conduct may occasion. In Scotland, at any rate,
it has never been a maxim of the law that a man acts at his peril. Legal liability is
limited to those consequences of our acts which a reasonable man of ordinary
intelligence and experience so acting would have in contemplation. "The duty to
take care," as I essayed to formulate it in *Bourhill* v. *Young* ([1943] A.C. 92, 104),
"is the duty to avoid doing or omitting to do anything the doing or omitting to do
which may have as its reasonable and probable consequence injury to others, and
the duty is owed to those to whom injury may reasonably and probably be
anticipated if the duty is not observed." This, in my opinion, expresses the law of
Scotland and I apprehend that it is also the law of England. The standard of
foresight of the reasonable man is, in one sense, an impersonal test. It eliminates
the personal equation and is independent of the idiosyncrasies of the particular
person whose conduct is in question. Some persons are by nature unduly timorous
and imagine every path beset with lions. Others, of more robust temperament, fail
to foresee or nonchalantly disregard even the most obvious dangers. The
reasonable man is presumed to be free both from over-apprehension and from
over-confidence, but there is a sense in which the standard of care of the reasonable
man involves in its application a subjective element. It is still left to the judge to

decide what, in the circumstances of the particular case, the reasonable man would have had in contemplation, and what, accordingly, the party sought to be made liable ought to have foreseen. Here there is room for diversity of view, as, indeed, is well illustrated in the present case. What to one judge may seem far-fetched may seem to another both natural and probable.

With these considerations in mind I turn to the facts of the occurrence on which your Lordships have to adjudicate. Up to a point the facts have been sufficiently ascertained . . . The question, as I see it, is whether Mrs. Alexander, when she was asked to allow a tea urn to be brought into the premises under her charge, ought to have had in mind that it would require to be carried through a narrow passage in which there were a number of children and that there would be a risk of the contents of the urn being spilt and scalding some of the children. If, as a reasonable person, she ought to have had these considerations in mind, was it her duty to require that she should be informed of the arrival of the urn, and, before allowing it to be carried through the narrow passage, to clear all the children out of it in case they might be splashed with scalding water? The urn was an ordinary medium-sized cylindrical vessel of about fifteen inches diameter and about sixteen inches in height made of light sheet metal with a fitting lid, which was closed. It had a handle at each side. Its capacity was about nine gallons, but it was only a third or a half full. It was not in itself an inherently dangerous thing and could be carried quite safely and easily by two persons exercising ordinary care. A caterer called as a witness on behalf of the pursuers, who had large experience of the use of such urns, said that he had never had a mishap with an urn while it was being carried. The urn was in charge of two responsible persons, McDonald, the church officer, and the lad, Taylor, who carried it between them. When they entered the passage way they called out to the children there congregated to keep out of the way and the children drew back to let them pass. Taylor, who held the front handle, had safely passed the children, when, for some unexplained reason, McDonald loosened hold of the other handle, the urn tilted over, and some of its contents were spilt, scalding several of the children who were standing by. The urn was not upset, but came to the ground on its base.

In my opinion, Mrs. Alexander had no reason to anticipate that such an event would happen as a consequence of granting permission for a tea urn to be carried through the passage way where the children were congregated, and, consequently, there was no duty incumbent on her to take precautions against the occurrence of such an event. I think that she was entitled to assume that the urn would be in charge of responsible persons (as it was) who would have regard for the safety of the children in the passage (as they did have regard), and that the urn would be carried with ordinary care, in which case its transit would occasion no danger to bystanders. The pursuers have left quite unexplained the actual cause of the accident. The immediate cause was not the carrying of the urn through the passage, but McDonald's losing grip of his handle. How he came to do so is entirely a matter of speculation. He may have stumbled or he may have suffered a temporary muscular failure. We do not know, and the pursuers have not chosen to enlighten us by calling McDonald as a witness. Yet it is argued that Mrs. Alexander ought to have foreseen the possibility, nay, the reasonable probability of an occurrence the nature of which is unascertained. Suppose that McDonald let go his handle through carelessness. Was Mrs. Alexander bound to foresee this as reasonably probable and to take precautions against the possible consequences? I do not think so. The only ground on which the view of the majority of the learned judges of the First Division can be justified is that Mrs. Alexander ought to have foreseen that some accidental injury might happen to the children in the passage if she allowed an urn containing hot tea to be carried through the passage, and ought, therefore, to have cleared out the children entirely during its transit, whch Lord Moncrieff describes as "the only effective step." With all respect, I think that this would impose on Mrs. Alexander a degree of care higher than the law exacts. . . .

LORD WRIGHT: My Lords, it is impossible not to feel a desire that the children, by or on behalf of whom these proceedings have been taken, should be compensated for the injuries sustained by them. It is true that the accident could not have occurred but for the action of Mrs. Alexander, the appellants' manageress, in giving permission that the tea urn should be carried through the short but narrow passage in which the children, about a dozen in number, were waiting as customers at the appellants' sweet counter to buy ices or sweets, but, to establish liability, the court has to be satisfied that the appellants owed a duty to the children, that that duty was broken, and that the children were injured in consequence of the breach.

That the appellants owed a duty to the children is not open to question. Your Lordships are not, therefore, on this occasion exercised by the problem which was presented recently in *Bourhill* v. *Young* ([1943] A.C. 92), which was whether the person injured came within the limits of foreseeable harm from the dangerous acts complained of. Here the children were on the appellants' premises in full view of Mrs. Alexander, the appellants' responsible servant, and were plainly liable to be injured if the place in which they were was rendered dangerous to them by Mrs. Alexander's act in consenting to the urn being carried through the place. The question thus is whether Mrs. Alexander knew or ought to have known that what she was permitting involved danger to the children. The same criterion applies in this connection as applied in the kindred problem in *Bourhill's* case, that is to say, the criterion of reasonable foreseeability of danger to the children. It is not a question of what Mrs. Alexander actually foresaw, but what the hypothetical reasonable person in Mrs. Alexander's situation would have foreseen. The test is what she ought to have foreseen. I may quote again as in *Bourhill's* case Lord Atkin's words in *Donoghue* v. *Stevenson:* "You must take reasonable care to avoid acts or omissions which you can reasonably foresee would be likely to injure your neighbour." On this occasion the children were "the neighbours." The act or omission to be avoided was creating a new danger in the premises by allowing the church party to transport the urn. If that issue is decided against the appellants, they must be held responsible in the action.

The issue can be stated on the general principles of the law of negligence without any reference to the special rules relating to the position of those who come as invitees upon premises. The children were clearly invitees within the rules laid down in *Indermaur* v. *Dames* ((1866) L.R. 1 C.P. 274), because they were customers at the appellants' shop, but that authority does no more than lay down a special sub-head of the general doctrine of negligence. . . .

Before dealing with the facts, I may observe that in cases of "invitation" the duty has most commonly reference to the structural condition of the premises, but it may clearly apply to the use which the occupier (or whoever has control so far as material) of the premises permits a third party to make of the premises. Thus, the occupier of a theatre may permit an independent company to give performances, or the person holding a fair may grant concessions to others to conduct side shows or subsidiary entertainments, which may, in fact, involve damage to persons attending the theatre or fair, and in such and similar cases the same test of reasonable foreseeability of danger may operate to impose liability on the person authorising what is done. The immediate cause of damage in such cases is generally the action of third parties who are neither servants nor agents of the defendant, but are mere licensees or concessionaires for whose acts as such the defendants are not directly liable. If the occupiers are held liable for what is done, it is because they are in law responsible in proper cases at an earlier stage because of the permission which they gave for the use of their premises. This is the cause of action against them. Thus, in the present case the appellants are not primarily concerned with the manner in which the members of the church party carried the urn as they would have been if these members had been their servants or agents. The two men were mere licensees in the matter. The appellants were not directly responsible for their acts. If they are to be held responsible, it must be because, by the permission which Mrs.

Alexander, their manageress, gave to the members of the church party, they created an unusual danger affecting the invitees, in particular, the children. The breach of duty (if any) may thus be stated to have been that in granting the permission they did not use reasonable foresight to guard the children from unusual danger arising from the condition or use of the premises. If the tea urn had been upset by the negligence of the appellants' servants, the appellants would have been liable in negligence. Whether or not they would have been liable as invitors in the alternative would depend on other considerations. The cause of action in invitation is different, because it depends primarily, not on what actually happened (except in the sense that what actually happened would be essential to complete the cause of action by showing damage), but on whether the invitor (it is convenient to use the word) knew or ought to have known that the invitee was being exposed to unusual danger. Where the unusual danger was due to structural defects the question can be stated to be whether the invitor knew or ought to have known of the defects. In a case like the present the question is whether it can be said of Mrs. Alexander that she either knew or ought to have known that the children would be exposed to unusual danger by reason of the uses to which the premises were put by her permission for the tea urn to be carried into and down the passage. It is not, of course, a question of what she actually thought at the moment but what the hypothetical reasonable person would have foreseen. That is the standard to determine the scope of her duty. This involves the question: Was the operation of carrying the tea urn something which a reasonable person in Mrs. Alexander's position should have realised would render the place in which it was performed dangerous to the children in the circumstances? This is the crucial issue of fact and the acid test of liability. On this crucial issue I agree with the Lord President. He said (1942 S.C. 126, 145): "I find myself unable to assent to the proposition that anything was authorised by the defenders or their servant in this case which obviously involved a danger which could not be avoided by the care of the men who carried the urn. The respondents [*i.e.,* the defenders] were not bound to take precautions against dangers which were not apparent to persons of ordinary intelligence and prudence."

A distinction has been drawn in some cases between things intrinsically dangerous or dangerous *per se* and other things which are not dangerous in the absence of negligence. The correctness or value of that distinction has been doubted by eminent judges. I think, however, that there is a real and practical distinction between the two categories. Some things are obviously and necessarily dangerous unless the danger is removed by appropriate precautions. These are things dangerous *per se*. Other things are only dangerous if there is negligence. It is only in that contingency that they can cause danger. Thus, to introduce, not a tea urn, but a savage animal, such as a lion or a tiger, into the passage way would have been of the former class. Another illustration of the same class may be afforded by the performance in a circus on the flying trapeze. The ocupier who permits such a performance owes a duty to the members of the audience to protect them by sufficient netting or otherwise against the obvious risk of the performer missing his hold. The present case, however, in my opinion, falls under the other category. It was not, in my opinion, *per se* dangerous. I do not think that the safe carriage of the tea urn presented any reasonably foreseeable difficulty. The urn was about sixteen inches high and about fifteen inches in diameter. It was a cylinder of metal about one-eighth of an inch thick with a lid which was in position. It weighed at most about one hundred pounds with the quantity of tea it contained. The handles for carrying it were about eighteen inches apart. Two men should have had no difficulty in carrying it safely even if one had to go in front and one behind because of the narrow space, as the men actually did. There is no explanation of how the accident happened. At the moment when one side of the urn was dropped, McDonald was at the handle at the back which he dropped, Taylor being at the front. It might have been easier for the two men to carry the urn side by side, but, having regard to its size and the closeness of the two handles to each other, I cannot see any difficulty in carrying it as the two men were doing. McDonald was not called. It is left to pure conjecture how he came to lose hold of the handle. It may have been a momentary physical faintness or a sudden stumble. Perhaps some hot tea may have splashed on his hand, but that is not likely with the urn only about half full and the lid on even if not screwed down. There is no evidence and no probability that children pushed against him and caused him to lose his grip. Any defect in the floor is excluded. There seem to be only two possible alternatives, either a mere accident or negligence. In my opinion, neither hypothesis could impose liability on the appellants. As to negligence, the two men were not their servants. They were not responsible for their acts. That the men should be negligent in so simple an operation was not likely to happen. It was a mere possibility, not a reasonable probability. The men, if negligent, were, no doubt, responsible for their own negligence, but from the standpoint of the appellants the risk of negligence was a mere unlikely accident which no reasonable person in Mrs. Alexander's position could naturally be expected to foresee. The same is true of an accidental slip or loss of grip. To hold the appellants liable on either basis would be to make them insurers, which under the authorities they are not. In my opinion, no breach of duty or negligence by the appellants to the respondents has been established. . . .

In the present case, as I have stated, as the permitted operation was intrinsically innocuous, I do not think any obligation rested on Mrs. Alexander to attempt to supervise it. As a reasonable person, not having any ground for anticipating harm, she was entitled to go on with her proper work and leave the church party to do what was proper. There might, of course, be circumstances in which, because there was an obvious risk, a duty might rest on the occupier to supervise the actual conducting of the operation if the permission was given. I do not see what Mrs. Alexander could have done in that respect unless she had seen that all the children were removed from the passage when the urn was being carried through. That might be her obligation if the operation she permitted had been intrinsically dangerous, but it was not so in the circumstances as I apprehend them. No doubt, some difficult questions of fact may arise in these cases. In the present case, however, as I think that there was no reasonably foreseeable danger to the children from the use of the premises which the appellants permitted to be made, I think the respondents' claim cannot be supported. In my judgment the appeal should be allowed.

Questions
1. Would the defenders have been liable if the urn had been carried in and dropped by a catering firm under contract with them?
2. Could the defenders have been held liable here without also making liable the inn-keeper whose guest drives his car into the car of another guest in the car-park?

Note:
McDonald would have been liable, because he could foresee that *if* he was careless the children might well be hurt, and he *was* careless. Mrs. Alexander could equally well foresee that *if* McDonald were careless the children might be hurt, but *she* was not careless, since she could not foresee that McDonald would in fact be clumsy, and only such a premonition would require her to put the children out in the rain.

Sometimes, however, one must foresee the carelessness of others. It is not careful to act on the assumption that other people will be careful when it is known that they are not. Drivers do in fact emerge without warning from side-roads. In *London Passenger Transport Board* v. *Upson* [1949] A.C. 155, 173, Lord Uthwatt said: "A driver is not, of course, bound to anticipate folly in all its forms, but he is not, in my opinion, entitled to put out of consideration the teachings of experience as to the form those follies commonly take."

The irreducible question is whether the defendant behaved *reasonably*.

WYNGROVE'S CURATOR BONIS v. SCOTTISH OMNIBUSES LTD.

House of Lords, 1966 S.C.(H.L.) 47; 1966 S.L.T. 273

Action by passenger against carrier in respect of personal injuries.

LORD REID: On July 25, 1961, the late Mr. Wyngrove was a passenger in a bus operated by the appellants. The bus was travelling from Edinburgh to Glasgow and he intended to alight at a stop in Broxburn. Some distance before the bus reached the stop he fell from the rear platform and sustained very serious injuries. . . . He died recently and [the respondent] is now his executrix. The Lord Ordinary held that the appellants were in fault but that the deceased had been guilty of contributory negligence. He assessed damages at £12,500 but awarded one-quarter of that sum. The Second Division (Lord Wheatley and Lord Walker, Lord Strachan dissenting) also held that the appellants were in fault but they increased the sum awarded to three-quarters of £12,500. The appellants appeal on the ground that no fault has been proved against them. Alternatively they seek to have the Lord Ordinary's award of damages restored.

The bus was double-decked, the body being of Bristol Lodeka type. The entrance and exit are through a doorway on the near side at the rear. The doorway is 3 feet 6 inches wide and the door can be folded back when it is open, and made secure against the partition between the rear platform and the lower saloon by means of a catch. When the door is open, the aperture through which passengers alight is reduced to a width of 3 feet 2 inches.

The practice in operating buses of this type is to keep the door open in built-up areas where stops are frequent, but to shut it at least in bad weather when there is a long interval between stops. There is no central vertical pillar or rail in this doorway similar to the pillars which are generally provided in buses with open rear platforms. The case for the respondent is that, if such a door was to be kept open between stops, a central pillar in the doorway ought to have been provided as a handhold for passengers on the rear platform, or alternatively that the door ought to have been kept shut between stops: if either of these courses had been followed, this accident would have been prevented.

. . . The deceased was seated in the lower saloon. Some considerable distance before the bus reached the stop, he rose from his seat and stepped on to the rear platform. The bus was being driven smoothly and properly. There were two adequate handholds on the right-hand side, a vertical rail by the side of the saloon door, and a horizontal handrail on the folded door between the door of the saloon and the near side of the bus. But before he had grasped either of them, for some reason he lost his balance and fell outwards. He seems to have tried to grasp the horizontal rail but failed to do so. His left arm swung outwards and the respondent says that, if there had been a vertical pillar or rail in the middle of the doorway, he could have saved himself by grasping it, or at least it would have arrested his fall. The Lord Ordinary reached the opinion that a central pillar probably would have prevented the accident. This finding was attacked by the appellants and no doubt it is a matter of speculation what would have happened had there been a central pillar. But I see no ground for disagreeing with this finding. So the main question is whether such a pillar ought to have been provided. The Lord Ordinary and the majority of the Second Division have held that it ought to have been provided.

It is admitted that the appellants were aware that it was a general practice for passengers to leave their seats and move on to the rear platform before the bus reached the stop at which they intended to alight. And it is not denied that they were therefore under a duty to take all reasonable precautions for the safety of passengers while they were on the rear platform. Their defence is that there were already ample handholds on the rear platform—nine in all—and that a central pillar in the doorway was unnecessary and would have been inconvenient in obstructing passengers boarding or alighting from the bus.

It is convenient at this point to deal with the respondent's alternative case that the door should have been kept shut between stops. It appears from the evidence for the appellants that the door is not intended as a safety precaution: its sole purpose is to keep out bad weather. It is left to the discretion of the conductor to close the door when practicable in bad weather. In my view it is clearly proved that it is impracticable to close the door in parts of the route where stops are close together. If it is closed, the conductor must be beside it in time to open it at the next stop, and his ordinary duty of collecting fares would, if the bus were at all crowded, prevent him from being at the door in time for every stop.

So the substantial question is whether there ought to have been a central pillar bisecting the doorway vertically. There was no engineering difficulty in fitting such a pillar and its cost would have been small. The appellants' defence was that experience had proved that it was unnecessary and that it would have been an obstruction to passengers boarding or alighting from the bus. Buses of this type had been on the road for six years or more before the accident. The evidence is that in a year a bus carries some 200,000 passengers. Evidence was given by the appellants' manager and the managers of two other large bus companies. Between them they operate over 600 of this type of bus. None of these buses is fitted with a central pillar in the doorway. They are all operated on the same system of leaving it to the conductor to shut the door when that is practicable and desirable for the comfort of the passengers. The managers said that they all received reports of all accidents but that they were unaware of any case where an accident had been attributable to the absence of a central pillar or of any complaint that such pillars should be provided. We do not know how many of the many hundreds of millions of passengers carried by these buses had stood on the rear platforms when the doors were open while the bus was in motion but the number must have been very large. Accordingly the chance that a passenger, who for any reason lost his balance while standing on the rear platform, would be unable to save himself by grasping one of the nine handholds provided but would be saved by the presence of a central pillar, must on the evidence be held to be extremely small.

The evidence with regard to the inconvenience of having a central pillar in the doorway was not very specific. If there were a central pillar, neither half of the bisected doorway would have been more than 1 foot 7 inches wide and the minimum width for a doorway required by paragraph 27 of the Public Service Vehicles (Conditions of Fitness) Regulations 1958 (S.I. 1958/473) is 1 foot 9 inches. The third proviso in that paragraph is not easy to understand and I do not find it necessary to decide whether putting a central pillar in a doorway 3 feet 2 inches wide would infringe the Regulations. But I am satisfied that it would be an inconvenient obstruction if there were many passengers trying to alight from or board the bus at the same stop.

The Lord Ordinary held "that the pursuer has established the need for a central pillar, if the bus was to be operated with the door open, and that the defenders have not shown any sufficient reason why a central pillar should not have been provided." His main reasons for the first of these findings were that a passenger at the forward end of the platform might need a rail that could be grasped with his left hand as well as a rail he could grasp with his right hand, and that a central pillar would have reduced the risk of a passenger falling or being thrown off the platform. I think that he underestimated the importance of the evidence as to the use of hundreds of these buses for years without any accident of this kind being known. And there was no sufficient evidence that it is customary in any type of bus for there always to be available for any passenger moving in the bus while it is in motion two things to grasp—one for each hand. Indeed common knowledge strongly suggests the contrary. As regards his second finding he had held that a central pillar could not be placed in a doorway of this width, but he said that this could be overcome by making the entrance slightly wider. Clearly that could not be done without redesigning the rear part of the body of the bus. So he has in effect found that this type of bus is unsuitable for use on routes where it is often impracticable to keep the door shut between stops. In face of the evidence of the use of hundreds of these buses for years I am quite unable to agree that their design is unsafe.

Lord Wheatley held that "the reasonable provision of safety required a hand-rail or support available to either hand," and that even if it was inconvenient to have a central pillar in this doorway, safety must come before convenience. He was of opinion that the defenders could have kept the door closed at all times when the bus was in motion, even if this might require in practice a conductor on each deck. Lord Walker held that "reasonable care required a system of closing the door when passengers might be expected to be on the platform on approaching stopping places."

These findings also appear to me necessarily to lead to the conclusion that the design of these buses makes them unsafe for use in the way in which they are habitually used. It needs no evidence to show that it would be impracticable to have two conductors: the cost would be prohibitive without an increase in fares. And if it is impracticable always to keep the door shut between stops with only one conductor, and the provision of a central pillar in the doorway would at least cause frequent inconvenience, I see no escape from the conclusion that the buses are badly designed—a conclusion which on the evidence I am not prepared to accept.

I think that it is necessary to recall the well-established principles of law regarding the duty of a person towards passengers or other persons who are in his vehicle or on his premises. He must take all precautions for their safety which a reasonable and careful person in his position would take, and he must anticipate such a degree of inadvertence on their part as experience shows to be not uncommon. But he is entitled to have regard to his own experience and to that of others in a similar situation with regard to what precautions have been found to be adequate hitherto. It may be that these precautions ought to have been seen by him to be in fact inadequate, but the more extensive the past experience of safe working has been, the more difficult it will be to prove that he ought to have seen that enough was not being done. It is clearly foreseeable that a person leaving his seat in a moving vehicle may for some reason lose his balance, and if he is near the door, he may fall out. So adequate means must be provided to enable him to save himself, and the recognised means are handholds. Nine handholds are provided on the rear platform of this type of bus. There is evidence that in operating hundreds of this type of bus for a period of years in the way in which this bus was operated, no accident has been reported as attributable to the absence of a central pillar. So it appears to me to be clear that a reasonable person operating such a bus would not have thought that there was more than a very remote chance of a passenger who failed to grasp one of these nine handholds gaining any benefit from the presence of a central pillar. And if the risk of injury is so small, the reasonable man will consider the disadvantages of providing something additional which might in some very exceptional circumstances serve to prevent an accident. Here the disadvantage was the general inconvenience to many passengers in the regular use of the bus. In my opinion the evidence shows that it would have been unreasonable to fit central pillars in the doorway of these buses.

That is sufficient to decide the case in favour of the appellants. . . .

Note:

Scottish Omnibuses Ltd. is not, of course, an organ of government, but the decision impugned by the plaintiff here, namely to purchase buses of the construction in question, was a fairly high-level decision, and if the courts had held that decision to be a ground of liability, the financial consequences would have been enormous. In making decisions of such an order, safety is naturally an important consideration, but it is by no means the only one; in a tort case brought by a particular injured plaintiff, the tendency is to give too much importance to safety, simply because other factors may seem less important. In *Levine* v. *Morris* [1970] 1 W.L.R. 71) there was an accident on a highway built to less than the optimum specifications and the plaintiff was injured in a collision with the stanchion of a road-sign. The highway authority was held liable for siting the road-sign where it did, but not liable for building a less than splendid road. The latter holding is clearly right; but the former holding is justifiable only on the ground that the authority did not show that it had considered the question of safety at all when it was decided to site the sign where it did. In another case a person was killed at a delusive intersection; a "Give-Way" sign would clearly have reduced the chances of a collision. The point was not argued, but soon it will be, whether an authority may not be liable for failing to erect such a sign (*Macintyre* v. *Coles* [1966] 1 W.L.R. 831) or having traffic lights which change quickly (*Radburn* v. *Kemp* [1971] 1 W.L.R. 1502) or not keeping up a side road while a main road is being constructed (*Rider* v. *Rider* [1973] 1 Q.B. 505). It does not seem that courts are better qualified to weigh the conflicting interests of safety and traffic flow, or safety and visibility, or safety and expense, than experts in the field. A decision disturbing for analogous reasons is *Barnes* v. *Hampshire County Council* ([1971] 1 W.L.R. 892). There the local authority had to pay a school-child aged five the sum of £10,000. She had been let out of school four minutes early on the day before the Whitsun break, had not waited for her mother (who was slightly late) and had been run over in the main street some yards away. Considering that many children were not met at all, the decision seems a doubtful one; but at least the House of Lords did not accede to the suggestion of the plaintiff's counsel that it was negligence in the school authority not to have a system of "pairing-off" whereby the kids would be kept by the teachers until someone appeared to take them individually away. Such a decision would not be an appropriate one for a court of justice to make.

The common law of trespass has been extremely useful in limiting the abuses of power by members of the executive; the common law of negligence seems a much less satisfactory form in which to challenge, at the instance of particular interests, decisions of a high order and political nature. Reference should be made again to the opinion of Lord Diplock in the *Dorset Yacht Co.* case [1970] A.C. 1004, 1057 and to the opinion of Lord Wilberforce in *Anns* (above, p. 58) with its distinction between the discretionary and the operational areas of government. One must also remember that it may be an abuse of process to try to question a public law decision in an ordinary action at law rather than by application for judicial review (*O'Reilly* v. *Mackman* [1982] 3 All E.R. 1124).

Question

Not long ago in the United States cars of a certain make tended to explode if rear-ended. This was because the petrol tank was situated in a relatively exposed position. When suit was brought on the part of incinerated passengers, it was discovered that the manufacturer had compared the cost of siting the tank in a safer place (as reflected in reduced income from sales by reason of the higher price) with the probable cost of paying damages to the victims injured by its being in the less safe place. People were outraged. Were they right to be so? Was the manufacturer's conduct reasonable (a) socially, (b) economically, (c) legally?

Section 3.—Special Plaintiffs

HALEY v. LONDON ELECTRICITY BOARD

House of Lords [1965] A.C. 778; [1964] 3 W.L.R. 479; 129 J.P. 14; 108 S.J. 637; [1964] 3 All E.R. 185

Action by pedestrian against person working on highway in respect of personal injury.

The plaintiff, a blind man, was walking carefully with a stick along the pavement in a London suburb when he fell into a trench dug there by the defendants pursuant to statutory powers. He suffered personal injury subsequently evaluated at £7,000. In front of the trench the defendants had put a long-handled hammer, its head resting on the pavement and the handle on some railings two feet high. This was an adequate protection for pedestrians with sight, but it was insufficient for blind people.

Marshall J. gave judgment for the defendants, and the Court of Appeal affirmed this decision [1964] 2 Q.B. 121. The plaintiff's appeal to the House of Lords was allowed.

LORD REID: . . . The trial judge held that what the respondents' men did gave adequate warning to ordinary people with good sight, and I am not disposed to disagree with that. The excavation was shallow and was to be filled in before nightfall, and the punner (or the pick and shovel) together with the notice boards and the heap of spoil on the pavement beside the trench were, I think, sufficient warning to ordinary people that they should not try to pass along the pavement past the trench. I agree with Somervell L.J. in saying that a person walking along a pavement does not have "to keep his eyes on the ground to see whether or not there is any obstacle in his path" (*Almeroth* v. *W. E. Chivers & Sons Ltd.* [1948] 1 All E.R. 53, 54). But even allowing for that degree of inadvertence of which most people are often guilty when walking along a pavement, I think that what the respondents' men did was just sufficient to attract the attention of ordinary people with good sight exercising ordinary care.

On the other hand, if it was the duty of the respondents to have in mind the needs of blind or infirm pedestrians I think that what they did was quite insufficient. Indeed, the evidence shows that an obstacle attached to a heavy weight and only nine inches above the ground may well escape detection by a blind man's stick and is for him a trap rather than a warning.

So the question for your Lordships' decision is the nature and extent of the duty owed to pedestrians by persons who carry out operations on a city pavement. The respondents argue that they were only bound to have in mind or to safeguard ordinary able-bodied people and were under no obligation to give particular consideration to the blind or infirm. If that is right, it means that a blind or infirm person who goes out alone goes at his peril. He may meet obstacles which are a danger to him but not to those with good sight because no one is under any obligation to remove or protect them. And if such an obstacle causes him injury he must suffer the damage in silence.

I could understand the respondents' contention if it was based on an argument that it was not reasonably foreseeable that a blind person might pass along that pavement on that day; or that, although foreseeable, the chance of a blind man coming there was so small and the difficulty of affording protection to him so great that it would have been in the circumstances unreasonable to afford that protection. Those are well recognised grounds for defence. But in my judgment neither is open to the respondents in this case.

In deciding what is reasonably foreseeable one must have regard to common knowledge. We are all accustomed to meeting blind people walking alone with their white sticks on city pavements. No doubt there are many places open to the public where for one reason or another one would be surprised to see a blind person walking alone, but a city pavement is not one of them. And a residential street cannot be different from any other. The blind people we meet must live somewhere and most of them probably left their homes unaccompanied. It may seem surprising that blind people can avoid ordinary obstacles so well as they do, but we must take account of the facts. There is evidence in this case about the number of blind people in London and it appears from Government publications that the proportion in the whole country is near one in 500. By no means all are sufficiently skilled or confident to venture out alone, but the number who habitually do so must be very large. I find it quite impossible to say that it is not reasonably foreseeable that a blind person may pass along a particular pavement on a particular day.

No question can arise in this case of any great difficulty in affording adequate protection for the blind. In considering what is adequate protection again one must have regard to common knowledge. One is entitled to expect of a blind person a high degree of skill and care because none but the most foolhardy would venture to go out alone without having that skill and exercising that care. We know that in fact blind people do safely avoid all ordinary obstacles on pavements; there can be no question of padding lamp posts as was suggested in one case. But a moment's reflection shows that a low obstacle in an unusual place is a grave danger: on the other hand, it is clear from the evidence in this case and also, I think, from common knowledge that quite a light fence some two feet high is an adequate warning. There would have been no difficulty in providing such a fence here. The evidence is that the Post Office always provide one, and that the respondents have similar fences which are often used. Indeed the evidence suggests that the only reason there was no fence here was that the accident occurred before the necessary fences had arrived. So if the respondents are to succeed it can only be on the ground that there was no duty to do more than safeguard ordinary able-bodied people. . . .

I can see no justification for laying down any hard-and-fast rule limiting the classes of persons for whom those interfering with a pavement must make provision. It is said that it is impossible to tell what precautions will be adequate to protect all kinds of infirm pedestrians or that taking such precautions would be unreasonably difficult or expensive. I think that such fears are exaggerated, and it is worth recollecting that when the courts sought to lay down specific rules as to the duties of occupiers the law became so unsatisfactory that Parliament had to step in and pass the Occupiers' Liability Act 1957. It appears to me that the ordinary principles of the common law must apply in streets as well as elsewhere, and that fundamentally they depend on what a reasonable man, careful of his neighbour's safety, would do having the knowledge which a reasonable man in the position of the defendant must be deemed to have. I agree with the statement of law at the end of the speech of Lord Sumner in *Glasgow Corporation* v. *Taylor* ([1922] 1 A.C. 44, 67): "a measure of care appropriate to the inability or disability of those who are immature or feeble in mind or body is due from others, who know of or ought to anticipate the presence of such persons within the scope and hazard of their own operations." I would therefore allow this appeal.

Question

If a sighted person had fallen into the trench, guarded as it was, would that person have recovered (a) nothing, or (b) a sum reduced by reason of his contributory negligence, (i) before this case, and (ii) after it?

Note:

Many of the people to whom accidents happen are people to whom accidents are particularly likely to happen. Wyngrove (last case) had no fingers on his right hand. The susceptible plaintiff causes difficulties. The susceptibility may be physical—the sensitive housewife who contracts dermatitis from a "safe" detergent (*Board* v. *Thos. Hedley* [1951] 2 All E.R. 431; *Ingham* v. *Emes* [1955] 2 Q.B. 366); or mental—the child who takes a bomb for a toy (*Yachuk* v. *Oliver Blais* [1949] A.C. 386); or emotional—(*Bourhill* v. *Young* [1943] A.C. 92). It is usually impossible to use the concept of contributory negligence to limit liability to the sensitive—though if an epileptic takes to working at heights, his recovery may be restricted (*Cork* v. *Kirby Maclean* [1952] W.N. 399). The "thin-skull" rule (below, p. 187) makes it difficult to limit the amount of recovery once liability is admitted; yet, though one's claim for pain and suffering will not be reduced just because others would not have suffered so acutely, one's claim for loss of earnings will be reduced if a pre-existing ailment would in any case have shortened one's earning life. It is sometimes possible to say that no special duty was owed to the abnormally accident-prone (see *Phipps* v. *Rochester Corpn.*, next case); but not when the susceptibility is known (*Paris* v. *Stepney Borough Council* [1951] A.C. 367), or foreseeable (the principal case). The question of liability then turns on breach, and becomes a question of fact.

PHIPPS v. ROCHESTER CORPORATION

Queen's Bench [1955] 1 Q.B. 450; [1955] 2 W.L.R. 23; 119 J.P. 92; 99 S.J. 45; [1955] 1 All
E.R. 129; 53 L.G.R. 80

Action by infant visitor against occupier of land in respect of personal injury.

The plaintiff, a boy of five, and his sister, aged seven, crossed the defendant's land in order to go blackberrying. The defendant knew that people crossed his land, and apparently did not mind. The land was being developed as a housing estate, and, preparatory to the insertion of a sewer, the defendant had dug a trench about two and a half feet wide, eight or nine feet deep, and about a hundred yards long. The girl negotiated this hazard safely, but the plaintiff fell in and broke his leg. His claim was dismissed.

DEVLIN J.: . . . The trench was neither an allurement to a child nor a danger concealed from an adult or even from a big child. It was, however, a danger imperceptible by a little child of the plaintiff's age simply because he was not old enough to see the necessity of avoiding it or of taking special care; whether or not it was obvious to his eye, it was concealed from his understanding. The question of law is whether he is entitled to protection against that sort of danger.

Mr. Van Oss submits that, irrespective of any question of allurement, the duty towards little children should not be judged by adult standards. But he admits that the duty cannot be so high as to require the licensor to make the premises absolutely safe for them. The difficulty is to see upon what principle one stops short of that, once one gets away from the test of obviousness as perceived by the adult. A commonplace feature of a building or of land may be a danger to a little child; he may see much but apprehend little; he is usually impervious to warning. Is, then, the licensor, in the words of Hamilton L.J. in *Latham* v. *R. Johnson & Nephew Ltd.* ([1913] 1 K.B. 398, 414), "practically bound to see that the wandering child is as safe as in a nursery?" If the duty of a licensor towards such a child is converted into an obligation to make the premises safe, it means that the normal relationship of licensor and licensee has entirely ceased to apply.

The cases which deal with the licensor's duty towards children in general are well known. The law recognises for this purpose a sharp difference between children and adults. But there might well, I think, be an equally well-marked distinction between "big children" and "little children." I shall use those broad terms to denote broadly the difference between children who know what they are about and children who do not. The latter are sometimes referred to in the cases as "children of tender years." Not having reached the age of reason or understanding, they present a special problem. When it comes to taking care of themselves, there is a greater difference between big and little children than there is between big children and adults, and much justification for putting little children into a separate category. Adults and big children can be guilty of contributory negligence; a little child cannot.

I have not been able to find in the cases which have been cited to me any clearly authoritative formulation of the licensor's duty towards little children. I think that the cases do show that judges have not allowed themselves to be driven to the conclusion that licensors must make their premises safe for little children; but they have chosen different ways of escape from that conclusion. One way, which can be supported by many dicta, is to say bluntly that children, no matter what their age, should get no different treatment from adults. Children must themselves bear the risks attendant of childhood: "that is the way the world is made," as Lord Dunedin said in effect in one of the cases (*Hastie* v. *Edinburgh Magistrates,* 1907 S.C. 1102, 1105). Another way is to put upon the parents the burden of the contributory negligence which the child cannot himself bear. A third way is to treat the licence as being conditional upon the little child being accompanied by a responsible adult. A fourth way is to frame the duty so as to compromise between the robustness that would make children take the world as they found it and the tenderness which would give them nurseries wherever they go. On this view the licensor is not entitled to assume that all children will, unless they ae allured, behave like adults; but he is entitled to assume that normally little children will in fact be accompanied by a responsible person and to discharge his duty of warning accordingly. The third and fourth solutions will in most cases produce the same result. They are, however, radically different in law, for in the former the unaccompanied child is a trespasser and in the latter a licensee. . . .

There is, especially among the earlier cases, support for Mr. O'Connor's first submission that the test of concealment is the same for little children as it is for adults; or, at any rate, that trenches, like ponds, rivers and heaps, are obvious dangers from which little children need not be specially protected. Apart from the Scottish cases, *Liddle's* case ([1934] 2 K.B. 101) and *Morley's* case ([1939] 4 All E.R. 92) are comparatively recent decisions of the Court of Appeal which carry that argument a long way. But I do not think that the solution is to be found simply by drawing up a list of "obvious dangers" which are of the same genus as ponds and contrasting it with a list of "allurements"; and I could adopt the general principle that adults and children are to be treated alike only if I were to disregard the persuasive dicta to the contrary of Lord Atkinson in *Cooke's* case ([1909] A.C. 229, 238), Lord Sumner in *Glasgow Corporation* v. *Taylor* ([1922] 1 A.C. 44, 65) and Jenkins L.J. in the most recent case, *Williams* v. *Cardiff Corporation* ([1950] 1 K.B. 514). For myself, I much prefer the flexibility afforded by these dicta and I think that I am free to follow them. A similar flexibility has been adopted in determining what is an "unusual danger" for invitees: see *London Graving Dock Ltd.* v. *Horton, per* Lord Normand ([1951] A.C. 737, 752). To assess the obligations of the licensor simply by reference to the physical powers of the average healthy adult seems to me to be unnecessarily rigid.

Can the licensor be exonerated on the ground that the casualty must in all cases be treated as attributable to what has been called the contributory negligence of the parents? I do not think that this question leads to the right answer. . . . I know of no English case in which the negligence of the parent has been visited upon the child. It would not, therefore, be correct to talk in England of a parent's contributory negligence; when Lord Sumner used the phrase, he was speaking in a Scottish appeal. Under English law, the parent's negligence would simply be that of another wrongdoer and would not enable the occupier to escape liability if his breach of duty was also a cause of the casualty; under the Law Reform (Contributory Negligence) Act 1945 a question of apportionment might arise. Anyway, I do not think that it would be a just rule. The parent of a straying child is not *ipso facto* negligent. A little child may sometimes escape from careful parental control, and it would be wrong to penalise an occupier whose premises were generally safe because he could not prove a parent to be at fault.

The third principle is that of the conditional licence, and the cases show that there is excellent authority for this. Nevertheless, I think that it involves difficulties of the sort which Lord Sumner considered in *Glasgow Corporation* v. *Taylor* ([1922] 1 A.C. 44) and regarded as still unresolved. It is easy to put a condition into an express licence; the licensor can then word it as he likes. It is not so easy to settle the terms of an implied condition. They must, however, be settled with some precision, because upon them will turn the question whether a person using the premises is a trespasser or not. He cannot become a trespasser according as to whether or not he falls into a pit. The law cannot wait to see whether in fact he is circumspect; he must be identifiable as a trespasser so that a legalistic licensor could turn him back at the gate. What is of more practical importance is that in certain cases his status may affect his right to recover. Suppose there is on the premises something which by any standard, adult or otherwise, constitutes a trap, and an unaccompanied little child falls into it. If he is a trespasser, he cannot recover. If he is a licensee he could recover, since in such a case the presence or absence of a guardian would be immaterial.

What then, is the definition of "tender years"? Is it an age qualification, or does it go by the appearance of physical capability? At the other end of mortality what degree of age or infirmity disqualifies? Should a blind man, who with the friendly help of passers-by walks the streets in comparative safety, be excluded from a public park because he cannot read the warning notices or see the dangers obvious to others? When the degree of incapacity that calls for the condition has been determined, the qualifications of the companion will have to be considered. Must the person who accompanies a child be an adult? If an older child will do, how much older must he be? If a blind man were led by a specially trained dog, would the dog do? If the qualifications of the guardian are settled, what duties does the condition impose upon him? If it is an obligation to exercise reasonable care and his attention at the critical moment is distracted in the performance of some other proper duty, is the child to recover in respect of a danger which an undistracted adult would have perceived?

I think that if this approach to the problem were followed up the conditional licensor would soon become a legal fiction and the terms of the supposed licence would be mainly lawyers' inventions. Legal fictions have played a useful part in the formulation of principles of law, but the formula of the conditional licence has the disadvantage that it does not get at the real need. What is wanted for the reasonable adjustment of the relationship between the licensor and the licensee of diminished capacity is not the formulation of a condition which must operate irrespective of any casualty, but something which places the casualty after it has occurred on one side or the other of the line.

For these reasons I respectfully doubt whether the notion of the conditional licence would, if further developed, be found in the end to work satisfactorily. Furthermore, I think that the general principle which governs the relationship between licensors and licensees can be made to work in the case of little children without the employment of any special device. The general principle is that a licensor must give warning of any danger which would not be perceived by a licensee using reasonable care for his own safety. In many cases the application of the rule raises the question whether the licensee has been guilty of contributory negligence. But that does not mean that, because a little child cannot be guilty of contributory negligence, the rule breaks down. The licensor's duty is not unbounded unless he can prove contributory negligence. There are limits to his duty which exist quite independently of the behaviour of the licensee in any particular case. His duty is to consider with reasonable care whether there are on his premises, so far as he knows their condition, any dangers that would not be obvious to the persons whom he has permitted to use them; and if there are, to give warning of them or to remove them. If he rightly determines a danger to be obvious, he will not be liable because some individual licensee, albeit without negligence in the special circumstances of his case, fails to perceive it. He must be taken to know generally the "habits, capacities and propensities" of those whom he himself has licensed, but not their individual peculiarities. In the light of that general knowledge and on the assumption that they will behave reasonably, he must determine what steps he will take. If he makes that determination carefully, he cannot be made liable, whatever may subsequently happen.

I think that it would be an unjustifiable restriction of the principle if one were to say that although the licensor may in determining the extent of his duty have regard to the fact that it is the habit, and also the duty, of prudent people to look after themselves, he may not in that determination have a similar regard to the fact that it is the habit, and also the duty, of prudent people to look after their little children. If he is entitled, in the absence of evidence to the contrary, to assume that parents will not normally allow their little children to go out unaccompanied, he can decide what he should do and consider what warnings are necessary on that basis. He cannot then be made liable for the exceptional child that strays, nor will he be required to prove that any particular parent has been negligent. It is, I think, preferable that this result should be achieved by allowing the general principle to expand in a natural way rather than by restricting its influence and then having to give it artificial aids in order to make it work at all in the case of little children.

The principle I am seeking to express is that contained in the passage from the speech of Lord Shaw in *Glasgow Corporation* v. *Taylor* ([1922] 1 A.C. 44, 61) where he says that the municipality is entitled to take into account that reasonable parents will not permit their children to be sent into danger without protection; that the guardians of the child and of the park must each act reasonably; and that each is entitled to assume of the other that he will. That passage was not spoken in reference to the English law of licence, but nevertheless it seems to me to express perfectly the way in which the English law can reasonably be applied. A licensor who tacitly permits the public to use his land without discriminating between its members must assume that the public may include little children. But as a general rule he will have discharged his duty towards them if the dangers which they may encounter are only those which are obvious to a guardian or of which he has given a warning comprehensible by a guardian. To every general rule there are, of course, exceptions. A licensor cannot divest himself of the obligation of finding out something about the sort of people who are availing themselves of his permission and the sort of use they are making of it. He may have to take into account the social habits of the neighbourhood. No doubt there are places where little children go to play unaccompanied. If the licensor knows or ought to anticipate that, he may have to take steps accordingly. But the responsibility for the safety of little children must rest primarily upon the parents; it is their duty to see that such children are not allowed to wander about by themselves, or at the least to satisfy themselves that the places to which they do allow their children to go unaccompanied are safe for them to go to. It would not be socially desirable if parents were, as a matter of course, able to shift the burden of looking after their children from their own shoulders to those of persons who happen to have accessible bits of land. Different considerations may well apply to public parks or to recognised playing grounds where parents allow their children to go unaccompanied in the reasonable belief that they are safe.

Although, as I have said, there is good authority for the presumption of a conditional licence, I do not feel compelled to hold that it is the only way out of the dilemma that would otherwise be created. It is not a doctrine which has since its inception been extensively adopted. It is noteworthy that apart from the reference to it by du Parcq L.J. ([1939] 4 All E.R. 92, 96), it has not even been mentioned in the Court of Appeal in any of the cases in the last thirty years in which one might have expected it to have been discussed. Although it was put forward by Hamilton L.J. in 1913 ([1913] 1 K.B. 398, 421) as the way out of the dilemma, he plainly in 1922 ([1922] 1 A.C. 44, 67) felt doubts about its efficacy and preferred to state the principle as one involving "a measure of care appropriate to the inability or disability of those who are immature." This is what Lord Atkinson was saying in *Cooke's* case ([1909] A.C. 229, 238) when he said that the duty must be measured by the licensor's knowledge of the habits, capacities and propensities of the licensees. These statements of the law are wide enough to allow as one of the factors determining the appropriate measure the licensor's knowledge of the habits of prudent parents in relation to little children. I think that Lord Sumner and Lord Atkinson are substantially at one with Lord Shaw in his statement of the relevant principle.

If this be the true principle to apply, then I have to consider whether the corporation ought in the present case to have anticipated the presence of the infant plaintiff unaccompanied. I say "unaccompanied" because the sister, while doubtless able to take care of herself as is shown by her own avoidance of the trench, was not old enough to take care of her little brother as well. There is no evidence in this case to show that little children frequently went unaccompanied on the open space in a way which ought to have brought home to the corporation that that was the use which was being made of its licence. Apart from evidence of that sort, I do not think that the corporation ought to have anticipated that it was a place in which children of five would be sent out to play by themselves. It is not an overcrowded neighbourhood; it is not as if it were the only green place in the centre of a city. The houses had gardens in which small children could play; if it be material, I believe that at the relevant time the plaintiff's garden was in fact fenced. The parents of children who might be expected to play there all live near and could have made themselves familiar with the space. They must have known that building operations were going on nearby and ought to have realised that that might involve the digging of trenches and holes. Even if it be prudent, which I do not think it is, for a parent to allow two small children out in this way on an October evening, the parents might at least have satisfied themselves that the place to which they allowed these little children to go held no dangers for them. Any parent who looked could have seen the trench and taken steps to prevent his child going there while it was still open. In my judgment, the corporation is entitled to assume that parents would behave in this naturally prudent way, and is not obliged to take it upon itself, in effect, to discharge parental duties. I conclude, therefore, that the infant plaintiff was on the land as a licensee, but that there was no breach of the corporation's duty towards him.

If I have failed to discover the true principle, then the alternative that I should apply is that of the conditional licence. If the general presumption be that a licence to a little child is conditional upon his being accompanied by an adult, there is nothing in the facts of this case to displace it. The infant plaintiff was not so accompanied and was, therefore, a trespasser, and so the claim would fail on that ground.

Questions
1. Which of the two devices preferred by Devlin J. should be used now that the law is controlled by the Occupiers' Liability Act 1957, s.2(2) (above, p. 114)?
2. How much would you bet that the child was trying to jump across the trench when he fell in? How could you prove it? Would it make any difference if you could?
3. Is the reference by Devlin J. to the Law Reform (Contributory Negligence) Act 1945 (below, p. 205) an appropriate one in the context?
4. Why not simply ask whether the defendants had behaved reasonably? Should they have (a) not dug the trench in the first place, (b) put a warning notice on top of the spoil, (c) filled the trench in for the weekend or (d) fenced off the whole area?

Note:
Wilde's Selfish Giant, who kept out of his garden the children who wanted to play in it, had read his law-books. He knew that if he didn't chase them out, he would be held to have permitted them to be there. Once there, they would fall off his apple-trees and eat the berries on his precious but poisonous shrubs. There would be endless litigation to determine the conceptual grounds of his liability or non-liability. So he kept them out. And they no doubt played in the street.

ROLES v. NATHAN

Court of Appeal [1963] 1 W.L.R. 1117; 107 S.J. 680; [1963] 2 All E.R. 908

Action by widow of visitor against occupier.

The Manchester Assembly Rooms, owned and occupied by the defendant, were heated by an old coke-burning boiler which smoked badly. Two chimney sweeps were called to clean it, but it was no better after they had done so. An expert, Collingwood, was called, saw that the boiler-room was dangerous through fumes and succeeded, though only by force, in removing the sweeps from it. He said that the sweep-hole and inspection chamber should be sealed before the boiler was lit, and the sweeps undertook to do that. On Friday evening the defendant's son-in-law, Mr. Corney, went to the boiler-room and found the sweeps working there with the fire on. They had not finished sealing off the apertures, and were to return the next day with more cement. On Saturday morning they were found there dead, the fire still burning brightly.

Elwes J. gave judgment for the widows of the sweeps, but the Court of Appeal allowed the defendant's appeal, Pearson L.J. dissenting.

LORD DENNING M.R.: . . . The judge found Mr. Corney guilty of negligence because "he failed to take such care as should have ensured that there was no fire lit until the sweep-hole had been sealed up." He said: "Unfortunately Mr. Corney did not tell the caretaker to draw the fire, or at any rate not to stoke it up." On this account he held that Mr. Corney was at fault, and the occupier liable. But he found the two sweeps guilty of contributory negligence, and halved the damages. The judge said: "That negligence"—that is to say, of the chimney sweeps—"consisted in the knowledge that there was gas about, or probably would be, the way they ignored explicit warnings and showed complete indifference to the danger which was pointed out to them in plain language, and this strange indifference to the fact that the fire was alight, when Mr. Collingwood had said it ought not to be, until the sweep-hole had been sealed."

The occupier now appeals and says that it is not a case of negligence and contributory negligence, but that, on the true application of the Occupiers' Liability Act 1957, the occupier was not liable at all. This is the first time we have had to consider that Act. It has been very beneficial. It has rid us of those two unpleasant characters, the invitee and the licensee, who haunted the courts for years, and it has replaced them by the attractive figure of a visitor, who has so far given no trouble at all. The Act has now been in force for six years, and hardly any case has come before the courts in which its interpretation has had to be considered. The draftsman expressed the hope that "the Act would replace a a principle of the common law with a new principle *of the common law;* instead of having the judgment of Willes J. construed as if it were a statute, one is to have a statute which can be construed as if it were a judgment of Willes J." [in *Indermaur v. Dames* (1866) L.R. 1 C.P. 274]. It seems that his hopes are being fulfilled. All the fine distinctions about traps have been thrown aside and replaced by the common duty of care.

"The common duty of care," the Act says, "is a duty to take such care as in all the circumstances of the case is reasonable to see that the visitor"—note the visitor, not the premises—"will be reasonably safe in using the premises for the purposes for which he is invited or permitted by the occupier to be there." That is comprehensive. All the circumstances have to be considered. But the Act goes on to give examples of the circumstances that are relevant. The particular one in question here is in subsection (3) of section 2: "The circumstances relevant for the present purpose include the degree of care, and of want of care, which would ordinarily be looked for in such a visitor, so that (for example) in proper cases . . . (*b*) an occupier may expect that a person, in the exercise of his calling, will appreciate and guard against any special risks ordinarily incident to it, so far as the occupier leaves him free to do so."

That subsection shows that *General Cleaning Contractors* v. *Christmas* ([1952] 1 K.B. 141) is still good law under this new Act. There a window cleaner (who was employed by independent contractors) was sent to clean the windows of a club. One of the windows was defective; it had not been inspected and repaired as it should have been. In consequence, when the window cleaner was cleaning it, it ran down quickly and trapped his hand, thus causing him to fall. It was held that he had no cause of action against the club. If it had been a guest who had his fingers trapped by the defective window, the guest could have recovered damages from the club. But the window cleaner could not do so. The reason is this: the householder is concerned to see that the windows are safe for his guests to open and close, but he is not concerned to see that they are safe for a window cleaner to hold on to. The risk of a defective window is a special risk, but it is ordinarily incident to the calling of a window cleaner, and so he must take care for himself, and not expect the householder to do so. Likewise in the case of a chimney sweep who comes to sweep the chimneys or to seal up a sweep-hole. The householder can reasonably expect the sweep to take care of himself so far as any dangers from the flues are concerned. These chimney sweeps ought to have known that there might be dangerous fumes about and ought to have taken steps to guard against them. They ought to have known that they should not attempt to seal up a sweep-hole whilst the fire was still alight. They ought to have had the fire withdrawn before they attempted to seal it up, or at any rate they ought not to have stayed in the alcove too long when there might be dangerous fumes about. All this was known to these two sweeps; they were repeatedly warned about it, and it was for them to guard against the danger. It was not for the occupier to do it, even though he was present and heard the warnings. When a householder calls in a specialist to deal with a defective installation on his premises, he can reasonably expect the specialist to appreciate and guard against the dangers arising from the defect. The householder is not bound to watch over him to see that he comes to no harm. I would hold, therefore, that the occupier here was under no duty of care to these sweeps, at any rate in regard to the dangers which caused their deaths. If it had been a different danger, as for instance if the stairs leading to the cellar gave way, the occupier might no doubt be responsible, but not for these dangers which were special risks ordinarily incidental to their calling.

Even if I am wrong about this point, and the occupier was under a duty of care to these chimney sweeps, the question arises whether the duty was discharged by the warning that was given to them. This brings us to subsection (4) which states: "In determining whether the occupier of premises has discharged the common duty of care to a visitor, regard is to be had to all the circumstances, so that (for example)—(a) where damage is caused to a visitor by a danger of which he had been warned by the occupier, the warning is not to be treated without more as absolving the occupier from liability, unless in all the circumstances it was enough to enable the visitor to be reasonably safe."

We all know the reason for this subsection. It was inserted so as to clear up the unsatisfactory state of the law as it had been left by the decision of the House of Lords in *London Graving Dock Co.* v. *Horton* ([1951] A.C. 737). That case was commonly supposed to have decided that, when a person comes onto premises as an invitee, and is injured by the defective or dangerous condition of the premises (due to the default of the occupier), it is nevertheless a complete defence for the occupier to prove that the invitee knew of the danger, or had been warned of it. Suppose, for instance, that there was only one way of getting into and out of premises, and it was by a footbridge over a stream which was rotten and dangerous. According to *Horton's* case, the occupier could escape all liability to any visitor by putting up a notice: "This bridge is dangerous," even though there was no other way by which the visitor could get in or out, and he had no option but to go over the bridge. In such a case, section 2(4) makes it clear that the occupier would nowadays be liable. But if there were two footbridges, one of which was rotten, and the other safe a hundred yards away, the occupier could still escape liability, even today, by putting up a notice: "Do not use this footbridge. It is dangerous. There is a safe one further upstream." Such a warning is sufficient because it does enable the visitor to be reasonably safe.

I think that the law would probably have developed on these lines in any case; see *Greene* v. *Chelsea Borough Council* ([1954] 2 Q.B. 127), where I ventured to say "knowledge or notice of the danger is only a defence when the plaintiff is free to act upon that knowledge or notice so as to avoid the danger." But the subsection has now made it clear. A warning does not absolve the occupier, unless it is enough to enable the visitor to be reasonably safe.

Apply subsection (4) to this case. I am quite clear that the warnings which were given to the sweeps were enough to enable them to be reasonably safe. The sweeps would have been quite safe if they had heeded these warnings. They should not have come back that evening and attempted to seal up the sweep-hole while the fire was still alight. They ought to have waited till next morning, and then they should have seen that the fire was out before they attempted to seal up the sweep-hole. In any case they should not have stayed too long in the sweep-hole. In short, it was entirely their own fault. The judge held that it was contributory negligence. I would go further and say that under the Act the occupier has, by the warnings, discharged his duty.

I would therefore be in favour of allowing this appeal and entering judgment for the defendants.

Note:

Firemen (who do not, like policemen, have a claim under the Criminal Injuries Compensation Scheme for the injuries they typically suffer at work) seem to be suing rather a lot these days.

In one case a fire broke out at a small station in Liverpool because the station-master, the sole person manning it, had left the station without closing the doors of the stove and without telling his employer, as he was instructed to do. The employer consequently told the Fire Brigade that he was still there, so the plaintiff searched a loft for him and was injured while doing so. The trial judge dismissed the claim, but the Court of Appeal held that the station-master's conduct was negligent vis-à-vis the plaintiff since it had exposed him to unnecessary risk. (*Hartley* v. *British Railways Board,* January 28, 1981 (C.A.)).

Then a fireman called Salmon was burnt in a fish and chip shop where an employee had carelessly left a light on under the deep-fryer. During the night the oil got hotter and hotter and then caught fire. The heat from the fire melted the seals of the gas meter and the escaping gas exploded. The defendant was held liable (*Salmon* v. *Seafarers Restaurants,* June 29, 1982. Woolf J.).

Previously the House of Lords had held that an occupier of business premises was not liable for fatal injuries to firemen caused when an accidental fire spread more rapidly than it would have done if the occupier had followed the instructions of a fire-marshal eight months previously and constructed a fire-screen round the open stairs on an upper floor. (*Bermingham* v. *Sher,* on appeal from 1979 S.C. 43).

Are these decisions reconcilable?

Section 4.—Skilful Defendants

WELLS v. COOPER

Court of Appeal [1958] 2 Q.B. 265; [1958] 3 W.L.R. 128; 102 S.J. 508; [1958] 2 All E.R. 527

Action by visitor against occupier in respect of personal injury.

The plaintiff went to the defendant's house to deliver fish and was asked to stay for a cup of tea. After drinking it, he left by the back door. As he pulled it shut, with the force required by a strong wind and the draught-excluder, the door-handle came away in his hand, and he fell four feet to the ground from the top of the back steps. The door-handle, which was of the lever type, had been screwed on with three-quarter inch screws by the defendant himself, a "do-it-yourself" man who frequently did such jobs around the house; he replaced the previous door-handle since he thought it was unsafe.

Stable J. dismissed the action on the ground that the accident was not one which was reasonably foreseeable; the plaintiff appealed to the Court of Appeal without success.

JENKINS L.J.: The judgment which I am about to read is the judgment of the court in this case. . . .

The relationship subsisting between the defendant and the plaintiff at the time of the accident was admittedly that of invitor and invitee. In these circumstances it is sought to make the defendant liable for the accident on two grounds. First, it is said that the defendant was in breach of his duty as invitor to the plaintiff as invitee. The insecure handle was an unusual danger of which the defendant knew or ought to have known and against which he should consequently have taken reasonable care to guard the plaintiff. Secondly, it is said that in carrying out the work of fixing the handle himself the defendant, irrespective of the invitor-invitee relationship, assumed a duty towards the plaintiff as a lawful visitor to the house to take reasonable care to protect him against any danger created by the insecurity of the handle. See *Riden* v. *A. C. Billings & Sons Ltd.,* Court of Appeal ([1957] 1 Q.B. 46), and in the House of Lords ([1958] A.C. 240).

We should have thought that in the circumstances of this case the first of these two possible grounds of liability is the more appropriate. But in truth there is little difference between them for the present purpose. Either way the duty owed by the defendant to the plaintiff was a duty to take reasonable care for his safety, and the question is whether on the facts of this case the defendant did take reasonable care to that end. . . .

As above related, the defendant did the work himself. We do not think the mere fact that he did it himself instead of employing a professional carpenter to do it constituted a breach of his duty of care. No doubt some kinds of work involve such highly specialised skill and knowledge, and create such serious dangers if not properly done, that an ordinary occupier owing a duty of care to others in regard to the safety of premises would fail in that duty if he undertook such work himself instead of employing experts to do it for him. See *Haseldine* v. *C. A. Daw & Son Ltd., per* Scott L.J. ([1941] 2 K.B. 343, 356). But the work here in question was not of that order. It was a trifling domestic replacement well within the competence of a householder accustomed to doing small carpentering jobs about his home, and of a kind which must be done every day by hundreds of householders up and down the country.

Accordingly, we think that the defendant did nothing unreasonable in undertaking the work himself. But it behoved him, if he was to discharge his duty of care to persons such as the plaintiff, to do the work with reasonable care and skill, and we think the degree of care and skill required of him must be measured not by reference to the degree of competence in such matters which he personally happened to possess, but by reference to the degree of care and skill which a reasonably competent carpenter might be expected to apply to the work in question. Otherwise, the extent of the protection that an invitee could claim in relation to work done by the invitor himself would vary according to the capacity of the invitor, who could free himself from liability merely by showing that he had done the best of which he was capable, however good, bad or indifferent that best might be.

Accordingly, we think the standard of care and skill to be demanded of the defendant in order to discharge his duty of care to the plaintiff in the fixing of the new handle in the present case must be the degree of care and skill to be expected of a reasonably competent carpenter doing the work in question. This does not mean that the degree of care and skill required is to be measured by reference to the contractual obligations as to the quality of his work assumed by a professional carpenter working for reward, which would, in our view, set the standard too high. The question is simply what steps would a reasonably competent carpenter wishing to fix a handle such as this securely to a door such as this have taken with a view to achieving that object.

In fact the only complaint made by the plaintiff in regard to the way in which the defendant fixed the new handle is that three-quarter inch screws were inadequate and that one inch screws should have been used. The question may, therefore, be stated more narrowly as being whether a reasonably competent carpenter fixing this handle would have appreciated that three-quarter inch screws such as those used by the defendant would not be adequate to fix it securely and would accordingly have used one inch screws instead. . . .

In relation to a trifling and perfectly simple operation such as the fixing of the new handle we think that the defendant's experience of domestic carpentry is sufficient to justify his inclusion in the category of reasonably competent carpenters. The matter then stands thus. The defendant, a reasonably competent carpenter, used three-quarter inch screws, believing them to be adequate for the purpose of fixing the handle. There is no doubt that he was doing his best to make the handle secure and believed that he had done so. Accordingly, he must be taken to have discharged his duty of reasonable care, unless the belief that three-quarter inch screws would be adequate was one which no reasonably competent carpenter could reasonably entertain, or, in other words, an obvious blunder which should at once have been apparent to him as a reasonably competent carpenter. The evidence adduced on the plaintiff's side failed, in the judge's view, to make that out. He saw and heard the witnesses, and had demonstrated to him the strength of attachment provided by three-quarter inch screws. We see no sufficient reason for differing from his conclusion. Indeed, the fact that the handle remained secure during the period of four or five months between the time it was fixed and the date of the accident, although no doubt in constant use throughout that period, makes it very difficult to accept the view that the inadequacy of the three-quarter inch screws should have been obvious to the defendant at the time when he decided to use them. . . .

Each case of this kind depends on its own particular facts, to which the broad principle of reasonable care must be applied with common sense. The task of finding the facts and applying the principle to them is eminently a matter for the court of first instance. On the facts of this case, we find it impossible to hold that the judge came to a wrong conclusion, having regard in particular to the view which he took, and was entitled to take, of the expert evidence on the strength of which it was sought, after the event, to show that the defendant knew or ought to have known at the time when he fixed the handle that the three-quarter inch screws were inadequate, notwithstanding that they in fact sufficed to hold the handle securely for the four or five months of constant use which preceded the accident.

Accordingly, we would dismiss this appeal.

Questions
1. Which of the following statements are correct?
   (i) The question is not whether the defendant did his best.
   (ii) The question is not whether he did as well as a professional carpenter would have done, acting under contract.
   (iii) The question is whether he did as well as a professional carpenter working for himself on a Sunday afternoon.
   (iv) If the defendant was a carpenter of some experience, the question is whether he did his best, except in the case where he should have known that what he was doing would strike a professional carpenter as an obvious blunder.
2. If the defendant here had hired a carpenter to do the job, and that carpenter had done it as the defendant did here, and the defendant had fallen downstairs as a result, would the carpenter have been liable to the defendant? To the plaintiff?

Note:
Most of the cases so far have been concerned with care rather than with skill, but the distinction is not very clear. Some tasks call for expertise if they are to be properly executed. Those who embark on them without having that expertise are careless in embarking; those who have the expertise but do not use it are liable for the faulty execution. It is where, as in this case, it is not clear that only an expert would undertake the job that one has the problem of whether to apply the standard of the expert or not.

Cases involving professional skill are less amenable to a jury. The jury knows what should be done by a person in the shoes of Mrs. Alexander (*Glasgow Corpn.* v. *Muir,* above, p. 116), but cannot say, except at second hand and after conflicting expert evidence, what a man in a surgeon's mask should have done. Nevertheless, the same standard is applied, and a ruling which required gross negligence in a doctor was overruled in *Hunter* v. *Hanley,* 1955 S.L.T. 213. A deviation from proper practice generates liability. But this involves considerations of time and place. A doctor will not be liable for not having the latest equipment, or for not having read the latest number of an American learned periodical. One cannot demand from a garage in the West Highlands of Scotland the same standard of expedition and professional competence which can be hoped for in the metropolis. These factors can easily be taken into account in the professional negligence cases, since the plaintiff and defendant are almost always in a "special relationship," whether payment passes or not. If you *choose* to go to a jeweller in Hatton Garden to have your ears pierced, you cannot expect a Harley Street puncture (*Philips* v. *Whiteley* [1938] 1 All E.R. 566). But see the views of Megaw L.J. above, p. 98.

BOLAM v. FRIERN HOSPITAL MANAGEMENT COMMITTEE

Queen's Bench [1957] 1 W.L.R. 582; 101 S.J. 357; [1957] 2 All E.R. 118

Action by patient against hospital in respect of personal injury.

The plaintiff broke his pelvis during electro-convulsive therapy treatment at the defendants' hospital. He alleged that the doctor was negligent in not warning him of the risks of the treatment, in not giving relaxant drugs before the treatment, and in not holding him down during the treatment. The trial took place before McNair J. and a jury. After the evidence the learned judge summed up as follows.

McNair J.: Members of the jury, it is now my task to try to help you to reach a true verdict, bearing in mind that you take the law from me and that the facts are entirely a matter for your consideration. You will only give damages if you are satisfied that the defendants have been proved to be guilty of negligence. Counsel for the plaintiff quite squarely faces up to that and accepts that he has to satisfy you that there was some act of negligence, in the sense which I will describe in a moment, on behalf of the defendants—and that primarily means Dr. Allfrey—and that that proved negligence did cause the injuries which the plaintiff suffered, or at least that the defendants negligently failed to take some precaution which would have minimised the risk of those injuries.

Before dealing with the law, it is right that I should say this, that you must look at this case in its proper perspective. You have been told by Dr. Page that he had only seen one acetabular fracture in 50,000 cases, involving a quarter of a million treatments, and it is clear, is it not, that the particular injury which produced these disastrous results in the plaintiff is one of extreme rarity. Another fact which I think it is right that you should bear in mind is this, that whereas some years ago when a patient went into a mental institution afflicted with mental illness, suffering from one of the most terrible ills from which a man can suffer, he had very little hope of recovery—in most cases he could only expect to be carefully and kindly treated until in due course merciful death released him from his sufferings—today, according to the evidence, the position is entirely changed. The evidence shows that today a man who enters one of these institutions suffering from particular types of mental disorder has a real chance of recovery. Dr. Marshall told you that in his view that change was due almost entirely to the introduction of physical methods of treatment of mental illness, and of those physical methods the electric convulsive therapy which you have been considering during the last few days is the most important. When you approach this case and consider whether it has been proved against this hospital that negligence was committed, you have to consider that against that background, and bearing in mind the enormous benefits which are conferred upon unfortunate men and women by this form of treatment.

Another general comment which I would make is this: on the evidence it is clear, is it not, that the use of E.C.T. is a progressive science. You have had it traced for you historically over the quite few years in which it has been used in this country, and you may think on the evidence that even today there is no standard settled technique upon all points, to which all competent doctors will agree. The doctors called before you have mentioned in turn different variants of the technique they use. Some use restraining sheets, some use relaxants, some use manual control; but the final question you have got to make up your minds about is this, whether Dr. Allfrey, following upon the practice he had learnt at Friern and following upon the technique which he had shown to him by Dr. Bastarrechea, was negligent in failing to use relaxant drugs or, if he decided not to use relaxant drugs, that he was negligent in failing to exercise any manual control over the patient beyond merely arranging for his shoulders to be held, the chin supported, a gag used, and a pillow put under his back. No one suggests that there was any negligence in the diagnosis or in the decision to use E.C.T. Furthermore, no one suggests that Dr. Allfrey or anyone at the hospital was in any way indifferent to the care of their patients. The only question is really a question of professional skill.

Before I turn to that I must tell you what in law we mean by "negligence." In the ordinary case which does not involve any special skill, negligence in law means a failure to do some act which a reasonable man in the circumstances would do, or the doing of some act which a reasonable man in the circumstances would not do; and if that failure or the doing of that act results in injury, then there is a cause of action. How do you test whether this act or failure is negligent? In an ordinary case it is generally said you judge it by the action of the man in the street. He is the ordinary man. In one case it has been said you judge it by the conduct of the man on the top of a Clapham omnibus. He is the ordinary man. But where you get a situation which involves the use of some special skill or competence, then the test as to whether there has been negligence or not is not the test of the man on the top of a Clapham omnibus, because he has not got this special skill. The test is the standard of the ordinary skilled man exercising and professing to have that special skill. A man need not possess the highest expert skill; it is well established law that it is sufficient if he exercises the ordinary skill of an ordinary competent man exercising that particular art. I do not think that I quarrel much with any of the submissions in law which have been put before you by counsel. Mr. Fox-Andrews put it in this way, that in the case of a medical man, negligence means failure to act in accordance with the standards of reasonably competent medical men at the time. That is a perfectly accurate statement, as long as it is remembered that there may be one or more perfectly proper standards; and if he conforms with one of those proper standards, then he is not negligent. Mr. Fox-Andrews also was quite right, in my judgment, in saying that a mere personal belief that a particular technique is best is no defence unless that belief is based on reasonable grounds. That again is unexceptionable. But the emphasis which is laid by the defence is on this aspect of negligence, that the real question you have to make up your minds about on each of the three major topics is whether the defendants, in acting in the way they did, were acting in accordance with a practice of competent respected professional opinion. Mr. Stirling submitted that if you are satisfied that they were acting in accordance with a practice of a competent body of professional opinion, then it would be wrong for you to hold that negligence was established. In a recent Scottish case, *Hunter* v. *Hanley* (1955 S.L.T. 213, 217), Lord President Clyde said: "In the realm of diagnosis and treatment there is ample scope for genuine difference of opinion and one man clearly is not negligent merely because his conclusion differs from that of other professional men, nor because he has displayed less skill or knowledge than others would have shown. The true test for establishing negligence in diagnosis or treatment on the part of a doctor is whether he has been proved to be guilty of such failure as no doctor of ordinary skill would be guilty of, if acting with ordinary care." If that statement of the true test is qualified by the words "in all the circumstances," Mr. Fox-Andrews would not seek to say that that expression of opinion does not accord with the English law. It is just a question of expression. I myself would prefer to put it this way, that he is not guilty of negligence if he has acted in accordance with a practice accepted as proper by a responsible body of medical men skilled in that particular art. I do not think there is much difference in sense. It is just a different way of expressing the same thought. Putting it the other way round, a man is not negligent, if he is acting in accordance with such a practice, merely because there is a body of opinion who would take a contrary view. At the same time, that does not mean that a medical man can obstinately and pig-headedly carry on with some old technique if it has been proved to be contrary to what is really substantially the whole of informed medical opinion. Otherwise you might get men today saying: "I do not believe in anaesthetics. I do not believe in antiseptics. I am going to continue to do my surgery in the way it was done in the eighteenth century." That clearly would be wrong.

Before I get to the details of the case, it is right to say this, that it is not essential for you to decide which of two practices is the better practice, as long as you accept that what the defendants did was in accordance with a practice accepted by responsible persons; if the result of the evidence is that you are satisfied that his practice is better than the practice spoken of on the other side, then it is really a stronger case. Finally, bear this in mind, that you are now considering whether it was negligent for certain action to be taken in August 1954, not in February 1957; and in one of the well-known cases on this topic it has been said you must not look with 1957 spectacles at what happened in 1954.

The plaintiff's case, as it has developed in the evidence, primarily depends upon three points. Firstly, that the defendants were negligent in failing to give to the plaintiff a warning of the risks involved in the treatment, so that he might have a chance to decide whether he was going to take those risks or not. Secondly, that they were negligent in failing to use any relaxant drugs which admittedly, if used, would have to all intents and purposes excluded the risk of fracture altogether. Thirdly—and this was, I think, the point upon which Mr. Fox-Andrews laid the most emphasis—that if relaxants are not used, then at least some form of manual control beyond shoulder control, support of the chin, and pillow under the back, must be used. . . .

Having considered the evidence on this point, you have to make up your minds whether it has been proved to your satisfaction that when the defendants adopted the practice they did (namely, the practice of saying very little and waiting for questions from the patient), they were falling below a proper standard of competent professional opinion on this question of whether or not it is right to warn. Members of the jury, though it is a matter entirely for you, you may well think that when dealing with a mentally sick man and having a strong belief that his only hope of cure is E.C.T. treatment, a doctor cannot be criticised if he does not stress the dangers which he believes to be minimal involved in that treatment.

If you do come to the conclusion that proper practice requires some warning to be given, the second question which you have to decide is: If a warning had been given, would it have made any difference? The only man who really can tell you the answer to that question is the plaintiff, and he was never asked the question. . . .

I have not said anything about Dr. Allfrey in detail, though he is primarily the man under attack, for it was during his operation that the disaster occurred. You have got to form your judgment of Dr. Allfrey, and make up your minds whether you think that he was a careful practitioner interested in his art, giving thought to the different problems, or whether he was a man who was quite content just to follow the swim. You may recall that on quite a number of occasions in the course of his evidence he gave instances where he had really applied his inquiring mind to the problem and come to a conclusion. On the use of restraint, he told you that during his training he knew that there was a school of thought that favoured restraint, but that he got the impression that the general view was against it. He recalls how he was taught by the man responsible for his training that there was a greater danger of fracture if two ends of a rigid member like a stick were held firm than if one was left swinging or both were left swinging, and that rather persuaded him that there was something in the view that restraint should not be used. He, at his hospital, Knole, adopted under tuition (and, as he got older, on his own responsibility) the practice of leaving the limbs free to move, merely holding down the shoulders. When he got to Friern he found the same practice was being carried out by his chief there, Dr. Bastarrechea. Having had his technique shown to him, he followed it. The question you have got to make up your minds about is whether he is, in following that practice, doing something which no competent medical practitioner using due care would do, or whether, on the other hand, he is acting in accordance with a perfectly well-recognised school of thought. Dr. Marshall at Netherne adopts the same practice. Dr. Baker at Banstead adopts the same practice. It is true, and in fact interesting as showing the diversity of practice, that Dr. Page at the Three Counties mental institution adopts a modification of that, inasmuch as he prefers to carry out the treatment in bed, with the patient controlled to some extent by the blanket, sheets and counterpane. That may be of interest to you as showing the diversity of practice; but it would not be right, would it, to take that as a condemnation of the practice adopted by the defendants? . . .

After a retirement of forty minutes the jury returned a verdict for the defendants.

Note:

The words of McNair J. were enthusiastically endorsed as "true doctrine" by Lord Edmund-Davies in *Whitehouse* v. *Jordan* [1981] 1 All E.R. 267. That case involved a claim of negligence against a senior registrar in charge of a childbirth in which the child suffered brain damage. The defendant realised that normal birth by contraction was impossible and attempted a trial by forceps in order to see whether delivery by forceps, a better method than Caesarean section, might be possible. The question was whether he pulled too long and too hard. The trial judge found that he had; the Court of Appeal, by a majority, differed; and the House of Lords unanimously upheld the Court of Appeal. Lord Russell said this: "Some passages in the Court of Appeal might suggest that if a doctor makes an error of judgment he cannot be found guilty of negligence. This must be wrong. An error of judgment is not *per se* incompatible with negligence . . . I would accept the phrase 'a mere error of judgment' if the impact of the word 'mere' is to indicate that not all errors of judgment show a lapse from the standard of skill and care required to be exercised to avoid a charge of negligence."

Compare with that of McNair J. the instruction given to the jury by Tindal C.J. in *Lanphier* v. *Phipos* (1838) 8 C. & P. 475; 173 E.R. 581. Frightened by a cow, Mrs. Lanphier had fallen and broken her wrist. The defendant applied splints, which he left on for seven weeks, and nursed the inflammation with vinegar; Mrs. Lanphier's condition did not improve.

"What you will have to say is this, whether you are satisfied that the injury sustained is attributable to the want of a reasonable and proper degree of care and skill in the defendant's treatment. Every person who enters into a learned profession undertakes to bring to the exercise of it a reasonable degree of care and skill. He does not undertake, if he is an attorney, that at all events you shall gain your case, nor does a surgeon undertake that he will perform a cure; nor does he undertake to use the highest possible degree of skill. There may be persons who have higher education and greater advantages than he has, but he undertakes to bring a fair, reasonable and competent degree of skill, and you will say whether, in this case, the injury was occasioned by the want of such skill in the defendant. . . . " The jury found a verdict for the plaintiff, £100 damages.

British people have hitherto displayed a decent distaste for suing their doctors (who are in some sense salvors—see above, p. 77, with the consequence that one of the medical protection societies can offer doctors unlimited liability insurance for as little as £150 per annum. There are, of course, some gross and disastrous errors, for which compensation should be paid, but one should bear in mind the foolish and unmeritorious claimants also: the parents of a girl who claimed damages for shock when the doctor diagnosed as gonorrhoea what was *herpes simplex,* the relatives of an attempted suicide whose doctor wrongly identified the poison, and the patient who sued the psychiatrist for letting her fall in love with him. That legal aid committees and judges should be slow to extend litigation and liability is suggested by the advice of the protection society to its members that they should communicate with it before embarking on experimental procedures.

Before long, tort lawyers are going to have to face problems caused by the development of techniques such as organ transplants and by the growth in popularity of fringe methods of treatment such as acupuncture and homoeopathic and herbal remedies.

ROE v. MINISTER OF HEALTH

Court of Appeal [1954] 2 Q.B. 66; [1954] 2 W.L.R. 915; 98 S.J. 319; [1954] 2 All E.R. 131

Action by patients against hospital and anaesthetist in respect of personal injury.

The two plaintiffs in these consolidated actions entered hospital for minor surgery and emerged permanently paralysed from the waist down. The reason was that the ampoules of the anaesthetic, nupercaine, which was injected spinally, had tiny cracks in them, and some phenol, the disinfectant in which they were kept, had percolated through those cracks and had contaminated the anaesthetic.

The action was brought against the Minister of Health, as successor in title to the trustees of the Chesterfield and North Derbyshire Royal Hospital, and the anaesthetist, Dr. Graham, who had a private practice but was under an obligation to provide a regular service at the hospital.

The trial judge dismissed the plaintiffs' actions ([1954] 1 W.L.R. 128), and the Court of Appeal dismissed their appeal.

DENNING L.J.: No one can be unmoved by the disaster which has befallen these two unfortunate men. They were both working men before they went into the Chesterfield Hospital in October 1947. Both were insured contributors to the hospital, paying a small sum each week, in return for which they were entitled to be admitted for treatment when they were ill. Each of them was operated on in the hospital for a minor trouble, one for something wrong with a cartilage in his knee, the other for a hydrocele. The operations were both on the same day, October 13, 1947. Each of them was given a spinal anaesthetic by a visiting anaesthetist, Dr. Graham. Each of them has in consequence been paralysed from the waist down.

The judge has said that those facts do not speak for themselves, but I think that they do. They certainly call for an explanation. Each of these men is entitled to say to the hospital: "While I was in your hands something has been done to me which has wrecked my life. Please explain how it has come to pass." The reason why the judge took a different view was because he thought that the hospital authorities could disclaim responsibility for the anaesthetist, Dr. Graham: and, as it might be his fault and not theirs, the hospital authorities were not called upon to give an explanation. I think that that reasoning is wrong. In the first place, I think that the hospital authorities are responsible for the whole of their staff, not only for the nurses and doctors, but also for the anaesthetists and the surgeons. It does not matter whether they are permanent or temporary, resident or visiting, whole-time or part-time. The hospital authorities are responsible for all of them. The reason is because, even if they are not servants, they are the agents of the hospital to give the treatment. The only exception is the case of consultants or anaesthetists selected and employed by the patient himself. I went into the matter with some care in *Cassidy* v. *Ministry of Health* ([1951] 2 K.B. 343) and I adhere to all I there said. In the second place, I do not think that the hospital authorities and Dr. Graham can both avoid giving an explanation by the simple expedient of each throwing responsibility on to the other. If an injured person shows that one or other or both of two persons injured him, but cannot say which of them it was, then he is not defeated altogether. He can call on each of them for an explanation: see *Baker* v. *Market Harborough Industrial Co-operative Society* ([1953] 1 W.L.R. 1472).

I approach this case, therefore, on the footing that the hospital authorities and Dr. Graham were called on to give an explanation of what has happened. But I think that they have done so. They have spared no trouble or expense to seek out the cause of the disaster. The greatest specialists in the land were called to give evidence. In the result, the judge has found that what happened was this: In October 1947, a spinal anaesthetic was in use at the hospital called nupercaine. It was a liquid supplied by the makers in closed glass ampoules. These were test tubes sealed with glass. When the time came to use it, a nurse filed off the glass top, the anaesthetist inserted his needle and drew off the nupercaine, which he then injected into the spine of the patient. It so happened that in this process there was some risk of the needle becoming infected. The reason was because the outside of the ampoule might become contaminated with a germ of some kind: and the needle might touch it as the anaesthetist was filling it. That this risk was a real one is shown by the fact that quite a number of cases became complicated by some infection or other.

In order to avoid this risk, the senior anaesthetist at the hospital, Dr. Pooler, decided to keep the ampoules in a jar of disinfectant called phenol, which was a form of carbolic acid. This disinfectant was made in two strengths. The stronger was tinted light blue and the weaker was tinted pale red. This was so as to distinguish it from water. Following Dr. Pooler, the junior anaesthetist, Dr. Graham, thought that it was a good thing to disinfect the ampoules in this way and he adopted the same system. By a great misfortune this new system of disinfecting had in it a danger of which Dr. Pooler and Dr. Graham were quite unaware. The danger was this: the ampoules in the jar might become cracked; the cracks might be so fine or so placed that they could not be detected by ordinary inspection, and the carbolic disinfectant would then seep through the cracks into the nupercaine, and no one would realise that it had taken place. Thus the anaesthetist, who thought he was inserting pure nupercaine into the spine of the patient, was in fact inserting nupercaine mixed with carbolic acid. That is the very thing which happened in the case of these two men. Carbolic acid was inserted into their spines and corroded all the nerves which controlled the lower half of their bodies.

That is the explanation of the disaster, and the question is: were any of the staff negligent? I pause to say that once the accident is explained, no question of *res ipsa loquitur* arises. The only question is whether on the facts as now ascertained anyone was negligent. Mr. Elwes said that the staff were negligent in two respects: (1) in not colouring the phenol with a deep dye; (2) in cracking the ampoules. I will take them in order: (1) The deep tinting. If the anaesthetists had foreseen that the ampoules might get cracked with cracks that could not be detected on inspection they would no doubt have dyed the phenol a deep blue; and this would have exposed the contamination. But I do not think that their failure to foresee this was negligence. It is so easy to be wise after the event and to condemn as negligence that which was only a misadventure. We ought always to be on our guard against it, especially in cases against hospitals and doctors. Medical science has conferred great benefits on mankind, but these benefits are attended by considerable risks. Every surgical operation is attended by risks. We cannot take the benefits without taking the risks. Every advance in technique is also attended by risks. Doctors, like the rest of us, have to learn by experience; and experience often teaches in a hard way. Something goes wrong and shows up a weakness, and then it is put right. That is just what happened here. Dr. Graham sought to escape the danger of infection by disinfecting the ampoule. In escaping that known danger he unfortunately ran into another danger. He did not know that there could be undetectable cracks, but it was not negligent for him not to know it at that time. We must not look at the 1947 accident with 1954 spectacles. The judge acquitted Dr. Graham of negligence and we should uphold his decision.

(2) The cracks. In cracking the ampoules, there must, I fear, have been some carelessness by someone in the hospital. The ampoules were quite strong and the

sisters said that they should not get cracked if proper care was used in handling them. They must have been jolted in some way by someone. This raises an interesting point of law. This carelessness was, in a sense, one of the causes of the disaster; but the person who jolted the ampoule cannot possibly have foreseen what dire consequences would follow. There were so many intervening opportunities of inspection that she might reasonably think that if the jolting caused a crack, it would be discovered long before any harm came of it. As Somervell L.J. has pointed out, she herself would probably examine the ampoule for a crack, and seeing none, would return it to the jar. The anaesthetist himself did in fact examine it for cracks, and finding none, used it. The trouble was that nobody realised that there might be a crack which could not be detected on ordinary examination. What, then, is the legal position?

It may be said that, by reason of the decision of this court in *Re Polemis* ([1921] 3 K.B. 560) the hospital authorities are liable for all the consequences of the initial carelessness of the nurse, even though the consequences could not reasonably have been foreseen. But the decision in *Re Polemis* is of very limited application. The reason is because there are two preliminary questions to be answered before it can come into play. The first question in every case is whether there was a duty of care owed to the plaintiff; and the test of duty depends, without doubt, on what you should foresee. There is no duty of care owed to a person when you could not reasonably foresee that he might be injured by your conduct: see *Hay or Bourhill* v. *Young* ([1943] A.C. 92), *Woods* v. *Duncan* ([1946] A.C. 401, 437), *per* Lord Russell and *per* Lord Porter.

The second question is whether the neglect of duty was a "cause" of the injury in the proper sense of that term; and causation, as well as duty, often depends on what you should foresee. The chain of causation is broken when there is an intervening action which you could not reasonably be expected to foresee: see *Woods* v. *Duncan* (421, 431, 432), *per* Lord Simon, Lord Macmillan, and Lord Simonds. It is even broken when there is an intervening omission which you could not reasonably expect. For instance, in cases based on *Donoghue* v. *Stevenson* a manufacturer is not liable if he might reasonably contemplate that an intermediate examination would probably be made. It is only when those two preliminary questions—duty and causation—are answered in favour of the plaintiff that the third question, remoteness of damage, comes into play.

Even then your ability to foresee the consequences may be vital. It is decisive where there is intervening conduct by other persons: see *Stansbie* v. *Troman* ([1948] 2 K.B. 48), *Lewis* v. *Carmarthenshire County Council* ([1953] 1 W.L.R. 1439). It is only disregarded when the negligence is the immediate or precipitating cause of the damage, as in *Re Polemis* and *Thurogood* v. *Van den Berghs & Jurgens Ltd.* ([1951] 2 K.B. 537). In all these cases you will find that the three questions, duty, causation, and remoteness, run continually into one another. It seems to me that they are simply three different ways of looking at one and the same problem. Starting with the proposition that a negligent person should be liable, within reason, for the consequences of his conduct, the extent of his liability is to be found by asking the one question: Is the consequence fairly to be regarded as within the risk created by the negligence? If so, the negligent person is liable for it: but otherwise not.

Even when the three questions are taken singly, they can only be determined by applying common sense to the facts of each particular case: see as to duty, *King* v. *Phillips* ([1953] 1 Q.B. 429, 437), as to causation, *Stapley* v. *Gypsum Mines Ltd.* ([1953] A.C. 663, 681), *per* Lord Reid; and as to remoteness, *Liesbosch, Dredger* v. *Edison S.S. (Owners)* ([1933] A.C. 449), *per* Lord Wright. Instead of asking three questions, I should have thought that in many cases it would be simpler and better to ask the one question: is the consequence within the risk? And to answer it by applying ordinary plain common sense. That is the way in which Singleton L.J. and Hodson L.J. approached a difficult problem in *Jones* v. *Livox Quarries Ltd.* ([1952]

2 Q.B. 608), and I should like to approach this problem in the same way.

Asking myself, therefore, what was the risk involved in careless handling of the ampoules, I answer by saying that there was such a probability of intervening examination as to limit the risk. The only consequence which could reasonably be anticipated was the loss of a quantity of nupercaine, but not the paralysis of a patient. The hospital authorities are therefore not liable for it.

When you stop to think of what happened in the present case, you will realise that it was a most extraordinary chapter of accidents. In some way the ampoules must have received a jolt, perhaps while a nurse was putting them into the jar or while a trolley was being moved along. The jolt cannot have been very severe. It was not severe enough to break any of the ampoules or even to crack them so far as anyone could see. But it was just enough to produce an invisible crack. The crack was of a kind which no one in any experiment has been able to reproduce again. It was too fine to be seen, but it was enough to let in sufficient phenol to corrode the nerves, whilst still leaving enough nupercaine to anaesthetise the patient. And this very exceptional crack occurred not in one ampoule only, but in two ampoules used on the self-same day in two successive operations; and none of the other ampoules was damaged at all. This has taught the doctors to be on their guard against invisible cracks. Never again, it is to be hoped, will such a thing happen. After this accident a leading textbook was published in 1951 which contains the significant warning: "Never place ampoules of local anaesthetic solution in alcohol or spirit. This common practice is probably responsible for some of the cases of permanent paralysis reported after spinal analgesia." If the hospitals were to continue the practice after this warning, they could not complain if they were found guilty of negligence. But the warning had not been given at the time of this accident. Indeed, it was the extraordinary accident to these two men which first disclosed the danger. Nowadays it would be negligence not to realise the danger, but it was not then.

One final word. These two men have suffered such terrible consequences that there is a natural feeling that they should be compensated. But we should be doing a disservice to the community at large if we were to impose liability on hospitals and doctors for everything that happens to go wrong. Doctors would be led to think more of their own safety than of the good of their patients. Initiative would be stifled and confidence shaken. A proper sense of proportion requires us to have regard to the conditions in which hospitals and doctors have to work. We must insist on due care for the patient at every point, but we must not condemn as negligence that which is only a misadventure. I agree with my Lord that these appeals should be dismissed.

Questions

1. Does the question formulated by Denning L.J. in terms of "risk" invite any other answer than "Yes" or "No"? And would it be better if judges answered it in one word? (See *Qualcast*, above, p. 101.

2. Contrast the attitudes of Lord Denning to fire brigades (*Watt*, above, p. 112), employers (*Christmas*, above, p. 107), village cricketers (*Miller*, above, p. 109) and hospitals (the principal case). Would the reasons he gives for denying liability in this case apply with equal force to industrial development during the last century? Or now? What about pharmaceutical companies?

Note:

The requirement of fault clearly entails that a defendant must be judged by the standard prevalent at the time of the conduct being impugned: a person cannot be blamed for not knowing what no one yet knows. But what if fault is not required? If manufacturers of products are to be strictly liable for defects, as Brussels will doubtless soon direct, are they to be liable for "development risks" or can they defend on "state of the art"? In other words, are they liable if the defect is shown to be such only by subsequent discoveries, as in the present case? The United Kingdom desires that there should be no liability in such a case, but then we believe in the importance of fault rather more than our friends abroad.

STOKES v. GUEST, KEEN & NETTLEFOLD (BOLTS AND NUTS) LTD.

Assizes [1968] 1 W.L.R. 1776; 112 S.J. 821

Action by widow against husband's employer.

The plaintiff's husband was frequently required, in the course of his employment as a toolsetter by the defendants, to lean over oily machines; he died of scrotal cancer. The plaintiff alleged that the defendants ought to have known of the risks of this disease and were negligent in not warning her husband and in not giving him periodic medical examinations. Judgment was given for the plaintiff.

SWANWICK J.: . . . This brings me to the third and most difficult question, were there any steps or precautions that as employers the defendants or their servants ought to have taken and did not take either to protect Mr. Stokes from the risk of contracting the disease or towards detecting it at an earlier stage?

There were cited to me and I have perused some of the standard line of authorities dealing with the duties of employers towards their workmen, especially where errors of omission are alleged. These included *Paris* v. *Stepney Borough Council* ([1951] A.C. 367), including the well-known passage from Lord Normand's speech quoting Lord Dunedin's famous dictum and putting what has been called his own "gloss" upon it, *Morris* v. *West Hartlepool Steam Navigation Co. Ltd.* ([1956] A.C. 552), *Cavanagh* v. *Ulster Weaving Co. Ltd.* ([1960] A.C. 145), and the dicta, *obiter* but still persuasive, of Devlin J. in *Graham* v. *Co-operative Wholesale Society Ltd.* ([1957] 1 W.L.R. 511); also the convenient summary of these and other cases in the sixth edition of Mr. Munkman's useful book on *Employers' Liability at Common Law,* 6th ed. (1966), pp. 34 to 47.

From these authorities I deduce the principles, that the overall test is still the conduct of the reasonable and prudent employer, taking positive thought for the safety of his workers in the light of what he knows or ought to know; where there is a recognised and general practice which has been followed for a substantial period in similar circumstances without mishap, he is entitled to follow it, unless in the light of common sense or newer knowledge it is clearly bad; but, where there is developing knowledge, he must keep reasonably abreast of it and not be too slow to apply it; and where he has in fact greater than average knowledge of the risks, he may be thereby obliged to take more than the average or standard precautions. He must weigh up the risk in terms of the likelihood of injury occurring and the potential consequences if it does; and he must balance against this the probable effectiveness of the precautions that can be taken to meet it and the expense and inconvenience they involve. If he is found to have fallen below the standard to be properly expected of a reasonable and prudent employer in these respects, he is negligent.

There is, however, an additional complication in this case, not directly covered by authority so far as I am aware. For in this case the negligence alleged against the defendants lies largely in the sphere of vicarious responsibility for the actions or inaction of Dr. Lloyd, who was in their full-time employment as factory doctor and was thus their servant. It is of course plain that, if an employer delegates to a servant the performance of any part of his duty towards his workmen, he is responsible for the servant's negligence, however skilled the task; and I myself would take the view that, where the task requires a special skill or art, the servant must be judged by the standards pertaining to that skill or art, in so far as he is possessed of and exercising it. In the case of a doctor those standards are well set out by McNair J. when charging the jury in *Bolam* v. *Friern Hospital Management Committee* [above, p. 137], to which along with *Mahon* v. *Osborne* ([1939] 2 K.B. 14) I was referred.

A factory doctor, however, as emerged from the evidence, when advising his employers on questions of safety precautions is subject to pressures and has to give weight to considerations which do not apply as between a doctor and his patient and is expected to give and in this case regularly gave to his employers advice based partly on medical and partly on economic and administrative considerations. For instance he may consider some precaution medically desirable but hesitate to recommend expanding his department to cope with it, having been refused such an expansion before; or there may be questions of frightening workers off the job or of interfering with production. An example of this last type of consideration is the final sentence of Dr. Lloyd's memorandum of January 8, 1962, to the defendants' labour manager, Mr. Powis, on the subject of a man Aldridge, who had been adivsed by Dr. Senter and his own general practitioner to cease working in oil for fear of contracting scrotal cancer. After disagreeing with this high-powered medical opinion and urging the man to stay at work and keep his earnings up, Dr. Lloyd finished his memorandum, "If we took the medical advice given in this case, we might as well close the works and much of British industry."

Where, therefore, the advice to management and its acceptance are based on mixed considerations of this sort, it is to the medical aspect only that I would apply the perhaps rather special tests indicated by McNair J. in the passage I have indicated; and the economic and administrative aspect would be covered by the more general principles that I have endeavoured to summarise. In any event McNair J. emphasises and I agree that, while adherence to the views of a recognised body of medical opinion even if a minority is not negligence in a doctor, where the doctor is acting on his own personal opinion only he must be judged by the standard of what is reasonable. . . .

Section 5.—Proof of Breach

In his statement of claim a plaintiff must disclose a cause of action, that is, he must aver facts which, if proved, would entitle him to succceed. If he does not, he may fail right at the outset (*Price* v. *Gregory* [1959] 1 W.L.R. 177; *Fowler* v. *Lanning,* below, p. 273). On the whole however, English judges prefer to let the case go to trial; facts involving liability may emerge, and the plaintiff may be allowed to amend his pleadings so as to bring them into line with those facts. On the other hand, if what was proved diverges very widely from what he alleged, he may still fail (*Esso Petroleum Co.* v. *Southport Corporation* [1956] A.C. 218, 241; *Waghorn* v. *George Wimpey & Co.* [1970] 1 All E.R. 474).

At the trial itself, the plaintiff must lead some evidence. He will always know what the damage is, and he will be able to show the circumstances in which he was placed when it was suffered. He may not be able to show exactly what caused the damage he complains of, and he may very well not be able to show the other thing that must ultimately be established, namely, that one of its causes was some fault in the behaviour of the defendant. If all the facts come out at the trial, as in *Roe,* then the only question is whether those facts show a breach of duty in the defendant. The question is not whether it was more probable or not that he was negligent, but simply whether he was negligent. As to that, of course, there may be two views; appellate courts are quite ready to substitute their view for that of the judge, unless he is a county court judge and not much money is involved.

But all the facts may not emerge—indeed, they rarely do. The defendant may not want to tell all he knows, though the process of discovery limits his power of secrecy. The question then is whether the plaintiff has proved enough. If you do not know what the defendant did (a matter of proof), you cannot decide (a matter of judgment) whether what he did was careless or not. It may, however, be possible to say that it is more probable than not that the defendant was careless; this is an elliptical and confusing way of saying that from the facts proved it is possible to *infer* other facts which, if proved, would entitle one to conclude that the defendant had fallen short of the required standard. For example, from the fact that a well-made machine worked badly one may infer that it was not very well maintained; whether that lack of maintenance, if one infers it, amounts to a shortfall in the defendant depends on how expert and frequent the maintenance incumbent on him, as a matter of law, is. But one may not infer bad maintenance at all. The machine may have been badly handled. If the person responsible for maintenance is also responsible for the faults of the operator of the machine, it does not matter which is inferred, and it is enough that it is more likely than not that it must have been one or the other.

When one can infer from the facts proved that the defendant was careless in some respect not specifically shown, then it is said that *res ipsa loquitur.* People have tried to say under what circumstances such an inference is possible or permissible or unavoidable, but it appears from the nature of the matter that there can be no real rules about it. If there are few rules to tell us when a defendant *was* careless, there must be even fewer to tell us when he *must have been* careless.

If *res ipsa loquitur,* a matter which need not be specifically pleaded (*Bennett* v. *Chemical Construction (G.B.) Ltd.* [1971] 1 W.L.R. 1571), the defendant will lead evidence. His aim is to show that he behaved properly. He may try to prove the physical cause of the accident and that it is not attributable to his fault; but it is enough, even if he cannot do that, to clear himself of fault by showing that he behaved properly throughout. If the facts he proves make it appear less likely than not that there are unproved facts suggesting that he was at fault, then the plaintiff loses.

Take an example. A shopper falls on some spilt yoghourt on the floor of a supermarket. She naturally has no idea how long it has lain there. The supermarket is not responsible just because the yoghourt was dropped, but only if it has lain there an unreasonable time. So the supermarket is probably not at fault unless the yoghourt is more likely than not to have been there an unreasonable time—and there is no evidence either way on that point. Certainly if the supermarket proves that the floor was swept ten minutes or so before the accident, the plaintiff will fail, but in a case where the supermarket did not prove when it last swept the floor but only that it normally swept the floor five or six times a day, a divided Court of Appeal upheld the judge's holding for the plaintiff. It might, of course, not have reversed a judge's finding for the defendant. (*Ward* v. *Tesco Stores* [1976] 1 All E.R. 219).

Take another example. Suppose that the defendant shows that the physical cause of the accident was a defect in his machine. Proof of that fact excludes the inference that the machine was badly operated. It leaves quite open the inference that the machine was badly maintained (*Colvilles* v. *Devine* [1969] 1 W.L.R. 475 (H.L.)). Suppose that the defendant then proves that his system of maintenance was in accordance with general practice, and that it was functioning properly. Then the defendant has very nearly rebutted the inference that there was some respect in which he behaved carelessly. But if he is a specialist, the court may require him to show in addition that he had a system of informing himself of those events which called for more than normal maintenance, and that that system operated properly (*Henderson* v. *Jenkins* [1970] A.C. 282). Or it may not.

A pedestrian who offers to prove only that she was run down in the street by the defendant motorist probably does not offer to prove enough—such accidents are commonly caused by plaintiffs who emerge suddenly from behind buses (*Kinnaird* v. *O'Donnell,* 1964 S.L.T.(Sh.Ct.) 51). A pedestrian who proves that she was on a controlled pedestrian crossing at the time probably does establish a prima facie case. So, too, if the pedestrian was on the sidewalk at the time she was struck by the defendant's vehicle. But in the last case, if the defendant proves that the driver was dead at the wheel by reason of a cardiac attack, then the inference of facts indicating negligence (the driver can't have been keeping a proper look-out, etc.) vanishes, and the defendant does not then have to go further and show that it was not negligent of the driver to set out when he was about to collapse (*Waugh* v. *James K. Allen Ltd.,* 1964 S.L.T. 269; [1964] 2 Lloyd's Rep. 1 (H.L.)).

Where the defendant's duty is high (as in the pedestrian crossing instance), it is easier to infer that facts occurred which constituted a breach of it, because there are more sets of such facts. Thus in the tort of public nuisance the burden of proof is said to be reversed. This reversal of the burden of proof may make it practically easier to recover, even if the defendant's duty is stated in terms of reasonable care. There is a positive rule of law that the bailee of a chattel who fails to return it to the bailor must either pay its value or show that he was not at fault in not having it to give back; the plaintiff need prove only the delivery and the unsuccessful demand (*Houghland* v. *Low,* below, p. 420). Yet the duty of the compensated bailee is always said to be the duty to take reasonable care only. In law he bears the risk of carelessness only; in fact he bears the risk of not being able to prove that he was careful.

CHAPTER 3

CRIME AND TORT

Introduction

ONE might think that if *unreasonable* behaviour can give rise to liability for resulting harm, *unlawful* behaviour must certainly do so. Behaviour is constantly being rendered unlawful by statutes and regulations emanating from Parliament or Ministers, telling people to do this or not do that. When someone has done or not done what such a rule forbids or requires, it is an important question whether he may be sued by a person injured in consequence. It is not, however, an easy question, since statutes and regulations cover a vast range of situations and are drafted in very various terms.

Sometimes the primary purpose of a statute is to change the rules of tort law (*e.g.*, Occupiers' Liability Act 1957, Defective Premises Act 1972). More often an enactment seeks to change human behaviour. It may do this either by empowering people to do what otherwise they could not lawfully do, or by requiring them to do or abstain from doing what they were previously free to do or not to do. It is important to note the distinction. The statutes in *Anns* and *Dorset Yacht* did not require, but merely empowered, the defendants to stop the building or confine the boys: it was the common law which required the defendants to take care how they exercised their statutory powers. The claims in this chapter, by contrast, are founded on the unlawfulness, not the unreasonableness, of the defendant's behaviour.

An enactment may simply provide that in certain circumstances liability is to exist (Civil Aviation Act 1982, s.76; Control of Pollution Act 1974, s.88). It may impose a duty to act in a certain way and then provide that liability is to ensue if the duty is broken (Health and Safety at Work Act 1974, s.47(2) (safety regulations), s.71 (building regulations); Consumer Safety Act 1978, s.6; Race Relations Act 1976, s.57; Consumer Credit Act 1974, s.92(3)). Sometimes an enactment imposes a duty but provides that there is to be no civil liability for breach (Post Office Act 1969, s.9; Health and Safety at Work Act 1974, s.47(1)(a)). Sometimes conduct is made into an offence and civil liability is excluded (Fair Trading Act 1973, s.26; Safety of Sports Grounds Act 1975, s.13). Quite often, however, an enactment imposes a duty or creates an offence and remains wholly silent about civil liability. In such a case it falls to the judges to determine whether civil liability is to exist or not.

In the French view it is obvious that a person who can be punished by the State can be sued by his victim: indeed, they let the victim claim his damages in the criminal prosecution itself. Criminal courts in England can now make certain compensation orders in favour of victims (see below p. 158) but the civil courts, which do not even impose liability on all common law criminals (*Hargreaves* v. *Bretherton* [1959] 1 Q.B. 45

(perjury), *Chapman* v. *Honig* [1963] 2 Q.B. 502 (contempt of court)), are most reluctant to impose liability on statutory offenders. This is not so unreasonable. It is one thing to make a person pay a small fine and quite another to make him pay for all the consequences of his conduct, especially if the fine is so small that it is exacted even if he is not really to blame at all. Furthermore, since the common law of tort already holds people liable if their unreasonable behaviour causes physical harm, the only result of imposing liability on statutory offenders would be to make people pay when they have behaved quite reasonably or have caused only financial harm to strangers.

How is one to determine whether breach of a particular statutory provision leads to civil liability? In Germany the judges ask if the law in question was designed to protect people like the plaintiff from harm of that type. In England that is certainly a factor to be taken into account, but the principal question is, was it the intention of Parliament that there should be civil liability? This is rather an odd question to ask when there is no evidence of the intention it seeks to ascertain, rather like the question in contract cases whether a statute which prohibits an act impliedly prohibits a contract which involves the act (*e.g., St. John Shipping Corpn.* v. *Rank* [1957] 1 Q.B. 267, 285). In both situations it is really the courts which make the decision, and in making the decision they are naturally affected by the same considerations which weigh with them in other cases. They are much more ready to impose liability in tort if the damage is physical, if the relationship is close and if the defendant was at fault—though if liability already exists at common law the judges may always say that statutory liability is unnecessary (*McCall* v. *Abelesz* [1976] Q.B. 585). In other cases if Parliament wants civil liability to exist, it had better say so in clear terms (Resale Prices Act 1976, s.25(3); Restrictive Trade Practices Act 1976, s.35(2)).

Damage

A water authority is under a duty to maintain a certain pressure in its pipes; it fails to do so and a ratepayer's house is burned down in consequence; the water authority is subject to a fine, but not to liability in damages (*Atkinson* v. *Newcastle Waterworks Co.* (1877) 2 Ex.D. 441). The same Act requires the water to be wholesome; it is not, and a ratepayer suffers personal injury from drinking it; the water authority is liable in damages as well as to a fine (*Read* v. *Croydon Corpn.* [1938] 4 All E.R. 631). Take another pair of cases. An education authority is under a duty to provide school accommodation; it fails to do so and a parent is put to the expense of fees at a private school; he cannot recover them (*Watt* v. *Kesteven C.C.* [195] 1 Q.B. 408). The same Act requires that safety in schools be reasonably assured; a child cuts her hand on a thin pane of glass; she can recover (*Reffell* v. *Surrey C.C.*, below, p. 160).

Relationship

The occupier of a factory buys and instals machinery whose dangerous parts are insufficiently fenced; a workman injures himself on it. The victim can recover from the occupier, but not from the vendor, though both are liable to a fine (*Biddle* v. *Truvox Engineering Co.* [1952] 1 K.B. 101: the relationship of vendor and consumer (unlike vendor/purchaser and manufacturer/consumer) is rather weak, whereas the relationship of occupier and visitor or employer and employee is extremely strong. Indeed, most of the successful suits for breach of statutory duty are brought by workmen against their employer or the occupier of their place of work. The relevant statutes (Mines and Quarries Act 1954, Factories Act 1961, and Offices, Shops and Railway Premises Act 1963) will eventually be replaced by regulations under the Health and Safety at Work Act 1974.

The relationship of common users of the highway, on the other hand, is much less protective and strong. The pedestrian, certainly, can recover from the driver who mows him down on a pedestrian crossing (*London Passenger Transport Board* v. *Upson* [1949] A.C. 155), but those duties breach of which may injure both pedestrians and other motorists, and property as well as person, are not generally so construed as to give a right of action to the person hurt thereby (*Phillips* v. *Britannia Hygienic Laundry Co.,* below, p. 163). And where the duty is imposed, not on a motorist using the highway, but on a manufacturer, vendor or repairer, the grounds for denying liability seem even stronger.

Where the common law relationship is extremely weak, as it is between rival traders, statutes regulating the subject-matter will hardly ever be held impliedly to give a right of action, even although the breach in such cases may be quite deliberate (*London Armoury Co.* v. *Ever Ready Co.* [1941] 1 K.B. 742).

Fault

German law has an admirable provision: "Liability also attaches to a person who contravenes a statute designed for the protection of another. If the statute may, according to its terms, be contravened even in the absence of fault, liability in damages attaches only where fault is present" (§ 823, German Civil Code). In England, however, Parliament declined to implement the recommendation of the Monckton Committee on Alternative Remedies that a workman should not be able to recover damages for breach of statutory duty when that breach could not reasonably have been avoided by the defendant or his servants working in the course of their employment (Cmd. 6860, para. 82).

If the statutory duty is one which gives rise to liability on breach, there will be liability no matter how the breach arose. Because of this rule, the courts, which dislike imposing liability without fault, are tempted either to deny that a particular statutory duty which can be broken without fault gives rise to liability at all or to construe it in such a manner that unless there is some fault there is no breach.

Subject to all this, the plaintiff who sues for breach of statutory duty has the one great advantage that, depending on its terms, he may not have to persuade the court that the defendant behaved unreasonably: proof that the situation was dangerous may suffice without the further proof that it was the defendant's fault. But there are special hurdles, too. The plaintiff must bring both himself and his harm within the ambit of the legislative intention. Thus only the ratepayer, and not his family, may found on the water company's duty to provide wholesome water (*Read* v. *Croydon Corp.* [1938] 4 All E.R. 631), and no compensation is payable to the owner of sheep which were drowned owing to breach of a duty intended to save them from contagion (*Gorris* v. *Scott,* below, p. 187).

"In every case where a plaintiff has alleged a breach of statutory duty, he is entitled to allege negligence at common law and to ask the court to answer the question whether he has proved negligence, irrespective of his having proved a breach of statutory duty" (*Bux* v. *Slough Metals* [1974] 1 All E.R. 262, 273, *per* Stephenson L.J.). The fact that the defendant has satisfied his statutory obligations does not entail, though it may go some way to suggest, that he has taken reasonable steps to safeguard the plaintiff: for example, an employer who is bound by statute to see that a safety appliance is available for use may be bound at common law to take steps to see that it is actually used.

The Pearson Commission paid particular attention to the compensation of injuries at work. While it made proposals for the extension of the industrial injuries scheme of social security benefits, it was content with the operation of the present law of tort, including the action for breach of statutory duty.

Common law crimes

So far as the common law is concerned, there appear to be only two cases where the qualification of the defendant's behaviour as criminal is relevant to render him liable to pay damages to a person hurt in consequence of that behaviour. One is conspiracy (see later, p. 508); the other, much more important, is public nuisance. Public nuisance is a crime committed, in the main, by unreasonably impeding proper use of the Queen's highway, whether by obstruction or danger. If the defendant has been guilty of public nuisance (by creation or failure to abate), a plaintiff who suffers special damage may sue. Public nuisance, indeed, is the matrix out of which the modern law of negligence between co-users of the highway has sprung; the two torts co-exist uneasily.

Now the public interest in interferences with the highway is primarily in their removal; the Attorney-General seeks an injunction. There is good reason to grant an injunction to abate a proved nuisance even if the defendant was not at fault in causing it; he will be at fault if he doesn's remove it after being put on notice by the action. It is, of course, another question whether he should be amenable to a fine or liable to pay damages if he was not at fault in creating the nuisance. Nevertheless, liability in public nuisance came to be independent of the qualification of the defendant's conduct as reasonable or not; if the obstruction or the danger was unreasonable, it is immaterial how the defendant acted in causing it. On this, however, one must put the gloss that obstructions or dangers which are produced without negligence in the course of a reasonable user of the highway do not constitute nuisances; thus a car does not become a nuisance the minute it has unforeseeably broken down, though the person responsible for its being there must show that it was not his fault it was there at all or so long (*Moore* v. *Maxwell's of Emsworth* [1968] 1 W.L.R. 1077).

There are three possible points of divergence between public nuisance and negligence—the fault, the damage, and the factor which links them.

Fault is necessary in negligence, as we have seen. Public nuisance, on the other hand, is based more on causing an unreasonable danger than on causing a danger unreasonably. Accordingly, bearing in mind the gloss mentioned above, we must say that fault in the defendant or his servant is not a necessary element of liability in public nuisance. The faultless instigator of faulty work on the highway and the landlord of dilapidated premises adjoining it are liable. (The first case may be subsumed under the general law of negligence by styling it an instance of liability for the fault of an independent contractor, but the second cannot.) Where, however, an unreasonable danger exists without the fault of anyone at all, the present tendency appears to be to deny liability in public nuisance (*British Road Services* v. *Slater* [1964] 1 W.L.R. 498).

Until recently the tort of negligence remedied primarily physical damage. In other words, negligence was about *dangers*. Public nuisance admittedly includes dangers on the highway, but it also extends to *obstructions*. Obstructions typically cause delay; and time is not blood, but money. "Obstruction damage," therefore, tended to found liability not in negligence but only, if at all, in public nuisance—delay to a traveller (*Anglo-Algerian S.S. Co.* v. *Houlder Line* [1908] 1 K.B. 659), the cutting-off of a valuable view (*Campbell* v. *Paddington Borough Council* [1911] 1 K.B. 869), loss of profit through inability to get goods out (*Iveson* v. *Moore* (1699) 1 Ld. Raym. 486; 91 E.R. 1224), or customers in (*Wilkes* v. *Hungerford Market Co.* (1835) 2 Bing.N.C. 281; 132 E.R. 110).

What of the link between the conduct and the damage? Negligence remedies primarily foreseeable damage. Suppose that a nuisance by obstruction unpredictably turns out to be a danger and directly causes unforeseeable physical damage. Is this damage compensable? A cogent judgment from New South Wales held that it was, but the Judicial Committee disagreed and said: "It is not sufficient that the injury suffered . . . was the direct result of the nuisance if that injury was in the relevant sense unforeseeable." *The Wagon Mound (No. 2)* [1967] 1 A.C. 617, 640, on appeal from [1963] 1 Lloyd's Rep. 402. In this respect, then, public nuisance has been analogised to negligence, at any rate where physical damage has been caused. Must obstruction damage also be foreseeable? The Judicial Committee said: "the choice is between [foreseeability] being a necessary element in all cases of nuisance or in none," but there will be difficulty in applying this to nuisance by obstruction, at any rate if "necessary" is taken to mean "sufficient"—for how many people foreseeably lose money when a bridge collapses or a level-crossing gate gets stuck or someone floods a road?

CHAPMAN v. HONIG

Court of Appeal [1963] 2 Q.B. 502; [1963] 3 W.L.R. 19; 107 S.J. 374; [1963] 2 All E.R. 513

This was an action of trespass brought by a tenant against his landlord. The plaintiff had given evidence against the defendant in a previous action by another tenant, and the defendant out of pique served a notice to quit on the plaintiff, under such circumstances that the defendant could have been punished for contempt of court. The plaintiff stayed on in the flat after the expiry of the notice to quit, and the defendant entered and padlocked the doors.

The county court judge awarded £50 damages. The defendant appealed, and his appeal was allowed by the Court of Appeal (Lord Denning M.R. dissenting).

DAVIES L.J.: . . . One cannot help but sympathise with the proposition that in general a person injured by a wrongful act should have a remedy in damages against the wrongdoer. But it has to be considered whether, in the first place, that proposition is universally true, and, secondly, whether in the circumstances of this case the defendant's action in serving a notice to quit was, as against the plaintiff, wrongful at all.

It is, no doubt, true that in most cases a person injured by a criminal offence has a right of action against the criminal. That is because most crimes are torts. Acts of criminal violence to person or property would be trespasses; larceny would be conversion; most frauds would give rise to an action of deceit; and so on. But not all crimes give rise to a cuase of action. For example, it is well established that perjury does not give rise to a cause of action at the suit of a person injured by the perjury; see the decision of Lord Goddard C.J. in *Hargreaves* v. *Bretherton* ([1959] 1 Q.B. 45), and the authorities there cited. It is true that there may be special features relating to the offence of perjury which might make it difficult to permit of an action based upon it. But this line of authority shows that there is no general rule that all crimes give rise to a cause of action.

Equally relevant to this inquiry is the great body of case-law dealing with the question whether the commission of an act forbidden or made punishable by statute gives a cause of action to a person injured by the act. On this question it is notoriously difficult to enunciate any guiding principle. The authorities are discussed in the dissenting *obiter* judgment of Somervell L.J. in *Solomons* v. *R. Gertzenstein Ltd.* [1954] 2 Q.B. 243. As examples may be cited the well-known case of *Groves* v. *Lord Wimborne* [1898] 2 Q.B. 402), the *alma genetrix* of so much litigation under the provisions of the Factories Acts, on the one side of the line, and, on the other, *Phillips* v. *Britannia Hygienic Laundry Co. Ltd.* [below, p. 163]. Perhaps the nearest that one gets to a statement of principle is in the words of Atkin L.J. in the last-cited case, in a passage adopted by Somervell L.J. in *Solomons'* case: "Therefore the question is," said Atkin L.J., "whether these regulations, viewed in the circumstances in which they were made and to which they relate, were intended to impose a duty which is a public duty only or whether they were intended, in addition to the public duty, to impose a duty enforceable by an individual aggrieved." It is, of course, implicit in this principle that not in every case is an individual who has been injured by a wrongful act entitled to sue, even though the wrongful act is prohibited or made punishable by statute. And the principle can, in my judgment, be applied in the present case by inquiring whether the concept of, and proceedings for, contempt of court are concerned with the preservation of the inviolability of the administration and course of justice and its proper conduct or whether, in addition, they are intended in all cases to give a remedy in damages to an individual injured by the contempt. . . .

PEARSON L.J.: . . . I have considered a number of cases in which the court had to decide, in relation to some particular enactment, whether an individual, adversely affected by breach of a statutory duty, had a right of action for damages against the person who had committed the breach. . . . The answer depends on the construction of the particular enactment, *i.e.,* on the intention which it manifests. Here there is no enactment which is directly relevant and I can only consider, perhaps in a rather metaphorical way, what intention is to be inferred from the nature and exercise of the jurisdiction. So far as I know, no individual ever has been awarded, or has even claimed, damages or other compensation for contempt of court until the present case. The jurisdiction exists and is exercised *alio intuitu,* for the protection of the administration of justice and not for the protection of individuals. So to speak, the hypothetical enactment should be notionally construed as not conferring on an individual affected by a contempt of court any right of action for damages for the contempt of court as such although of course he may have a right of action for damages on other grounds. . . .

LONRHO LTD. v. SHELL PETROLEUM CO. LTD.

House of Lords [1982] A.C. 173; [1981] 3 W.L.R. 33; [1981] 2 All E.R. 456

The claimants owned a pipeline, leading from the Mozambique coast to Southern Rhodesia, which the respondent oil companies used and paid for. After the government of that country had declared itself independent, Orders in Council in the United Kingdom rendered it an offence to supply crude oil to Southern Rhodesia, and oil ceased to flow along the claimants' pipeline to their loss. In the present arbitration proceedings, in which over £100 m. was claimed, the claimants asserted that the respondents had agreed to supply, and had supplied, the illegal regime with oil in breach of the Orders, and that this had prolonged the existence of the illegal regime and consequently the period during which their pipeline remained unused. It was held by the House of Lords that none of the claimants' allegations stated a cause of action, and the extract printed below gives the opinion of Lord Diplock in answer to question 5, namely " . . . if there were breaches by the Respondents of the 1965 and 1968 Orders [sc. the sanctions orders] (a) Whether breaches of those Orders would give rise to a right of action in the Claimants for damage alleged to have been caused by those breaches . . . "

LORD DIPLOCK: . . . My Lords, it is well settled by authority of this House in *Cutler* v. *Wandsworth Stadium Ltd.* ([1949] A.C. 398) that the question whether legislation which makes the doing or omitting to do a particular act a criminal offence renders the person guilty of such offence liable also in a civil action for damages at the suit of any person who thereby suffers loss or damage is a question of construction of the legislation. . . .

[His Lordship considered the provisions of the Southern Rhodesia Act 1965 and the 1965 sanctions order] . . .

The sanctions order thus creates a statutory prohibition on the doing of certain classes of acts and provides the means of enforcing the prohibition by prosecution for a criminal offence which is subject to heavy penalties including imprisonment. So one starts with the presumption laid down originally by Lord Tenterden C.J. in *Doe d. Bishop of Rochester* v. *Bridges* ((1831) 1 B. & Ad. 847, 859) where he spoke of the "general rule" that "where an Act creates an obligation, and enforces the performance in a specified manner . . . that performance cannot be enforced in any other manner," a statement that has frequently been cited with approval ever since, including on several occasions in speeches in this House. Where the only manner of enforcing performance for which the Act provides is prosecution for the criminal offence of failure to perform the statutory obligation or for contravening the statutory prohibition which the Act creates, there are two classes of exception to this general rule.

The first is where on the true construction of the Act it is apparent that the obligation or prohibition was imposed for the benefit or protection of a particular class of individuals, as in the case of the Factories Acts and similar legislation. As Lord Kinnear put it in *Black* v. *Fife Coal Co. Ltd.* ([1912] A.C. 149, 165), in the case of such a statute:

> "There is no reasonable ground for maintaining that a proceeding by way of penalty is the only remedy allowed by the statute . . . We are to consider the scope and purpose of the statute and in particular for whose benefit it is intended. Now the object of the present statute is plain. It was intended to compel mine owners to make due provision for the safety of the men working in their mines, and the persons for whose benefit all these rules are to be enforced are the persons exposed to danger. But when a duty of this kind is imposed for the benefit of particular persons there arises at common law a correlative right in those persons who may be injured by its contravention."

The second exception is where the statute creates a public right (*i.e.* a right to be enjoyed by all those of Her Majesty's subjects who wish to avail themselves of it) and a particular member of the public suffers what Brett J. in *Benjamin* v. *Storr* ((1874) L.R. 9 C.P. 400, 407) described as "particular, direct and substantial" damage "other and different from that which was common to all the rest of the public." Most of the authorities about this second exception deal not with public rights created by statute but with public rights existing at common law, particularly in respect of use of highways. *Boyce* v. *Paddington Borough Council* ([1903] 1 Ch. 109) is one of the comparatively few cases about a right conferred on the general public by statute. It is in relation to that class of statute only that Buckley J.'s oft-cited statement (at 114) as to the two cases in which a plaintiff, without joining the Attorney-General, could himself sue in private law for interference with that public right must be understood. The two cases he said were:

> "first, where the interference with the public right is such as that some private right of his is at the same time interfered with . . . and, secondly, where no private right is interfered with, but the plaintiff, in respect of his public right, suffers special damage peculiar to himself from the interference with the public right."

The first case would not appear to depend on the existence of a public right in addition to the private one; while to come within the second case at all it has first to be shown that the statute, having regard to its scope and language, does fall within that class of statutes which create a legal right to be enjoyed by all of Her Majesty's subjects who wish to avail themselves of it. A mere prohibition on members of the public generally from doing what it would otherwise be lawful for them to do is not enough.

My Lords, it has been the unanimous opinion of the arbitrators with the concurrence of the umpire, of Parker J. and of each of the three members of the Court of Appeal that the sanctions orders made pursuant to the Southern Rhodesia Act 1965 fell within neither of these two exceptions. Clearly they were not within the first category of exception. They were not imposed for the *benefit* or *protection* of a particular class of individuals who were engaged in supplying or delivering crude oil or petroleum products to Southern Rhodesia. They were intended to put an end to such transactions. Equally plainly they did not create any public right to be enjoyed by all those of Her Majesty's subjects who wished to avail themselves of it. On the contrary, what they did was to withdraw a previously existing right of citizens of, and companies incorporated in, the United Kingdom to trade with Southern Rhodesia in crude oil and petroleum products. Their purpose was, perhaps, most aptly stated by Fox L.J. He said:

> "I cannot think that they were concerned with conferring rights either on individuals or the public at large. Their purpose was the destruction, by economic pressure, of the UDI regime in Southern Rhodesia; they were instruments of state policy in an international matter."

Until the United Nations called on its members to impose sanctions on the illegal regime in Southern Rhodesia it may not be strictly accurate to speak of it as an international matter, but from the outset it was certainly state policy in affairs external to the United Kingdom.

In agreement with all those present and former members of the judiciary who have considered the matter I can see no ground on which contraventions by Shell and BP of the sanctions orders, though not amounting to any breach of their contract with Lonrho, nevertheless constituted a tort for which Lonrho could recover in a civil suit any loss caused to them by such contraventions.

Briefly parting from this part of the case, however, I should mention briefly two cases, one in the Court of Appeal of England, *Ex parte Island Records Ltd.* ([1978] Ch. 122), and one in the High Court of Australia, *Beaudesert Shire Council* v.

Smith ((1966) 120 C.L.R. 145), which counsel for Lonrho, as a last resort, relied on as showing that some broader principle has of recent years replaced those long-established principles that I have just stated for determining whether a contravention of a particular statutory prohibition by one private individual makes him liable in tort to another private individual who can prove that he has suffered damage as a result of the contravention.

Ex parte Island Records Ltd. was an unopposed application for an Anton Piller order against a defendant who, without the consent of the performers, had made records of musical performances for the purposes of trade. This was an offence, punishable by a relatively small penalty under the Dramatic and Musical Performers' Protection Act 1958. The application for the Anton Piller order was made by performers whose performances had been "bootlegged" by the defendant without their consent and also by record companies with whom the performers had entered into exclusive contracts. So far as the application by performers was concerned, it could have been granted for entirely orthodox reasons. The Act was passed for the protection of a particular class of individuals, dramatic and musical performers; even the short title said so. Whether the record companies would have been entitled to obtain the order in a civil action to which the performers whose performances had been bootlegged were not parties is a matter which or present purposes it is not necessary to decide. Lord Denning M.R., however, with whom Waller L.J. agreed (Shaw L.J. dissenting) appears to enunciate a wider general rule, which does not depend on the scope and language of the statute by which a criminal offence is committed, that whenever a lawful business carried on by one individual in fact suffers damage as the consequence of a contravention by another individual of any statutory prohibition the former has a civil right of action against the latter for such damage.

My Lords, with respect, I am unable to accept that this is the law; and I observe that in his judgment rejecting a similar argument by the appellants in the instant appeal Lord Denning M.R. accepts that the question whether a breach of sanctions orders gives rise to a civil action depends on the object and intent of those orders, and refers to *Ex parte Island Records Ltd.* as an example of a statute passed for the protection of private rights and interests, *viz.* those of the performers.

Beaudesert Shire Council v. *Smith* is a decision of the High Court of Australia. It appeared to recognise the existence of a novel innominate tort of the nature of an "action for damages upon the case" available to "a person who suffers harm or loss as the inevitable consequence of the unlawful, intentional and positive acts of another." The decision, although now 15 years old, has never been followed in any Australian or other common law jurisdiction. In subsequent Australian cases it has invariably been distinguished, most recently by the Privy Council in *Dunlop* v. *Woollahra Municipal Council* ([1982] A.C. 158), on appeal from the Supreme Court of New South Wales. It is clear now from a later decision of the Australian High Court in *Kitano* v. *Commonwealth of Australia* ((1974) 129 C.L.R. 151) that the adjective "unlawful" in the definition of acts which give rise to this new action for damages on the case does not include *every* breach of statutory duty which in fact causes damage to the plaintiff. It remains uncertain whether it was intended to include acts done in contravention of a wider range of statutory obligations or prohibitions than those which under the principles that I have discussed above would give rise to a civil action at common law in England if they are contravened. If the tort described in *Beaudesert* was really intended to extend that range, I would invite your Lordships to declare that it forms no part of the law of England. . . .

LORD EDMUND-DAVIES, LORD KEITH, LORD SCARMAN AND LORD BRIDGE all agreed with LORD DIPLOCK.

Note:
    The terms in which this opinion are rendered seem to have been affected by the decision in *Gouriet,* which was concerned with another point of contact between private law and criminal

law, with the question when an individual can seek an injunction to restrain a threatened breach of statutory law. It is true that in that case the plaintiff did not allege that he would suffer any damage as a result of the crime, were it committed, and it is true that even if he had, he could not have sued the trade union for encouraging it (trade unions being then immune to liability in tort) nor yet the Post Office or any of its employees (Post Office Act 1969 s.9). In that case, however, Viscount Dilhorne said that although " . . . only the Attorney-General can sue on behalf of the public for the purpose of preventing public wrongs . . . a private individual . . . may be able to do so if he will sustain injury as a result of a public wrong" ([1978] A.C. 435, 494). Lord Diplock here says that a private individual cannot sue for proven damage resulting from a public wrong; indeed his dismissive analysis of the observations of Buckley J. which he cites robs them of content entirely. Do you think that Lonrho would have been allowed to seek an injunction to prevent the respondents' conduct if (unimaginably) the Attorney-General had refused his consent to a relator action?

POWERS OF CRIMINAL COURTS ACT 1973

35.—(1) Subject to the provisions of this Part of this Act, a court by or before which a person is convicted of an offence, in addition to dealing with him in any other way, may, on application or otherwise, make an order (in this Act referred to as "a compensation order") requiring him to pay compensation for any personal injury, loss or damage resulting from that offence or any other offence which is taken into consideration by the court in determining sentence.

(2) In the case of an offence under the Theft Act 1968, where the property in question is recovered, any damage to the property occurring while it was out of the owner's possession shall be treated for the purposes of subsection (1) above as having resulted from the offence, however and by whomsoever the damage was caused.

(3) No compensation order shall be made in respect of loss suffered by the dependants of a person in consequence of his death, and no such order shall be made in respect of injury, loss or damage due to an accident arising out of the presence of a motor vehicle on a road, except such damage as is treated by subsection (2) above as resulting from an offence under the Theft Act 1968.

(4) In determining whether to make a compensation order against any person, and in determining the amount to be paid by any person under such an order, the court shall have regard to his means so far as they appear or are known to the court.

(5) The compensation to be paid under a compensation order made by a magistrates' court in respect of any offence of which the court has convicted the offender shall not exceed £1,000; and the compensation or total compensation to be paid under a compensation order or compensation orders made by a magistrates' court in respect of any offence or offences taken into consideration in determining sentence shall not exceed the difference (if any) between the amount or total amount which under the preceding provisions of this subsection is the maximum for the offence or offences of which the offender has been convicted and the amount or total amounts (if any) which are in fact ordered to be paid in respect of that offence or those offences.

. . .

38.—(1) This section shall have effect where a compensation order has been made in favour of any person in respect of any injury, loss or damage and a claim by him in civil proceedings for damages in respect thereof subsequently falls to be determined.

(2) The damages in the civil proceedings shall be assessed without regard to the order; but where the whole or part of the amount awarded by the order has been paid, the damages awarded in the civil proceedings shall not exceed the amount (if any) by which, as so assessed, they exceed the amount paid under the order.

(3) Where the whole or part of the amount awarded by the order remains unpaid and the court awards damages in the civil proceedings, then, unless the person against whom the order was made has ceased to be liable to pay the amount unpaid (whether in consequence of an appeal, of his imprisonment for default or otherwise), the court shall direct that the judgment—

(a) if it is for an amount not exceeding the amount unpaid under the order, shall not be enforced; or

(b) if it is for an amount exceeding the amount unpaid under the order, shall not be enforced as to a corresponding amount;

without the leave of the court.

Note:

128,000 such orders were made in 1980; in the same year the Criminal Injuries Compensation Scheme paid out £9.5m. to 14,000 claimants.

If the claim is worth less than £400, the Criminal Injuries Compensation Board can make no order. If a claim is brought in the County Court, one gets no costs if the award is less than £200. For small claims, therefore, it is wise to apply for a compensation order. Unfortunately, in *R.* v. *Vivian* [1979] 1 W.L.R. 291 the Court of Appeal said that "no order for compensation should be made unless the sum claimed by way of compensation is either agreed or has been proved."

CIVIL EVIDENCE ACT 1968

11.—(1) In any civil proceedings the fact that a person has been convicted of an offence by or before any court in the United Kingdom or by a court-martial there or elsewhere shall (subject to subsection (3) below) be admissible in evidence for the purpose of proving, where to do so is relevant to any issue in those proceedings, that he committed that offence, whether he was so convicted upon a plea of guilty or otherwise and whether or not he is a party to the civil proceedings; but no conviction other than a subsisting one shall be admissible in evidence by virtue of this section.

. . .

Section 1.—Statutory Duties and Civil Liability

BARNA v. HUDES MERCHANDISING CORPORATION

Court of Appeal (1962) 106 S.J. 194; Crim.L.R. 321

Action by motorist against motorist in respect of property damage.

The plaintiff was driving his Citroen along West Heath Avenue to where it ended by forming a T-junction with North End Road, where he planned to turn right. At the junction he stopped. To his left, on the crown of the main road, was a line of cars waiting to turn right into the street from which he was emerging. To his right was a line of parked cars which impeded his vision. He edged slowly forward, and then saw, about forty yards away, the defendant's car approaching from his right at a speed which the defendant admitted was in excess of the legal limit. The plaintiff stopped, but as there was not enough room between his car and those waiting to turn right, the defendant collided with him, and both vehicles were damaged. The plaintiff claimed the cost of repairs, and the defendant counterclaimed. The county court judge dismissed the claim and allowed the counterclaim. The plaintiff appealed without success to the Court of Appeal.

ORMEROD L.J. said that, since the amount of the claim was under £200, there was no appeal on a question of fact and the Court of Appeal could only interfere if the judge's inference could not be reasonably drawn from the evidence. There was no doubt that the . . . defendant had exceeded the speed limit and had committed an offence, but that did not make his speed excessive for the purposes of civil liability and did not of itself constitute negligence. The . . . defendant, driving on a fast busy main road, had no reason to anticipate that it would be blocked as it was. In those circumstances the judge's inference, that the speed of the . . . defendant was not excessive and that the plaintiff alone was negligent, was one that could be reasonably drawn from the evidence.

REFFELL v. SURREY COUNTY COUNCIL

Queen's Bench [1964] 1 W.L.R. 358; 128 J.P. 261; 108 S.J. 119; 62 L.G.R. 186; [1964] 1 All E.R. 743

Action by pupil against education authority in respect of personal injury.

The plaintiff, a girl of twelve and a pupil at the defendant's school, hurried down a corridor to the cloakroom. One of its two glazed doors was swinging towards her, so she put out her right hand to stop it. Her hand went through one of the panes of glass which was only one-eighth of an inch thick. It had been installed by a competent architect when the school was built in 1919, and there had never been an accident with that door before. Broken panes were always replaced by toughened glass. The local authority was responsible for over 700 educational establishments, and had about eleven accidents per year involving broken glass.

VEALE J.: . . . It is in those circumstances that the plaintiff puts her case in two ways. She alleges that the local education authority have been guilty of a breach of their statutory duty. Secondly, she alleges that they are guilty of negligence at common law.

I will deal first with the question of statutory duty. The Education Act 1944, provides by section 10(1): "The Minister shall make regulations prescribing the standards to which the premises of schools maintained by local education authorities are to conform, and such regulations may prescribe different standards for such descriptions of schools as may be specified in the regulations." Section 10(2) provides: "Subject as hereinafter provided, it shall be the duty of a local education authority to secure that the premises of every school maintained by them conform to the standards prescribed for schools of the description to which the school belongs." Be it noted that the duty is a duty to secure conformity with the prescribed standards.

In accordance with the duty laid upon him, the Minister has made regulations. The relevant ones for my consideration are the Standards for School Premises Regulations 1959. Regulation 51, under the heading "Precautions for Health and Safety," reads as follows [His Lordship read regulation 51 and continued:] Omitting irrelevant words, that regulation therefore reads: "In all parts of the buildings of every school . . . the design, the construction . . . and the properties of the materials shall be such that the health and safety of the occupants . . . shall be reasonably assured."

Three points really arise. First, do the statute and regulation 51 give a right of action to a pupil at the school? Secondly, if so, what is the nature and extent of the duty? Thirdly, was there any breach of duty which caused this accident?

So far as the first point is concerned, if one looks at the Education Act 1902, s.7, the duty then imposed was a duty "to maintain and keep efficient public elementary schools" in the area of the education authority. Those words in that section were held to give a right of action to both master and pupil at a school. It would, I think, be curious if subsequent legislation was so drafted as to take away that right of action. The question whether or not a private person has a right of action for the breach of a statutory duty is always a very difficult one. Reliance is placed by the plaintiff on cases such as *Groves* v. *Wimborne* ([1898] 2 Q.B. 402) and on the observations of their Lordships in *Cutler* v. *Wandsworth Stadium* ([1949] A.C. 398). It is said that there is a strong presumption that a private right of action can be enforced by a private individual in cases where the statute provides no penalty for the breach. That is the case here, because the Education Act 1944, by section 99, gives powers to the minister to issue directions to an education authority and, if necessary, an application can be made for mandamus.

I think that the best approach to this kind of question is that set out in *Charlesworth on Negligence* (4th ed., 1962), paragraph 963, at p. 454: "It has been said: 'No universal rule can be formulated which will answer the question whether in any given case an individual can sue in respect of a breach of statutory duty.' In addition to the general rule set out in the preceding section, however, the most important matters to be taken into consideration appear to be: (a) Is the action brought in respect of the kind of harm which the statute was intended to prevent? (b) Is the person bringing the action one of the class which the statute desired to protect? (c) Is the special remedy provided by the statute adequate for the protection of the person injured? If the first two questions are answered in the affirmative and the third in the negative then, in most cases, the individual can sue."

I do not think that there has been any express decision on section 10 of the Education Act 1944, and regulation 51 of the Standards for School Premises Regulations 1959, and I confess that I have had some doubt about the matter; but I have come to the conclusion that the answers in this case to the three questions set out in the paragraph I have just read are "yes" to the first two and "no" to the third. Bearing in mind that no penalty is laid down by the statute for a breach, I think that an action does lie by a pupil or master at a school who can prove a breach of the regulation.

What then is the nature of the duty? Counsel for the plaintiff says that, if in fact there is a breach in the sense that premises are not reasonably safe or that safety is not reasonably assured, this statutory duty is wider than any duty at common law, because—so the argument runs—the test is objective; that is to say, it matters not what this authority or other authorities knew or did not know, did or did not do, or what the past experience was. If safety was not reasonably assured, that, says counsel, is an end of the matter, though he concedes that, at common law, such matters as past experience, would indeed be relevant. The local education authority, on the other hand, say that the regulation adds nothing to the common law duty. On the facts as I find them to be in this case I think this argument is largely academic; but it is an important point and I think it right to express my view upon it.

In my judgment, the argument of the plaintiff on this point is right. I think the duty to secure (that is the word in the section) that safety shall be reasonably assured (which are the words of the regulation) is an absolute duty and the test of breach or no is objective. Putting it another way, if safety is not reasonably assured in the premises in fact, then there is a breach.

That leads to the third question. Were the premises on July 15, 1960, with this ⅛ inch glass in the cloakroom door, at a height of four feet, reasonably safe? I have no hesitation in saying that they were not. This ⅛ inch glass in a cloakroom door was, in my view, asking for trouble. True, there had been no previous accident at this door, but there had been accidents of some sort at such doors elsewhere, and there had been an accident at the boys' cloakroom door in 1937, and the boys' cloakroom door was altered because of the danger of unruly boys. Boys are more unruly than girls, or so a witness told me. Boys will be boys; but, equally, I should have thought, girls will be girls. Even if they do not fight like small boys and generally behave with more decorum, they nevertheless have been known to chase each other and to run in corridors. It is easy to visualise one girl following another, the one in front swinging the cloakroom door to and the following girl putting out a hand to arrest it, without any element of horse play at all. I cannot help thinking that the defendants have been lucky that there has been no previous accident at this door.

The distinction between boys and girls has not been drawn by the local education authority since the war. All doors in new schools have toughened glass in doors and all breakages of glass in doors have involved toughened glass as a replacement. One sympathises, of course, with the position of a local education authority with a number of old schools to manage. I have no doubt at all that this local education authority appreciated the risk. But no evidence has been called before me by the local education authority to show that they considered this question; or if they did, to what conclusion they came and why; or that the replacements involved enormous expense which was out of proportion to the risk; or that some form of grille or wooden slat was impracticable. For all I know (and, indeed, the position seems to be this) the local education authority merely waited for either a major adaptation of the buildings, or a breakage to occur, before they did anything at all.

The Middlesex County Council are said now to be gradually changing ⅛ inch glass in school doors. The Essex County Council are said to have issued, only last month, a directive to the same effect to a Mr. Jefferson, who takes his orders from the Essex County architect and follows their advice. But I have the evidence of a practical man and a convincing witness whose evidence I accept. This ⅛ inch glass, he said, should have been changed years ago. I am not, I hope, being wise after the event, and I exclude, I hope, the wisdom of hindsight; but, if instead of considering whether there was a breach of regulation 51 on an objective basis I were to approach the matter on a common law basis, I should still say, and indeed I find, that the defendants were negligent. This is not the case of an isolated hit for six out of a cricket ground as in *Bolton* v. *Stone*.

It is said for the local education authority that their common law duty *qua* their premises is the common duty of care under the Occupiers' Liability Act 1957 and is a somewhat lower duty than the duty of a school master as a good and prudent father of a family. That is, I think, correct. But it makes very little, if any, difference, on the facts of this case. I am content to take their duty as the common duty of care, which is defined by section 2(2) of the Occupiers' Liability Act 1957 as a duty "to take such care as in all the circumstances of the case is reasonable to see that the visitor will be reasonably safe in using the premises for the purposes for which he is invited or permitted by the occupier to be there." The circumstances here include the circumstance that this was a school and that the door was in constant use by children. I do not accept that the risk was minimal, as was urged upon me by counsel for the local education authority. If it is too much to ask an education authority, confronted with this problem of glass in doors, to change every door with ⅛ inch in it, it is not too much to ask them to do something more than merely wait for major adaptations or breakages. Whatever may be the vulnerability of other doors, I should have said that a cloakroom door at the end of a straight corridor was more vulnerable than most. Not only, in my judgment, was the risk of accident a real risk, but it was both a foreseeable risk and was in fact foreseen. If it had not been foreseen there would not have been the policy of replacing broken ⅛ inch glass with toughened glass.

In the result, I find the local education authority liable to the plaintiff both under the statute and regulation and at common law.

Questions

1. Are there any situations in which the plaintiff would have recovered in an action for breach of statutory duty and would have failed to recover at common law?

2. Suppose you want to *make* someone perform his statutory duty, rather than wait for harm and then claim compensation from him. For what remedy should you apply if the duty is (a) public, (b) private? Would the appropriate remedy ever be granted or refused when damages for any harm suffered would not?

Note:

The plaintiff here, who had suffered no financial loss, recovered (tax free) a sum about equal to half her teacher's annual salary, or the cost of a thousand panes of toughened glass.

No injunction will issue to prevent an education authority's setting up a new school in premises which fall short of the standards laid down by Regulations: the only remedy of the parent is to apply to the Secretary of State: *Bradbury* v. *Enfield Borough* ([1967] 3 All E.R. 434 (C.A.)).

Many statutory duties imposed on public bodies involve the provision of benefits to specified classes of people. Can a disappointed claimant sue for breach of statutory duty? A two-man Court of Appeal so held in *Thornton* v. *Kirklees Metropolitan B.C.* [1979] Q.B. 626, a decision entirely out of line with previous holdings, but of course quite consonant with *Anns* (above p. 56) which imposed liability for financial harm caused by the unreasonable exercise of statutory powers, though only in the operational area. The consequent harassment of local authorities has led the courts to undo some of this wretched work by insisting that what are really matters of public law must be resolved in proper proceedings, namely by judicial review, in which damages may be awarded, rather than by an ordinary action of tort.

PHILLIPS v. BRITANNIA HYGIENIC LAUNDRY CO.

Court of Appeal [1923] 2 K.B. 832; 93 L.J.K.B. 5; 129 L.T. 777; 39 T.L.R. 530; 68 S.J. 102; 21 L.G.R. 709; [1923] All E.R.Rep. 127

Action by highway user against highway user in respect of property damage.

BANKES L.J.: This is an appeal from the Divisional Court reversing the county court judge in an action brought by the plaintiff for damage done to his motor van. The axle of the defendants' motor lorry broke and caused the damage. The action in the county court was founded on an alleged breach of a statutory provision contained in the Motor Cars (Use and Construction) Order 1904 and alternatively on the alleged negligence of the defendant. The county court judge absolved the defendant from negligence in relation either to the management of the motor lorry or to the state of its axle, but he found negligence on the part of the repairers to whom the motor lorry had been sent, in not having executed the repairs efficiently, and gave judgment for the plaintiff on the ground that the lorry was not in the condition required by cl. 6 of art. II of the Order. On an appeal by the defendants the Divisional Court reversed this judgment. The plaintiff appeals to this court.

I agree with the conclusion of the Divisional Court. If the judgment of the county court judge were to stand it would have very far-reaching consequences. It is unnecessary to consider what they would be, as in this case there is only one point to be considered, and that has long been governed by well-established rules; and when those rules are applied to the facts of this case, it is clear that the Divisional Court came to the right conclusion.

The only point of substance argued for the appellant was that the Motor Cars (Use and Construction) Order 1904 conferred on him a statutory right of action for breach of its conditions. Two well-known rules relate to this question; the first is stated by Kennedy L.J. in *Dawson & Co.* v. *Bingley Urban Council* ([1911] 2 K.B. 149, 159) in these words: "Now, the general law as to the remedy of a person who has been injured by the infringement of a statutory right or the breach of a statutory obligation for his benefit is clear. Where the statute has not in express terms given a remedy, the remedy which by law is properly applicable to the right or the obligation follows as an incident. The law is, I think, correctly stated in *Addison on Torts*, 8th ed., p. 104, referring to *Comyn's Digest:* 'In every case where a statute enacts or prohibits a thing for the benefit of a person, he shall have a remedy upon the same statute for the thing enacted for his advantage, or for the recompense of a wrong done to him contrary to the said law': Com.Dig. Action upon Statute (F). Accordingly, where the statute is silent as to the remedy, the Legislature is to be taken as intending the ordinary result; and the proper remedy for breach of the statute is an action for damages and, in a proper case, for an injunction." In these cases it may be material to consider whether the right conferred or the act prohibited is for the benefit of a particular class of persons or of the public generally. The second rule is thus stated by Lord Halsbury in *Pasmore* v. *Oswaldtwistle Urban Council* ([1898] A.C. 387, 394): "The principle that where a specific remedy is given by a statute, it thereby deprives the person who insists upon a remedy of any other form of remedy than that given by the statute, is one which is very familiar and which runs through the law. I think Lord Tenterden accurately states that principle in the case of *Doe* v. *Bridges* ((1831) 1 B. & Ad. 847, 859; 109 E.R. 1001, 1006). He says: 'Where an Act creates an obligation, and enforces the performance in a specified manner, we take it to be a general rule that performance cannot be enforced in any other manner.' " In the same case of *Pasmore* v. *Oswaldtwistle Urban Council* Lord Macnaghten said: "Whether the general rule is to prevail, or an exception to the general rule is to be admitted, must depend on the scope and language of the Act which creates the obligation and on considerations of policy and convenience." In the case we are considering the statute creates an obligation and provides a remedy for its non-observance, and the question is whether the scope and language of the statute indicate that the general rule is to prevail so that the remedy provided is the only remedy, or whether an exception to that general rule is to be admitted. The order of the Local Government Board was made under section 6 of the Locomotives on Highways Act 1896, which empowered the Local Government Board to make regulations with respect to the use of light locomotives on highways, their construction, and the conditions under which they may be used. Section 7 of the Act provides that a breach of any regulation made under the Act may be punished by a fine not exceeding £10. The language of the Act includes the expressions the "use of light locomotives" their "construction" and "conditions under which they may be used"; and its scope is the public user of highways, which has been for years subject to rules regulating and controlling it. Thus the Act deals with rights which have always been sufficiently protected by the common law. Under this Act the Local Government order was made. It is divided into sections or articles, five in number. The provision relied on is art. II: "No person shall cause or permit a motor car to be used on any highway, or shall drive or have charge of a motor car when so used, unless the conditions hereinafter set forth are satisfied." Then follow the conditions on which a motor car may be used on any highway. They are contained in seven clauses. It is clear that some of them are introduced not to protect persons using the highway but to preserve the highway itself; those for instance relating to the width of wheels and the weight of motor cars. If the appellant's contention is to prevail everyone injured by a motor car which does not comply with the regulations has a right of action. There is no reason for differentiating between those who are injured as a legal consequence of a breach from those who are injured in fact irrespective of the breach of the regulations. Take cl. 7 for example. That clause provides that a car must have lamps exhibiting a white light in front and a red light in the rear. According to the appellant's contention a foot passenger crossing in front of a motor car would have a right of action if injured without any negligence of the driver, merely because the car had no red light in the rear. That cannot have been the intention of the Legislature. The absence of a red light in the rear may concern the safety of the car itself, or it may be a wise police regulation for other vehicles overtaking it, but it cannot affect the safety of a foot passenger passing in front of the car. This seems to indicate that it is not the intention of the Act to confer a right of action on every person injured by a car which does not conform to the regulations and to confer this right even though the breach of the regulations has no effect on the injury of which he complains. The matter might have been more doubtful if cl. 6 had stood alone. It provides that the car and all its fittings "shall be in such a condition as not to cause, or to be likely to cause, danger to any person on the motor car or on any highway." We have not to consider the case of a person injured on the highway. The injury here was done to the appellant's van; and the appellant, a member of the public, claims a right of action as one of a class for whose benefit cl. 6 was introduced. He contends that the public using the highway is the class so favoured. I do not agree. In my view the public using the highway is not a class; it is itself the public and not a class of the public. The clause therefore was not passed for the benefit of a class or section of the public. It applies to the public generally, and it is one among many regulations for breach of which it cannot have been intended that a person aggrieved should have a civil remedy by way of action in addition to the more appropriate remedy provided, namely a fine. In my opinion therefore this case is not an exception to the general rule; that rule applies, and the appeal must be dismissed.

Note:

In *Monk* v. *Warbey,* the plaintiff, a bus-driver, was injured by X, who was carelessly driving a car he had borrowed from the defendant. X was not insured against liability to the plaintiff—he had no policy of his own, and he was not an additional insured under the defendant's policy. The defendant had therefore unwittingly committed an offence under the Road Traffic Act 1930, s.35 (now Road Traffic Act 1972, s.143). X had no money with which to pay the plaintiff, so the plaintiff was allowed to recover from the defendant (who had at least the car).

The decision is striking, both because the plaintiff was complaining of financial harm (the defendant's breach of duty did not cause the injuries, but only the plaintiff's failure to get compensation for them), and because offences under the section in question are so easily committed. Nevertheless, the decision fits very well into the policy of the law that victims of *negligence* on the highway should not only be entitled to compensation, but should actually receive it. The scheme is now completed by the institution of the Motor Insurers' Bureau, which compensates those victims of motor-vehicles who should, by statute, have been able to recover from an insurance company). (See Hepple and Matthews, *Tort: Cases and Materials* (2d ed. 1980) 696–700).

But if the policy of the law were to indemnify the victims of traffic *accidents,* then *Phillips* would appear as the anomalous decision. If the offence of putting an *uninsured* vehicle on the roads leads to liability, then why not also the offence of putting a *dangerous* car on the road? The distinction is particularly curious when one considers that, had *Phillips* gone the other way, most of the people caught under it would have the statutory insurance cover against liability to pay those damages, whereas defendants caught under *Monk* v. *Warbey* will normally have to pay out of their own pocket.

FACTORIES ACT 1961

14.—(1) Every dangerous part of any machinery . . . shall be securely fenced. . . .

Note:

It might be supposed that this section gave a claim for damages to every workman injured in a factory by a machine. Not so.

Dangerous part: The mere fact that a piece of machinery hurt someone does not show that it was dangerous. A part is dangerous only if a person looking at it could reasonably imagine it hurting a person acting the way people do.

Machinery: All factory equipment, installed or not, but not the factory product, is capable of being machinery; but not all parts of a machine are parts of its machinery (just as "poems very seldom consist of poetry and nothing else" (Housman)).

Securely fenced: A fence is secure if it keeps the workman from bringing his person (and perhaps his clothing, but perhaps not his tools) into contact with the dangerous part, notwithstanding that it does not prevent his being bombarded by pieces of the material being worked on or of the machinery itself. Since secure fencing can be got round by workmen determined to do so, mere proof that the workman came in contact with the dangerous part does not conclusively show that the fence was not secure.

Shall be: The imperative is absolute in the sense that it is unqualified by reasonableness; but, as has been seen, it is conditioned on foreseeability.

F. E. CALLOW (ENGINEERS) v. JOHNSON

House of Lords [1971] A.C. 335; [1970] 3 W.L.R. 982; 114 S.J. 846; [1970] 3 All E.R. 639

Action for personal injuries by employee against occupier of factory.

A stainless-steel workpiece rotated every two seconds while a boring-bar to which a cutting tool was attached moved very slowly forward inside it. Between the workpiece and the bar was a space varying from half an inch on the operative's side to four inches on the far side. While the plaintiff was manually injecting the necessary coolant—a practice disapproved of by his employers who provided an automatic system—his hand, inserted into the larger space, was caught in the narrower space and his fingers were crushed.

The trial judge found no breach of Factories Act 1961, s.14, and dismissed the action. The Court of Appeal allowed the plaintiff's appeal ([1970] 1 All E.R. 129). The defendant appealed and his appeal was dismissed by the House of Lords (Viscount Dilhorne dissenting).

LORD HAILSHAM OF ST. MARYLEBONE L.C.: My Lords, this appeal is another example of litigation arising from section 14 of the Factories Act 1961.

Section 14 forms part of a group of five sections (sections 12 to 16) which deal with the liability of an employer in a factory to fence part of the machinery for the protection of his employees. These sections are clearly intended to form, as it were, a single code and should be read together. Section 12 deals with prime movers. Section 13 deals with transmission machinery. Section 14 deals with dangerous parts of machinery, other than prime movers and transmission machinery.

The obligation cast on the employer is not unqualified, and section 15 deals with the operation of machinery which, under the exceptions to the preceding sections, is unfenced. Section 16 deals with the construction and maintenance of fences in cases where the duty to fence applies under the preceding sections. It provides (in language which may be material to this appeal) that the fences are to be kept in position while the parts required to be fenced are "in motion or in use," thereby implying that there may be cases in which the parts are in motion but not in use and equally cases in which the parts required to be fenced are in use but not in motion.

At first sight the code provided by this group of five sections is deceptively simple. In point of fact, however, its provisions, especially those of section 14 which are now under discussion, have given rise to a considerable degree of difference of opinion. In some ways the duty cast on employers has seemed at times unduly harsh. In others the protection afforded to the worker has seemed illusory and unreal.

The sanction behind the sections imposed by the Act is primarily penal and this is the only sanction contained expressly in the Act. But for many years a breach of the provisions of the code has been held to give rise to a civil action for damages for personal injury at the suit of the injured workman. As a matter of social policy the necessity for this connection between the judicially recognised remedy and the statutory offence is not logically plain. For, while it might appear to be reasonable and even self-evident that if an employer is guilty of an offence against the code any workman injured thereby should be entitled to damages for the breach, the converse is by no means so obvious; it is not so plain that in the absence of negligence the only correct basis for the compensation by an employer of his workman injured or killed by dangerous machinery is his commission of a criminal offence. It is clearly the law now. But it is not self-evident that it should be so.

But, while the policy of the Act is well established, some of the protection to the workman which at first sight might be thought to be available turns out on closer scrutiny to be illusory. Thus: (1) since it is only *parts* of the machinery which have to be fenced there is no obligation to fence a machine under section 14 if it is dangerous *as a whole* but without having dangerous parts (*cf. Liptrot* v. *British Railways Board* [1969] 1 A.C. 136, *per* Lord Reid at p. 159); (2) it is now established that under section 14 what is referred to as a part of the machinery does not include a workpiece moving under power and held in the machinery by a chuck; nor does it include other material in the machine as distinct from parts of the machinery (see, for instance, *Eaves* v. *Morris Motors Ltd.* [1961] 2 Q.B. 385; *Bullock* v. *G. John Power (Agencies) Ltd.* [1956] 1 W.L.R. 171); (3) the dangers against which the fencing is required do not include dangers to be apprehended from the ejection of flying material from the machine whether this is part of the material used in the machine (see *Nicholls* v. *F. Austin (Leyton) Ltd.* [1946] A.C. 493) or part of the machine itself (see *Close* v. *Steel Co. of Wales Ltd.* [1962] A.C. 367); (4) the workman is not ordinarily protected if what comes into contact with the dangerous part of a machine is a hand tool operated by the workman as distinct from the workman's body or his clothes (see *Sparrow* v. *Fairey Aviation Co. Ltd.* [1964] A.C. 1019), nor if the danger created arises because of the proximity of moving machinery to some stationary object extraneous to the machine (*Pearce* v. *Stanley-Bridges Ltd.* [1965] 1 W.L.R. 931).

In these circumstances it is not surprising that arguments about the protection afforded by section 14 of the Factories Act were described by Holroyd Pearce L.J. as "technical" and "artificial" and the protection itself as "in some respects illusory" (see *Eaves* v. *Morris Motors Ltd.* [1961] 2 Q.B. 385, 396). It is equally not surprising that the decisions in *Nicholls* v. *F. Austin (Leyton) Ltd.* ([1946] A.C. 493) and *Close* v. *Steel Co. of Wales Ltd.* ([1962] A.C. 367) were strongly criticised by Lord MacDermott and by Lord Reid in *Sparrow* v. *Fairey Aviation Co. Ltd.* ([1964] A.C. 1019, 1046–1048, 1033–1034), in spite of the fact that Lord Reid regarded himself as bound by the decisions which he criticised. It has been pointed out more than once that the position would be ameliorated by the use by the Minister of his regulatory powers under section 14(6) of the Act of 1961 (for this purpose equivalent to section 14(3) of its predecessor of 1937). But no use has so far been made of this power, not, I apprehend, through inadvertence, but as a matter of departmental policy. No one contemplating the situation set up by this series of decisions can wholly avoid the conclusion reached by Holroyd Pearce L.J. in the passage cited above that the gap in the protection afforded by the statute is one "which neither logic nor common sense appears to justify." It is however too late for the courts to close the gap. The gap can only be closed by legislation or to some extent by the use of the regulatory powers of the Minister. It has however to be said that I for one would be slow to enlarge the gap or to extend the ambit of the criticised decisions beyond the limits required by the facts of the cases concerned and the reasoning of the judgments in them. . . .

LORD HAILSHAM, having intimated that in his view the defendants were guilty of common law negligence in permitting an unsafe system of work, held that the boring bar, though nearly stationary, could be a dangerous part of machinery by reason of its juxtaposition to the moving workpiece (which there was no obligation to fence), an accident of this type being in the light of the defendant's knowledge foreseeable. LORD HODSON and LORD GARDINER concurred. LORD DONOVAN held that it was possible to regard the boring bar as a dangerous part of the machine only because the employers knew of the system of injecting coolant by hand. VISCOUNT DILHORNE, dissenting, held that the boring bar was not made into a dangerous part of the machinery of the lathe by the mere fact that coolant was being injected by hand, and that consequently there was no duty to fence it.

NIMMO v. ALEXANDER COWAN & SONS

House of Lords [1968] A.C. 107; [1967] 3 W.L.R. 1169; 111 S.J. 668; [1967] 3 All E.R. 187; 3 K.I.R. 277; 1967 S.L.T. 277

Action by employee against employer in respect of personal injuries.

The pursuer was injured while working, and alleged that the working-place was not safe, and claimed that the employer was in breach of Factories Act 1961, s.29(1), which requires that "every such place shall, so far as is reasonably practicable, be made and kept safe for any person working there." He did not plead that it was reasonably practicable for the employer to make the place safe, and the Lord Ordinary accordingly dismissed his claim. The pursuer's appeal to the Inner House of the Court of Session was dismissed (1966 S.L.T. 266). His further appeal to the House of Lords was allowed, and the case returned for trial.

LORD GUEST, LORD UPJOHN and LORD PEARSON allowed the appeal on the ground that it must have been the intention of Parliament that the onus be on the employer of showing that it was not reasonably practicable to make the working-place safe, since this would give better protection to the workman, and the employer was in a better position to know, and was under a duty to know, whether safety was reasonably practicable or not.

LORD REID (dissenting): My Lords, a considerable number of statutes prescribe, or enable regulations to prescribe, what steps an employer or occupier must take to promote the safety of persons working in factories, mines and other premises where work is carried on. Sometimes the duty imposed is absolute: certain things must be done and it is no defence that it was impossible to prevent an accident because it was caused by a latent defect which could not have been discovered—still less is it a defence to prove that it was impracticable to carry out the statutory requirement.

But in many cases the statutory duty is qualified in one way or another so that no offence is committed if it is impracticable or not reasonably practicable to comply with the duty. Unfortunately there is great variety in the drafting of such provisions. Sometimes the duty is expressed in absolute terms in one section and in another section it is provided that it shall be a defence to prove that it was impracticable or not reasonably practicable to comply with the duty. Sometimes the form adopted is that the occupier shall, so far as reasonably practicable, do certain things. Sometimes it is that the occupier shall take all practicable steps to achieve or prevent a certain result. And there are other provisions which do not exactly fit into any of these classes. Often it is difficult to find any reason for these differences.

There has been much doubt where the onus rests in these cases. About the first class it may well be it is sufficient for the prosecutor or pursuer to aver and prove a breach of the duty set out in the one section, leaving it to the accused or defender to avail himself of the statutory defence if he can. But in the other cases there is much room for doubt. In the present case the pleadings have been deliberately drawn in such a way as to require a decision at least with regard to the section on which the pursuer relies.

The pursuer, the present appellant, avers that on May 18, 1964, he had, within a factory, to unload railway wagons filled with bales of pulp. In doing this he had to stand on some of the bales, and while he was standing on one of the bales it tipped up and caused him to fall and fracture his skull and three ribs. He founds on section 29(1) of the Factories Act 1961, which is in these terms: "There shall, so far as is reasonably practicable, be provided and maintained safe means of access to every place at which any person has at any time to work, and every such place shall, so far as is reasonably practicable, be made and kept safe for any person working there."

He avers that the bales were insecurely placed in the wagons so that the place at which he had to work was not made and kept safe for his working there. He deliberately avoids averring that it was reasonably practicable for the respondents, his employers, to make that place safe. He says that he has averred a relevant case because under this section it is for the defender to aver and prove, if he can, that it was not reasonably practicable to make the place safe. The respondents, of course, had no control over the loading of the bales in the wagon: that no doubt was done by the seller who sold the pulp to them. They make averments to show that it was not reasonably practicable for them to make the place safe, and they also plead that, the pursuer's averments being irrelevant, the action should be dismissed. This plea to the relevancy was sustained by the Lord Ordinary and the First Division adhered to his interlocutor.

This matter is not a mere technicality. It has important practical consequences. If the respondents are right the pursuer must not only aver in general terms that it was reasonably practicable to make the place safe—such an averment without more would be lacking in specification—he must also make sufficient positive averments to give notice to the defender of the method of making the place safe which he proposes to support by evidence. But if the appellant is right he can simply wait for the evidence which the respondent would have to lead to discharge the onus on him to show that it was not reasonably practicable to make the place safe, and then cross-examine the respondent's witness in any relevant way he chooses. He would only have to make positive averments if he intended to lead evidence that some particular method of making the place safe could have been adopted by the defender.

In my opinion, this question should be approached by considering first what a prosecutor would have to allege and prove in order to obtain a conviction. For civil liability only arises if there has been a breach of the statutory duty, and I cannot see how a pursuer could succeed in a civil action without averring and proving all the facts essential to establish the commission of an offence. It is true that the standard of proof is lower in a civil case so that the pursuer only has to show that it is probable that an offence was committed. But that cannot mean that the onus of proof is different with regard to any of the essential elements of the offence.

The appellant's argument is that, although the statute says that every working place "shall, so far as is reasonably practicable, be made and kept safe," a prosecutor need only allege and prove that the place was not made and kept safe, leaving it to the accused to show that this was not reasonably practicable. . . .

Lord President Clyde, having analysed the section with which we are concerned, said (1966 S.L.T. 266, 271): "The words 'so far as is reasonably practicable' consequently become, in my view, an integral part of the duty imposed and define the ambit of what is made obligatory." Lord Guthrie said (*ibid.* at 272): "No breach of the section is committed, and no failure on the part of the defenders can take place, unless it is reasonably practicable to take steps to make and keep the working place safe." And Lord Migdale said (*ibid.* at 273) that the section "is not a command to make the place safe but to make it safe so far as is reasonably practicable." I agree with these views.

It would be very convenient if one could avoid examination of the method of drafting and have a general rule either that in all these cases the onus is on the pursuer or that it is on the defender. But I do not think that is possible. On the one hand, where the provision is that it "shall be a defence to prove" something, it would not be reasonable to require the pursuer to disprove that defence. But, on the other hand, take, for example, section 31 of this Act which requires that "all practicable steps shall be taken" to prevent an explosion, to restrict its spread, and to remove fumes, etc. I cannot see how a prosecutor or pursuer could frame a relevant complaint or condescendence by merely alleging that an explosion occurred, or that it spread, or that fumes were not removed, leaving it to the accused or the defender to show that no practicable steps could have been taken to avoid that. The offence here must be failure to take practicable steps and the prosecutor or pursuer must allege and prove such failure.

I get no assistance in this case from any general presumption that a person is not required to prove a negative or that a person is required to prove facts peculiarly within his own knowledge. I do not lay any stress on the fact that, if the appellant is right, the defender would have to prove a negative—that it was not reasonably practicable to make the place safe. And I do not think that the question whether this was reasonably practicable is a matter peculiarly within the knowledge of the defender—an expert witness for the pursuer should be just as well able to deal with this as the defender.

I would dismiss this appeal.

LORD WILBERFORCE also dissented.

Note:
It is perfectly true, as Lord Reid said in *Jenkins* v. *Allied Ironfounders* ([1970] 1 W.L.R. 304, 307), that " . . . after the evidence has been led it is only in very rare cases that onus of proof is material," but it is very material indeed when one is deciding whether to sue or not.

THE INTERPRETATION OF STATUTES

Law Commission Paper No. 21 (1969)

APPENDIX A

DRAFT CLAUSES

. . .

4. Where any Act passed after this Act imposes or authorises the imposition of a duty, whether positive or negative and whether with or without a special remedy for its enforcement, it shall be presumed, unless express provision to the contrary is made, that a breach of the duty is intended to be actionable (subject to the defences and other incidents applying to actions for breach of statutory duty) at the suit of any person who sustains damage in consequence of the breach.

Questions
1. Is the rule that compensation is given only for harm of the type Parliament intended to prevent (below, p. 187) an "incident applying to actions for breach of statutory duty"? If so, will the present proposal, if implemented, greatly curtail the inquiry by the courts into the intentions of Parliament?
2. Does a statute which enacts that it will be an offence to do an act impose a duty not to do that act?
3. Could Parliament consistently attempt to prevent harm happening and not attempt to remedy it if it does happen?
4. Would Lonrho (above p. 155) be wise to lobby for the enactment of this proposal?

Section 2.—Public Nuisance and Civil Liability

BENJAMIN v. STORR

Common Pleas (1874) L.R. 9 C.P. 400; 43 L.J.C.P. 162; 30 L.T. 362; 22 W.R. 631

Action by frontager against highway-user in respect of financial loss.

The plaintiff ran a coffee-house in Rose Street, near Covent Garden, adjoining the exit from the defendant's auction rooms. The defendant had many horse-drawn vans to collect and deliver goods. The constant presence of the vans and the intermittent urination of the horses made the plaintiff's premises incommodious by obstructing the light and fouling the air.

The jury gave a verdict for the plaintiff, damages £75. The defendant, pursuant to leave, obtained a rule *nisi* for a non-suit or a new trial, but the rule was discharged.

BRETT J.: This action is founded upon alleged wrongful acts by the defendants, *viz.*, the unreasonable use of a highway—unreasonable to such an extent as to amount to a nuisance. That alone would not give the plaintiff a right of action; but the plaintiff goes on to allege in his declaration that the nuisance complained of is of such a kind as to cause him a particular injury other than and beyond that suffered by the rest of the public, and threfore he claims damages against the defendants. The first point discussed was whether it was necessary that the plaintiff should show something more than an injury to his business, an actual injury to his property; and cases decided under the Lands Clauses Consolidation Act (8 & 9 Vict. c. 18) were cited. In this case I think the action is maintainable without showing injury to property. In the class of cases referred to, the action is brought to recover compensation for lands taken or injuriously affected; and there, of course, injury to property must be shown, and not merely injury to the trade of the occupier. Those cases, therefore, do not at all affect the present. Before the passing of the Lands Clauses Consolidation Act, by the common law of England, a person guilty of a public nuisance might be indicted; but, if injury resulted to a private individual, other and greater than that which was common to all the Queen's subjects, the person injured had his remedy by action. The cases referred to upon this subject show that there are three things which the plaintiff must substantiate, beyond the existence of the mere public nuisance, before he can be entitled to recover. In the first place, he must show a particular injury to himself beyond that which is suffered by the rest of the public. It is not enough for him to show that he suffers the same inconvenience in the use of the highway as other people do, if the alleged nuisance be the obstruction of a highway. The case of *Hubert* v. *Groves* ((1794) 1 Esp. 148; 170 E.R. 308) seems to me to prove that proposition. There, the plaintiff's business was injured by the obstruction of a highway, but no greater injury resulted to him therefrom than to anyone else, and therefore it was held that the action would not lie. . . . Other cases show that the injury to the individual must be direct, and not a mere consequential injury; as, where one way is obstructed, but another (though possibly a less convenient one) is left open; in such a case the private and particular injury has been held not to be sufficiently direct to give a cause of action. Further, the injury must be shown to be of a substantial character, not fleeting or evanescent. If these propositions be correct, in order to entitle a person to maintain an action for damage caused by that which is a public nuisance, the damage must be particular, direct, and substantial. The question then is, whether the plaintiff here has brought himself within the rule so laid down.

The evidence on the part of the plaintiff showed that from the too long standing of horses and wagons of the defendants in the highway opposite his house, the free passage of light and air to his premises was obstructed, and the plaintiff was in consequence obliged to burn gas nearly all day, and so to incur expense. I think that brings the case within all the requirements I have pointed out; it was a particular, a direct, and a substantial damage. As to the bad smell, that also was a particular injury to the plaintiff, and a direct and substantial one. So, if by reason of the access to his premises being obstructed for an unreasonable time and in an unreasonable manner, the plaintiff's customers were prevented from coming to his coffee-shop, and he suffered a material diminution of trade, that might be a particular, a direct, and a substantial damage. As to that part of the rule which seeks to enter a non-suit, assuming the evidence objected to to have been properly received, I think it cannot be sustained. . . .

Note:

Public nuisance is a crime because it is likely to cause at least widespread inconvenience; stopping it is a matter for the state enforcement authorities. It would be intolerable if all those who were inconvenienced could bring a private action, even if the defendant is acting wrongfully; the courts therefore insist that the plaintiff show a particular damage suffered by himself. The requirement of particular damage was strictly insisted on in the mid-nineteenth century, lest the construction of railways, which was necessarily disruptive, become too expensive (*Ricket* v. *Metropolitan Ry.* (1867) L.R. 2 H.L. 175); today it is certain that proved business loss is recoverable.

Question

Every evening people waiting at the bus-stop outside your house throw into your front garden the remnants of the fish-and-chips they have bought from a fish restaurant close by. Have you any remedy against the bus company or the fish restaurant?

MINT v. GOOD

Court of Appeal [1951] 1 K.B. 517; 94 S.J. 822; [1950] 2 All E.R. 1159; 49 L.G.R. 495

Action by highway-user against owner of adjoining property in respect of personal injury.

A boy of ten years of age was walking along a public footpath when a wall collapsed on him and injured him. The wall, some four feet in length and two feet six inches high, separated the footpath from the forecourt of two houses owned by the defendant and let by him to persons (not sued) on weekly tenancies. The defendant had not specifically reserved the right to enter the premises for examination or repairs.

Stable J. found that the wall was in imminent danger of collapse, and that a competent person would have realised this after a reasonable inspection; accordingly the wall was technically a nuisance. But he dismissed the action on the ground that the defendant was not liable for it, since he had not reserved the right to enter the premises, and therefore had no control of the wall.

The plaintiff's appeal to the Court of Appeal was allowed in unreserved judgments.

DENNING L.J.: The law of England has always taken particular care to protect those who use a highway. It puts on the occupier of adjoining premises a special responsibility for the structures which he keeps beside the highway. So long as those structures are safe, all well and good; but if they fall into disrepair, so as to be a potential danger to passers-by, then they are a nuisance, and, what is more, a public nuisance; and the occupier is liable to anyone using the highway who is injured by reason of the disrepair. It is no answer for him to say that he and his servants took reasonable care; for, even if he has employed a competent independent contractor to repair the structure, and has every reason for supposing it to be safe, the occupier is still liable if the independent contractor did the work badly: see *Tarry* v. *Ashton* ((1876) 1 Q.B.D. 314).

The occupier's duty to passers-by is to see that the structure is as safe as reasonable care can make it; a duty which is as high as the duty which an occupier owes to people who pay to come on to his premises. He is not liable for latent defects, which could not be discovered by reasonable care on the part of anyone, nor for acts of trespassers of which he neither knew, nor ought to have known: see *Barker* v. *Herbert* ([1911] 2 K.B. 633, 645); but he is liable when structures fall into dangerous disrepair, because there must be some fault on the part of someone or other for that to happen; and he is responsible for it to persons using the highway, even though he was not actually at fault himself. That principle was laid down in this court in *Wringe* v. *Cohen* ([1940] 1 K.B. 233), where it is to be noted that the principle is confined to "premises on a highway," and is, I think, clearly correct in regard to the responsibility of an occupier to passers-by.

The question in this case is whether the owner, as well as the occupier, is under a like duty to passers-by. I think that in many cases he is. The law has shown a remarkable development on this point during the last sixteen years. The three cases of *Wilchick* v. *Marks and Silverstone* ([1934] 2 K.B. 56), *Wringe* v. *Cohen* ([1940] 1 K.B. 229), and *Heap* v. *Ind, Coope & Allsopp Ltd.* ([1940] 2 K.B. 476), show that the courts are now taking a realistic view of these matters. They recognise that the occupying tenant of a small dwelling-house does not in practice do the structural repairs, but the owner does; and that if a passer-by is injured by the structure being in dangerous disrepair, the occupier has not the means to pay damages, but the owner has, or, at any rate, he can insure against it. If a passer-by is injured by its falling on him, he should be entitled to damages from someone, and the person who ought to pay is the owner, because he is in practice responsible for the repairs. This practical responsibility means that he has *de facto* control of the structure for the purpose of repairs and is therefore answerable in law for its condition. Parliament has long made owners responsible under the Public Health Acts for nuisances arising from defects of a structural character: see section 94 of the Public Health Act 1875 and section 93(*b*) of the Public Health Act 1936; and the common law now also in many cases makes them responsible for public nuisances due to the disrepair of the structure.

This seems to me to be a logical consequence of the cases to which we have been referred. In *Wilchick* v. *Marks and Silverstone* the landlord had covenanted to repair; in *Heap* v. *Ind, Coope & Allsopp Ltd.* he had not covenanted to repair, but had reserved a right to enter. In the present case he has not reserved a right to enter, but he has in practice always done the structural repairs. I cannot think that the liability of the owner to passers-by depends on the precise terms of the tenancy agreement between the owner and the tenant, that is to say, on whether he has expressly reserved a right to enter or not. It depends on the degree of control exercised by the owner, in law or in fact, for the purpose of repairs. If a landlord is liable when he reserves an express right to enter, he is also liable when he has an implied right; and even if he has no strict right, but has been given permission to enter whenever he asked, it should make no difference. The landlord has in practice taken the structural repairs on himself and should be responsible for any disrepair.

That is sufficient for the decision of this case, but I venture to doubt whether in these days a landlord can in all cases exempt himself from liability to passers-by by taking a covenant from a tenant to repair the structure adjoining the highway. I know that in *Pretty* v. *Bickmore* ((1873) L.R. 8 C.P. 401) a landlord managed to escape liability for a coal-plate which was, at the beginning of the lease, in dangerous disrepair, because he took from the tenant a covenant to repair. I doubt whether he would escape liability today. Again, suppose that a landlord of small houses took from weekly tenants a covenant to repair the structure, and then did not trouble to enforce the covenant or to repair himself? Could he escape liability by so doing? I doubt it. It may be that in such cases the landlord owes a duty to the public which he cannot get rid of by delegating it to another. These questions do not however arise here because there was no such covenant. In this case the judge found that the condition of the wall was a nuisance, and that a reasonable examination of the wall by a competent person would have detected the condition in which it was. That means that the duty of the landlord was not fulfilled. His duty was to see that the structure was as safe as reasonable care could make it. It was not so safe.

I agree, therefore, that the appeal should be allowed, and judgment entered accordingly.

Note:

This vigorous unreserved judgment makes the law appear perhaps simpler than it is.

One starts with the proposition that if a person is hurt by something on the highway, he must first find out whether the act which hurt him was incidental to a reasonable user of the highway. If it was, then, subject to *res ipsa loquitur,* he must prove carelessness in the actor. If the act was something the actor had no right to do on the highway at all, the victim need not prove carelessness but will recover only for foreseeable damage.

People may also be hurt by things falling on to the highway from adjoining land. Some legal systems make the occupier of the premises from which they fall strictly liable to the person injured by them; but in England there is no law of *res dejectae vel effusae* (see Buckland, *Textbook of Roman Law,* 598). If a chattel (*e.g.,* Miss Stone's cricket ball) falls into the highway, the person struck by it must prove negligence; but the chattel may help him to establish it by speaking for itself (*Byrne* v. *Boadle* (1863) 2 H. & C. 722, 159 E.R. 299; but see *Walsh* v. *Holst & Co.* [1958] 1 W.L.R. 800).

The biggest things that frequently fall into the highway are trees and bits of houses; the law of England appears to distinguish between them. A house involves liability if, had a competent person looked at it just before it collapsed, he would have seen that it needed repair. A tree makes the occupier liable only if he should have procured a competent person to look at it, and that person would have seen that action was called for (*Caminer* v. *Northern & London Investment Trust* [1951] A.C. 88; *British Road Services* v. *Slater* [1964] 1 W.L.R. 498; *Quinn* v. *Scott* [1965] 2 All E.R. 588). This is the difference between liability in nuisance and liability in negligence.

Now what are the grounds for distinction between a tree and a bit of a house? Is it that a house is used and a tree is not? (*Sedleigh-Denfield* v. *O'Callaghan,* [1940] A.C. 880. Is it because a house is always built and a tree is not always planted? (It would be absurd to distinguish between planted and self-sown trees, *Davey* v. *Harrow Corporation* [1958] 1 Q.B. 60). Is it because a tree is uncommonly lovely and a house is commonly unlovely? Or is it because people are supposed to know about houses and not about trees, trees being subject, as houses are usually not, to *secret unobservable processes of nature*?

The italicised phrase occurs in *Wringe* v. *Cohen* [1940] 1 K.B. 229, an action in respect of property damage between neighbours adjoining the highway. That case established that an occupier was liable if his house, or part of it, collapsed owing to want of repair, independently of the question whether he was negligent or not. It would be a defence to show that the collapse was caused by the act of a trespasser (and enemy bombers were treated as trespassers in *Cushing* v. *Peter Walker & Son* [1942] 2 All E.R. 693) or a secret unobservable process of nature. The decision has been very adversely commented on, but, as Somervell L.J. said in the present case, "It is a plain decision, laying down plain principles." The French Civil Code, Art. 1386, provides: "The owner of a building is liable for the damage caused by its collapse, if it collapses by reason of want of repair or fault in construction."

In English law we think of the occupier and not the owner as being the person responsible, but the principal case shows one of the great advantages of public nuisance as a ground of action. Once the plaintiff has been injured by a thing which can be characterised as a nuisance, he is in a better position than the plaintiff in negligence who has to look around for a person who *acted* badly. The plaintiff in nuisance only has to study the thing and he can catch anyone connected with that thing—here the landlord as well as the occupier. So if I fall into an unguarded trench dug illegally on the highway, I can sue not only the careless person who dug it, but also the perfectly careful person who procured the digging.

But the rules of public nuisance protect only those on the highway, that is, those outside buildings. People injured inside buildings must generally use the Occupiers' Liability Act 1957. For this purpose the landlord as well as the tenant may be the occupier (see *Wheat* v. *Lacon,* above, p. 81; even if he is not the occupier, the landlord may still be held liable to an injured visitor under the Defective Premises Act 1972, s.4 (above, p. 84), provided that he is in breach of obligations owed, or deemed by s.4(4) to be owed, to the tenant. Note, however, that the landlord's liability under the Defective Premises Act 1972 extends also to persons outside the premises, while not, presumably, diminishing their rights, if wider, under the common law of which the principal case is an example.

CHAPTER 4

CAUSATION

Section 1.—No Cause

McWILLIAMS v. SIR WILLIAM ARROL & CO.

House of Lords [1962] 1 W.L.R. 295; 106 S.J. 218; 1962 S.C.(H.L.) 70; 1962 S.L.T. 121;
[1962] 1 All E.R. 623

Action by widow against employer of husband.

The pursuer appealed to the House of Lords from an order of the First Division of the Court of Session (1961 S.L.T. 265) affirming judgment given by the Lord Ordinary in favour of the defender. Her appeal was dismissed.

LORD REID: My Lords, the appellant is the widow of William McWilliams, a steel erector who was killed on May 27, 1956, when he fell from a steel tower which was being erected in a shipyard occupied by the second respondents. The first respondents were his employers. McWilliams was setting up a working platform for riveters on the outside of the tower about seventy feet from the ground. This had to be placed on "needles" which are battens projecting some four feet from the tower. They were secured to the tower by lashings. A lashing of one of the needles was not properly fixed so that when the deceased put his weight on this needle it tilted and he fell to the ground. It is not clear whether he was responsible for not fixing it properly or not inspecting it, and in this action no fault is alleged against the respondents with regard to the needle.

The case made by the appellant is that both respondents were at fault in not providing safety belts. These belts have about fifteen feet of rope attached to them so that the end of the rope can be tied to some convenient part of the structure near where the man is working: then if he falls the rope prevents him from falling more than its length. It is not denied that if McWilliams had been wearing a safety belt when he fell he would not have been killed. The employers do not deny that it was general practice to provide such belts but they do not admit any duty to provide them. The courts below have held that they had this duty and also that, by reason of the shipyard being a factory within the meaning of the Factories Act 1937, section 26(2) of that Act required the second respondents to provide these belts. I need not consider whether this was right, because the main defence of both respondents is that if such belts had been available on the day of the accident McWilliams would not have worn one and, therefore, any failure to provide a belt was not the cause of his death. I shall assume in the case of both respondents that they were in breach of duty in not providing belts.

There can be no certainty as to whether the deceased would or would not have worn a belt on this day, but the defenders maintain that it is highly probable that he would not. Work on this tower had been proceeding for many weeks and at least for a good part of that time he had been doing work similar to that which he was doing when he fell. Throughout this period safety belts had to his knowledge been available in a hut near-by and it is clear that it was not his practice to wear a belt. Steel erectors were neither required nor exhorted to wear belts, and several witnesses with long experience say that they had never seen any steel erector wear a belt, and in particular that they had never seen McWilliams wear one. And there is evidence that the condition of the belts showed that they had seldom if ever been

175

used. But one witness says that he saw McWilliams wearing a belt on two occasions when working in an exposed position. The Lord Ordinary thought this extremely doubtful, but I am prepared to assume in the appellant's favour that this evidence can be accepted. It was left to the discretion of each man to decide whether to wear a belt, and it appears that the reason why belts were not generally worn was not mere prejudice against them. They are cumbersome and some witnesses say they might be dangerous in certain circumstances.

For some reason, the belts were taken away to another site two or three days before the accident. So after that the defenders were in breach of their duty to provide belts. We do not know whether the deceased knew that they had been removed, and there is nothing to suggest that during those two or three days he may have considered changing his normal practice not to wear a belt. So it appears to me to be a natural, and indeed almost inevitable, inference that he would not have worn a belt on this occasion even if it had been available. And that inference is strengthened by the general practice of other men not to wear belts.

It was argued that the law does not permit such an inference to be drawn because what a man did on previous occasions is no evidence of what he would have done on a later similar occasion. This argument was based on the rule that you cannot infer that a man committed a particular crime or delict from the fact that he has previously committed other crimes or delicts. But even that is not an unqualified rule (see, for example, *Moorov* v. *Lord Advocate*, 1930 J.C. 68), and there are reasons for that rule which would not apply to a case like the present. It would not be right to draw such an inference too readily because people do sometimes change their minds unexpectedly. But the facts of this case appear to me to be overwhelming.

I would have had much more difficulty if the only evidence had been that there was a general practice not to wear belts. One would assume, in the absence of evidence to the contrary, that the deceased was a reasonable and careful man, and it may be that if the evidence proved that a reasonable and careful man would not have worn a belt on such an occasion that would be sufficient. But I would reserve my opinion about a case which merely depended on evidence of general practice. I regard the evidence about general practice in this case as corroborating the inference to be drawn from McWilliams' own past conduct.

The appellant founded on the case of *Roberts* v. *Dorman Long & Co. Ltd.* ([1953] 1 W.L.R. 942). There a steel erector who was not wearing a safety belt was killed during the erection of a steel building to which building regulations of 1948 applied. They required that belts should be available which would "so far as practicable enable such persons who elect to use them to carry out the work without risk of serious injury." The employers did have belts but they were kept so far away from the site that they were held not to be available. One question in the case was whether the employers' breach of statutory duty could be founded on in face of evidence of a general practice to elect not to use such belts. The evidence is not fully reported and it is not clear whether the deceased himself had ever had an opportunity to use such belts, or whether the evidence merely related to the practice of other men not to use them at other sites where they were available. Lord Goddard C.J. said: "It may very well be that the judge could form the opinion on the evidence that it was unlikely that if safety belts had been available the deceased would have used one." But he went on to say: "I think that if a person is under a duty to provide safety belts or other appliances and fails to do so, he cannot be heard to say: 'Even if I had done so they would not have been worn.' "

In my view, this is not correct. "He cannot be heard to say" suggests to me personal bar or estoppel: indeed, I know of no other ground on which a defender can be prevented from proving a fact vital for his defence. If I prove that my breach of duty in no way caused or contributed to the accident I cannot be liable in damages. And if the accident would have happened in just the same way whether or not I fulfilled my duty, it is obvious that my failure to fulfil my duty cannot have caused or contributed to it. No reason has ever been suggested why a defender should be barred from proving that his fault, whether common law negligence or breach of statutory duty, had nothing to do with the accident.

Hodson L.J. (as he then was) put the matter rather differently. His view was that there was no possibility of finding out whether the man would have exercised his election one way or another. If my noble and learned friend meant that if a man is dead you can never prove what he would have done I would not agree with him. Proof in civil cases depends on probability, and I think that the ordinary man would be surprised if told that you can never say that it is probable that in certain circumstances a deceased man would have done one thing and not another. But if his observation was directed to the facts of that particular case I am not prepared to say that it was wrong without fuller knowledge of the evidence which had been led. I have already said that I wish to reserve my opinion about a case where the only evidence relates to the practice of other men engaged on other work: much may depend on the precise nature of that evidence. . . .

It has been suggested that the decision of this House in *Bonnington Castings Ltd. v. Wardlaw* ([1956] A.C. 613) lays down new law and increases the burden on pursuers. I do not think so. It states what has always been the law—a pursuer must prove his case. He must prove that the fault of the defender caused, or contributed to, the danger which he has suffered. But proof need not be by direct evidence. If general practice or a regulation requires that some safety appliance shall be provided, one would assume that it is of some use, and that a reasonable man would use it. And one would assume that the injured man was a reasonable man. So the initial onus on the pursuer to connect the failure to provide the appliance with the accident would normally be discharged merely by proving the circumstances which led to the accident, and it is only where the evidence throws doubt on either of these assumptions that any difficulty would arise. Normally it would be left to the defender to adduce evidence, if he could, to displace these assumptions. So in practice it would be realistic, even if not theoretically accurate, to say that the onus is generally on the defender to show that the man would not have used the appliance even if it had been available. But in the end, when all the evidence has been brought out, it rarely matters where the onus originally lay, the question is which way the balance of probability has come to rest. . . .

LORD DEVLIN: . . . Mr. Stott, for the appellant, based his case upon the proposition that the failure to provide the safety belt was the cause of the [workman's] death. In my opinion, this proposition is incomplete. There is a missing link. The immediate cause of the deceased's death was the fact that at the time of the fall he was not wearing a safety belt. The cause or reason he was not wearing a safety belt may have been the fact that one was not provided, but the failure to provide operates only through the failure to wear. The correct way of stating the appellant's case is, I think, as follows: The immediate cause of the deceased's death was that at the time of the fall he was not wearing a safety belt: but for the fault of his employers, he would have been wearing a safety belt: therefore the fault of his employers was an effective cause of his death. So stated, it is plain that the reason why the deceased was not wearing a safety belt must be a proper subject for inquiry. . . .

This question of the burden of proof is frequently important when what is in issue is what a dead workman in fact did. Without his evidence it may be difficult to prove that negligence by the employers was an effective cause of the death: once negligence is proved, the fact that the workman cannot be called to account for his actions often defeats the proof of contributory negligence. But in the present case the question is not what the deceased actually did but what he would have done in circumstances that never arose. Whether the workman is alive or dead, this cannot be proved positively as a matter of fact but can only be inferred as a matter of likelihood or probability. Even when the workman himself is perforce silent, there may be plenty of material, as there is in this case, from which an inference can be drawn one way or the other; and then the question of burden of proof is unimportant. . . .

Question

Was "death by falling" within the risk envisaged by the legislature when it required safety belts to be provided?

Note:

The decedent would have been just as dead even if the defendant had done his duty and provided the safety belts. More briefly put, the defendant's breach of duty did not contribute to the death.

It is not necessary that the defendant's fault should have been the sole, or even a principal, cause of the harm; it is enough if his fault *contributed* to the harm (*Bonnington Castings* v. *Wardlaw* [1956] A.C. 613). The defendant's contribution to the harm must be proved by the plaintiff, but he proves it by showing that it was more probable than not that the defendant's fault did contribute to the harm. If a person does something which is in general likely to contribute to harm and such harm occurs, then he probably contributed to it, unless, of course, it is shown that in the particular case he did not. Thus in *McGhee* v. *N.C.B.* ([1973] 1 W.L.R. 1) an employee contracted dermatitis after some days spent cleaning out brick kilns. It was not the employer's fault that the conditions in the brick kilns were hot and dusty, but after work the employee had to cycle home unwashed because no washing facilities were provided. It was not proved that washing would have been effective (the aetiology of dermatitis being quite obscure), but "washing probably helps" and the defenders were held liable.

Puzzles

1. The defendant carelessly injures the plaintiff, causing him to lose 30 per cent. of the use of his left leg. Three years later gangsters shoot the plaintiff in the same leg and it has to be amputated. Does the defendant have to pay for 30 per cent. of the leg for life or only 30 per cent. of the leg for three years? *Baker* v. *Willoughby* ([1970] A.C. 467) said for life.

2. A person who might have been expected to work until 1985 had an accident in 1973 owing to his employer's fault. This reduced his earning capacity by 50 per cent. In 1976 a disease quite unconnected with the accident incapacitated him totally. Does he get 50 per cent. of his lost earnings for three years or for twelve? *Jobling* v. *Associated Dairies* ([1982] A.C. 794) said for three.

In that case Lord Wilberforce drew "the conclusion that no general, logical, or universally fair rules can be stated which will cover, in a manner consistent with justice, cases of supervening events, whether due to tortious, partially tortious, non-culpable or wholly accidental events."

3. A school is under a duty not to let children out till 3.30 p.m., since that is when their mothers fetch them. One day the school lets a child out at 3.25 p.m., and at 3.29 p.m. the child is run over in the street. It is proved that on that day the mother would have been fifteen minutes late. Is the school liable for causing the death of the child?

4. George is injured when Henry runs him over in the street. Henry wasn't looking where he was going and didn't apply the brakes at all. If he had been paying attention he could have braked and if the brakes had worked he would not have hit George. The brakes would not have worked, however, because Ian, a mechanic, had failed to fix them properly. Has either Henry or Ian contributed to George's injuries? Have both?

Section 2.—Directness and Foreseeability

IN RE AN ARBITRATION between POLEMIS and FURNESS, WITHY & Co.

Court of Appeal [1921] 3 K.B. 560; 90 L.J.K.B. 1353; 126 L.T. 154; 37 T.L.R. 940; 27 Com.Cas. 25; 15 Asp.M.L.C. 398; [1921] All E.R.Rep. 40

Claim by owners against charterers in respect of destruction of ship.

This was a dispute between the charterers and owners of a ship which was destroyed while under charter. At Casablanca, the charterers had employed Arab stevedores to unload the cargo. One of them dropped a heavy plank into the hold, which was full of petrol vapour. On impact, the plank caused a spark, the spark ignited the vapour, and the ship was destroyed. The arbitrator found that it was careless to drop the plank, that some damage to the ship was foreseeable, but that the causing of the spark and the ensuing fire were not. He awarded the owners damages of £196,165-odd (the equivalent of twenty months' hire). Sankey J. confirmed the award, and so did the Court of Appeal.

BANKES L.J.: . . . In the present case the arbitrators have found as a fact that the falling of the plank was due to the negligence of the defendants' servants. The fire appears to me to have been directly caused by the falling of the plank. Under these circumstances I consider that it is immaterial that the causing of the spark by the falling of the plank could not have been reasonably anticipated. The appellants' junior counsel sought to draw a distinction between the anticipation of the extent of damage resulting from a negligent act, and the anticipation of the type of damage resulting from such an act. He admitted that it could not lie in the mouth of a person whose negligent act had caused damage to say that he could not reasonably have foreseen the extent of the damage, but he contended that the negligent person was entitled to rely upon the fact that he could not reasonably have anticipated the type of damage which resulted from his negligent act. I do not think that the distinction can be admitted. Given the breach of duty which constitutes the negligence, and given the damage as a direct result of that negligence, the anticipations of the person whose negligent act has produced the damage appear to me to be irrelevant. I consider that the damages claimed are not too remote. . . .

WARRINGTON L.J.: . . . The result may be summarised as follows: The presence or absence of reasonable anticipation of damage determines the legal quality of the act as negligent or innocent. If it be thus determined to be negligent, then the question whether particular damages are recoverable depends only on the answer to the question whether they are the direct consequence of the act. Sufficient authority for the proposition is afforded by *Smith* v. *London and South Western Ry.* ((1870) L.R. 6 C.P. 14), in the Exchequer Chamber, and particularly by the judgments of Channell B. and Blackburn J. . . .

SCRUTTON L.J.: . . . The second defence is that the damage is too remote from the negligence as it could not be reasonably foreseen as a consequence. On this head we were referred to a number of well-known cases in which vague language, which I cannot think to be really helpful, has been used in an attempt to define the point at which damage becomes too remote from, or not sufficiently directly caused by, the breach of duty, which is the original cause of action, to be recoverable. For instance, I cannot think it useful to say the damage must be the natural and probable result. This suggests that there are results which are natural but not probable, and other results which are probable but not natural. I am not sure what either adjective means in this connection; if they mean the same thing, two need not be used; if they mean different things, the difference between them should be defined. And as to many cases of fact in which the distinction has been drawn, it is difficult to see why one case should be decided one way and one another. Perhaps the House of Lords will some day explain why, if a cheque is negligently filled up, it is a direct effect of the negligence that someone finding the cheque should commit forgery: *London Joint Stock Bank* v. *Macmillan* ([1918] A.C. 777); while if someone negligently leaves a libellous letter about, it is not a direct effect of the negligence that the finder should show the letter to the person libelled: *Weld-Blundell* v. *Stephens* ([1920] A.C. 956). In this case, however, the problem is simpler. To determine whether an act is negligent, it is relevant to determine whether any reasonable person would foresee that the act would cause damage; if he would not, the act is not negligent. But if the act would or might probably cause damage, the fact that the damage it in fact causes is not the exact kind of damage one would expect is immaterial, so long as the damage is in fact directly traceable to the negligent act, and not due to the operation of independent causes having no connection with the negligent act, except that they could not avoid its results. Once the act is negligent, the fact that its exact operation was not foreseen is immaterial. This is the distinction laid down by the majority of the Exchequer Chamber in *Smith* v. *London and South Western Ry.*, and by the majority of the Court in Banc in *Rigby* v. *Hewitt* and *Greenland* v. *Chaplin* ((1850) 5 Ex. 240, 243; 155 E.R. 103, 104), and approved recently by Lord Sumner in *Weld-Blundell* v. *Stephens* and Sir Samuel Evans in *H.M.S. London* ([1914] P. 76). In the present case it was negligent in discharging cargo to knock down the planks of the temporary staging, for they might easily cause some damage either to workmen, or cargo, or the ship. The fact that they did directly produce an unexpected result, a spark in an atmosphere of petrol vapour which caused a fire, does not relieve the person who was negligent from the damage which his negligent act directly caused. . . .

Questions

1. A borrows a car from B. When the day comes for returning it, A says, "Oh, I'm very sorry, I haven't got it. My chauffeur was getting into the car with a heavy picture I had just bought, and he rather carelessly struck the cigar-lighter on the dash-board. This must have set up some kind of electrical trouble, for the next thing we knew was that the car was on fire, and we were lucky to escape before the whole thing blew up. As to the car, it was just an unfortunate accident, I'm afraid." Is this a satisfactory answer to B's claim for the car?

2. If, under *Hadley* v. *Baxendale* ((1854) 9 Exch. 341; 156 E.R. 145), there is implied in a contract of carriage a term that the carrier will not be liable for more than the value of the thing to be carried, what is the limit of liability in a contract whereby one person contracts for the use of another person's chattel (*e.g.*, a ship)?

3. The charterparty in question in this case exempted the charterers from liability for "act of God, the King's enemies, loss or damage from fire on board, etc.," and all the judges agreed that this did not cover fire caused by the charterer's negligence. Does the presence of this clause suggest which party agreed to bear the risk of loss not covered by the exemption clause?

4. Suppose the cause of the fire were wholly unknown. Would the charterers pay (a) in the absence of the exemption clause, (b) when it is present?

OVERSEAS TANKSHIP (U.K.) LTD. v. MORTS DOCK & ENGINEERING CO. THE WAGON MOUND

Privy Council [1961] A.C. 388; [1961] 2 W.L.R. 126; 105 S.J. 85; [1961] 1 All E.R. 404; [1961] 1 Lloyd's Rep. 1

Action by frontager against highway user in respect of property damage.

A large quantity of oil was carelessly allowed to spill from *The Wagon Mound*, a ship under the defendant's control, during bunkering operations in Sydney Harbour on October 30, 1951. This oil spread to the plaintiff's wharf about 200 yards away, where a ship, *The Corrimal*, was being repaired. The plaintiff asked whether it was safe to continue welding, and was assured (in accordance with the best scientific opinion) that the oil could not be ignited when spread on water. On November 1, a drop of molten metal fell on a piece of floating waste; this ignited the oil, and the plaintiff's wharf was consumed by fire.

Kinsella J. found that the destruction of the wharf by fire was a direct but unforeseeable consequence of the carelessness of the defendant in spilling the oil, but that some damage by fouling might have been anticipated. He gave judgment for the plaintiff [1958] 1 Lloyd's Rep. 575. The Full Court of the Supreme Court of New South Wales affirmed his decision [1959] 2 Lloyd's Rep. 697. The defendant appealed to the Judicial Committee of the Privy Council, and the appeal was allowed.

VISCOUNT SIMONDS: . . . the authority of *Polemis* has been severely shaken through lip-service has from time to time been paid to it. In their Lordships' opinion it should no longer be regarded as good law. It is not probable that many cases will for that reason have a different result, though it is hoped that the law will be thereby simplified, and that in some cases, at least, palpable injustice will be avoided. For it does not seem consonant with current ideas of justice or morality that for an act of negligence, however slight or venial, which results in some trivial foreseeable damage the actor should be liable for all consequences however unforeseeable and however grave, so long as they can be said to be "direct." It is a principle of civil liability, subject only to qualifications which have no present relevance, that a man must be considered to be responsible for the probable consequences of his act. To demand more of him is too harsh a rule, to demand less is to ignore that civilised order requires the observance of a minimum standard of behaviour.

This concept applied to the slowly developing law of negligence has led to a great variety of expressions which can, as it appears to their Lordships, be harmonised with little difficulty with the single exception of the so-called rule in *Polemis*. For, if it is asked why a man should be responsible for the natural or necessary or probable consequences of his act (or any other similar description of them) the answer is that it is not because they are natural or necessary or probable, but because, since they have this quality, it is judged by the standard of the reasonable man that he ought to have foreseen them. Thus it is that over and over again it has happened that in different judgments in the same case, and sometimes in a single judgment, liability for a consequence has been imposed on the ground that it was reasonably foreseeable or, alternatively, on the ground that it was natural or necessary or probable. The two grounds have been treated as coterminous, and so they largely are. But, where they are not, the question arises to which the wrong answer was given in *Polemis*. For, if some limitation must be imposed upon the consequences for which the negligent actor is to be held responsible—and all are agreed that some limitation there must be—why should that test (reasonable foreseeability) be rejected which, since he is judged by what the reasonable man ought to foresee, corresponds with the common conscience of mankind, and a test (the "direct" consequence) be substituted which leads to nowhere but the never-ending and insoluble problems of causation. "The lawyer," said Sir Frederick Pollock, "cannot afford to adventure himself with philosophers in the logical and metaphysical controversies the beset the idea of cause." Yet this is just what he has most unfortunately done and must continue to do if the rule in *Polemis* is to prevail. A conspicuous example occurs when the actor seeks to escape liability on the ground that the "chain of causation" is broken by a "nova causa" or "novus actus interveniens."

The validity of a rule or principle can sometimes be tested by observing it in operation. Let the rule in *Polemis* be tested in this way. In the case of the *Liesbosch* ([1933] A.C. 449) the appellants, whose vessel had been fouled by the respondents, claimed damages under various heads. The respondents were admittedly at fault; therefore, said the appellants, invoking the rule in *Polemis*, they were responsible for all damage whether reasonably foreseeable or not. Here was the opportunity to deny the rule or to place it secure upon its pedestal. But the House of Lords took neither course; on the contrary, it distinguished *Polemis* on the ground that in that case the injuries suffered were the "immediate physical consequences" of the negligent act. It is not easy to understand why a distinction should be drawn between "immediate physical" and other consequences, nor where the line is to be drawn. It was perhaps this difficulty which led Denning L.J. in *Roe* v. *Minister of Health* ([1954] 2 Q.B. 66, 85; above, p. 143) to say that foreseeability is only disregarded when the negligence is the immediate or *precipitating* cause of the damage. This new word may well have been thought as good a word as another for revealing or disguising the fact that he sought loyally to enforce an unworkable rule.

In the same connection may be mentioned the conclusion to which the Full Court finally came in the present case. Applying the rule in *Polemis* and holding therefore that the unforeseeability of the damage by fire afforded no defence, they went on to consider the remaining question. Was it a "direct" consequence? Upon this Manning J. said: "Notwithstanding that, if regard is had separately to each individual occurrence in the chain of events that led to this fire, each occurrence was improbable and, in one sense, improbability was heaped upon improbability, I cannot escape from the conclusion that if the ordinary man in the street had been asked, as a matter of common sense, without any detailed analysis of the circumstances, to state the cause of the fire at Mort's Dock, he would unhesitatingly have assigned such cause to spillage of oil by the appellant's employees." Perhaps he would, and probably he would have added: "I never should have thought it possible." But with great respect to the Full Court this is surely irrelevant, or, if it is relevant, only serves to show that the *Polemis* rule works in a very strange way. After the event even a fool is wise. But it is not the hindsight of a fool; it is the foresight of the reasonable man which alone can determine responsibility. The *Polemis* rule by substituting "direct" for "reasonably foreseeable" consequence leads to a conclusion equally illogical and unjust.

At an early stage in this judgment their Lordships intimated that they would deal with the proposition which can best be stated by reference to the well-known dictum of Lord Sumner: "This however goes to culpability not to compensation." It is with the greatest respect to that very learned judge, and to those who have echoed his words, that their Lordships find themselves bound to state their view that this proposition is fundamentally false.

It is, no doubt, proper when considering tortious liability for negligence to analyse its elements and to say that the plaintiff must prove a duty owed to him by the defendant, a breach of that duty by the defendant, and consequent damage. But there can be no liability until the damage has been done. It is not the act but the consequences on which tortious liability is founded. Just as (as it has been said) there is no such thing as negligence in the air, so there is no such thing as liability in the air. Suppose an action brought by A for damage caused by the carelessness (a neutral word) of B, for example, a fire caused by the careless spillage of oil. It may, of course, become relevant to know what duty B owed to A, but the only liability that is in question is the liability for damage by fire. It is vain to isolate the liability from its context and to say that B is or is not liable, and then to ask for what damage he is liable. For his liability is in respect of that damage and no other. If, as admittedly it is, B's liability (culpability) depends on the reasonable foreseeability of the consequent damage, how is that to be determined except by the foreseeability of the damage which in fact happened—the damage in suit? And, if that damage is unforeseeable so as to diplace liability at large, how can the liability be restored so as to make compensation payable?

But, it is said, a different position arises if B's careless act has been shown to be negligent and has caused some foreseeable damage to A. Their Lordships have already observed that to hold B liable for consequences however unforeseeable of a careless act, if, but only if, he is at the same time liable for some other damage however trivial, appears to be neither logical nor just. This becomes more clear if it is supposed that similar unforeseeable damage is suffered by A and C but other foreseeable damage, for which B is liable, by A only. A system of law which would hold B liable to A but not to C for the similar damage suffered by each of them could not easily be defended. Fortunately, the attempt is not necessary. For the same fallacy is at the root of the proposition. It is irrelevant to the question whether B is liable for unforeseeable damage that he is liable for foreseeable damage, as irrelevant as would the fact that he had trespassed on Whiteacre be to the question whether he has trespassed on Blackacre. Again, suppose a claim by A for damage by fire by the careless act of B. Of what relevance is it to that claim that he has another claim arising out of the same careless act? It would surely not prejudice his claim if that other claim failed: it cannot assist it if it succeeds. Each of them rests on its own bottom, and will fail if it can be established that the damage could not reasonably be foreseen. We have come back to the plain common sense stated by Lord Russell of Killowen in *Bourhill* v. *Young* ([1943] A.C. 92, 101). As Denning L.J. said in *King* v. *Phillips* ([1953] 1 Q.B. 429, 441): "there can be no doubt since *Bourhill* v. *Young* that the test of *liability for shock* is foreseeability of *injury by shock.*" Their Lordships substitute the word "fire" for "shock" and endorse this statement of the law.

Their Lordships conclude this part of the case with some general observations. They have been concerned primarily to displace the proposition that unforeseeability is irrelevant if damage is "direct." In doing so they have inevitably insisted that the essential factor in determining liability is whether the damage is of such a kind as the reasonable man should have foreseen. This accords with the general view thus stated by Lord Atkin in *Donoghue* v. *Stevenson:* "The liability for negligence, whether you style it such or treat it as in other systems as a species of 'culpa,' is no doubt based upon a general public sentiment of moral wrongdoing for which the offender must pay." It is a departure from this sovereign principle if liability is made to depend solely on the damage being the "direct" or "natural" consequence of the precedent act. Who knows or can be assumed to know all the processes of nature? But if it would be wrong that a man should be held liable for damage unpredictable by a reasonable man because it was "direct" or "natural," equally it would be wrong that he should escape liability, however "indirect" the damage, if he foresaw or could reasonably foresee the intervening events which led to its being done: *cf. Woods* v. *Duncan* ([1946] A.C. 401, 442). Thus foreseeability becomes the effective test. In reasserting this principle their Lordships conceive that they do not depart from, but follow and develop, the law of negligence as laid down by Baron Alderson in *Blyth* v. *Birmingham Waterworks Co.* ((1856) 11 Exch. 781, 784; 156 E.R. 1047).

It is proper to add that their Lordships have not found it necessary to consider the so-called rule of "strict liability" exemplified in *Rylands* v. *Fletcher* ((1868) L.R. 3 H.L. 330; below, p. 369) and the cases that have followed or distinguished it. Nothing that they have said is intended to reflect on that rule. . . .

Their Lordships will humbly advise Her Majesty that this appeal should be allowed, and the respondents' action so far as it related to damage caused by the negligence of the appellants be dismissed with costs, but that the action so far as it related to damage caused by nuisance should be remitted to the Full Court to be dealt with as that court may think fit. The respondents must pay the costs of the appellants of this appeal and in the courts below.

Questions

1. Did their Lordships deny that the spillage of oil caused the fire?

2. Could *you* defend a legal system which held "B liable to A but not to C for the similar damage suffered by each of them" if there was a contract or other special relationship between B and A but not between B and C, or vice versa?

3. Do you have any difficulty in distinguishing the immediate physical consequences of an act from its immediate non-physical consequences (*e.g., The Edison,* below, p. 546) or from its mediate physical consequences (*e.g., Best* v. *Samuel Fox,* [1952] A.C. 716)?

4. Suppose that their Lordships had wanted to maintain the result of *Re Polemis* and to decide the present case in favour of the defendants. On which of the following grounds of distinction could they most properly have done so?

    (a) the difference between three days and one second;

    (b) the difference between 200 yards horizontally and about twenty feet vertically;

    (c) the difference between a case where there was an intervening act (*viz.,* the dropping of the molten metal) and a case where there was not;

(d) the difference between strangers and contractors?

5. Does what the plaintiff complains of have to be merely foreseeable, or does it have to be a foreseeable *consequence* of the defendant's behaviour? If the latter, how do we escape from the "never-ending and insoluble problems of causation"?

Small Notes:

1. "But it is not the hindsight of a fool. . . . " One of the characters in Congreve's *Love for Love* is named Foresight. He is described as "An illiterate old Fellow, peevish and positive, superstitious and pretending to understand Astrology, Palmistry, Phisiognomy, Omens, Dreams &c."

2. All the incendiary bombs and high explosives of the Royal Air Force were incapable of setting fire to the oil which spread on to the English Channel from the wreck of the *Torrey Canyon* after it collided with Lands End in 1967. Presumably experts thought they might.

Long Note:

In *The Wagon Mound* (*No.* 2) the same defendant was sued by the owners of the ship which was being repaired at Morts Dock. The trial judge held that there could be no recovery in negligence, since the fire was unforeseeable, but that unforeseeability of consequences was irrelevant in nuisance. The Judicial Committee held that there was no difference in this respect between nuisance and negligence, but found that the fire was foreseeable after all and gave judgment for the plaintiff in negligence ([1967] 1 A.C. 617, on appeal from [1963] 1 Lloyd's Rep. 402).

So the defendants paid the owner of the burnt ship. Could they then claim contribution (above, p. 65) from Morts Dock? That depends on whether Morts Dock would have been liable to the owners of the ship they were repairing. Now that the fire has been held to have been foreseeable, could one properly say that it was negligent of the *Wagon Mound's* engineer to let the oil spill, but not negligent of the wharf-owners to carry on welding? Probably one could, since liability depends on the unreasonableness of behaviour as well as the foreseeability of the results. Remember the words of Lord Reid: "If a real risk is one which would occur to the mind of a reasonable man . . . and which he would not brush aside as far-fetched, and if the criterion is to be what that reasonable man would have done in the circumstances, then surely he would not neglect such a risk if action to eliminate it presented no difficulty, involved no disadvantage and required no expense." ([1967] 1 A.C. 617, 643–644).

The Wagon Mound (*No.* 2) discusses how foreseeable the damage must be in order to satisfy the test laid down by *The Wagon Mound* (*No.* 1). As Lord Upjohn put it in *The Heron II* [1969] 1 A.C. 350, 422, "the tortfeasor is liable for any damage which he can reasonably foresee may happen as a result of the breach however unlikely it may be, unless it can be brushed aside as far-fetched." According to *The Heron II* the rules of remoteness are different in contract and tort: a contractor is not, like the tortfeasor, liable for consequences which are just foreseeable, but only for those which are so foreseeable that one would actually have predicted them. Now although the rules of remoteness certainly operate differently depending on the features of the case in hand, it is far from clear that the distinction between contract and tort is the correct one to draw or that it is useful to spend time on such verbal formulae. If we accept that the outcome of a damages suit is a function of (a) the type of harm complained of, (b) the relationship between the parties and (c) the blameworthiness of the defendant, then we can be sure that liability for consequences will be more extensive if (a) the harm is physical, especially personal injury, (b) there is a special relationship, and (c) the defendant was greatly to blame. Whereas features (a) and (c) are often missing in contract cases, feature (b) is invariably present; in tort cases, on the other hand, (a) and (c) are usually present but (b) often is not (as in *The Wagon Mound* itself). In *Parsons* v. *Uttley Ingham* [1978] Q.B. 791 the defendants sold the plaintiff a hopper for pig-food. Because its ventilator was stuck, the nuts inside went mouldy. The plaintiff's pigs got a rare disease from the mouldy nuts and 254 of them died. Here was physical harm (as Lord Denning emphasised) caused by a careless breach of contract. The defendants were held liable.

SMITH v. LEECH BRAIN & CO.

Queen's Bench [1962] 2 Q.B. 405; [1962] 2 W.L.R. 148; 106 S.J. 77; [1961] 3 All E.R. 1159

Action by widow against employer of husband.

Smith was employed by the defendant as labourer and galvaniser; his job was to remove galvanised articles from a tank of molten metal. One day in 1950 he was burnt on the lip by a drop of molten metal when a large object was immersed in the tank. The defendants were negligent in not providing adequate protection. Smith died of cancer in 1953. He had previously worked in a gasworks for nine years and was consequently at the time of the accident in a condition such that a burn or scratch might induce the malignancy from which he died.

LORD PARKER C.J.: . . . Accordingly, I find that the burn was the promoting agency of cancer in tissues which already had a pre-malignant condition. In those circumstances, it is clear that the plaintiff's husband, but for the burn, would not necessarily ever have developed cancer. On the other hand, having regard to the number of matters which can be promoting agencies, there was a strong likelihood that at some stage in his life he would develop cancer. But that the burn did contribute to, or cause in part, at any rate, the cancer and the death, I have no doubt.

The third question is damages. Here I am confronted with the recent decision of the Privy Council in *Overseas Tankship (U.K.) Ltd.* v. *Morts Dock and Engineering Co. Ltd. (The Wagon Mound).* But for that case, it seems to me perfectly clear that, assuming negligence proved, and assuming that the burn caused in whole or in part the cancer and the death, the plaintiff would be entitled to recover. It is said on the one side by Mr. May that although I am not strictly bound by the *Wagon Mound* since it is a decision of the Privy Council, I should treat myself as free, using the arguments to be derived from that case, to say that other cases in these courts—other cases in the Court of Appeal—have been wrongly decided, and particularly that *Re Polemis and Furness Withy & Co.* was wrongly decided, and that a further ground for taking that course is to be found in the various criticisms that have from time to time in the past been made by members of the House of Lords in regard to the *Polemis* case.

It is said, on the other hand, by Mr. Martin Jukes, that I should hold that the *Polemis* case was rightly decided and, secondly, that even if that is not so I must treat myself as completely bound by it. Thirdly, he said that in any event, whatever the true view is in regard to the *Polemis* case, the *Wagon Mound* has no relevance at all to this case.

For my part, I am quite satisfied that the judicial Committee in the *Wagon Mound* case did not have what I may call, loosely, the thin skull cases in mind. It has always been the law of this country that a tortfeasor takes his victim as he finds him. It is unnecessary to do more than refer to the short passage in the decision of Kennedy J. in *Dulieu* v. *White & Sons,* where he said ([1901] 2 K.B. 669, 679): "If a man is negligently run over or otherwise negligently injured in his body, it is no answer to the sufferer's claim for damages that he would have suffered less injury, or no injury at all, if he had not had an unusually thin skull or an unusually weak heart."

To the same effect is a passage in the judgment of Scrutton L.J. in *The Arpad* ([1934] P. 189, 202). But quite apart from those two references, as is well known, the work of the courts for years and years has gone on on that basis. There is not a day that goes by where some trial judge does not adopt that principle, that the tortfeasor takes his victim as he finds him. If the Judicial Committee had any intention of making an inroad into that doctrine, I am quite satisfied that they would have said so.

It is true that if the wording in the advice given by Lord Simonds in the *Wagon Mound* case is applied strictly to such a case as this, it could be said that they were dealing with this point. But, as I have said, it is to my mind quite impossible to conceive that they were and, indeed, it has been pointed out that they disclose the distinction between such a case as this and the one they were considering when they comment on *Smith* v. *London & South Western Ry.* ((1870) L.R. 6 C.P. 14). Lord Simonds, in dealing with that case, said: "Three things may be noted about this case: the first, that for the sweeping proposition laid down no authority was cited; the second, that the point to which the court directed its mind was not unforeseeable damage of a different kind from that which was foreseen, but more extensive damage of the same kind." In other words, Lord Simonds is clearly there drawing a distinction between the question whether a man could reasonably anticipate a type of injury, and the question whether a man could reasonably anticipate the extent of injury of the type which could be foreseen.

The Judicial Committee were, I think, disagreeing with the decision in the *Polemis* case that a man is no longer liable for the type of damage which he could not reasonably anticipate. The Judicial Committee were not, I think, saying that a man is only liable for the extent of damage which he could anticipate, always assuming the type of injury could have been anticipated. I think that view is really supported by the way in which cases of this sort have been dealt with in Scotland. Scotland has never, so far as I know, adopted the principle laid down in *Polemis,* and yet I am quite satisfied that they have throughout proceeded on the basis that the tortfeasor takes the victim as he finds him.

In those circumstances, it seems to me that this is plainly a case which comes within the old principle. The test is not whether these employers could reasonably have foreseen that a burn would cause cancer and that he would die. The question is whether these employers could reasonably foresee the type of injury he suffered, namely, the burn. What, in the particular case, is the amount of damage which he suffers as a result of that burn depends upon the characteristics and constitution of the victim.

Accordingly, I find that the damages which the widow claims are damages for which the defendants are liable. Before leaving that part of the case, I should say, in case the matter goes further, that I would follow, sitting as a trial judge, the decision in the *Wagon Mound* case; or rather, more accurately, I would treat myself, in the light of the arguments in that case, able to follow other decisions of the Court of Appeal prior to the *Polemis* case, rather than the *Polemis* case itself. As I have said, that case has been criticised by individual members of the House of Lords, although followed by the Court of Appeal in *Thurogood* v. *Van Den Berghs & Jurgens Ltd.* ([1951] 2 K.B. 537). I should treat myself as at liberty to do that, and for my part I would do so the more readily because I think it is important that the common law, and the development of the common law, should be homogeneous in the various sections of the Commonwealth. I think it would be lamentable if a court sitting here had to say that while the common law in the Commonwealth and Scotland has been developed in a particular way, yet we in this country, and sitting in these courts, are going to proceed in a different way. However, as I have said, that does not strictly arise in this case.

[His Lordship considered the qestion of damages, observed that he must make a substantial reduction from the figure taken for the dependency because of the fact that the plaintiff's husband might have developed cancer even if he had not suffered the burn, and awarded the plaintiff £3,064 17s. 0d.]

Questions

1. Was this a claim in respect of "immediate physical consequences" which were unforeseeable?

2. Was the claim in respect of damage of the same *type* as could have been foreseen?

3. Complete the following: "The test of liability for fire is foreseeability of injury by fire. The test of liability for cancer is foreseeability of injury by—."

4. Does the "thin-skull" rule apply every time some injury to the plaintiff is foreseeable and a different injury occurs? Did *Doughty* v. *Turner Manufacturing Co.* [1964] 1 Q.B. 518 turn on whether there was a breach of duty or on whether the consequences of an admitted breach of duty were foreseeable?

5. If it be true, as Lord Denning suggests below p. 198, that policy is an element in questions of remoteness of damage, would it be right to make a distinction between claims for personal injury (this case) and property damage (*The Wagon Mound*)? If the claim is for

purely financial loss, is the rule of remoteness likely to be applied in a manner favourable to the plaintiff?

Note:

"You must take your victim as you find him" is a perplexing saying in some ways. The principal case seems to hold that a claim for unforeseeable consequences of careless conduct is not defeated if their unforeseeability results from an unsuspected pre-existing susceptibility of the victim, given that some injury was foreseeably caused. The susceptibility is an old cause, not a new one. Here, then, is a difference between culpability and compensation, since if one knows or should know of the susceptibility one may have to take extra steps to avoid that damage (*Paris* v. *Stepney B.C.* [1951] A.C. 367; *Haley* v. *London Electricity Board* (above p. 124).

But there may be a new cause which triggers the old susceptibility. In one case the plaintiff proved tragically allergic to an anti-tetanus serum which was foreseeably injected after he suffered an abrasion on a ladder which was oily owing to the defendant employer's negligence. In upholding judgment for the plaintiff, the Court of Appeal said: " . . . the principle that a defendant must take the plaintiff as he finds him involves that if a wrongdoer ought reasonably to foresee that as a result of his wrongful act the victim may require medical treatment he is, subject to the principle of novus actus interveniens, liable for the consequences of the treatment applied although he could not reasonably foresee those consequences or that they could be serious." (*Robinson* v. *Post Office* [1974] 2 All E.R. 737, 750). Can this be reconciled with the decision for the defendant in a South African case where the victim of a traffic accident who was taking Parstellin as prescribed died as a result of eating a cheese sandwich, it not being known at that time that the drug and cheese made a fatal mixture? (*Alston* v. *Marine & Trade Ins. Co.* 1964 (4) S.A. 112).

The saying also sometimes works to the benefit of the defendant. If the young man whom the motorist injures has a secret ailment which would in any case have curtailed his working life, the motorist pays less by way of damages. Again, if you carelessly dent a car you expect to have to pay for a respray; but if it already needed a respray by reason of a prior dent, you don't have to pay (*sed quaere*) (*Performance Cars* v. *Abraham* [1962] 1 Q.B. 33).

Where personal injury is suffered and there is no intervening event, the injury has to be really freaky to excuse a negligent person who caused it. One can contrast two master and servant cases. In *Bradford* v. *Robinson Rentals Ltd.* ([1967] 1 W.L.R. 337) in the depths of the worst winter for years the plaintiff radio engineer was required to drive in unheated vans from Honiton to Bedford and back, a trip of twenty-four hours in two days; he suffered frostbite, a rare complaint in England, and recovered damages. In *Tremain* v. *Pike* ([1969] 1 W.L.R. 1556) a farm worker contracted Weil's disease owing to contact with the urine of rats which his employer allowed to proliferate; the employer was held not liable.

Note that Lord Russell in *McLoughlin* (above p. 72) emphasised that the shock victim in that case was not abnormally susceptible. Can his implication be reconciled with true doctrine? In *Malcolm* v. *Broadhurst* [1970] 3 All E.R. 508, Geoffrey Lane J. had observed that there was no difference in principle between an egg-shell skull and an egg-shell personality. In that case the defendant was liable for causing physical injury to husband and wife. The wife recovered from the physical injuries by June 1967, but their psychical consequences lasted until February 1968 because she had a nervous condition before the accident. For six months thereafter she was still unfit for work because with her vulnerable personality she was unable to cope with her husband's changed behaviour due to the accident. She recovered damages for all three periods of unfitness for work.

Section 3.—The Risk Envisaged

GORRIS v. SCOTT

Court of Exchequer (1874) L.R. 9 Exch. 125; 43 L.J.Ex. 92; 30 L.T. 431; 22 W.R. 575

Action by owner against carrier in respect of loss of property.

KELLY C.B.: This is an action to recover damages for the loss of a number of sheep which the defendant, a shipowner, had contracted to carry, and which were washed overboard and lost by reason (as we must take it to be truly alleged) of the neglect to comply with a certain order made by the Privy Council, in pursuance of the Contagious Diseases (Animals) Act 1869. The Act was passed merely for sanitary purposes, in order to prevent animals in a state of infectious disease from communicating it to other animals with which they might come in contact. Under the authority of that Act, certain orders were made; amongst others, an order by which any ship bringing sheep or cattle from any foreign ports to ports in Great Britain is to have the place occupied by such animals divided into pens of certain dimensions, and the floor of such pens furnished with battens or foot-holds. The object of this order is to prevent animals from being overcrowded, and so brought into a condition in which the disease guarded against would be likely to be developed. This regulation has been neglected, and the question is, whether the loss, which we must assume to have been caused by that neglect, entitles the plaintiffs to maintain an action.

The argument of the defendant is, that the Act has imposed penalties to secure the observance of its provisions, and that, according to the general rule, the remedy prescribed by the statute must be pursued; that although, when penalties are imposed for the violation of a statutory duty, a person aggrieved by its violation may sometimes maintain an action for the damage so caused, that must be in cases where the object of the statute is to confer a benefit on individuals and to protect them against the evil consequences which the statute was designed to prevent, and which have in fact ensued; but that if the object is not to protect individuals against the consequences which have in fact ensued, it is otherwise; that if, therefore, by reason of the precautions in question not having been taken, the plaintiffs had sustained that damage against which it was intended to secure them, an action would lie, but that when the damage is of such a nature as was not contemplated at all by the statute, and as to which it was not intended to confer any benefit on the plaintiffs, they cannot maintain an action founded on the neglect. The principle may be well illustrated by the case put in argument of a breach by a railway company of its duty to erect a gate on a level crossing, and to keep the gate closed except when the crossing is being actually and properly used. The object of the precaution is to prevent injury from being sustained through animals or vehicles being upon the line at unseasonable times; and if by reason of such a breach of duty, either in not erecting the gate, or in not keeping it closed, a person attempts to cross with a carriage at an improper time, and injury ensues to a passenger, no doubt an action would lie against the railway company, because the intention of the legislature was that, by the erection of the gates and by their being kept closed individuals should be protected against accidents of this description. And if we could see that it was the object, or among the objects of this Act, that the owners of sheep and cattle coming from a foreign port should be protected by the means described against the danger of their property being washed overboard, or lost by the perils of the sea, the present action would be within the principle.

But, looking at the Act, it is perfectly clear that its provisions were all enacted with a totally different view; there was no purpose, direct or indirect, to protect against such damage; but, as is recited in the preamble, the Act is directed against the possibility of sheep or cattle being exposed to disease on their way to this country. The preamble recites that "it is expedient to confer on Her Majesty's most honourable Privy Council power to take such measures as may appear from time to time necessary to prevent the introduction into Great Britain of contagious or infectious diseases among cattle, sheep, or other animals, by prohibiting or regulating the importation of foreign animals," and also to provide against the "spreading" of such diseases in Great Britain. Then follow numerous sections directed entirely to this object. Then comes section 75, which enacts that "the Privy Council may from time to time make such orders as they think expedient for all or any of the following purposes." What, then, are these purposes? They are "for securing for animals brought by sea to ports in Great Britain a proper supply of food and water during the passage and on landing," "for protecting such animals from unnecessary suffering during the passage and on landing," and so forth; all the purposes enumerated being calculated and directed to the prevention of disease, and none of them having any relation whatever to the danger of loss by the perils of the sea. That being so, if by reason of the default in question the plaintiffs' sheep had been overcrowded, or had been caused unnecessary suffering, and so had arrived in this country in a state of disease, I do not say that they might not have maintained this action. But the damage complained of here is something totally apart from the object of the Act of Parliament, and it is in accordance with all the authorities to say that the action is not maintainable.

PIGOTT B.: . . . The object, then, of the regulations which have been broken was, not to prevent cattle from being washed overboard, but to protect them against contagious disease. . . . If, indeed, by reason of the neglect complained of, the cattle had contracted a contagious disease, the case would have been different. But as the case stands on this declaration, the answer to the action is this: Admit there has been a breach of duty; admit there has been a consequent injury; still the legislature was not legislating to protect against such an injury, but for an altogether different purpose; its object was not to regulate the duty of the carrier for all purposes, but only for one particular purpose.

POLLOCK B.: . . . Here no other negligence is alleged than the omission of that precaution; we must assume that the sheep were washed overboard merely in consequence of that omission and the question is whether that washing away gives a cause of action to the plaintiffs. Now, the Act of Parliament was passed *alio intuitu;* the recital in the preamble and the words of section 75 point out that what the Privy Council have power to do is to make such orders as may be expedient for the purpose of preventing the introduction and the spread of contagious and infectious diseases amongst animals. Suppose, then, that the precautions directed are useful and advantageous for preventing animals from being washed overboard, yet they were never intended for that purpose, and a loss of that kind caused by their neglect cannot give a cause of action.

Quote
"It is one thing to say that if the damage suffered is of a kind totally different from that which it is the object of the regulation to prevent, there is no civil liability. But it is quite a different thing to say that civil liability is excluded because the damage, though precisely of the kind which the regulation was designed to prevent, happened in a way not contemplated by the maker of the regulation. The difference is comparable with that which caused the decision in *Overseas Tankship (U.K.) Ltd.* v. *Morts Dock & Engineering Co. Ltd.* (*The Wagon Mound*) ([1961] A.C. 388; above, p. 180) to go one way and the decision in *Hughes* v. *Lord Advocate* ([1963] A.C. 837, next below) to go the other way." *Donaghey* v. *Boulton & Paul Ltd.* ([1968] A.C. 1, 26, *per* Lord Reid).

Note:
In *Millard.* v. *Serck Tubes Ltd.* ([1969] 1 W.L.R. 211), a case turning on the Factories Act 1961, s.14 (duty to fence dangerous machinery), Salmon L.J. said "the fact that the accident occurred in an entirely unforeseeable way is wholly irrelevant in this case." Whether any accident was foreseeable is, of course, material to determine whether the machinery was dangerous and therefore bound to be fenced. We therefore here have an example of the application of Lord Sumner's dictum that foreseeability "goes to culpability not to compensation," though that observation was said to be fundamentally false in *The Wagon Mound* (above, p. 180).

Question
If statutory duties are imposed because the legislature has certain consequences in mind and not others, the same must be true when the legislature grants statutory powers. If an action lies in respect of breach of statutory duty only for those items of harm the legislature had in mind, what is the position when one sues for breach of the common law duty to

exercise one's statutory powers, so far as their mode of execution is concerned, with reasonable care (*Dorset Yacht,* above p. 50)?

HUGHES v. LORD ADVOCATE

House of Lords [1963] A.C. 837; [1963] 2 W.L.R. 779; 107 S.J. 232; [1963] 1 All E.R. 705; 1963 S.C.(H.L.) 31; 1963 S.L.T. 150

Action by pedestrian against person working on highway in respect of personal injury.

The defenders, acting under statutory powers, opened a manhole in an Edinburgh street in order to do underground telephone repairs. Above the manhole their workmen placed a tent, and round the tent they placed warning paraffin lamps. At five o'clock one winter evening all the workmen left for tea. The pursuer, a boy of eight, and his uncle, a boy of ten, came along, took a lamp and entered the manhole. As they emerged, the lamp was knocked into the hole and a violent explosion took place, with flames shooting thirty feet into the air. The pursuer was knocked back into the hole where he sustained serious burns.

The Lord Ordinary, after hearing evidence, gave judgment for the defenders, and this decision was upheld by the First Division of the Court of Session (Lord Carmont dissenting), 1961 S.C. 310. The pursuer's appeal to the House of Lords was allowed.

LORD GUEST: . . . It might very well be that paraffin lamps by themselves, if left in the open, are not potentially dangerous even to children. But different considerations apply when they are found in connection with a shelter tent and a manhole, all of which are allurements to the inquisitive child. It is the combination of these factors which renders the situation one of potential danger.

In dismissing the appellant's claim the Lord Ordinary and the majority of the judges of the First Division reached the conclusion that the accident which happened was not reasonably foreseeable. In order to establish a coherent chain of causation it is not necessary that the precise details leading up to the accident should have been reasonably foreseeable: it is sufficient if the accident which occurred is of a type which should have been foreseeable by a reasonably careful person (*Miller* v. *South of Scotland Electricity Board* (1958 S.C.(H.L.) 20, 34), Lord Keith of Avonholm; *Harvey* v. *Singer Manufacturing Co. Ltd.* (1960 S.C. 155, 168, Lord Patrick) or as Lord Mackintosh expressed in the *Harvey* case, the precise concatenation of circumstances need not be envisaged. Concentration has been placed in the courts below on the explosion which, it was said, could not have been foreseen because it was caused in a unique fashion by the paraffin forming into vapour and being ignited by the naked flame of the wick. But this, in my opinion, is to concentrate on what is really a non-essential element in the dangerous situation created by the allurement. The test might better be put thus: Was the igniting of paraffin outside the lamp by the flame a foreseeable consequence of the breach of duty? In the circumstances, there was a combination of potentially dangerous circumstances against which the Post Office had to protect the appellant. If these formed an allurement to children it might have been foreseen that they would play with the lamp, that it might tip over, that it might be broken, and that when broken the paraffin might spill and be ignited by the flame. All these steps in the chain of causation seem to have been accepted by all the judges in the courts below as foreseeable. But because the explosion was the agent which caused the burning and was unforeseeable, therefore the accident, according to them, was not reasonably foreseeable. In my opinion, this reasoning is fallacious. An explosion is only one way in which burning can be caused. Burning can also be caused by the contact between liquid paraffin and a naked flame. In the one case paraffin vapour and in the other case liquid paraffin is ignited by fire. I cannot see that these are two different types of accident. They are both burning accidents and in both cases the injuries would be burning injuries. Upon this view the explosion was an immaterial event in the chain of causation. It was simply one way in which burning might be caused by the potentially dangerous paraffin lamp. I adopt, with respect, Lord Carmont's observation in the present case: "The defender cannot, I think, escape liability by contending that he did not foresee all the possibilities of the manner in which allurements—the manhole and the lantern—would act upon the childish mind."

The respondent relied upon the case of *Muir* v. *Glasgow Corporation* ([1943] A.C. 448; above, p. 116) and particularly on certain observations by Lords Thankerton and Macmillan. There are, in my view, essential differences between the two cases. The tea urn was, in that case, not, like the paraffin lamp in the present circumstance, a potentially dangerous object. Moreover, the precise way in which the tea came to be spilled was never established, and, as Lord Romer said (at 467): "It being thus unknown what was the particular risk that materialised, it is impossible to decide whether it was or was not one that should have been within the reasonable contemplation of Mrs. Alexander or of some other agent or employee of the appellants, and it is, accordingly, also impossible to fix the appellants with liability for the damage that the respondents sustained."

I have therefore reached the conclusion that the accident which occurred and which caused burning injuries to the appellant was one which ought reasonably to have been foreseen by the Post Office employees and that they were at fault in failing to provide a protection against the appellant entering the shelter and going down the manhole.

I would allow the appeal.

LORD PEARCE: My Lords, I agree with the opinion of my noble and learned friend, Lord Guest.

The dangerous allurement was left unguarded in a public highway in the heart of Edinburgh. It was for the defenders to show by evidence that, although this was a public street, the presence of children there was so little to be expected that a reasonable man might leave the allurement unguarded. But, in my opinion, their evidence fell short of that, and the Lord Ordinary rightly so decided.

The defenders are therefore liable for all the foreseeable consequences of their neglect. When an accident is of a different type and kind from anything that a defender could have foreseen he is not liable for it (see *The Wagon Mound*). But to demand too great precision in the test of foreseeability would be unfair to the pursuer since the facets of misadventure are innumerable. . . . In the case of an allurement to children it is particularly hard to foresee with precision the exact shape of the disaster that will arise. The allurement in this case was the combination of a red paraffin lamp, a ladder, a partially closed tent, and a cavernous hole within it, a setting well fitted to inspire some juvenile adventure that might end in calamity. The obvious risks were burning and conflagration and a fall. All these in fact occurred, but unexpectedly the mishandled lamp instead of causing an ordinary conflagration produced a violent explosion. Did the explosion create an accident and damage of a different type from the misadventure and damage that could be foreseen? In my judgment it did not. The accident was but a variant of the foreseeable. It was, to quote the words of Denning L.J. in *Roe* v. *Minister of Health* (above, p. 143), "within the risk created by the negligence." No unforeseeable, extraneous, initial occurrence fired the train. The children's entry into the tent with the ladder, the descent into the hole, the mishandling of the lamp, were all foreseeable. The greater part of the path to injury had thus been trodden, and the mishandled lamp was quite likely at that stage to spill and cause a conflagration. Instead, by some curious chance of combustion, it exploded and no conflagration occurred, it would seem, until after the explosion. There was thus an unexpected manifestation of the apprehended physical dangers. But it would be, I think, too narrow a view to hold that those who created the risk of fire are excused from the liability for the damage by fire because it came by way of explosive combustion. The resulting damage, though severe, was not greater than or different in kind from that which might have been produced had the lamp spilled and produced a more normal conflagration in the hole.

I would therefore allow the appeal.

LORD REID: . . . So we have (first) a duty owed by the workmen, (secondly) the fact that if they had done as they ought to have done there would have been no accident, and (thirdly) the fact that the injuries suffered by the appellant, though perhaps different in degree, did not differ in kind from injuries which might have resulted from an accident of a foreseeable nature. The ground on which this case has been decided against the appellant is that the accident was of an unforeseeable type. Of course, the pursuer has to prove that the defender's fault caused the accident, and there could be a case where the intrusion of a new and unexpected factor could be regarded as the cause of the accident rather than the fault of the defender. But that is not this case. The cause of this accident was a known source of danger, the lamp, but it behaved in an unpredictable way. . . .

Note:

This decision has been taken as an authority in favour of the risk principle in so far as it "typifies" the means whereby the injury accrues. Lord Jenkins said: "To my mind, the distinction drawn between burning and explosion is too fine to warrant acceptance." Yet the distinction between fire and explosion as separate risks is a commonplace of insurance law. For example, the 1943 Standard Fire Policy of New York specifically excludes the liability of the insurer for damage caused by explosion. And the following is an extract from a Consequential Loss policy in everyday use in Great Britain: "The Company agrees . . . that if . . . any building . . . be destroyed or damaged by 1. Fire (whether resulting from explosion or otherwise); 2. Lightning; 3. Explosion . . . the Company will pay to the Insured . . . the amount of loss. . . . As will be seen from that extract, however, a fire caused by explosion falls within the *fire* risk. What the Court of Session did was to distinguish between risks created by a wrongdoer more subtly than do those whose business it is to distinguish the risks they choose to accept. It is satisfactory that the House of Lords has corrected them. But it remains a question whether a person who has admittedly and wrongfully created a danger should have his liability for the consequent damage determined as if he were a person who had been paid to accept that risk and that risk alone.

Section 4.—Intervening Act

THE OROPESA

Court of Appeal [1943] P. 32; 112 L.J.P. 91; 168 L.T. 364; 74 Lloyd's Rep. 86; 59 T.L.R. 103; [1943] 1 All E.R. 211

Action by dependants of seaman against owners of colliding vessel.

The parents of the sixth engineer on board the steamship *Manchester Regiment* claimed damages as administrators of their son's estate, and on their own behalf as dependants, from the Pacific Steam Navigation Company, owner of the steamship *Oropesa*. The two vessels collided off Nova Scotia in December 1939, the *Manchester Regiment* being four-fifths to blame. Both ships were badly damaged. The captain of the *Manchester Regiment* thought his ship could be saved. He sent fifty of his crew of seventy-four by lifeboat to the *Oropesa* in safety. Then, about eighty minutes after the collision, he decided to go to speak to the captain of the *Oropesa,* already over a mile away, about salving the *Manchester Regiment.* He embarked in a lifeboat with the rest of his crew, including the deceased, but the boat capsized in the heavy seas after half an hour, and the deceased was among the nine men who were drowned. The *Oropesa* returned to Nova Scotia with the survivors and the *Manchester Regiment* sank.

Langton J. gave judgment for the plaintiffs [1942] P. 140, and the Court of Appeal dismissed the defendants' appeal.

LORD WRIGHT: . . . On the main question, the plaintiffs sue on the basis that the owners of the *Oropesa* owed a duty, not only to the owners of the *Manchester Regiment,* but also to her officers and crew, to navigate with care and skill so as not to injure them. Negligent navigation would obviously be a breach of that duty, and, therefore, it is said there was here a breach of duty towards the deceased. The defendants deny liability on the ground that there was no legal connection between the breach of duty and the death of the deceased. Certain well-known formulae are invoked, such as that the chain of causation was broken and that there was a *novus actus interveniens.* These phrases, sanctified as they are by standing authority, only mean that there was not such a direct relationship between the act of negligence and the injury that the one can be treated as flowing directly from the other. Cases have been cited which show great difference of opinion on the true answer in the various circumstances to the question whether the damage was direct or too remote. I find it very difficult to formulate any precise and all-embracing rule. I do not think that the authorities which have been cited succeed in settling that difficulty. It may be said that in dealing with the law of negligence it is possible to state general propositions, but when you come to apply those principles to determine whether there has been actionable negligence in any particular case, you must deal with the case on its facts.

What were the facts here? The master of the *Manchester Regiment* was faced with a very difficult proposition. His ship was helpless, without any means of propulsion or of working any of her important auxiliary apparatus, a dead lump in the water, and he had only the saving thought that she might go on floating so long as her bulkheads did not give way. He had great faith in his ship, but he realised that there was a heavy sea, with a heavy gale blowing and that he was in a very perilous plight. As Sir Robert Aske pointed out in his argument, the captain of a ship is guilty of a misdemeanour under section 220 of the Merchant Shipping Act 1894 if he "refuses or omits to do any lawful act proper and requisite to be done by him for preserving his ship from immediate loss, destruction or serious danger, or for preserving any person belonging to or on board ship from immediate danger to life or limb." In those circumstances the master decided to go to the *Oropesa* where, no doubt, he thought he would find valuable help and advice. Nobody suggests that he was acting unreasonably or improperly in doing so, or, indeed, that he was doing anything but his duty. Nor can anyone say that the deceased acted unreasonably in getting into the boat. If he had not obeyed the lawful orders of his captain, he would have committed a criminal offence under section 225(1)(*b*) of the Merchant Shipping Act 1894. If, therefore, the test is whether what was done was reasonable, there can be no question that the actions of both the master and the deceased were reasonable. Whether the master took exactly the right course is another matter. He may have been guilty of an error of judgment, but, as I read the authorities, that would not affect the question whether the action he took and its consequences flowed directly from the negligence of the *Oropesa.* I am not sure that Mr. Sellers does not agree with that view, anyhow to some extent, but he also argued that the deceased was merely a spectator of the collision. He received no personal injury nor shock, and there was no need for special steps to be taken on his behalf in the emergency. That being so, in obeying the master's orders and getting into the boat, he was merely doing a voluntary act which was in no legal sense associated or connected with the negligence of the *Oropesa.* As for the master, Mr. Sellers argued that what he did had no legal connection with the casualty. In my view, that is not a correct reading of the position. Having regard to the situation of the *Manchester Regiment* and those on board her, I think that the hand of the casualty lay heavily on her and that the conduct both of the master and of the deceased was directly caused by and flowed from it. There was an unbroken sequence of cause and effect between the negligence which caused the *Oropesa* to collide with the *Manchester Regiment,* and their action, which was dictated by the exigencies of the position. It cannot be severed from the circumstances affecting both ships. To that must be joined the duty which they were under in their positions as captain and sixth engineer.

There are some propositions which are beyond question in connection with this class of case. One is that human action does not *per se* sever the connected sequence of acts. The mere fact that human action intervenes does not prevent the sufferer from saying that injury which is due to that human action as one of the elements in the sequence is recoverable from the original wrongdoer. *The City of Lincoln* ((1889) 15 P.D. 15) is a useful case. It is short and the judges of the Court of Appeal were all agreed so we do not get the complications which are present in some of the cases in the House of Lords on this point. In *The City of Lincoln* the question was whether the injury was directly caused by the casualty. On the point of what was meant by "the ordinary course of things," Lindley L.J. said: "Sir Walter Phillimore has asked us to exclude from it all human conduct. I can do nothing of the kind. I take it that reasonable human conduct"—I stress that expression—"is part of the ordinary course of things. So far as I can see my way to any definite proposition I should say that the ordinary course of things does not exclude all human conduct, but includes at least the reasonable conduct of those who have sustained the damage, and who are seeking to save further loss." Mr. Sellers said that those words must not be pressed too hard, but you must look at the facts. The facts were that there had been a collision between a steamer and a barque, and the steamer was held alone to blame. "The steering compass, charts, log and log glass of the barque were lost through the collision," the headnote states. "The captain of the barque made for a port of safety, navigating his ship by a compass which he found on board. The barque, while on her way, without any negligence on the part of the captain or crew, and owing to the loss of the requisites for navigation above mentioned, grounded, and was necessarily abandoned." It was held by the Court of Appeal that "the grounding of the barque was a natural and reasonable consequence of the collision, and that the owners of the steamer were liable for the damages caused thereby." In principle, that case is not different from the present. The captain, being placed in a difficulty, went on navigating the ship. He thought that that was the reasonable course to adopt, and it was held to be reasonable in the emergency. The plaintiffs thus recovered, although there was a long interval, both in time and distance, between the collision and the physical grounding of the vessel. If the vessel had remained where she was, she might have been picked up or many other things might have happened. She might still have become a total wreck, but not a total wreck in the way in which the event happened in fact, but there it was held, notwithstanding the human action, that the grounding was a natural and reasonable consequence of the collision. In *Summers* v. *Salford Corporation* ([1942] W.N. 224), a woman cleaning a window was injured because the sash cord broke. That is far removed from the facts with which we have to deal here, but it involves the same principle. Assuming, as was held in that case, that there was a breach of duty to her, the mere fact that no harm would have happened to her if she had not been cleaning the window was immaterial because she was doing something which was reasonable and in the ordinary course of events. If the master and the deceased in the present case had done something which was outside the exigencies of the emergency, whether from miscalculation or from error, the plaintiffs would be debarred from saying that a new cause had not intervened. The question is not whether there was new negligence, but whether there was a new cause. I think that is what Lord Sumner emphasised in *The Paludina* ([1927] A.C. 16). To break the chain of causation it must be shown that there is something which I will call ultroneous, something unwarrantable, a new cause which disturbs the sequence of events, something which can be described as either unreasonable or extraneous or extrinsic. I doubt whether the law can be stated more precisely than that. Lord Haldane gave a fuller description in *Canadian Pacific Ry.* v. *Kelvin Shipping Co. Ltd.* ((1927) 138 L.T. 369, 370), where the whole of the ultimate damage was due to a handling of the vessel after the collision. Lord Haldane said: "I therefore turn at once to the crucial question in the case, was there fault in those responsible for the ship in reference to the use of her engines when she was on the north bank? Now this is a question of evidence, and in weighing the evidence in order to draw the proper inferences, there are certain principles which have to be kept steadily in view. When a collision takes place by the fault of the defending ship in an action for damages, the damage is recoverable if it is the natural and reasonable result of the negligent act, and it will assume this character if it can be shown to be such a consequence as in the ordinary course of things would flow from the situation which the offending ship had created. Further, what those in charge of the injured ship do to save it may be mistaken, but if they do whatever they do reasonably, although unsuccessfully, their mistaken judgment may be a natural consequence for which the offending ship is responsible, just as much as is any physical occurrence. Reasonable human conduct is part of the ordinary course of things which extends to the reasonable conduct of those who have sustained the damage and who are seeking to save further loss." He takes that final proposition from *The City of Lincoln.* I think that is an important statement of principle—"if they do whatever they do reasonably, although unsuccessfully, their mistaken judgment may be a natural consequence for which the offending ship is responsible." Here it may be said that, even if the master of the *Manchester Regiment* was not doing quite the right thing, his mistake might be regarded as the natural consequence of the emergency in which he was placed by the negligence of the *Oropesa.* There was a difference of opinion in *Canadian Pacific Ry.* v. *Kelvin Shipping Co. Ltd.* on the final issue of fact. There was again a difference of opinion in *The Paludina,* but I should like to quote a few words of Lord Sumner: "Cause and consequence in such a matter do not depend on the question whether the first action, which intervenes, is excusable or not, but on the question whether it is new and independent or not." There the master of the *Singleton Abbey* had not stopped his engines at a particular moment, and that resulted in trouble with the *Paludina* and the *Sara.* It was held that there had been a miscalculation which broke the chain of causation. That, again, was a decision on the facts. It does not take the matter any further, except, possibly, by way of comparison. The statement of the pinciples applicable by the majority of their Lordships does not in any way contradict what I have said. A mere voluntary act would clearly cause a breaking in the sequence of cause and effect as, for instance, in *The Amerika* ([1917] A.C. 38), one of the claims made by the Admiralty by way of damages for loss due to the collision was that they had paid bounties to relatives of members of the ship's crew who had lost their lives. It was held that those payments were purely voluntary. That is an extreme, but obvious, illustration of a loss resulting from a collision which did not impose any legal liability. It was a loss incurred by purely ultroneous conduct.

The real difficulty in the present case is the application of the principle, which is a question of fact. I agree entirely with Langton J. in the way in which he has dealt with the question. I am not prepared to say in all the circumstances that the fact that the deceased's death was due to his leaving the ship in the lifeboat and to the unexpected capsizing of that boat prevented his death being a direct consequence of the casualty. It was a risk, no doubt, but a boat would not generally capsize in those circumstances. In my opinion, the appeal should be dismissed.

SCOTT L.J.: I agree. We have been advised, as Langton J. was advised, that the position throughout in these happenings was one of critical danger to all those on board the *Manchester Regiment.* I am satisfied that the action taken by the master to save the lives of those for whom he was responsible was reasonable, and, therefore, that there was no break in the chain of causation. I agree entirely with the judgment which has just been delivered.

Questions

1. Suppose that the captain of the *Manchester Regiment* had been the only person drowned. Would his dependants have recovered?

2. Suppose that, owing to the unreasonable behaviour of the captain, the life-boats of the *Manchester Regiment* were incapable of being used, would the defendants have been liable to the dependants of persons drowned in consequence?

3. Suppose that, though the life-boats could be used, the captain of the *Manchester Regiment* unreasonably declined to allow the crew to leave the sinking ship; would the dependants of the crew recover from the defendants?

Note:

When the question is asked whether the captain behaved "reasonably" or not, one is not asking whether he behaved without negligence, but whether his decision to act as he did, that decision having turned out to be wrong, was voluntary or not. If the decision was made in the stress of danger, it will not be really voluntary ("the hand of casualty lay heavily on her"), and it may be called a reasonable response to the emergency, notwithstanding that it turned out to be wrong. Behaviour which is unreasonable only in the sense of being careless is much less potent causally than a voluntary act even if that act can be called "reasonable." Though "sciens" is not "volens," voluntariness is affected by knowledge, perhaps dependent on it. Thus a failure to remedy a known defect or danger is a better insulator than a failure to discover it. For example, in *Taylor* v. *Rover Co.* [1966] 1 W.L.R. 1491, an employee was injured by a chisel which had carelessly been overhardened by the supplier's sub-contractor. The employer, however, had prior knowledge that the chisel was dangerous and had failed to remove it from circulation. Baker J. held that this insulated the supplier from possible liability. In *Lambert* v. *Lewis* [1982] A.C. 225, on the other hand, where the plaintiffs were injured on the highway when the first defendant's trailer came loose from his Land-Rover owing to a defect in the coupling badly designed by the manufacturer, the fourth defendant, the manufacturer, was held liable to the victims although the first defendant knew that the coupling was defective and dangerous.

Question

Is there an explanation in terms of causation of s.1(4) of the Congenital Disabilities (Civil Liability) Act 1976 (above p. 80)?

LAMB v. CAMDEN LONDON BOROUGH COUNCIL

Court of Appeal [1981] Q.B. 625; [1981] 2 W.L.R. 1038; [1981] 2 All E.R. 408

Action by houseowner against careless local authority for damage done by vandals.

In 1973 the defendant's contractors broke a water-main outside the plaintiff's house near Hampstead Heath. The water washed away the foundations and the plaintiff's tenant moved out. In the summer of 1974 the plaintiff returned from the United States, moved her furniture out and arranged for some building works to be started. In October squatters moved in. The plaintiff had them evicted when she returned again at Christmas, and had some boarding put up. In the summer of 1975 more squatters moved in and were not expelled until May 1977, by which time they had done damage amounting to £30,000. This was the item in issue.

The plaintiff's claim for it was rejected by the official referee, and her appeal to the Court of Appeal was dismissed.

WATKINS L.J.: . . . This appeal involves but a single issue. Was the damage done to Mrs. Lamb's house by squatters too remote to be a consequence of the council's initial negligent and damaging act which partly destroyed support for the house and for which they have to compensate her?

Counsel for the plaintiffs contends that, since the official referee intimated in his judgment that if thereby he was applying the only relevant and correct test he would be disposed to hold that an invasion of the undermined house by squatters was a risk reasonably foreseeable by the defendants, the case should go back to him so that he can positively make that finding and give judgment for Mrs. Lamb for the sum claimed in respect of the squatters' damage. For, he says, reasonable foreseeability simpliciter of the fresh kind of damage done is, since *The Wagon Mound (No.* 2) [1967] 1 A.C. 617, the sole test which determines whether fresh damage caused by an act which is independent of and committed later than the initial tortious act is too remote: whether, in other words, it is truly a novus actus interveniens for the damage caused by which a defendant is not liable.

He submits that Lord Reid was out of step with the *Wagon Mound* test which should always be followed nowadays when in *Home Office* v. *Dorset Yacht Co. Ltd.* ([1970] A.C. 1004, 1030) he said:

> " . . . where human action forms one of the links between the original wrongdoing of the defendant and the loss suffered by the plaintiff, that action must at least have been something very likely to happen if it is not to be regarded as novus actus interveniens breaking the chain of causation. I do not think that a mere foreseeable possibility is or should be sufficient, for then the intervening human action can more properly be regarded as a new cause than as a consequence of the original wrongdoing. But if the intervening action was likely to happen I do not think that it can matter whether that action was innocent or tortious or criminal. Unfortunately, tortious or criminal action by a third party is often the "very kind of thing" which is likely to happen as a result of the wrongful or careless act of the defendant."

So by adopting, as he did, the opinion of Lord Reid the official referee was also out of step with *The Wagon Mound (No.* 2) and applied the wrong test to the issue of remoteness. If he had allowed himself to be governed by *The Wagon Mound (No.* 2) he would inevitably have found for Mrs. Lamb for the considerable damage deliberately and criminally caused by the squatters.

I feel bound to say with respect that what Lord Reid said in the *Dorset Yacht* case does nothing to simplify the task of deciding for or against remoteness, especially where the fresh damage complained of has been caused by the intervening act of a third party. It may be that in respect of such an act he is to be understood as saying, without using his remarkable and usual clarity of expression, that damage is inevitably too remote unless it can reasonably be foreseen as likely to occur. If that be so, it could be said that he was not intending to depart from the *Wagon Mound* test save in cases involving intervening human action to which he would apply a rather stricter than usual test by placing acts which are *not likely to occur* within the realm of remoteness. . . .

It seems to me that if the sole and exclusive test of remoteness is whether the fresh damage has arisen from an event or act which is reasonably foreseeable, or reasonably foreseeable as a possibility, or likely or quite likely to occur, absurd, even bizarre, results might ensue in actions for damages for negligence. Why, if this test were to be rigidly applied to the facts in the *Dorset Yacht* case, one can envisage the Home Office being found liable for the damage caused by an escaped borstal boy committing a burglary in John O'Groats. This would plainly be a ludicrous conclusion.

I do not think that words such as, among others, "possibility," "likely" or "quite likely" assist in the application of the test of reasonable foreseeability. If the crisply stated test which emanates from *The Wagon Mound (No.* 2) is to be festooned with additional words supposedly there for the purpose of amplification or qualification, an understandable application of it will become impossible.

In my view the *Wagon Mound* test should always be applied without any of the gloss which is from time to time being applied to it.

But when so applied it cannot in all circumstances in which it arises conclude consideration of the question of remoteness, although in the vast majority of cases it will be adequate for this purpose. In other cases, the present one being an example of these in my opinion, further consideration is necessary, always providing, of course, a plaintiff survives the test of reasonable foreseeability.

This is because the very features of an event or act for which damages are claimed themselves suggest that the event or act is not on any practical view of it remotely in any way connected with the original act of negligence. These features will include such matters as the nature of the event or act, the time it occurred, the place where it occurred, the identity of the perpetrator and his intentions, and responsibility, if any, for taking measures to avoid the occurrence and matters of public policy.

A robust and sensible approach to this very important area of the study of remoteness will more often than not produce, I think, an instinctive feeling that the event or act being weighed in the balance is too remote to sound in damages for the plaintiff. I do not pretend that in all cases the answer will come easily to the inquirer. But that the question must be asked and answered in all these cases I have no doubt.

To return to the present case, I have the instinctive feeling that the squatters' damage is too remote. I could not possibly come to any other conclusion, although on the primary facts I, too, would regard that damage or something like it as reasonably foreseeable in these times.

We are here dealing with unreasonable conduct of an outrageous kind. It is notorious that squatters will take the opportunity of entering and occupying any house, whether it be damaged or not, which is found to be unoccupied for more than a very temporary duration. In my opinion this kind of antisocial and criminal behaviour provides a glaring example of an act which inevitably, or almost so, is too remote to cause a defendant to pay damages for the consequences of it.

Accordingly, I would hold that the damage caused by the squatters in the present case is too remote to be recovered from these defendants.

LORD DENNING M.R. [rejected the "very likely to happen" test of Lord Reid, on the ground that it led to too wide a range of liability in some cases and that it was inconsistent with *Stansbie* v. *Troman* ([1948] 2 K.B. 48), and also rejected the "reasonably foreseeable" test for the same reason. The test should be one of policy]. . . .

Looking at the question as one of policy, I ask myself: whose job was it to do something to keep out the squatters? And, if they got in, to evict them? To my mind the answer is clear. It was the job of the owner of the house, Mrs. Lamb, through her agents. That is how everyone in the case regarded it. It has never been suggested in the pleadings or elsewhere that it was the job of the council. No one ever wrote to the council asking them to do it. The council were not in occupation of the house. They had no right to enter it. All they had done was to break the water main outside and cause the subsidence. After they had left the site, it was Mrs. Lamb *herself* who paved the way for the squatters by moving out all her furniture and leaving the house unoccupied and unfurnished. There was then, if not before, on the judge's findings, a reasonably foreseeable risk that squatters might enter. She ought to have taken steps to guard against it. She says that she locked the doors and pulled the shutters. That turned out to be insufficient, but it was her responsibility to do more. At any rate, when the squatters did get in on the first occasion in 1974, it was then her agents who acted on her behalf. They got the squatters out. Then, at any rate, Mrs. Lamb or her agents ought to have done something effective. But they only put up a few boards at a cost of £10. Then there was the second invasion in 1975. Then her agents did recognise her responsibility. They did what they could to get the squatters out. They eventually succeeded. But no one ever suggested throughout that it was the responsibility of the council. . . .

On broader grounds of policy, I would add this: the criminal acts here, malicious damage and theft, are usually covered by insurance. By this means the risk of loss is spread throughout the community. It does not fall too heavily on one pair of shoulders alone. The insurers take the premium to cover just this sort of risk and should not be allowed, by subrogation, to pass it on to others. Just as in *Stansbie* v. *Troman* [1948] 2 K.B. 48, the householder was no doubt insured against theft of the diamond bracelet. She should have recovered its value from the insurers and not from the decorator whose only fault was that he forgot to put the latch down. It might be decided differently today. It is commonplace nowadays for the courts, when considering policy, to take insurance into account. It played a prominent part in *Photo Production Ltd.* v. *Securicor Transport Ltd.* ([1980] A.C. 827). The House of Lords clearly thought that the risk of fire should be borne by the fire insurers, who had received the full premium for fire risk, and not by Securicor's insurers, who had only received a tiny premium. That, too, was a policy decision. It was a direct consequence of the Unfair Contract Terms Act 1977. Before that Act, the doctrine of fundamental breach was an essential part of our legal system: so as to protect the small consumer from unjust exemption clauses.

So here, it seems to me, that, if Mrs. Lamb was insured against damage to the house and theft, the insurers should pay the loss. If she was not insured, that is her misfortune.

Taking all these policy matters into account, I think the council are not liable for the acts of these squatters.

I would dismiss this appeal.

OLIVER L.J.: [considered the observation of Lord Reid cited by Watkins L.J. above, and continued]. As it seems to me, all that Lord Reid was saying was this, that, where as a matter of fact the consequence which the court is considering is one which results from, or would not have occurred but for, the intervention of some independent human agency over which the tortfeasor has no control it has to approach the problem of what could be reasonably foreseen by the tortfeasor, and thus of the damage for which he is responsible, with particular care. The immediate cause is known: it is the independent human agency; and one has therefore to ask: on what basis can the act of that person be attributed back to the tortfeasor? It may be because the tortfeasor is responsible for his actions or because the third party act which has precipitated the damage is the very thing that the tortfeasor is employed to prevent. But what is the position in the absence of some such consideration? Few things are less certainly predictable than human behaviour, and if one is asked whether in any given situation a human being may behave idiotically, irrationally or even criminally the answer must always be that that is a possibility, for every society has its proportion of idiots and criminals. It cannot be said that you cannot foresee the possibility that people will do stupid or criminal acts, because people are constantly doing stupid or criminal acts. But the question is not what is foreseeable merely as a possibility but what would the reasonable man actually foresee if he thought about it, and all that Lord Reid seems to me to be saying is that the hypothetical reasonable man in the position of the tortfeasor cannot be said to foresee the behaviour of another person unless that behaviour is such as would, viewed objectively, be very likely to occur. Thus, for instance, if by my negligent driving I damage another motorist's car, I suppose that theoretically I *could* foresee that, whilst he leaves it by the roadside to go and telephone his garage, some ill-intentioned passer-by may jack it up and remove the wheels. But I cannot think that it could be said that, merely because I have created the circumstances in which such a theft might become possible, I ought reasonably to foresee that it would happen. . . .

The critical finding here is, to my mind, that the incursion of squatters was in fact unlikely.

Given this finding, it seems to me that, accepting Lord Reid's test as correct (which counsel for the plaintiff challenges), it must be fatal to the plaintiff's contentions on this appeal, because it constitutes in effect a finding that the damage claimed is not such as could be reasonably foreseen. And that, indeed, seems to me to accord with the common sense of the matter. . . .

. . . whether or not it is right to regard questions of remoteness according to some flexible test of the policy of the law from time to time (on which I prefer at the moment to express no view) I concur with Lord Denning M.R. in regarding the straight test of foreseeability, at least in cases where the acts of independent third parties are concerned, as one which can, unless subjected to some further limitation, produce results which extend the ambit of liability beyond all reason. Speaking for myself, I would respectfully regard Lord Reid's test as a workable and sensible one, subject only to this, that I think that he may perhaps have understated the *degree* of likelihood required before the law can or should attribute the free act of a responsible third person to the tortfeasor. Such attribution cannot, as I think, rationally be made simply on the basis of some geographical or temporal proximity, and even "likelihood" is a somewhat uncertain touchstone. It may be that some more stringent standard is required. There may, for instance, be circumstances in which the court would require a degree of likelihood amounting almost to inevitability before it fixes a defendant with responsibility for the act of a third party over whom he has and can have no control. On the official referee's finding, however, that does not arise here, and the problem can be left for a case in which it directly arises.

Note:

1. There is an element of despair in these opinions. Watkins L.J. reverts to intuition like some medieval German lay-judge; Lord Denning appeals to a perfectly indeterminate policy; and Oliver L.J. is reduced to semantics. There have been difficult problems in this area before, though they are certainly accentuated as liability in tort is imposed more widely, but the despair comes, it is fair to say, from the delusive terms of *The Wagon Mound*. It is a terrible thing to say, but "Foreseeability rules, O.K.?" will simply not answer the complexities of life and litigation. In the light of the desert into which foreseeability has brought us when remoteness of consequences is in issue, one may have some reservations about the trend to use it as the sole determinant of duty in cases of economic and psychical harm.

2. Another recent case in which the opinion seems rather incoherent, though the result is not wrong, is *Knightley* v. *Johns* [1982] 1 All E.R. 851 (C.A.). The plaintiff police constable was knocked off his motor-bike by a car being driven quite carefully through a one-way tunnel in Birmingham. The plaintiff was going the wrong way down the double carriageway and another policeman was going the wrong way down the other side. The reason for this was that the first defendant had carelessly caused an obstruction farther down the tunnel. Only some time after the police had come to the scene did the inspector realise that, contrary to standing instructions, he had failed to close the entrance to the tunnel; it was he who told the plaintiff to drive back up it in order to close it to traffic. The deputy judge held that only the original motorist was to blame, but the Court of Appeal held that he was not responsible and that the police inspector was.

Stephenson L.J. said: "The ordinary course of things took an extraordinary course. The length and irregularities of the line leading from the first accident to the second have no parallel in the reported rescue cases, in all of which the plaintiff succeeded in establishing the original wrongdoer's liability. It was natural, it was probable, it was foreseeable, it was indeed certain, that the police would come to the overturned car and control the tunnel traffic. It was also natural and probable and foreseeable that some steps would be taken in controlling the traffic and clearing the tunnel and some things be done that might be more courageous than sensible. The reasonable hypothetical observer would anticipate some human errors, some forms of what might be called folly, perhaps even from trained police officers, and some unusual and unexpected accidents in the course of their rescue duties. But would he anticipate such a result as this from so many errors as these, so many departures from the common sense procedure prescribed by the standing orders for just such an emergency as this?"

3. In motorway pile-ups, which are normally caused by successive acts of carelessness, the person responsible for the original danger tends to be liable for all the damage. In *Rouse* v.

Squires ([1973] Q.B. 889) the driver of an articulated lorry, A, carelessly let it skid: it jack-knifed and blocked the slow and centre lanes. B, in a car, collided with it. C, in a lorry, drove past, parked and returned to help. D pulled his lorry up 15 feet short and illuminated the scene with his headlights. Five or ten minutes after the original accident E, driving too fast, braked too late and skidded into D's lorry which was pushed forward on to C, who was killed. E, held liable to C's widow, was able to claim 25 per cent. contribution from A.

4. In the cases excerpted so far in this section the harm complained of would not have occurred at all but for the act of the third party. In other cases harm for which the defendant is clearly responsible is prolonged or aggravated by an incompetent doctor, an indolent garage, a neurotic mother or a dilatory solicitor. Are there any grounds for distinguishing cases of the two types?

5. In *Salsbury* v. *Woodland* (below, p. 256) the Court of Appeal expressed relief that the judge's finding on causation was not questioned. Do you think that the facts of that case raised any difficult question of causation?

McKEW v. HOLLAND & HANNEN & CUBITTS (SCOTLAND) LTD.

House of Lords [1969] 3 All E.R. 1621; 8 K.I.R. 921; 1970 S.C.(H.L.) 20

Action by employee against employer for personal injuries:

The pursuer, who had suffered trivial injuries at work by reason of the defender's fault, which had made him stiff and weakened his left leg, went some days later to inspect a tenement flat, in the company of some members of his family. The stair was steep, with walls on either side, but no hand-rail. As the pursuer left the apartment with his daughter, he raised his right foot to go down the stairs. His left leg "went" and he was about to fall. Rather than fall, he jumped, and landed heavily on his right foot, breaking the right ankle and a bone in his left leg.

The Court of Session disallowed the claim for the consequences of the second accident, and the House of Lords dismissed the pursuer's appeal.

LORD REID: My Lords, the appellant sustained in the course of his employment trivial injuries which were admittedly caused by the fault of the respondents. His back and hips were badly strained, he could not bend, and on several occasions his left leg suddenly "went away from" him. I take this to mean that for a short time he lost control of his leg and it became numb. He would have recovered from his injuries in a week or two but for a second accident in which he suffered a severe fracture of his ankle. The question in this case is whether the respondents are liable for the damge caused by this second accident. If they are so liable then damages have been agreed at £4,915; if they are not so liable then damages are agreed at £200, the sum awarded in the Court of Session. . . .

The appellant's case is that this second accident was caused by the weakness of his left leg which in turn had been caused by the first accident. The main argument for the respondents is that the second accident was not the direct or natural and probable or foreseeable result of their fault in causing the first accident.

In my view the law is clear. If a man is injured in such a way that his leg may give way at any moment he must act reasonably and carefully. It is quite possible that in spite of all reasonable care his leg may give way in circumstances such that as a result he sustains further injury. Then that second injury was caused by his disability which in turn was caused by the defender's fault. But if the injured man acts unreasonably he cannot hold the defender liable for injury caused by his own unreasonable conduct. His unreasonable conduct is novus actus interveniens. The chain of causation has been broken and what follows must be regarded as caused by his own conduct and not by the defender's fault or the disability caused by it. Or one may say that unreasonable conduct of the pursuer and what follows from it is not the natural and probable result of the original fault of the defender or of the ensuing disability. I do not think that foreseeability comes into this. A defender is not liable for a consequence of a kind which is not foreseeable. But it does not follow that he is liable for every consequence which a reasonable man could foresee. What can be foreseen depends almost entirely on the facts of the case, and it is often easy to foresee unreasonable conduct or some other novus actus interveniens as being quite likely. But that does not mean that the defender must pay for damage caused by the novus actus. It only leads to trouble that if one tries to graft on to the concept of foreseeability some rule of law to the effect that a wrongdoer is not bound to foresee something which in fact he could readily foresee as quite likely to happen. For it is not at all unlikely or unforeseeable that an active man who has suffered such a disability will take some quite unreasonable risk. But if he does he cannot hold the defender liable for the consequences.

So in my view the question here is whether the second accident was caused by the appellant doing something unreasonable. It was argued that the wrongdoer must take his victim as he finds him and that that applies not only to a thin skull but also to his intelligence. But I shall not deal with that argument because there is nothing in the evidence to suggest that the appellant is abnormally stupid. This case can be dealt with equally well by asking whether the appellant did something which a moment's reflection would have shown him was an unreasonable thing to do.

He knew that his left leg was liable to give way suddenly and without warning. He knew that this stair was steep and that there was no hand-rail. He must have realised, if he had given the matter a moment's thought, that he could only safely descend the stair if he either went extremely slowly and carefully so that he could sit down if his leg gave way, or waited for the assistance of his wife and brother-in-law. But he chose to descend in such a way that when his leg gave way he could not stop himself. . . .

But I think it right to say a word about the argument that the fact that the appellant made to jump when he felt himself falling is conclusive against him. When his leg gave way the appellant was in a very difficult situation. He had to decide what to do in a fraction of a second. He may have come to a wrong decision; he probably did. But if the chain of causation had not been broken before this by his putting himself in a position where he might be confronted with an emergency, I do not think that he would put himself out of court by acting wrongly in the emergency unless his action was so utterly unreasonable that even on the spur of the moment no ordinary man would have been so foolish as to do what he did. In an emergency it is natural to try to do something to save oneself and I do not think that his trying to jump in this emergency was so wrong that it could be said to be no more than an error of judgment. But for the reasons already given I would dismiss this appeal.

GINTY v. BELMONT BUILDING SUPPLIES LTD.

Queen's Bench [1959] 1 All E.R. 414

Action by employee against employer in respect of personal injury.

The plaintiff was employed by the first defendant. He was told to replace the asbestos roofing at the factory of the second defendant and told that the existing roofing was unsafe. Crawling boards were provided by the second defendant but the plaintiff did not use them and consequently fell through the roof and was seriously injured. The plaintiff's failure to use the boards constituted a breach of statutory regulations on the part both of himself and of his employers.

Pearson J. gave judgment for the defendants.

Pearson J.: . . . This accident was caused manifestly by the plaintiff working on an asbestos roof, which was a fragile roof, without using boards. The special feature of this case is that that wrongful act of his constitutes a breach by him of his instructions and of the regulations as they apply to him; but it also constitutes, technically at any rate, a breach by his employer under his obligation under reg. 31(3)(*a*) [Building (Safety, Health and Welfare) Regulations 1948] to use the boards. The actual wrongful act was the plaintiff's wrongful act, but in one aspect it constitutes a breach by himself and in another aspect it constitutes a breach by his employer. So what is the position?

There has been a number of cases, to which I shall refer in a moment, in which it has been considered whether or not the employer delegated to the employee the performance of the statutory duty. In my view, the law which is applicable here is clear and comprehensible if one does not confuse it by seeking to investigate this very difficult and complicated question whether or not there was a delegation. In my view, the important and fundamental question in a case like this is not whether there was a delegation, but simply the usual question: Whose fault was it? I shall refer to some of the decided cases to demonstrate what I have said. If the answer to that question is that in substance and reality the accident was solely due to the fault of the plaintiff, so that he was the sole author of his own wrong, he is disentitled to recover. But that has to be applied to the particular case and it is not necessarily conclusive for the employer to show that it was a wrongful act of the employee plaintiff which caused the accident. It might also appear from the evidence that something was done or omitted by the employer which caused or contributed to the accident; there may have been a lack of proper supervision or lack of proper instructions; the employer may have employed for this purpose some insufficiently experienced men, or he may in the past have acquiesced in some wrong behaviour on the part of the men. Therefore, if one finds that the immediate and direct cause of the accident was some wrongful act of the man, that is not decisive. One has to inquire whether the fault of the employer under the statutory regulations consists of, and is co-extensive with, the wrongful act of the employee. If there is some fault on the part of the employer which goes beyond or is independent of the wrongful act of the employee, and was a cause of the accident, the employer has some liability. I have stated what, in my view, the proper rule is. For this rule several explanations can be given and several bases can be provided, and I will mention three. First, there is the common law principle that a person cannot derive any advantage from his own wrong. As applied to this case, that means that a person cannot by his own wrongful act impose on his employers the liability to pay damages to him. On that, I will refer to a recent case, *Goulandris Bros. Ltd.* v. *B. Goldman & Sons Ltd.* ([1957] 3 All E.R. 100), in which that principle of the common law was considered in relation to a different subject-matter.

Secondly (and this is, at any rate, closely allied to the first explanation or principle which I have mentioned), let us consider the effect of the plaintiff's own negligence at common law, that is, before the passing of the Law Reform (Contributory Negligence) Act 1945. If the accident was caused wholly or in part by the plaintiff's own negligence, he was barred from recovering anything, and his action failed. The Law Reform (Contributory Negligence) Act 1945, s.1(1), modified that position and provides: "Where any person suffers damage as the result partly of his own fault and partly of the fault of any other person or persons, a claim in respect of that damage shall not be defeated by reason of the fault of the person suffering the damage, but the damages recoverable in respect thereof shall be reduced to such extent as the court thinks just and equitable having regard to the claimant's share in the responsibility for the damage. . . . "

That applies only in a case where the accident is caused partly by the fault of the plaintiff and partly by the fault of somebody else; but the peculiarity of a situation such as we have here is that the accident is caused wholly by one wrongful act, and that act constitutes in one aspect a breach of obligation by the plaintiff and in another aspect a breach of obligation by his employer. Therefore, although one could say that the accident was wholly caused by the fault of the plaintiff, one could also say that the accident was wholly caused by the fault of the first defendant. In my view, that takes a case of this kind outside the scope of the Law Reform

(Contributory Negligence) Act 1945 and one has to revert to common law principles to see what the position is. If one does that, the common law principle is still valid to this extent, that, if the accident is wholly caused by the plaintiff's own fault, he is disentitled to recover.

Then there is a third explanation, or basis, which can be provided; that is, the need for avoiding circuity of action. Circuity of action would arise in this way. Suppose that the plaintiff said that his employer committed a breach of statutory obligation whereby damage was caused to him, and he was entitled to recover damages from his employer. The employer would reply that by the contract of employment the employee owed a duty to his employer, who, therefore, was entitled to recover damages against the employee, and that the amount of damages which the employer was entitled to recover was equal to the amount of the damages which the employee was supposedly entitled to recover against the employer. If that were the position, the litigation would go round in a circle, and for that reason there is, in my view, a valid plea of circuity of action. The plea of circuity of action is not usually found in these days because that situation is usually sufficiently provided for by the modern provisions for set-off and counterclaim; but it is a valid plea, and again I would cite *Goulandris Bros. Ltd.* v. *B. Goldman & Sons Ltd.* and certain previously decided cases which are mentioned in that case.

Those are three explanations of the rule, which, in my view, is a valid one, and there may be other explanations too. I ought to say that I think the theory of delegation of the performance of the employer's statutory duty is not a sound explanation. It may be that another explanation suggested, namely, the principle *"ex turpi causa non oritur actio,"* is also unsound. . . .

That being the position, we have here the case in which the fault of the employer—and it is a fault under the definition of "fault" contained in the definition section, section 4, of the Law Reform (Contributory Negligence) Act 1945—was a breach of statutory obligation by the employer because, through the employee, the employer did not use the boards; but that fault of the employer consisted of, and was co-extensive with, that of the plaintiff, and in substance this unfortunate accident was due to the fault of the plaintiff in breach of, and in defiance of, his instructions and of regulations which were well known to him. He decided to do the work on this roof without the use of boards. It would not be right, however, to take too severe a view; he was not in any direct sense going to gain anything for himself; he was taking the risk for himself with a view to getting the work done. Yet it is quite impossible to impose a liability on his employer, because the plaintiff himself decided to take the risk and not to use the boards, and in those circumstances the plaintiff must fail.

Question

How can you solve a problem of causation by asking: "Whose fault was it?"?

Note:

The defendant's liability for breach of statutory duty is not neutralised by the fact that it was the plaintiff's breach of duty which constituted it. If the defendant does not show that there was adequate supervision of the job, instruction about dangers and explanation of the regulations he remains liable, even if a failure in those regards would not amount to common law negligence. *Boyle* v. *Kodak Ltd.* [1969] 1 W.L.R. 661 (H.L.).

CHAPTER 5

DEFENCES

Section 1.—Contributory Negligence

LAW REFORM (CONTRIBUTORY NEGLIGENCE) ACT 1945

1.—(1) Where any person suffers damage as the result partly of his own fault and partly of the fault of any other person or persons, a claim in respect of that damage shall not be defeated by reason of the fault of the person suffering the damage, but the damages recoverable in respect thereof shall be reduced to such extent as the court thinks just and equitable having regard to the claimant's share in the responsibility for the damage: . . .

(2) Where damages are recoverable by any person by virtue of the foregoing subsection subject to such reduction as is therein mentioned, the court shall find and record the total damages which would have been recoverable if the claimant had not been at fault. . . .

4. **Interpretation.**—The following expressions have the meanings hereby respectively assigned to them, that is to say—

"damage" includes loss of life and personal injury;

"fault" means negligence, breach of statutory duty or other act or omission which gives rise to a liability in tort or would, apart from this Act, give rise to the defence of contributory negligence.

Notes:

Until this very important Act, a plaintiff was unlikely to recover any damages at all if his own fault had contributed to the injury of which he complained. Many questions are raised by the Act, not all of which have yet been answered.

1. In determining the proportion by which the plaintiff's damages are to be reduced, attention must be paid to the respective blameworthiness of the parties as well as to the causative potency of their acts or omissions: if attention were not paid to causative potency, a careless plaintiff would recover nothing from a defendant who was free from fault but strictly liable, and if blameworthiness were not taken into account the results would be unfair. But the reduction is to be by an amount which is "just and equitable" having regard to the plaintiff's responsibility for the harm, and it has been suggested that it may not be just and equitable to reduce at all the damages payable by an employer to a mildly careless employee (*Hawkins* v. *Ian Ross (Castings) Ltd.* [1970] 1 All E.R. 180). It had, indeed, already been held, before the Act was passed, that an employee who made a careless mistake in the heat and stress of factory conditions was not, as against an occupier in breach of safety regulations, to be treated as careless, but this new approach is more extensive. Contrariwise, it has sometimes been held that the plaintiff's contribution to his injury was so very great that no damages should be paid at all, though the defendant's liability and contribution to the harm could not be denied (*Richardson* v. *Stephenson Clarke Ltd.* [1969] 1 W.L.R. 1695). Nevertheless reductions are very commonly made, and courts of appeal are readier than they say to vary the apportionment.

2. Failure to wear a seat-belt does not cause accidents, but it may aggravate injuries. It is now clear that it is normally unreasonable not to wear a seat-belt and that damages will be reduced if the defendant can show that it made a difference. Lord Denning has suggested standard reductions of 15 per cent. if the injuries would have been less serious, 25 per cent. if they would have been avoided altogether: *Froom* v. *Butcher* [1976] Q.B. 286. The fact that failure to wear a seat-belt is now often unlawful will make no difference here.

3. Contributory negligence must be pleaded by the defendant: *Fookes* v. *Slaytor* [1979] 1 All E.R. 137 (C.A.). For a case where the particulars of contributory negligence offered by

the defendant resulted in his own liability for failure to take those very precautions, see *General Cleaning Contractors* v. *Christmas,* above p. 104.

4. Apart from the doctrine of mitigation of damage (sec for example *Darbishire* v. *Warran* below, p. 548) this Act provides the only admitted means of giving the plaintiff something by way of damages, but less than the full amount. (Other systems are more flexible—in Switzerland damages may be reduced if the defendant was not greatly at fault, and in France judges have a *de facto* discretion because no final appeal lies on questions of quantum.) It is therefore a pity that the courts of England have not applied the Act against trespassers (*Westwood* v. *Post Office* [1974] A.C. 1), and that they are so unwilling to find that a child has been contributorily negligent (*Gough* v. *Thorne* [1966] 1 W.L.R. 1387). The Pearson Commission has recommended that the defence of contributory negligence should not be available in cases of motor vehicle injury where the victim was under the age of twelve at the time.

5. Damages claimed for loss of support by dependants of a person killed by the defendant are reduced by the amount of carelessness of the deceased. A child's damages are not reduced by reason of the concurrent carelessness of a parent or guardian, but the parent or guardian may, at a pinch, be brought in as a third party by the tortfeasor and held liable to pay contribution (above, p. 65). Neither a passenger in a vehicle not its owner is affected by the contributory negligence of the driver unless he is driving as their servant or agent. Note, however, the position under s.1(7) of the Congenital Disabilities (Civil Liability) Act 1976, and consider the position if there is a collision between a car negligently driven by a pregnant mother and one negligently driven by a stranger and the child is born deformed as a result.

6. Rescuers are frequently and nobly indifferent to their own safety but their recovery is not often barred or limited on that account. In a case where the rescuer's negligence contributed to the emergency which called for the rescue, Boreham J. overcame his "distaste about finding a rescuer guilty of contributory negligence" (*Harrison* v. *British Railways Board* [1981] 3 All E.R. 679).

7. This Act is designed to split the loss between plaintiff and defendant; where there is more than one defendant the loss may be apportioned between them under the 1978 Act (above, p. 65). Where the plaintiff as well as two others have been at fault, both Acts apply, and one must establish the extent to which each contributed to the harm complained of by the plaintiff (*The Miraflores and The Abadesa* [1967] 1 A.C. 826). Now there is a rule, except in maritime collision cases (where all parties could be supposed solvent, at least until the appearance of one-ship companies from Nicaragua and elsewhere), that a person liable for a loss is liable for the whole of that loss even though someone else was just as much or more at fault in causing it. This rule produces strange results where the plaintiff also was at fault. Suppose, as happened in the case last cited, that the plaintiff is found 40 per cent. to blame, and the two defendants (D1 and D2) are found 40 per cent. and 20 per cent. to blame respectively. Owing to the effect of the rule just mentioned, D2 is bound to pay 60 per cent. of the plaintiff's loss although the plaintiff was twice as much to blame as he; it is then left to D2 to try to recover two-thirds of that sum from D1.

In Germany the matter is resolved in a much more sophisticated manner. Suppose that the plaintiff's loss is £12,000. The plaintiff, being 40 per cent. to blame, can collect in all 60 per cent. of his loss, or £7,200. Since D1 is equally to blame with the plaintiff, the plaintiff can collect up to 50 per cent. of his loss from D1, or £6,000; D2, only half as much to blame as the plaintiff, need pay only one-third of his loss, or £4,000. If, as one would expect, the plaintiff collects £6,000 from D1 and the balance of £1,200 from D2, how much contribution can D1 collect from D2? Since the first £3,200 paid by D1 did not reduce the amount of D2's liability at all (for at that stage the plaintiff was still entitled to collect £4,000, the total amount of D2's liability) only £2,800 of the money paid by D1 had the effect of reducing the liability of D2. To this sum D2 must contribute, but since D1 was twice as negligent as D2, D2 pays only one-third of it, or £933. In the result, then, D1 pays £5,067 and D2 pays £2,133. Since in England D1 would pay £4,800 and D2 would pay £2,400, the difference may not seem material. But if D1 were insolvent, D2 in Germany would pay £4,000 and in England would pay £7,200, and this difference is not immaterial.

8. The Act applies only if the defendant's liability is tortious. Thus if the defendant has broken his contract and the plaintiff's fault has concurred to cause him harm, the plaintiff will recover all or nothing (*Quinn* v. *Burch Bros.* [1966] 2 Q.B. 370, affirming [1965] 3 All E.R. 801; *Lambert* v. *Lewis*: all in the Court of Appeal, nothing in the House of Lords ([1982] A.C. 225)). Very often, however, the defendant's breach of contract will also constitute a tort, in which case the Act will apply (*Sole* v. *W. J. Hallt* [1973] Q.B. 574); but if the plaintiff can in a contractual action recover his whole loss, neither this Act nor the 1978 Act will reduce the

amount of his recovery (*Driver* v. *William Willett (Contractors) Ltd.* [1969] 1 All E.R. 665).

9. There is bound to be a problem with this Act in cases arising under *Hedley Byrne* (above p. 34), for if the defendant is liable only if the plaintiff acted reasonably in relying on his statement, how can the defendant be liable at all if the plaintiff's reliance on it was unreasonable enough to call for a reduction of damages? The fact that recovery is unimpaired if reliance is unreasonably placed on a fraudulent statement should not be invoked.

10. Since the legislature has seen fit to enact that "Contributory negligence is no defence in proceedings founded on conversion, or on intentional trespass to goods" (Torts (Interference with Goods) Act 1977, s.11), it is still important to distinguish the form of action being used. In cases of nuisance, where the plaintiff is complaining that the defendant's conduct is rendering life on his real property intolerable, the obvious defence in some cases is that the plaintiff was aware of the situation when he bought the property. Traditionally however, it is no defence that "the plaintiff came to the nuisance." See *Miller* v. *Jackson*, below p. 365.

11. The existence of this Act has induced the judges to reduce the scope of the defence of *volenti non fit injuria*, by which a plaintiff who has accepted the risk of the injury which has occurred is barred from recovery in respect of it. The reaction is perfectly understandable, but it is not wholly justifiable, since respect for the self-determination of the individual requires the legal system to make him suffer the consequences of *voluntarily* exposing himself to physical risk, even if it was not in the circumstances an *unreasonably* dangerous thing to do.

12. A person can naturally recover under a liability insurance policy although he was at fault: this is the point of the policy. So also a person can recover under insurance policies of other types (*e.g.* fire, theft) although he was at fault regarding loss: a clause that he must take care will be construed as a clause that he must not act recklessly (*W. J. Lane* v. *Spratt* [1970] 2 Q.B. 480). However, it is not normal for persons other than insurers to promise to pay for the faults of others, so contracts of other types must be very explicit if they are to be so construed (*Smith* v. *South Wales Switchgear Ltd.* [1978] 1 All E.R. 18 (H.L.)). As against a consumer such a clause will be invalid unless it is reasonable (Unfair Contract Terms Act 1977, s.4).

13. In France, where liability for harm caused by things under one's control is strict, the increasing feeling that it is unfair to reduce the plaintiff's damages by reason of his contributory fault has induced the Court of Cassation to ordain that in future no such reduction shall be made. There has been little echo of that feeling in England, where liability for traffic accidents is based on fault; but since a person can recover from his own insurer although he has been careless, it might be thought that he could recover from someone else's insurer notwithstanding that fact.

BILL v. SHORT BROS. & HARLAND LTD.

House of Lords [1963] N.I. 1

Action by employee against employer in respect of personal injury.

The plaintiff was an experienced workman with fourteen years' service with the defendants. One day after his lunch-break, he fell over a 1½-inch rubber pipe laid across the floor of the building for the purpose of carrying compressor air. His view of the floor was slightly obstructed by the presence in front of him of a fellow-workman, but he knew that the pipe might be there.

At the trial before Sheil J. and a jury, the plaintiff gave evidence of those facts, said that he knew of two previous accidents caused in a similar way, and that in other factories the air-pipes were laid along a wall or suspended from the roof. Sheil J. withdrew the case from the jury, and dismissed the plaintiff's claim. The Court of Appeal of Northern Ireland dismissed the plaintiff's appeal (Lord MacDermott C.J. dissenting). Curran L.J. said: "This was the case of a man who decided to cross the working floor of a factory and who stumbled on an obstacle which he knew was there." The House of Lords allowed the plaintiff's appeal and ordered a new trial.

LORD DENNING: My Lords, it appears to me that the claim at common law depends on three simple propositions. First, it is the duty of the employer to take reasonable care so to carry on his operations as not to subject those employed by him to unnecessary risk. Secondly, if the employer has failed in that duty, then the fact that the employee was fully aware of the risk may go to show that he was guilty of contributory negligence, but it does not by itself disentitle him from recovering. Thirdly, it is for the judge to say where there is any evidence from which the jury *could* infer that there was negligence on the part of the employer or contributory negligence on the part of the employee, but if there is such evidence then it must be left to the jury to say whether it *ought* to be inferred.

There was, in my opinion, evidence on which the jury *could* find that the employers were negligent. I base this particularly on the previous accidents which were drawn to their attention and on the means taken in other workshops to eliminate the risk. There was evidence on which the jury *could* find that the workman was guilty of contributory negligence. I base this particularly on his knowledge of the facts and of the risk. The jury *might* even find that his negligence was so predominant a factor that he was solely responsible for the accident—in short that he was one hundred per cent. to blame—but they were not bound so to find. They *could* find him less to blame. And if so, it was for the jury to apportion the responsibility.

I think, therefore, that the common law claim should have been left to the jury. . . .

Section 2.—Volenti Non Fit Injuria

IMPERIAL CHEMICAL INDUSTRIES v. SHATWELL

House of Lords [1965] A.C. 656; [1964] 3 W.L.R. 329; 108 S.J. 578; [1964] 2 All E.R. 999

Action by employee against employer in respect of personal injury.

On the facts, sufficiently stated in the judgment of Lord Reid, Elwes J. gave judgment for the plaintiff, subject to a reduction of damages by 50 per cent. for contributory negligence. The Court of Appeal affirmed this judgment. The defendant's appeal was allowed by the House of Lords.

LORD REID: My Lords, this case arises out of the accidental explosion of a charge at a quarry belonging to the appellants which caused injuries to the respondent George Shatwell and his brother James, who were both qualified shot firers. On June 28, 1960, these two men and another shot firer, Beswick, had bored and filled fifty shot holes and had inserted electric detonators and connected them up in series. Before firing it was necessary to test the circuit for continuity. This should have been done by connecting long wires so that the men could go to a shelter some eighty yards away and test from there. They had not sufficient wire with them and Beswick went off to get more. The testing ought not to have been done until signals had been given so that other men could take shelter and these signals were not due to be given for at least another hour.

Soon after Beswick had left George said to his brother: "Must we test them?" meaning shall we test them, and James said "Yes." The testing is done by passing a weak current through the circuit in which a small galvanometer is included and if the needle of the instrument moves when a connection is made the circuit is in order. So George got a galvanometer and James handed two short wires to him. Then George applied the wires to the galvanometer and the needle did not move. This showed that the circuit was defective so the two men went round inspecting the connections. They saw nothing wrong and George said that that meant there was a dud detonator somewhere, and decided to apply the galvanometer to each individual detonator. James handed two other wires to him and George used them to apply the galvanometer to the first detonator. The result was an explosion which injured both men.

This method had been regularly used without mishap until the previous year.

Then some research done by the appellants showed that it might be unsafe and in October 1959, the appellants gave orders that testing must in future be done from a shelter and a lecture was given to all the shot firers, including the Shatwells, explaining the position. Then in December 1959, new statutory regulations were made (1959, No. 2259) probably because the Ministry had been informed of the results of the appellants' research. These regulations came into operation in February 1960, and the Shatwells were aware of them. But some of the shot firers appear to have gone on in the old way. An instances of this came to the notice of the management in May 1960, and the management took immediate action and revoked the shot firing certificate of the disobedient man, and told the other shot firers about this. George admitted in evidence that he knew all this. He admitted that they would only have had to wait ten minutes until Beswick returned with the long wires. When asked why he did not wait, his only excuse was that he could not be bothered to wait.

George now sues the appellants on the ground that he and his brother were equally to blame for this accident, and that the appellants are vicariously liable for his brother's conduct. He has been awarded £1,500, being half the agreed amount of his loss. There is no question of the appellants having been in breach of the regulations because the duty under the regulation is laid on the shot firer personally. So counsel for George frankly and rightly admitted that if George had sued James personally instead of suing his employer the issue would have been the same. If this decision is right it means that if two men collaborate in doing what they know is dangerous and is forbidden and as a result both are injured, each has a cause of action against the other.

The appellants have two grounds of defence, first that James' conduct had no causal connection with the accident, the sole cause being George's own fault, and secondly, *volenti non fit injuria*. I am of opinion that they are entitled to succeed on the latter ground but I must deal shortly with the former ground because it involves the decision of this House in *Stapley* v. *Gypsum Mines Ltd.* ([1953] A.C. 663), and I think that there has been some misunderstanding of that case. Stapley and a man named Dale were working together in the mine. They found that a part of the roof was dangerous. They tried to bring it down but failed. Then, contrary to the foreman's orders and to statutory regulations, they decided to go on with their ordinary work and Stapley went to work below that part of the roof. It fell on him and he was killed. The only issue before the House was whether the conduct of Dale had contributed to cause the accident, and the House decided by a majority that it had. There was little, if any, difference of opinion as to the principles to be applied; the difference was in their application to the facts of the case. The case gives authoritative guidance on the question of causation but beyond that it decides nothing. It clearly appears from the argument of counsel that the defence *volenti non fit injuria* was never taken and nothing about it was said by any of their Lordships.

Applying the principles approved in Stapley's case, I think that James' conduct did have a causal connection with this accident. It is far from clear that George would have gone on with the test if James had not agreed with him. But perhaps more important James did collaborate with him in making the test in a forbidden and unlawful way. His collaboration may not have amounted to much but it was not negligible. If I had to consider the allocation of fault I would have difficulty in finding both men equally to blame. If James had been suing in respect of his damage it would, I think, be clear that both had contributed to cause the accident but that the greater part of the fault must be attributed to George. So I do not think that the appellants could succeed entirely on this defence and I turn to consider their second submission.

The defence *volenti non fit injuria* has had a chequered history. At one time it was very strictly applied. Today one can hardly read the robust judgment of Cockburn C.J. in *Woodley* v. *Metropolitan District Railway* ((1877) 2 Ex.D. 384) without some astonishment. But one must remember that his views were in line with those of the judges who a generation or two before had invented the doctrine of common employment. Then the tide began to turn. The modern view can be seen emerging in the judgments of the majority in *Yarmouth* v. *France* ((1887) 19 Q.B.D. 647). No one denied that a man who freely and voluntarily incurs a risk of which he has full knowledge cannot complain of injury if that risk materialises and causes him damage. The controversy was whether acceptance of the risk can (or must) be inferred from the mere fact that the man goes on working in full knowledge of the risk involved. The point was finally settled by this House in *Smith* v. *Baker & Sons* ([1891] A.C. 325). The opposing views were tersely stated by Hawkins J. in *Thrussell* v. *Handyside* ((1888) 20 Q.B.D. 359, 364)—"his poverty, not his will, consented to incur the danger"—and by Lord Bramwell in *Membery* v. *Great Western Railway* ((1889) 14 App.Cas. 179, 188): "The master says here is the work, do it or let it alone. . . . The master says this, the servant does the work and earns his wages, and is paid, but is hurt. On what principle of reason or justice should the master be liable to him in respect of that hurt?"

The ratio in *Smith* v. *Baker and Sons* was, I think, most clearly stated by Lord Herschell: "The maxim is founded on good sense and justice. One who has invited or assented to an act being done towards him cannot, when he suffers from it, complain of it as a wrong. The maxim has no special application to the case of employer and employed, though its application may well be invoked in such a case." Then he pointed out that a person undertaking to do work which is intrinsically dangerous, notwithstanding that care has been taken to make it as little dangerous as possible, cannot if he suffers complain that a wrong has been done him. And then he continued: "But the argument for the respondents went far beyond this. The learned counsel contended that, even though there had been negligence on the part of the defendants, yet the risk created by it was known to the plaintiff; and inasmuch as he continued in the defendants' employment, doing their work under conditions, the risk of which he appreciated, the maxim, '*Volenti non fit injuria*,' applied, and he could not recover." And later he said: "If, then, the employer thus fails in his duty towards the employed, I do not think that because he does not straightaway refuse to continue his service, it is true to say that he is willing that his employer should thus act towards him. I believe it would be contrary to fact to assert that he either invited or assented to the act or default which he complains of as a wrong."

More recently it appears to have been thought in some quarters that, at least as between master and servant, *volenti non fit injuria* is a dead or dying defence. That I think is because in most cases where the defence would now be available it has become usual to base the decision on contributory negligence. Where the plaintiff's own disobedient act is the sole cause of the injury it does not matter in the result whether one says 100 per cent. contributory negligence or *volenti non fit injuria*. But it does matter in a case like the present. If we adopt the inaccurate habit of using the word "negligence" to denote a deliberate act done with full knowledge of the risk it is not surprising that we sometimes get into difficulties. I think that most people would say, without stopping to think of the reason, that there is a world of difference between two fellow-servants collaborating carelessly so that the acts of both contribute to cause injury to one of them, and two fellow-servants combining to disobey an order deliberately though they know the risk involved. It seems reasonable that the injured man should recover some compensation in the former case but not in the latter. If the law treats both as merely cases of negligence it cannot draw a distinction. But in my view the law does and should draw a distinction. In the first case only the partial defence of contributory negligence is available. In the second *volenti non fit injuria* is a complete defence if the employer is not himself at fault and is only liable vicariously for the acts of the fellow-servant. If the plaintiff invited or freely aided and abetted his fellow-servant's disobedience, then he was *volens* in the fullest sense. He cannot complain of the resulting injury either against the fellow-servant or against the master on the ground of his vicarious responsibility for his fellow-servant's conduct. I need not here consider the common case where the servant's disobedience puts the master in breach of a statutory obligation and it would be wrong to decide in advance whether that would make any difference. There remain two other arguments for the respondent which I must deal with.

It was argued that in this case it has not been shown that George had a full appreciation of the risk. In my view it must be held that he had. He knew that those better qualified than he was took the risk seriously. He knew that his employers had forbidden this practice and that it had then been prohibited by statutory regulation. And he knew that his employers were taking strong measures to see that the order was obeyed. If he did not choose to believe what he was told I do not think that he could for that reason say that he did not fully appreciate the risk. He knew that the risk was that a charge would explode during testing, and no shot firer could be in any doubt about the possible consequences of that.

Finally the respondent argues that there is a general rule that the defence of *volenti non fit injuria* is not available where there has been a breach of a statutory obligation. It would be odd if that were so. In the present case the prohibition of testing except from a shelter had been imposed by the appellants before the statutory prohibition was made. So it would mean that if the respondent had deliberately done what he did in full knowledge of the risk the day before the statutory prohibition was made this defence would have been open to the appellants, but if he had done the same thing the day after the regulation came into operation it would not. . . .

I entirely agree that an employer who is himself at fault in persistently refusing to comply with a statutory rule could not possibly be allowed to escape liability because the injured workman had agreed to waive the breach. If it is still permissible for a workman to make an express agreement with his employer to work under an unsafe system, perhaps in consideration of a higher wage—a matter on which I need express no opinion—then there would be a difference between breach of statutory obligation by the employer and breach of his common law obligation to exercise due care: it would be possible to contract out of the latter but not out of the former type of obligation. But all that is very far removed from the present case. . . .

I can find no reason at all why the facts that these two brothers agreed to commit an offence by contravening a statutory prohibition imposed on them as well as agreeing to defy their employer's orders should affect the application of the principle *volenti non fit injuria* either to an action by one of them against the other or to an action by one against their employer based on his vicarious responsibility for the conduct of the other. I would therefore allow this appeal.

VISCOUNT RADCLIFFE: . . . On one view George simply blew himself up. . . . After all, if a man decides to test an unexploded mine by tapping it with a hammer and he asks someone standing by to find the hammer and hand it to him, the complier would not naturally be thought of as being in any degree the author of any injury that is inflicted on the tester if the mine explodes. . . .

I do not see how either can succeed against the other, since, where both were joined in carrying through the whole operation and each in what he did was the agent of the other to achieve it, there was nothing that one did against the other that the other did not equally do against himself. This, in my view, is the true result of a joint unlawful enterprise, in which what is wrong is the whole enterprise and neither of the joint actors has contributed a separate wrongful act to the result. Each emerges as the author of his own injury. . . .

Note:
This case shows the practical advantages of keeping all possible concepts available, however offensive their overlap may be to the intellectual aesthete. *Stapley's* case was on its

facts indistinguishable. If the concept of *volenti* has been destroyed—and many have wished for its destruction (*e.g.,* James, "Assumption of Risk," 61 Yale L.J. 141, 169 (1952))—the difficulty of reaching the proper result would have been enhanced.

Questions
    1. Is there a big difference between doing something bad and doing something badly?
    2. If *Shatwell* applies only where the defendant's liability is purely vicarious and *Ginty* (above, p. 202) applies only where the plaintiff has been fully apprised of the regulations, is *Shatwell* very like *Ginty* or not?
    3. Should all those who agree to play Russian Roulette be liable to the loser's widow?

WOOLDRIDGE v. SUMNER

Court of Appeal [1963] 2 Q.B. 43; [1962] 3 W.L.R. 616; 106 S.J. 489; [1962] 2 All E.R. 978

The facts are given above, p. 91.

DIPLOCK L.J.: . . . The practical result of this analysis of the application of the common law of negligence to participant and spectator would, I think, be expressed by the common man in some such terms as these: "A person attending a game or competition takes the risk of any damage caused to him by any act of a participant done in the course of and for the purposes of the game or competition notwithstanding that such act may involve an error of judgment or a lapse of skill, unless the participant's conduct is such as to evince a reckless disregard of the spectator's safety."

The spectator takes the risk because such an act involves no breach of the duty of care owed by the participant to him. He does not take the risk by virtue of the doctrine expressed or obscured by the maxim *volenti non fit injuria*. That maxim states a principle of estoppel applicable originally to a Roman citizen who consented to being sold as a slave. Although pleaded and argued below it was only faintly relied upon by Mr. Everett in this court. In my view, the maxim in the absence of expressed contract has no application to negligence *simpliciter* where the duty of care is based solely upon proximity or "neighbourship" in the Atkinian sense. The maxim in English law presupposes a tortious act by the defendant. The consent that is relevant is not consent to the risk of injury but consent to the lack of reasonable care that may produce that risk (see *Kelly* v. *Farrans Ltd.* ([1954] N.I. 41, 45 *per* Lord MacDermott) and requires on the part of the plaintiff at the time at which he gives consent full knowledge of the nature and extent of the risk he ran (*Osborne* v. *London and North Western Railway* ((1888) 21 Q.B.D. 220, 224), *per* Wills J., approved in *Letang* v. *Ottawa Electric Railway* ([1926] A.C. 725)). In *Dann* v. *Hamilton* ([1939] 1 K.B. 509) Asquith J. expressed doubts as to whether the maxim ever could apply to license in advance a subsequent act of negligence, for if the consent precedes the act of negligence the plaintiff cannot at that time have full knowledge of the extent as well as the nature of the risk which he will run. Asquith J., however, suggested that the maxim might nevertheless be applicable to cases where a dangerous physical condition had been brought about by the negligence of the defendant, and the plaintiff with full knowledge of the existing danger elected to run the risk thereof. With the development of the law of negligence in the last twenty years a more consistent explanation of this type of case is that the test of liability on the part of the person creating the dangerous physical condition is whether it was reasonably foreseeable by him that the plaintiff would so act in relation to it as to endanger himself. This is the principle which has been applied in the rescue cases (see *Cutler* v. *United Dairies (London) Ltd.* ([1933] 2 K.B. 297), and contrast *Haynes* v. *Harwood* ([1935] 1 K.B. 146)) and that part of Asquith J.'s judgment in *Dann* v. *Hamilton* dealing with the possible application of the maxim to the law of negligence which was not approved by the Court of Appeal in *Baker* v. *T. E. Hopkins & Son* ([1959] 1 W.L.R. 966). In the type of case envisaged by Asquith J., if I may adapt the words of Morris L.J. in *Baker* v. *T. E. Hopkins & Son*, the plaintiff could not have agreed to run the risk that the defendant might be negligent for the plaintiff would only play his part after the defendant had been negligent.

Since the maxim has in my view no application to this or any other case of negligence *simpliciter*, the fact that the plaintiff owing to his ignorance of horses did not fully appreciate the nature and extent of the risk he ran did not impose upon Mr. Holladay any higher duty of care towards him than that which he owed to any ordinary reasonable spectator with such knowledge of horses and vigilance for his own safety as might be reasonably expected to be possessed by a person who chooses to watch a heavyweight hunter class in the actual arena where the class is being judged. He cannot rely upon his personal ignorance of the risk any more than the plaintiff in *Murray* v. *Harringay Arena* ([1951] 2 K.B. 529) could rely upon his ignorance of the risk involved in ice-hockey, excusable though such ignorance may have been in a six-year-old child. . . .

Note:

It is clear that the voluntary act of a person in exposing himself to a danger of which he knows, already created by the carelessness of another, may well deprive him of a claim on the grounds of causation (*McKew* v. *Holland & Hannen & Cubitts (Scotland)* (above, p. 201)). It is clear also from *Shatwell* that a person may be deprived of a claim if he participated deliberately in a dangerous enterprise. Furthermore, it is clear that a person may deprive himself in advance of a claim in respect of subsequent negligence, by means of an agreement by which the defendant exempts himself from liability or the plaintiff undertakes not to sue, so far as the Unfair Contract Terms Act 1977 permits. The question is whether there is a doctrine related neither to causation nor to participation nor to contract which may operate to deprive a person of a claim on the ground that he accepted the risk of injury caused by the defendant's carelessness. Diplock L.J. denies it in the previous case, but it does seem strange that a person who has voluntarily exposed himself to the risk of subsequent carelessness can invariably sue, subject only to a reduction of damages under the 1945 Act if it was unreasonably dangerous of him so to act.

Legislators admit the existence of the defence. The Occupiers' Liability Act 1957, s.2(5) reads: "The common duty of care does not impose on an occupier any obligation to a visitor in respect of risks willingly accepted as his by the visitor (the question whether a risk was so accepted to be decided on the same principles as in other cases in which one person owes a duty of care to another)." Acceptance of risk is also a specific defence to a claim under the Control of Pollution Act 1974, s.88. Note, however, that the Road Traffic Act 1972, s.148(3), provides that "the fact that a person so carried [*i.e.* carried in a vehicle whose use is such that a policy of insurance is required] has willingly accepted as his the risk of negligence on the part of the user shall not be treated as negativing any such liability of the user." This section reverses the effect of such decisions as *Birch* v. *Thomas* ([1972] 1 W.L.R. 294 (C.A.)), which will, however, remain useful to repel claims by pillion passengers on toboggans and by waterskiers against the motorman.

In his *Last Journal*, Captain Scott wrote: "I do not regret this journey; we took risks, we knew we took them, things have come out against us, therefore we have no cause for complaint."

Question

A's dog and B's dog are fighting on the highway. C intervenes to separate them and is bitten by A's dog. *Volenti non fit injuria*? It is different if they are fighting in C's garden? Is it different if B intervenes and is bitten by A's dog?

Section 3.—Agreement and Notice

UNFAIR CONTRACT TERMS ACT 1977

1.—(1) For the purposes of this Part of this Act, "negligence" means the breach—

(*a*) of any obligation, arising from the express or implied terms of a contract, to take reasonable care or exercise reasonable skill in the performance of the contract;

(*b*) of any common law duty to take reasonable care or exercise reasonable skill (but not any stricter duty);

(*c*) of the common duty of care imposed by the Occupiers' Liability Act 1957 or the Occupiers' Liability Act (Northern Ireland) 1957.

. . .

(3) In the case of both contract and tort, sections 2 to 7 apply (except where the contrary is stated in section 6(4)) only to business liability, that is liability for breach of obligations or duties arising—

(*a*) from things done or to be done by a person in the course of a business (whether his own business or another's); or

(*b*) from the occupation of premises used for business purposes of the occupier; and references to liability are to be read accordingly.

(4) In relation to any breach of duty or obligation, it is immaterial for any purpose of this Part of this Act whether the breach was inadvertent or intentional, or whether liability for it arises directly or vicariously.

2.—(1) A person cannot by reference to any contract term or to a notice given to persons generally or to particular persons exclude or restrict his liability for death or personal injury resulting from negligence.

(2) In the case of other loss or damage, a person cannot so exclude or restrict his liability for negligence except insofar as the term or notice satisfies the requirement of reasonableness.

(3) Where a contract term or notice purports to exclude or restrict liability for negligence a person's agreement to or awareness of it is not of itself to be taken as indicating his voluntary acceptance of any risk.

11. . . .

(3) In relation to a notice (not being a notice having contractual effect), the requirement of reasonableness under this Act is that it should be fair and reasonable to allow reliance on it, having regard to all the circumstances obtaining when the liability arose or (but for the notice) would have arisen.

(4) Where by reference to a contract term or notice a person seeks to restrict liability to a specified sum of money, and the question arises (under this or any other Act) whether the term or notice satisfies the requirement of reasonableness, regard shall be had in particular (but without prejudice to subsection (2) above in the case of contract terms) to—

(*a*) the resources which he could expect to be available to him for the purpose of meeting the liability should it arise; and

(*b*) how far it was open to him to cover himself by insurance.

(5) It is for those claiming that a contract term or notice satisfies the requirement of reasonableness to show that it does.

13.—(1) To the extent that this Part of this Act prevents the exclusion or restriction of any liability it also prevents—

(*a*) making the liability or its enforcement subject to restrictive or onerous conditions;

(*b*) excluding or restricting any right or remedy in respect of the liability, or subjecting a person to any prejudice in consequence of his pursuing any such right or remedy;

(*c*) excluding or restricting rules of evidence or procedure;

and (to that extent) sections 2 and 5 to 7 also prevent excluding or restricting liability by reference to terms and notices which exclude or restrict the relevant obligation or duty.

14. In this Part of this Act—

"business" includes a profession and the activities of any government department or local or public authority;

. . .

"negligence" has the meaning given by section 1(1);

"notice" includes an announcement, whether or not in writing, and any other communication or pretended communication;

. . .

Note:

Once upon a time, before this country went in every sense bankrupt, adults used to be bound by what they had agreed to. Those who had agreed that their employment or tenancy was to last for a fixed period might have to leave when that period expired. *A fortiori*, people were disentitled to sue if they had accepted a benefit on the express terms that they were to have no claim if something went wrong and they got hurt. How different now! Politicians have accorded to voters their special privilege of going back on their word once elected, and have extended to every citizen the irresponsibility previously reserved for the ignorant, the imbecile and the infantile. Great emotion has admittedly been generated in recent years by the contractual exclusion of tortious liability, but it is permissible to wonder whether the emotion, winningly presented as outrage at exploitation and abuse of power, may not simply be the irritation of Leviathan and his creatures at any private derogation from his law.

The value-judgments of the draftsmen of the Act are clear enough: (i) personal injury is more serious than property damage (even a reasonable exclusion of liability for causing personal injury by negligence is void); (ii) conduct is particularly objectionable if it is careless (strict liability for even personal injury may be excluded, though not vicarious liability for negligence causing it); (iii) businesses are subject to greater liability than persons in private life.

The classic instance of the defence which this Act so severely restricts arises where a person is allowed to take a short-cut across the land of another on the published terms that he is to have no claim against the occupier even if he is negligently injured. The Court of Appeal upheld this defence in *Ashdown* v. *Williams* [1957] 1 Q.B. 409, and the legislator endorsed the decision in the Occupiers' Liability Act 1957, s.2(1). So, too, the charitable organisers of jalopy races were exempt from liability for the death of a spectator who had competed in earlier races and knew that the organisers were disclaiming responsibility (*White* v. *Blackmore* [1972] 2 Q.B. 651). These decisions remain relevant except where personal injury or death has been caused by the negligent operation of a business, as defined, and may be applied where the damage is to property or purse (and the exclusion is reasonable) or where the defendant is a private person. Even private people, however, cannot exclude their liability for personal injury to passengers in their cars (Road Traffic Act 1972, s.148(3)).

Section 4.—Illegality

MURPHY v. CULHANE

Court of Appeal [1977] Q.B. 94; [1976] 3 W.L.R. 458; 120 S.J. 506; [1976] 3 All E.R. 533

Action by widow of assailant against criminal killer

Lord Denning M.R. In this case we do not know the true facts. We only know the allegations in the pleadings. According to them Timothy Murphy was a man of 29. He was a self-employed builder, that is on the "lump" earning between £60 and £70 a week. On 19th September 1974 he, with some other men, made a wicked plot together. They decided to beat up another man called John Joseph Culhane, the defendant. They went to an address at 20 Grove Place in Greater London. We do not know anything of what took place except that there was a "criminal affray." During it John Culhane is said to have struck Timothy Murphy on the head with a plank and killed him. John Culhane was charged with murder. He was tried at the Central Criminal Court on 25th April 1975. At first, he pleaded not guilty, but after the case had been opened and some evidence heard, he changed his plea to guilty of manslaughter. He was sentenced to eight years which was reduced to five years by the Court of Appeal.

Timothy Murphy's widow now brings an action against John Culhane for damages under the Fatal Accidents Acts, claiming damages on behalf of herself and her baby daughter. I do not suppose he has any money to pay any damages as he is still in prison. But legal aid has, I believe, been granted to both sides. The question is whether or not Mrs. Murphy is entitled to judgment on the pleadings without any trial. The statement of claim says:

"On or about the nineteenth day of September, 1974, near Grove Place, in the area of Greater London, the Defendant assaulted and beat the Deceased by striking him on the head with a plank. The said assault was unlawful. The Plaintiff intends to adduce evidence pursuant to Section 11 of the Civil Evidence Act, 1968, that the Defendant was on the 25th day of April, 1975, convicted on his own plea of guilty before the Central Criminal Court of manslaughter of the Deceased."

The defence admits those allegations and further admits that, by reason of the assault, Mr. Murphy was killed. It then says:

"The said assault occurred during and as part of a criminal affray which was initiated by the Deceased and others who had together come to 20 Grove Place on the occasion in question with the joint criminal intent of assaulting and beating the Defendant."

That is followed by legal contentions of *ex turpi causa non oritur actio, volenti non fit injuria*, and that the deceased's said death was caused in part by his own aforesaid fault.

On those pleadings Mrs. Murphy applied for judgment under RSC Ord. 27, r. 3, which gives the court power to give judgment on admissions. The master and the judge both felt that, on the state of the authorities, they were bound to give judgment for Mrs. Murphy and shut out these defences of Mr. Culhane. Judgment was given for damages to be assessed. I gather that the judge felt most unwilling to do this, but thought he was bound by the cases. So I must deal with them. There are two cases which seem to show that, in a civil action for damages for assault, damages are not to be reduced because the plaintiff was himself guilty of provocation. Provocation, it was said, can be used to wipe out the element of exemplary damages but not to reduce the actual figure of pecuniary damages. It was so said by the High Court of Australia in 1962 in *Fontin* v. *Katapodis* ((1962) 108 C.L.R. 177) and followed by this court in 1967 in *Lane* v. *Holloway* ([1968] 1 Q.B. 379). But those were cases where the conduct of the injured man was trivial—and the conduct of the defendant was savage—entirely out of proportion to the occasion. So much so that the defendant could fairly be regarded as solely responsible for the damage done. I do not think they can or should be applied where the injured man, by his own conduct, can fairly be regarded as partly responsible for the damage he suffered. So far as general principle is concerned, I would like to repeat what I said in the later case of *Gray* v. *Barr* ([1971] 2 Q.B. 554, 569):

"In an action for assault, in awarding damages, the judge or jury can take into account, not only circumstances which go to aggravate damages, but also those which go to mitigate them."

That is the principle I prefer rather than the earlier cases. Apart altogether from damages, however, I think there may well be a defence on liability. If Murphy was one of a gang which set out to beat up Culhane, it may well be that he could not sue for damages if he got more than he bargained for. A man who takes part in a criminal affray may well be said to have been guilty of such a wicked act as to deprive himself of a cause of action or, alternatively, to have taken on himself the risk. I put the case in the course of argument: suppose that a burglar breaks into a house and the householder, finding him there, picks up a gun and shoots him, using more force maybe than is reasonably necessary. The householder may be guilty of manslaughter and liable to be brought before the criminal courts. But I doubt very much whether the burglar's widow could have an action for damages. The householder might well have a defence either on ground of ex turpi causa non oritur actio or volenti non fit injuria. So in the present case it is open to Mr. Culhane to raise both those defences. Such defences would go to the whole claim.

There is another point, too, even if Mrs. Murphy were entitled to damages under the Fatal Accidents Acts, they fall to be reduced under the Law Reform (Contributory Negligence) Act 1945 because the death of her husband might be the result partly of his own fault and partly of the default of the defendant: see s.1(1) and (4) of the 1945 Act. On this point I must explain a sentence in *Gray* v. *Barr* where the widow of the dead man was held to be entitled to full compensation without any reduction. Her husband had not been guilty of any "fault" within s.4 of the 1945 Act because his conduct had not been such as to make him liable in an action of tort or, alternatively, was not such that he should be regarded as responsible in any degree for the damage. So also in *Lane* v. *Holloway*, as Winn L.J. pointed out. But in the present case the conduct of Mr. Murphy may well have been such as to make him liable in tort.

It seems to me that this is clearly a case where the facts should be investigated before any judgment is given. It should be open to Mr. Culhane to be able to put forward his defences so as to see whether or not and to what extent he is liable in damages.

I would therefore allow the appeal. The judgment should be set aside and the case go for trial accordingly.

ORR L.J. and WALLER J. agreed.

Note:

Earlier in the book we saw that unlawful as well as unreasonable behaviour might render a defendant liable. Unreasonable conduct on the part of the plaintiff may reduce or extinguish his claim, as we have just seen. What if his conduct is unlawful?

Judges are naturally unwilling to award damages to plaintiffs they think should be in the dock. Bad people get less. This is reflected in the Latin tag *ex turpi causa non oritur actio*. Although it is of general application throughout the law, it has different effects in the different branches of the law of obligations. In contract, for example, if we agree that I shall kill your mother-in-law for £500 and I do kill her, I cannot claim the £500—the judges will not reward a person for doing wrong: and if I change my mind, you cannot sue me for non-performance— the judges will not make a person pay for not doing wrong. These principles are so strong in contract law that they apply even if the illegality is quite technical and the parties morally innocent. In restitution the principle operates less fiercely. It is true that if I decide not to murder your mother-in-law, I can keep any down-payment you made me, not because I have earned it but because you will be disentitled from reclaiming it; here the normal right to reclaim is lost only if the claimant is tainted with turpitude. Again, when one tortfeasor is claiming contribution from another, he is founding on his own wrong. This was enough to bar his claim at common law, unless he was wholly innocent: negligent tortfeasors may now claim under the statute (above, p. 65) but a wicked claimant might well find himself in difficulties.

In tort cases the wickedness of the plaintiff plays a slighter role, because the interests traditionally in issue are basic—liberty, life and limb, property. Of course the liberty of criminals is not as well protected as that of honest citizens, for criminals are subject to arrest and imprisonment, but they are no longer hanged or beaten, and their property is not forfeit, though they may be bankrupted (Powers of Criminal Courts Act 1973, ss.39–41). So if I run someone over in the street, it can hardly be relevant that he was on his way to or from a robbery (unless in the former case he was claiming for lost swag or in the latter for damage to his booty).

Yet in recent years there has been a revival of the defence, actually upheld in *Ashton* v. *Turner* [1981] Q.B. 137 (burglar hurt by bad driving of fellow-burglar in get-away car). On one view, this is due to the growing moralism which accompanies the levelling process in society. Technically, perhaps, it is due to the restriction in the scope of the other defences—no duty, contributory negligence, *volenti non fit injuria*. Suppose a person is injured by a defective product he has stolen from the retailer. Can we say that the manufacturer owed the shoplifter no duty? Suppose that a burglar is injured by a danger on the burgled premises: contributory negligence does not apply if he was looking out for his own safety (*Westwood* v. *Post Office* [1974] A.C. 1), and it has been suggested that an occupier should owe the same duty to a trespasser as to a visitor (*Herrington* v. *British Railways Board* [1971] 2 Q.B. 107, 120 *per* Salmon L.J.). Suppose that a hitch-hiker pulls a gun on the person who gives him a lift and forces him to drive to a specified destination: the Road Traffic Act 1972, s.148(3) makes it impossible for us to say that the gunman takes the risk of bad driving, and *Nettleship* v. *Weston* (above, p. 94) makes it difficult for us to qualify the competence required of the driver.

It is therefore not surprising that in recent years it has been suggested in *obiter dicta* that the defence of illegality might bar a claim by a burglar bitten by a guard-dog (*Cummings* v. *Grainger* [1977] Q.B. 397), a patron of a pub who had been drinking after hours and was injured on the way out (*Stone* v. *Taffe* [1974] 3 All E.R. 1016) and a passenger in a car whose driver was known to be the worse for drink or drugs (*Nettleship* v. *Weston*, above, p. 94).

In *Burns* v. *Edman* [1970] 2 Q.B. 541 a criminal had been killed in a motor accident for which the defendant was principally responsible. Not only was the claim for loss of life reduced because the criminal's lot, like the policeman's, is not a happy one, but his widow and children were not allowed to claim for the loss of their share of the proceeds of his prevented crimes.

Significant, too, is the decision in *Ashmore, Benson, Pease & Co.* v. *A. V. Dawson* [1973] 2 All E.R. 856, where the Court of Appeal dismissed a claim in respect of damage negligently caused to the plaintiffs' property while it was being carried by the defendants on a vehicle which, as the plaintiffs knew, was illegally and dangerously inadequate for the load. Lord Denning said: " . . . the question is whether the illegality prevents Ashmores from suing for that negligence. This depends on whether the contract itself was unlawful, or its performance was unlawful." But suppose a doctor agrees to perform an illegal abortion and carelessly injures the patient. Surely the patient would not be debarred from suing just because she knew the operation was unlawful?

There is another straw in the wind. Having recommended that social security benefits be payable to victims of motor accidents regardless of any question of negligence or contributory negligence, the Pearson Commission suggests that the Secretary of State be given discretionary power to withhold such payments from convicts who are injured during the commission of the offence or on the way there or back.